Women on Screen

Feminism and Femininity in Visual Culture

Edited by

Melanie Waters

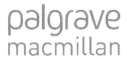

First published 2011 by
PALGRAVE MACMILLAN

Palgrave Macmillan in the UK is an imprint of Macmillan Publishers Limited,
registered in England, company number 785998, of Houndmills, Basingstoke,
Hampshire RG21 6XS.

Palgrave Macmillan in the US is a division of St Martin's Press LLC,
175 Fifth Avenue, New York, NY 10010.

Palgrave Macmillan is the global academic imprint of the above companies
and has companies and representatives throughout the world.

Palgrave® and Macmillan® are registered trademarks in the United States,
the United Kingdom, Europe and other countries.

ISBN 978-1-349-31098-2   ISBN 978-0-230-30197-9 (eBook)
DOI 10.1007/978-0-230-30197-9

This book is printed on paper suitable for recycling and made from fully
managed and sustained forest sources. Logging, pulping and manufacturing
processes are expected to conform to the environmental regulations of the
country of origin.

A catalogue record for this book is available from the British Library.

A catalog record for this book is available from the Library of Congress.

10   9   8   7   6   5   4   3   2   1
20   19 18 17 16 15 14 13 12 11

Transferred to Digital Printing in 2011

Women on Screen

Contents

Acknowledgements   vii

Notes on Contributors   viii

Introduction: Screening Women and Women on Screen   1
Melanie Waters

Part I Generations

1 Nancy Meyers and "Popular Feminism"   17
   Kathrina Glitre

2 "I'm nothing like you!" Postfeminist Generationalism
   and Female Stardom in the Contemporary Chick Flick   31
   Shelley Cobb

3 *Alias*: Quality Television and the New Woman Professional   45
   Rosie White

4 The Horrors of Home: Feminism and Femininity in the
   Suburban Gothic   58
   Melanie Waters

Part II Sex and Sexuality

5 Bad Girls in Crisis: The New Teenage Femme Fatale   77
   Katherine Farrimond

6 Butch Lesbians: Televising Female Masculinity   90
   Helen Fenwick

7 "Challenging and Alternative": Screening Queer Girls
   on Channel 4   103
   Martin Zeller-Jacques

Part III Makeovers

8 Under the Knife: Feminism and Cosmetic Surgery in
   Contemporary Culture   123
   Stéphanie Genz

 9 Imperialist Projections: Manners, Makeovers, and Models
    of Nationality   136
    Brenda R. Weber

10 Femininity Repackaged: Postfeminism and *Ladette to Lady* 153
    Angela Smith

11 Performing Postfeminist Identities: Gender, Costume, and
    Transformation in Teen Cinema   167
    Sarah Gilligan

Part IV Violence

12 Return of the "Angry Woman": Authenticating Female
    Physical Action in Contemporary Cinema   185
    Lisa Purse

13 Negotiating Shifts in Feminism: The "Bad" Girls of
    James Bond   199
    Lisa Funnell

14 "A Caligula-like despot": Matriarchal Tyranny in
    The Sopranos   213
    Anna Gething

15 A Pathological Romance: Authority, Expert Knowledge
    and the Postfeminist Profiler   225
    Lindsay Steenberg

Index   237

Acknowledgements

This book would not have been completed without the hard work and dedication of all the contributors, to whom I am immensely grateful. In addition, I would like to thank Christabel Scaife, Felicity Plester, and Catherine Mitchell at Palgrave for their advice and patience, and my colleagues at the Department of Humanities at Northumbria University for enabling the completion of this project. I would also like to acknowledge the people who have kept me amused during the editing process, especially Helena Barron, Kati Hall, Emma Hogarth, Becky Munford, Tomos Owen, Catherine Souter, Anne Whitehead, and Mark Gillingwater. Special thanks goes to Stacy Gillis for her involvement in the initial organization and administration of this project.

Finally, many thanks to Judith, Les, and Keith Waters, and to Jen Kennerley, for all their encouragement and good humour, and to Paul Crosthwaite, for being a constant source of delight and inspiration.

Notes on Contributors

Shelley Cobb is Teaching Fellow in Literature and Film at the University of Southampton. Currently, she is writing a book entitled *Making Her Move: Women, Adaptation and Post-Feminist Filmmaking*. She has published on film adaptation, Jane Campion, and celebrity culture.

Katherine Farrimond is a doctoral student at Newcastle University. Her thesis maps the articulations of the femme fatale in contemporary cinema. Her major research interests are feminist theory and representations of gender and sexuality in Hollywood film. Her essay, " 'Mom! You Look So Thin!': Constructions of Femininity Across the Space-Time Continuum", appears in the collection *The Worlds of Back to the Future: Critical Essays on the Films* (2010).

Helen Fenwick is a Ph.D. student in English Literature at Newcastle University, where her work focuses on the sexual politics within Neo-Victorian novels and their televisual and filmic adaptations.

Lisa Funnell has a Ph.D. in Film Studies from Wilfrid Laurier University. Her work has been accepted for publication in *The Quarterly Review of Film and Video* and *The Journal of Popular Culture*, and she has contributed a chapter to the forthcoming collection *Asian Popular Culture* (2010).

Stéphanie Genz is Senior Lecturer in Media and Culture at Edge Hill University. She specializes in contemporary gender and cultural theory. Her book publications include *Postfemininities in Popular Culture* (2009), *Postfeminism: Cultural Texts and Theories* (2009), and *Postfeminist Gothic: Critical Interventions in Contemporary Culture* (2007).

Anna Gething is a part-time Lecturer in English at Bath Spa University. Her research focuses on contemporary women's writing, gender studies, postcolonial writing, and the senses in literature. She has recently contributed to *Feminism, Domesticity and Popular Culture* (2008), *Rites of Passage in Postcolonial Women's Writing* (2010), and *The Encyclopedia of Literary and Cultural Theory* (2010). Forthcoming publications include a book chapter on women, history and imagination in Kate Grenville's historical fiction, an article on the gendering of smell in literature, and a monograph study of the writing of Kate Grenville.

Sarah Gilligan is Lecturer in Media at Hartlepool College of FE, UK. Her interdisciplinary research focuses on the ways in which costume, fashion, and gadgets are self-consciously used in contemporary popular culture to construct visual narrative discourses of gendered identities. Recent and forthcoming publications include work on star-celebrity fashion icons (Grace Kelly, James Bond, Will Smith, Gwyneth Paltrow), contemporary costume cinema, and sci-fi cinema. She is also currently developing a monograph entitled *Transforming Identity: Gender and Clothing in Contemporary Cinema*.

Kathrina Glitre is Senior Lecturer in Film Studies at the University of the West of England, UK. She is the author of *Hollywood Romantic Comedy: States of the Union 1934–65* (2006) and *Starring Cary Grant: Casting and Performance in Classical Hollywood Film* (2010), and the co-editor of *Neo-Noir* (2009).

Lisa Purse is Lecturer in Film in the Department of Film, Theatre & Television at the University of Reading. Her research interests focus on the relationship between film style and the politics of representation in post-studio mainstream and independent US cinema, and she has published a number of essays on digital effects in film. She is the author of "Reading the Digital" in the *Close-Up* series (Wallflower, 2011), and is currently completing a book on contemporary US action cinema.

Angela Smith lectures in Language and Culture at the University of Sunderland. She has published in the areas of gender, politics, media discourses, and children's fictions, and is currently writing *The Language of Journalism: A Multi-Genre Approach* (2011).

Lindsay Steenberg is Lecturer in Film and Television Studies at the University of East Anglia. She has published on the subject of violence in cinema, the postfeminist martial artist, the forensic gaze, and the works of filmmaker Guillermo Del Toro. Her doctoral thesis focused on female investigators and forensic science in contemporary crime thrillers, and her wider research interests include representations of gender and violence in postmodern and postfeminist media culture.

Melanie Waters is Senior Lecturer in Modern and Contemporary Literature at Northumbria University. She has published essays on feminist theory, popular culture, and twentieth-century women's poetry, and is the author of a forthcoming monograph on the contemporary gothic. She is also the co-author of *Feminism and Popular Culture* (2012) and the co-editor of *Poetry and Autobiography* (2011).

Brenda R. Weber is Associate Professor in Gender Studies at Indiana University, where she teaches courses in gender and popular culture, celebrity studies, masculinity, and theories of the body. She is the author of *Makeover TV: Selfhood, Citizenship, and Celebrity* (2009) and *Women and Literary Celebrity in the Nineteenth Century: The Transatlantic Production of Fame and Gender* (2011).

Rosie White is Senior Lecturer in English at Northumbria University. Her research interests include Michèle Roberts, women spies, and women in television comedy. Her monograph, *Violent Femmes: Women as Spies in Popular Culture*, was published by Routledge in 2008.

Martin Zeller-Jacques is a postgraduate student in the Department of Theatre, Film and Television at the University of York. He specializes in studies of contemporary television narrative and maintains related research interests in gender and sexuality across a range of television and film genres.

Introduction

Screening Women and Women on Screen

Melanie Waters

Women on Screen provides a new critical overview of the representation of women and girls in contemporary television and cinema. In doing so, it builds on recent analyses of the relationship between feminism, femininity, and popular culture by Imelda Whelehan, Joanne Hollows, Diane Negra, Yvonne Tasker, and Angela McRobbie in order to shed light on the particular issues that swirl around on-screen portrayals of embodied female identity. Intervening in established and emerging debates about postfeminism, the 15 chapters in this book investigate the roles accorded to feminism and femininity in late twentieth- and early twenty-first-century depictions of women's lives and ask why certain configurations of femininity – especially configurations of femininity that second wave feminism would seem to have rendered redundant or inappropriate – are not only persistent but also valorized within popular forms of visual culture.

Central to the examination of women on screen in this book is an analysis of the concept of screening itself: to be on screen, after all, is to have been subjected, already, to processes of screening. While the term "screening" typically denotes the practical processes of showing and viewing – the means by which the visual texts referenced in this collection are presented to, and consumed by, the public – it likewise refers to the systems of selection that inform the production and reception of these texts. In the first place, the chapters here are interested in the "screening" systems that lie behind the representation of women in any cultural text. In other words, they aim to focalize the decision-making strategies by which certain constellations of femininity are deemed appropriate (or otherwise) at particular historical moments, while also exploring how such judgements might be informed by feminist anxieties and/or anxieties about feminism. Secondly, they are committed to an analysis of how portrayals of women in female-centred texts are "screened" within the space of feminist critical scholarship: What kinds of visual texts are screened within (and screened out of) this kind of scholarship? How are the attributes of women on screen identified, isolated, and delineated by feminist critics? What kind of value is apportioned to these various attributes, and why? In essence, then, "screening" simultaneously accounts for the showing and viewing of visual texts, as well as the processes by which particular images of women and girls are created or concealed, promoted or suppressed, then vetted and examined.

As I have already suggested, the precise ways in which women are screened in film and on television are illuminated by – and might also illuminate – ongoing debates about the relationship between feminism and femininity. As Charlotte Brunsdon notes in a 2005 article, it has become something of a commonplace within feminist discourses to characterize this relationship as "complex" and "contradictory" (113). While the contributors featured here acknowledge that such terms remain apposite to critical considerations of women on screen, the collection as a whole strives to avoid the critical impasse at which the use of such terms can leave us – an impasse where, it seems, any and every representation of female experience is understood as "vexed" or "ambivalent", and where feminism itself is regarded as an objective political standard against which popular constructions of femininity are measured and, invariably, denigrated or dismissed. *Women on Screen* seeks to move beyond this impasse by recognizing that the relationship between feminism and femininity – just like the relationship between any diverse ideological groupings – is always and already complicated, not least as a result of the various meanings which are ascribed to these respective terms. The chapters that follow, then, understand complexity and ambivalence as hallmarks of contemporary female-centred texts, but do so as a starting point for thinking about their wider implications. Rather than falling into the trap of using a "politically correct feminist identity" to render "other feminine identities... 'invalid' " (Brunsdon, 1991, 379), we wish to highlight how such critical manoeuvres have come to operate within existing scholarship and draw attention to the ways in which they can both limit and redefine the terms of feminist debates about visual culture. At the same time, *Women on Screen* aims to recuperate to the realm of feminist scholarship those areas of women's representation that such strategies tend to "screen out". We are, then, looking to uncover new layers of complexity within contemporary cultural texts, rather than implying that their complexity resides solely in their negotiation of the relationship between feminism and femininity.

Postfeminism

At the heart of this collection lies a deep and necessary engagement with postfeminism and the various critical controversies by which it is orbited. Since the term began to acquire cultural currency in the early 1980s, feminist theorists have argued spiritedly over its meaning and usefulness, while trying to delineate its potential implications for critical and historical accounts of feminism.[1] For a number of thinkers in the 1980s and early 1990s, the concept of postfeminism invited interpretation alongside the media's increasingly antagonistic treatment of, or backlash against, the feminist agenda. As Brenda Polan contended in *The Guardian* in 1988, the endeavour of postfeminism to render itself nominally distinct from "older" incarnations of feminism – through its "post" prefix – indicates that it is not merely symptomatic of the backlash, it "*is* the backlash" (qtd. in Faludi 15; emphasis added). This proposal is significant in that it not only foregrounds the status of second wave feminism and postfeminism as discrete and monolithic movements (with postfeminism auguring a clear and deliberate break with the goals and politics of the second wave), but also indicates that postfeminism is a historically locatable reaction to the former – an idea which, as we shall see, is carried through into critical approaches to postfeminist cultural texts.

The "anti-feminist backlash" to which Polan refers is, of course, the subject of Susan Faludi's 1991 bestseller *Backlash: The Undeclared War Against Women*. Elaborating on Polan's logic, Faludi argues that the term "post-feminism" is part of a re-branding strategy, one of the means by which the media in the 1980s endeavoured to signpost the "past-ness" of feminism, using it to conjure up a "new story" for a "younger generation who supposedly reviled the women's movement" (14). Although she identifies postfeminism as a 1980s phenomenon, however, Faludi uses the term flexibly to denote other historical eruptions of anti-feminist sentiment, and traces the initial emergence of postfeminism back to the American media's treatment of feminist organizations in the 1920s. As Faludi's varied usage implies, the prefixation or "posting" of feminism is open to wide and wild interpretation, depending on one's understanding of "post" – namely, whether "post" is viewed as designating a rejection of, continuity with, or ambivalence towards the feminism(s) by which it is predated.[2]

As Imelda Whelehan observes, the "post" prefix implies the functional inadequacy of "feminism" as a term; though this, she makes clear, does not guarantee the distinctiveness of feminism and postfeminism:

> "New" and "post" are prefixes added to the term "feminism" when the writer or speaker wants to make it clear that they have a certain antagonism to the term, because of the connotations it generates, or because feminism by itself is seen to be inadequate to their own definition.... [A]ll imply that the word feminism is not enough to embrace their own political programmes or personal agendas, and that it has been manipulated to certain ends from which they want to exclude themselves. But as with most additions of prefixes, the central concept remains the same, so that "new" and "post" imply cosmetic changes rather than radical rethinking. Feminism is portrayed as a territory over which various women have to fight to gain their ground; it has become so unwieldy as a term that it threatens to implode under the weight of its own contradictions. (77–78)

These semantic ambiguities are alluded to more explicitly by Diane Negra in *What a Girl Wants* (2008). Situating postfeminism firmly within the cultural landscape of the 1990s and early 2000s, Negra shows how it operates as a "widely-applied and highly contradictory term [which] performs as if it is commonsensical and presents itself as pleasingly moderated in contrast to a 'shrill' feminism" that it regards as "rigid, serious, anti-sex and romance, difficult and extremist" (2). Although postfeminism is routinely associated with the negative characterizations of feminism that Negra here describes, the frequent signposting of its seemingly "contradictory" applications implies its status as a more complex and elastic phenomenon. In this vein, Genz, one of the contributors to this book, has remarked on the extraordinary number of terms – including "Girl Power", "popular feminism", and "do-me feminism" – that have been used in conjunction and/or interchangeably with postfeminism in recent years. For Genz, this polysemy not only liberates postfeminism from any fixed or singular definition but also speaks to its cultural currency, establishing its existence "as a conceptual entity in its own right". According to Genz, then, postfeminism need not be a "negation [or] sabotage" of feminism; rather, the "post" prefix may instead designate "reliance and continuity" or even "a contradictory dependence on and independence from the term that follows it" (18–19).

Perhaps the most salient, and least controversial, feature of postfeminism is its inextricability from popular, and particularly visual, culture. From Naomi Wolf's investigation into how mainstream images of female beauty shape women's social experiences in *The Beauty Myth* (1991) to the analyses of the impact of "raunch culture" on the behaviour and aspirations of young women in Ariel Levy's *Female Chauvinist Pigs* (2006) and Natasha Walter's *Living Dolls* (2010), the discourses of postfeminism are, increasingly, only intelligible within the context of the contemporary visual iconography by which we, as global citizens, are perpetually bombarded.

If the term "visual culture" can encompass everything from fine art, photography, and architecture to film, television, advertising, and digital media, its particular value lies in its gesturing towards the interpenetration of different visual forms and codes as a hallmark of postmodern culture, as well as in its recognition of the growing predominance of visual media over verbal/textual forms of communication within the mediasphere. These factors are especially significant in a collection of this kind, which focuses predominantly (though not exclusively) on film and television produced in the United States and the United Kingdom since 1990. Such contemporary texts, after all, are always and already marked by the issues of cross-mediation to which the term "visual culture" pertains. In using it, then, I hope to speak directly to the particularities of the current cultural moment, while at the same time telegraphing the persistence of links between feminist discourse and issues of female visibility – links which are writ large in everything from Laura Mulvey's seminal psychoanalytical account of women-on-screen in "Visual Pleasure and Narrative Cinema" (1975) and Susie Orbach's delineation of the overweight female body in *Fat is a Feminist Issue* (1978), to Carol Dyhouse's recent work on fashion and femininity in *Glamour: Women, History, Feminism* (2010).

Feminism and popular culture

As Joanne Hollows and Rachel Moseley have observed, feminism is difficult to conceptualize outside of the popular: "apart from women actively involved in the second wave of feminism in the 1960s and 1970s, most people's initial knowledge and understanding of feminism has been formed within the popular and through representation" (2). Even so, like other political campaigns of the time, the second wave was – and is – regularly "conceived of as a social movement that was 'outside' of, and frequently oppositional to, the dominant culture" (4). In other words, it is assumed to take place in a hypothetical "real" space that lies, impossibly, beyond the sensationalizing tentacles of the mainstream media. Still, even the women who *were* "actively involved" in the second wave were eminently preoccupied with the issue of women's representation in the media. As is clearly evidenced in some of feminism's key texts, such as Simone de Beauvoir's *The Second Sex* (1949), Betty Friedan's *The Feminine Mystique* (1963), and Kate Millett's *Sexual Politics* (1970), the second wave's social agenda was guided precisely by anxieties about representation, relating particularly to the circulation of "unrealistic" and "misleading" images of women in popular magazines, advertising, literature, television, and film.[3] Over the course of *The Second Sex*, for example, De Beauvoir traces gender inequality through a discussion of the roles occupied by women within the popular imaginary, from the witches, wicked stepmothers, and damsels-in-distress of common folklore to the modern-day Cinderellas of Hollywood cinema (in the films of Orson Welles and Edmund Goulding), and the complicated, conflicted women who populate the novels of D. H. Lawrence and Virginia Woolf. Friedan, with a background in journalism, was likewise concerned with the prescriptive models of domesticated womanhood that were offered up in post-war culture, exploring the conservative gender politics of the articles and short fiction that constituted the stock-in-trade of popular women's magazines like *Ladies Home Journal, McCalls,* and *Good Housekeeping* during the 1950s.[4] A few years later, in 1970, Kate Millett's *Sexual Politics* drew attention to the misogynistic dimensions of fiction by Henry Miller and Norman Mailer,[5] while Germaine Greer's *The Female Eunuch* (1970) dissected the persistence of various feminine stereotypes across a widening spectrum of popular media.

The second wave thus maintained an interest in investigating the ways in which "real" or authentic womanhood has been distorted or elided within popular culture, while also viewing its agenda, in part, as a means of correcting these perceived representational injustices. For this reason, it is necessary for contemporary scholars to acknowledge and interrogate the tendencies within some existing scholarship to imply the existence of feminism(s) beyond the realm of representation. After all, as Hollows and Moseley suggest, such criticism "assumes that feminism, or the feminist, can tell us about popular culture, but does not examine what popular culture can tell us about feminism" (1). Given the inextricability of feminism and popular culture, any unilateral reading of the kind that Hollows and Moseley describe is destined to be partial and misleading. Part of the aim of this collection, then, is to foreground the extent to which feminism, femininity, and popular forms of visual culture constitute a dynamic and influential nexus of activity. In this spirit, it seeks to focalize the potential limitations of conceptual frameworks that rely exclusively on straightforward distinctions between different "species" of feminism. Stacy Gillis and Rebecca Munford have already highlighted the potential restrictions imposed by the use of the wave paradigm, which tends to construct a monolithic account of each "wave" of feminist activity and in doing so "lends power to backlash politics and rhetoric" (177). As we will see, the backlash logic that Gillis and Munford identify with the wave paradigm is inscribed in many of the texts with which *Women on Screen* is concerned. In line with Gillis and Munford, the chapters here query the anchoring of particular conceptual models in presumptions about feminist conflict and inter-generational disagreements, while also acknowledging the ways in which such models continue to inform creative and critical configurations of contemporary female identities.

The chapters

The chapters here are divided into four discrete but interlocking parts: "Generations"; "Sex and Sexuality"; "Makeovers"; and "Violence". These parts reflect some of the key concerns by which popular representations of feminism and femininity are striated, but they also offer a framework for conceptualizing the dominant preoccupations of feminist media criticism at the start of the twenty-first century. While drawn together by a shared awareness of the extent to which postfeminist texts and contexts have been shaped by a particular issue – be it generational conflict, female sexuality, embodied identity, or gendered violence – the chapters in each part are marked by their sustained engagement with broader questions of power and visibility. Such questions are, after all, critical to considerations of the "postfeminist canon" and, more specifically, to the interrogation of postfeminism's exclusionary tendencies – most conspicuously apparent in its "limited race and class vision" (Tasker and Negra 14–15) – with which *Women on Screen* is necessarily concerned.

The first part of this book, "Generations", explores the ways in which generational models of feminism have informed fictional and critical approaches to feminine identities in popular culture. Each author acknowledges the role that such paradigms have played in shaping scholarly analyses of feminism and/or femininity, while endeavouring to show how they might also undermine or reduce the complexity of these representations. Glitre and Cobb, for example, show how chick flicks dramatize feminist debates about independence and empowerment through the representation of women's personal and/or familial relationships. Focusing on the comedies of writer and director Nancy Meyers, Glitre argues that the evolution of these debates can be (re)viewed through reference to changing approaches to the figure of the working woman. From Goldie Hawn's society-girl-turned-soldier in *Private Benjamin* (1980) to Helen Hunt's high-flying advertising executive in *What Women Want* (2000), Glitre shows how Meyers' chick flicks register shifting attitudes to women in the workplace, while interrogating the persistence of the heterosexual romance motif in the wake of such shifts. In particular, she queries the use of the romantic resolution as a means of resolving the raft of dilemmas that the working woman presents.

The working woman is equally central to Cobb's investigation of the twenty-first-century chick flick. Demonstrating how feminist intergenerational conflict is often figured through the portrayal of antagonistic relationships between older and younger women, Cobb contends that chick flicks like *Monster-in-Law* (2005) and *The Devil Wears Prada* (2006) routinely use the mature career woman as a visual shorthand for feminism that is selfish, anti-familial, outmoded, and generally ineffective in the context of contemporary Western societies. With close reference to their individual star personae, Cobb shows how the casting of baby-boomer female actors – like Jane Fonda and Meryl Streep – opposite their younger counterparts – namely Jennifer Lopez and Anne Hathaway – is used as a means of signalling the final, triumphant displacement of second wave feminism's "old", selfish careerism by "new" family-oriented models of postfeminist identity.

If the chick flick speculatively proposes a different, and emotionally fulfilled, future for the postfeminist woman, then this is, perhaps, challenged within certain types of quality American television. Redeploying the term "New Woman" to refer to female professionals in film and television at the end of the twentieth century and the beginning of the twenty-first, White discusses the politics of empowerment through close reference to the representation of working woman in *Alias* (2001–06). Accounting for the vexed positioning of women within the context of the New Economy, White analyses Jennifer Garner's portrayal of Sydney Bristow – the "empowered" New Woman spy – through the lens of the show's approach to the ageing female professional. In this way, White shows how the sinister machinations and betrayals of the older women in *Alias* are used to symbolize a potential – if undesirable – future for the New Woman professional, thus highlighting the persistence of gender inequality with the global capitalist system, as well as the limited options that are available to the successful career woman as she gets older.

My own chapter, finally, shows how the trope of haunting has been used in recent feminist discourses to symbolize the spectral status of second wave feminism in contemporary culture. With this as a starting point, I investigate the representation of feminine identities in contemporary female-centred television fictions. Placing a special focus on the tensions between women, maternity, and domesticity, I analyse the extent to which mainstream representations of gender are haunted by anxieties about femininity and show how this is inscribed in a range of shows, from *Desperate Housewives* (2004–) and *Mad Men* (2007–) to *Medium* (2005–) and *Ghost Whisperer* (2005–10).

The second part, "Sex and Sexuality", begins with Katherine Farrimond's investigation of ways in which the compelling figure of the femme fatale has been re-appropriated and modified within contemporary cinema. Establishing the principal characteristics of the femme fatale through reference to the classic film noir of the 1940s and 1950s, Farrimond shows how her mystery, allure, and sexual maturity have been adapted to the figure of the teenage girl. Given the teenage girl's usual marginalization or infantilization within popular culture, Farrimond interrogates the extent to which her reformulation as an intelligent, worldly, and sexually experienced antagonist – as it takes place within the thriller and neo-noir genres – might be indicative of her agency and her inherent threat to patriarchal systems of power.

Helen Fenwick returns the focus to quality television and the representation of female masculinity in *The L Word* (2004–09) and *The Wire* (2002–08). Over the course of her chapter, Fenwick traces the elusive presence of the butch lesbian within popular culture, and draws attention to the ways in which racial markers and the discourses of transgenderism are traditionally used to impose order on this otherwise renegade figure. As Fenwick goes on to explain, representations of lesbian relationships tend to pivot on a butch/femme dynamic in which the butch partner is black or mixed race, while the femme to whom she is coupled is lighter-skinned or white. Although this intricate tethering of butchness and blackness is progressively re-negotiated within *The Wire*, Fenwick signposts the remaining taboo of the white butch lesbian, acknowledging the threat this figure poses to white masculinity as one of the key justifications for her continued invisibility.

Martin Zeller-Jacques is also concerned with issues relating to the representation of sexuality on the small screen. Shining a critical light on the Channel 4 Corporation's public service remit, which spells out its commitment to the production of "challenging and alternative" content that reflects the diversity of the British population, Martin analyses the increased visibility of lesbians within Channel 4 programming. Orienting this analysis around popular "post-lesbian" shows like *Sugar Rush* (2005–06) and *Skins* (2007–), Maz queries the formulation of teen lesbianism in particular, and considers the extent to which such content might be considered "challenging" or subversive when it tends to be so rigidly contained within the "hegemonic structures of family and friendship".

The chapters by Stéphanie Genz, Brenda R. Weber, Angela Smith, and Sarah Gilligan offer various theorizations of the ongoing prevalence of the makeover in contemporary film and television. The surgical modification of the female body – as it takes place in an ever-expanding raft of popular makeover shows, including *The Swan* (2004–05), *Extreme Makeover* (2002–05), and *Ten Years Younger* (2004–) – is used by Genz as a basis for investigating the intersections and divergences of femininity, beauty, agency, and choice. Bringing new light to bear on the modern culture of *chirurgia decoratoria*, in which the individual is encouraged to remodel herself in the pursuit of social status, sexual desirability, and personal contentment, Genz views makeover television in relation to the "paradox of choice" that Rosemary Gillespie identifies as a hallmark of postfeminist culture (79).

According to Brenda R. Weber, the term "affective domination" can assist in bringing some of the contradictions and ironies by which makeover shows are riven into sharper focus. Used to denote the strategies of shaming and support that are deployed by the makeover "experts" in order to gain social mastery of the participant, the concept of "affective domination" provides a framework for thinking about the trajectory of the transformation narrative. Reflecting particularly on *American Princess* (2005–07) and *Australian Princess* (2005), Weber shows how the makeover is presented as a positive means of reconciling the participant's outer appearance with his or her inner subjectivity. She exposes, moreover, the irony of the fact that it is the woman who submits most wholeheartedly to the affective domination who is situated as the most empowered.

Smith's chapter views the makeover show in light of the postfeminist media phenomenon of "Girl Power" and the contemporaneous moral panic about teenage behaviour in British society. With close reference to the *Ladette to Lady* (2005–) franchise – a UK reality show in which young, hard-drinking, promiscuous, rebellious young women are refashioned as dress-making, flower-arranging "ladies" – Smith questions the politics of postfeminism and its putative valorization of traditional models of domesticated femininity.

Taking account of the proliferation of makeover shows in Anglo-American television schedules, Sarah Gilligan explores the transformation narrative as an enduring staple of feminine popular culture. From Hollywood classics such as *Now Voyager* (1942) and *My Fair Lady* (1964) to contemporary programming like *Gok's Fashion Fix* (2008–09), Gilligan establishes the rootedness of the transformation narrative in processes of consumerism and feminization. If a number of cultural texts trade on the premise that a woman's conformity to contemporary notions of "ideal" femininity will enable her to achieve the twin prizes of masculine approval and heterosexual romance, then some contemporary teen films generate a "postfeminist space" within which the female protagonists are permitted to experiment with identity more freely. In films like *She's All That* (1999), Gilligan argues, the centrality of vintage and homemade clothing to the "making over" of the protagonist implicates her in an endless cycle of (re)fashioning femininity that speaks, ultimately, to the performativity of gender identity.

This collection concludes with a section on "Violence", in which Lisa Funnell, Lisa Purse, Anna Gething, and Lindsay Steenberg explore the role that aggression and physicality have played in the construction of new feminine and feminist identities.

Funnell discusses the ways in which anxieties about feminism and feminist women are registered in the changing depiction of female villainy within the James Bond film franchise. As Funnell explains, if the Bond films of the 1960s speak to second wave feminism through their representation of powerful, sexually liberated "bad" women – who are, ultimately, punished for their perceived disobedience – then the female villains of the 1990s and 2000s are best understood as the Bond film's response to "Girl Power" and the broader discourses of postfeminism. Stressing the franchise's (often antagonistic) engagement with feminist politics, Funnell shows how the female villain is used variously as a means of challenging and/or (re)asserting Bond's masculine authority. In addition, however, she argues that some of Bond's female adversaries also function as figures through which new, empowered feminine identities can be productively envisioned and critiqued.

Lisa Purse is likewise interested in addressing shifts in the representation of empowered (or disempowered) feminine identities on the big screen. Establishing the "angry woman" as a staple of the rape-revenge and slasher cycles of the 1970s, Purse attempts to make sense of the recent reappearance of this traumatized, aggressive figure in films such as *Kill Bill* (2003–04), *Monster* (2003), and *Hard Candy* (2005). Reading the representation of the "new" angry woman in relation to that of her would-be sisters – namely, the postfeminist action heroines of popular film series like *The Matrix*, *Resident Evil*, and *X-Men* – Purse shows how the active female body is ascribed different meanings in different cultural contexts. For Purse, then, the postfeminist action heroine has come to constitute the acceptable face (and body) of female empowerment in the twenty-first century; white, heterosexual, and demonstrably feminine, her physical prowess is routinely spectacularized and sexualized, without being explained through reference to her gender. Her "angry" counterpart, by contrast, exhibits a physical agency that is rationalized explicitly through reference to her motives, which are clearly gendered (usually relating to rape or maternal instinct). In the course of unpacking these differences, Purse situates the new angry woman as a "return of the repressed" – a dramatic re-materialization of female rage and aggression that is strategically disavowed in mainstream representations of the "action babe".

For Anna Gething, HBO's gangster drama *The Sopranos* (1999–2007) offers an interesting take on the relationship between femininity and violence. Establishing the ass-kicking, wise-cracking fantasy heroine as the prime exponent of female violence in contemporary television and film fictions, Gething examines *The Sopranos'* creative reinterpretation of gendered brutality. In particular, she considers the show's positioning of the ageing, physically impaired matriarch as the agent of aggression which – though psychological rather than physical – is as damaging in its long-term effects as any of the tortures inflicted by the male mobsters in the series.

Retaining a focus on representations of active and/or professional female identities, Lindsay Steenberg brings a critical light to bear on portrayals of the postfeminist criminal profiler in recent television and film fictions. As Steenberg explains, such fictions tend to centralize the relationship between the male serial killer and the female profiler, trading heavily on its predatory and eroticized dimensions. Taking into account the gendered nature of serial violence, Steenberg examines the ways in which the "pathological romance" between the killer and the profiler functions to enhance the latter's expertise, while also placing her in a situation where both her professionalism and her physical safety are compromised. In this way, Steenberg argues, the female expert is used to reflect a stubborn "postfeminist" scepticism about the ambitious woman who prioritizes her career over her femininity.

Covering a spectrum of feminist perspectives and drawing on a wide range of critical and cultural theory, this collection is intended to expand the parameters of existing debates about the plotting of modern female identities in the Western imaginary. The kinds of identities addressed here are broadly reflective of those with which postfeminist culture is predominantly preoccupied; as white, middle-class, heterosexual femininities continue to occupy positions of high visibility within mainstream cinema and television, then, so these femininities form the basis of many of the chapters that follow. This book is also, however, responsive to current shifts in representation and criticism. The recent mainstreaming of queer identities and storylines in contemporary programming and film has, for example, generated an urgent need for new critical investigations into the portrayal of non-heterosexual sexualities and the impact of these portrayals on adjacent representations of women and girls. This need is addressed here by the likes of Fenwick and Zeller-Jacques, who explore the construction of non-heterosexual identities in television fictions like *The Wire*, *Sugar Rush*, and *Skins* – fictions which have yet to be exposed to any sustained feminist scrutiny. *Women on Screen* is also interested in the role that class, age, race, and ethnicity have to play in shaping contemporary femininities: How do these factors interact in order to produce new female identities? How do they enhance or diminish women's visibility and/or power? How, if at all, are these factors implicated in the spectacularization or minstrelization of particular female identities? While the contributors to this book are attentive and responsive to the issues of class, age, race, and ethnicity – and to the kinds of questions mentioned above – the usual practical constraints of time and space apply, meaning that this collection is always and already a starting point for further discussions. Certainly, there remains a great deal of critical work to be done in these areas, and an ever-growing multitude of texts – and textual identities – to be accounted for. Through reference to some of these texts and some of these identities, *Women on Screen* seeks to add new fuel to the fires of feminist debate, reassessing the scope of popular culture and critical scholarship in the expanding mediascape of the twenty-first century.

Notes

1. As Stéphanie Genz reflects, much of the controversy about postfeminism has centred on the implications of the "post" prefix – namely, whether it heralds the success, failure, or irrelevance of the second wave agenda in the late twentieth century. While some scholars hyphenate the term (as in "post-feminism") or parenthesize the prefix (as in "(post)feminism") in order to

signal its discontinuity with feminism and/or its dubious status as a term in its own right, it remains unhyphenated here (unless it appears as part of a direct quotation). This is not to disregard the very valid reasons for hyphenation or parenthesization, but simply as a means of indicating the fact that these debates – which are addressed consistently throughout this book – are now so thoroughly inextricable the term that they form a vital part of its meaning. For more on this, see Genz 18–26.

2. For more on the "post-ing" of feminism, see Genz 18–26.
3. See De Beauvoir (1949), Millett (1970), and Greer (1970).
4. De Beauvoir's attempts to delineate the cultural mythologization of femininity are sustained throughout *The Second Sex*, but are analysed with particular vigour from 171 to 282.
5. See Millett 294–335.

Works cited

Brunsdon, Charlotte. "Feminism, Postfeminism, Martha, Martha, and Nigella". *Cinema Journal* 44.2 (Winter 2005): 110–16.
———. "Pedagogies of the Feminine: Feminist Teaching and Women's Genre". *Screen* 32.4 (1991): 364–82.
De Beauvoir, Simone. *The Second Sex*. 1949. Ed and trans. H. M. Parshley. London: Vintage, 1997.
Faludi, Susan. *Backlash: The Undeclared War Against Women*. London: Vintage, 1992.
Friedan, Betty. *The Feminine Mystique*. London: Penguin, 1992.
Gillespie, Rosemary. "Women, the Body and Brand Extension in Medicine: Cosmetic Surgery and the Paradox of Choice". *Women and Health* 24.4 (1996): 69–85.
Gillis, Stacy, and Rebecca Munford. "Genealogies and Generations: The Politics and Praxis of Third Wave Feminism". *Women's History Review* 13.2 (2004): 165–82.
Greer, Germaine. *The Female Eunuch*. 1970. London: Paladin, 1976.
Hollows, Joanne. *Feminism, Femininity and Popular Culture*. Manchester: Manchester University Press, 2000.
Hollows, Joanne, and Rachel Moseley. *Feminism in Popular Culture*. London: BERG, 2005.
Millett, Kate. *Sexual Politics*. 1970. London: Virago, 1977.
Negra, Diane. *What A Girl Wants: Fantasizing the Reclamation of Self in Postfeminism*. London: Routledge, 2008.
Tasker, Yvonne, and Diane Negra. Introduction. *Interrogating Postfeminism*. Ed. Yvonne Tasker and Diane Negra. Durham, NC: Duke University Press, 2007. 1–25.
Whelehan, Imelda. *Overloaded: Popular Culture and the Future of Feminism*. London: Women's Press, 2000.

Part I
Generations

1

Nancy Meyers and "Popular Feminism"

Kathrina Glitre

Nancy Meyers has an exceptional career. While many women in Hollywood struggle to sustain employment, Meyers has worked steadily for 30 years, from co-writing and co-producing films such as *Private Benjamin* (1980) and *Baby Boom* (1987) with her then-husband, Charles Shyer, to becoming probably the most commercially successful female writer-producer-director in the history of Hollywood. *What Women Want* (2000) is the highest-grossing romantic comedy ever, earning $374,111,707 worldwide, while *Something's Gotta Give* (2003), *The Holiday* (2006), and *It's Complicated* (2009) all broke the $200,000,000 barrier (*Box Office Mojo*).[1] Despite this success (or perhaps because of its commercial nature), Meyers has attracted little critical and academic attention, even within feminist film studies. This is particularly surprising given that Meyers's films are centrally concerned with that icon of the postfeminist era – the independent (white, middle-class) woman with a successful professional career.

By exploring Meyers's work, I want to unpack the relationships between feminism, postfeminism, popular culture, and pleasure, in order to consider the problems that "popular feminism" might pose for feminist politics. There are three interrelated, but distinct, meanings embedded in my understanding of "popular feminism":

1. representations of "feminist" ideas in popular culture;
2. the popularity of such representations;
3. the popular understanding of "feminism" that is generated through this exchange.

Paradigms come and go – from power-dressing to "Girl Power" to empowerment – but, broadly speaking, popular feminism has become

closely identified with the figure of the "independent woman" during
the postfeminist era. As Kristyn Gorton argues, "popular representations of feminism in the media sell: whether in music, film or television,
images of independent women appeal to a wide audience.... Throughout these representations it is implied that women have achieved the
goals of second wave feminism – financial autonomy, a successful career,
sexual freedom" (154). The second wave was about more than this,
but popular culture's reductive understanding tends to involve little
more than sex, money, and freedom of choice. While these particular ideas have certainly become part of mainstream representation of
women, this probably has as much, if not more, to do with the demands
of neoliberalism and consumer capitalism than the achievements of
the second wave.[2] Moreover, simply because a fictional character has
achieved these goals does not mean the women watching her have:
the figure of the independent woman sells because she provides a pleasurable fantasy of power and success, not because she is a "feminist".
Indeed, in recent years, postfeminist film and television narratives (certainly in the US and the UK) have tended to resolve their conflicts by
depicting women as "outgrowing" independence and becoming happily
co-dependent through heterosexual romance.[3]

In this context, *Private Benjamin*, *Baby Boom*, and *What Women
Want* offer a fascinating condensation of the historical trajectory of
Hollywood's representation of independent women and "popular feminist" ideas.[4] With the possible exception of *Private Benjamin*, I do not
think any of Meyers's films can be called "feminist". They do, however, bear the traces of feminism,[5] invoking popular feminist ideas in
very direct ways, including pointed dialogue about the choices open to
women in *Private Benjamin*, "having it all" in *Baby Boom*, and empowerment and "being yourself" in *What Women Want*. Thus, while all
three feature a successful, independent woman, they articulate the
trope in different ways. *Private Benjamin*'s poster, for example, shows
a bedraggled Judy Benjamin (Goldie Hawn) wearing army fatigues, with
smudged mascara and a band-aid on her face. It is difficult to imagine a
contemporary chick flick using such an unglamorous image as a selling
point. While much of the film's comedy comes from the idea of a petite,
hapless woman doing "men's work" by joining the army, the narrative is
also about the submissive, hyper-feminine Judy's transformation into an
independent woman, breaking free from patriarchal authority (her husband, her father, her colonel, her fiancé) and heterosexist institutions
(family, the army, marriage). In *Baby Boom*, J.C. Wiatt (Diane Keaton)
initially epitomizes the eighties' yuppie (a young, upwardly-mobile

professional), but her career promotion is jeopardized when she inherits guardianship of her cousin's baby, Elizabeth (Kristina and Michelle Kennedy). The narrative's conflicts are again encapsulated in the poster image. J.C./Keaton is attractively presented, but her stance indicates the struggle of trying to "have it all": clutching a briefcase in one hand and the baby in the other, she appears off-balance and overburdened. By the time of *What Women Want*, the idea of the independent career woman has become so familiar that Darcy Maguire (Helen Hunt) is no longer the protagonist; her story is displaced by the reformation of pseudo-rat packer, Nick Marshall (Mel Gibson), into postfeminist hero, in a film that relies on heterosexual romance as the "solution" to gender inequality. The film's various posters all emphasize the couple, usually showing Nick/Gibson dominating the frame and meeting our gaze, while the conventionally feminine Darcy/Hunt is positioned side-on, gazing at him, not us.[6]

Without wanting to impose an overly simplistic linear trajectory on these phenomena, these shifts in representation do seem quite typical of contemporary Hollywood – and of popular understandings of the history of feminism. We might say that popular culture has spun a familiar tale: Act 1, a woman breaks free of patriarchal oppression, proving her self-worth by becoming independent; Act 2, she discovers the difficulty of having it all; Act 3, lonely and frustrated, she decides the cost of independence is too high, settling down with a nice "new man" for a happily-ever-after ending. To unpick the implications of such representations for feminist politics, I want to analyse the role of heterosexual romance within these three films.

Private Benjamin begins and ends with a wedding, symbolizing the extent to which Judy has changed. Judy's second husband, Yale Goodman (Albert Brooks), dies of a heart attack on their wedding night, while – briefly – consummating their marriage on the bathroom floor. In many ways, this is represented as a lucky escape for Judy: the stereotypical Jewish "princess", her marriage looked set to revolve around home furnishings and unsatisfying sex-on-demand. Judy is distraught because, as she puts it, "I've never *not* belonged to somebody – *never*". Tricked into enlisting, she ends up belonging to Uncle Sam. Judy is transformed by basic training and becomes the first female Thornbirds paratrooper, but she is sexually harassed by her Colonel (Robert Webber) and negotiates a transfer to Belgium as a purchasing specialist – "The one job I've trained for all my life". She falls in love with a Parisian gynaecologist, Henri Tremont (Armand Assante), whose stereotypical expertise finally enables her to achieve sexual fulfilment. Forced to choose between the army and marriage to Henri, she picks him, immediately reverting to stereotype: we next see her wearing a garish pink and blue outfit that Henri had earlier admired in a boutique, but in which Judy had shown no interest. Standing at the altar, Judy has an epiphany. Three quick shots are intercut as flashes of her memory: marrying Yale; her father admonishing her for running away; and Henri asking her to sign a prenuptial agreement. Each shot represents her submissive relationship to a man. In this way, the film articulates her subsequent refusal to marry as a refusal of patriarchy, not just a refusal of Henri's womanizing. When Henri tells her, "For once in your life, don't be stupid" – echoing her father's words, "You were never a smart girl" – she punches him, declaring, "Don't call me stupid". The film ends with Judy throwing her veil to the wind, striding away from Henri's house in her wedding gown, head held high.

This moment of "feminist" triumph remains relatively unusual for a mainstream Hollywood film. *Private Benjamin*'s final rejection of heterosexual romance seems to speak quite directly to the second wave's critique of the ways in which compulsory heterosexuality, romance, and marriage subjugate women within patriarchy. The image of the bride striding away plays out very differently here to the recuperative representation of weddings and marriage in more recent films, such as *Runaway Bride* (1999), *Forces of Nature* (1999), or even *Wedding Crashers* (2005), not to mention Meyers's own work on *Father of the Bride* (1991). However, it should be borne in mind that *Private Benjamin* is at the tail end of a cycle of comedies, such as *Shampoo* (1975), *Annie Hall* (1977), and *Semi-Tough* (1977), which ended unconventionally as part of the broader countercultural moment. *Private Benjamin*, like all Meyers's work, is very much of its time; indeed, her films seem particularly adept at tapping into the zeitgeist.

Baby Boom, for example, begins with a montage of (white) women striding along the New York streets on their way to work. The sequence is reminiscent of the opening credits of *Cagney and Lacey* (1982–1988), with Bill Conti's score bearing a striking resemblance to his well-known theme for that series. We also hear a voiceover, spoken by the NBC news reporter, Linda Ellerbee, lending the words factual authority as well as connoting the real-world success of women:

> Fifty-three percent of the American work force is female. Three generations of women have turned a thousand years of tradition on its ear. As little girls, they were told to grow up and marry doctors and lawyers. Instead, they became doctors and lawyers... Take J.C. Wiatt,

for example.... She works five to nine. She makes six figures a year and they call her "The Tiger Lady". Married to her job, she lives with an investment banker married to his.... One would take it for granted that a woman like this has it all. One must never take *anything* for granted.

From the outset, then, the film expresses an ambivalent attitude to women's professional success. When J.C. fails to get the promotion she deserved, because she has been struggling with the newfound responsibilities of parenthood, she decides to move to Vermont. After various domestic and financial disasters, she launches her own gourmet baby food company, rapidly becoming even more successful as an entrepreneur, but this time on her own terms.

The film is a prescient example of the postfeminist "retreatist" narratives discussed by Diane Negra: in films and telvision shows like *Hope Floats* (1998), *Judging Amy* (1999–2005), *The Gilmore Girls* (2000–2007), and *Sweet Home Alabama* (2002), a career woman relocates back home, or to an idealized New England small town, " 'downshifting' her career or ambitions in order to re-prioritize family commitments and roles" (18), enabling her to (re)discover love along the way; like *Baby Boom*, the television series particularly privilege the mother–daughter relationship. Negra argues that these retreatist narratives work "to manage a pervasive cultural contradiction in which claims of feminist victories need to be squared with abundant evidence of feminism's losses" (15) – the same kind of contradiction expressed in *Baby Boom*'s opening voiceover: equality has (supposedly) been achieved, but at what cost? All too often, postfeminist culture represents (white, middle-class) women's achievement of social and economic independence as being at the expense of femininity, relationships, and happiness.

Like other retreatist narratives, *Baby Boom* suggests there is more to a woman's life than loving a man, but heterosexual romance is nonetheless constructed as a vital ingredient for happiness. J.C.'s initial relationship of convenience with investment banker, Steven Buchner (Harold Ramis), contrasts strongly with her later romance with country vet, Jeff Cooper (Sam Shepherd). Steven is Jewish and – much like Yale in *Private Benjamin* – his ethnicity is stereotypically used to bring his virility into question: we first see him wearing a facemask in bed. His idea of foreplay involves asking "Do you want to make love?" and removing his glasses; four minutes later, he is putting them back on, declaring, "That was incredible". In contrast, when J.C. asks Jeff if he is tired the morning after they have sex, he remarks, "Well, I usually require more than 20 minutes sleep a night". While Steven is represented as safe but dull, Jeff is represented as sexually confident and dynamic. The catalyst for change, however, is Elizabeth, who inspires J.C.'s retreat and her business success. Elizabeth humanizes, as well as feminizes, the Tiger Lady. J.C.'s career change involves replacing the masculinized office environment of sharp suits and cut-throat competition with a feminized domestic environment of natural soft foods, boosting the local economy as well as feeding the next generation. By rejecting the man-eating Tiger Lady in favour of the nurturing mother-entrepreneur the film's resolution finally enables J.C. to have it all: a beautiful home, a successful business, a passionate man, a place in the community, and – above all else – a loving mother–daughter relationship.[7] Motherhood is represented as central to female happiness and the film's final image emphasizes this cosy, reassuring sentiment: J.C. sits with the pink-clad Elizabeth in an old-fashioned rocking chair, surrounded by flowers and comfy country-style furnishings with diffuse sunlight streaming through the windows.

What Women Want places even more importance on heterosexual romance and is typically postfeminist in the way it uses this romance as an individualized solution to systemic problems. As Rosalind Gill has helpfully elucidated, "postfeminism should be conceived of as a sensibility" (148) involving a number of interrelated elements, including:

> the notion that femininity is a bodily property; the shift from objectification to subjectification; the emphasis upon self-surveillance, monitoring and discipline; a focus upon individualism, choice and empowerment; the dominance of a makeover paradigm; a resurgence in ideas of natural sexual difference; a marked sexualization of culture; and an emphasis upon consumerism and the commodification of difference. (149)

While all of these elements are present in *What Women Want*, I want to focus on the issues around femininity, commodification, and "natural" sexual difference in relation to the film's fantastic articulation of heterosexual romance.

The commodification of femininity as a bodily property is signalled by the pink box of consumables distributed by Darcy, which Nick then drunkenly tests out: anti-wrinkle cream, make-up, bath beads, home waxing and pregnancy kits, a "more wonderful wonderbra", control-top panty-hose, pore-cleansing strips, painkillers, and (essentially) a credit card. The parodic makeover scene flirts with critique (Nick's bafflement at how anyone manages to wax hair more than once, for example), but overall the film constructs a sense of sympathy with, even admiration for, women's commitment to external beauty (rather than suggesting women might choose to *stop* waxing). When Nick wakes up with the power to hear women's thoughts, what he hears further reinforces the idea of "natural" gender difference, conforming to gendered (and ethnic) stereotype. The first women he encounters are his Latina cleaner (Diana-Maria Riva) and African-American doorwoman (Loretta Devine): both are thinking about him. In the following scene at the park (where every female he encounters, including a French poodle, is white) he hears women thinking about domestic appliances, kissing a woman *once*, calories, oestrogen, a hyperactive kid, and a man who doesn't listen; not one woman is thinking about work, or politics, or anything apart from her personal, domestic life. The scene's overwhelming association of the female mind with bodily concerns is confirmed by the poodle: "Monsieur, I need to poop". Nick's ability to hear women's thoughts places him in an exceptionally privileged position. As his ex-counsellor (Bette Midler) spells out: "Freud died... still asking one question: 'What do women want?'... If men are from Mars, and women are from Venus, and you speak Venusian... the world can be yours". For the most part, the exploitative aspects of this power are glossed over, diverting attention to Nick's re-education – but here, too, conservative gender discourse prevails: while female makeovers emphasize external transformation (products applied to the body), Nick's makeover is about internal transformation (knowledge that changes his mind).

Given this emphasis on gender difference, Nick's power becomes indispensible to the romance plot: his ability to "speak Venusian" enables him to understand Darcy in a way no other man can. At the same time, Nick's "mind-reading" ability is complemented by Darcy's tendency to "speak her mind" – a trait which she describes as a curse, but which he sees as an "enormous relief", specifically asking, "Do you know how rare that is?" Both are marked as *exceptional* among their sex, evoking the romantic notion that they are "made for each other". Thus, the romance plot provides a powerful, but contradictory, fantasy, imagining that men can change and women can (finally) be happy – but only if men learn to read women's minds and women (then) speak theirs.

Nick's "mind-reading" ability also enables him to hear the disjunction between Darcy's thoughts and actions, revealing her vulnerability and insecurity. For example, finding her working late, he is momentarily confused because her words and thoughts overlap; the camerawork reinforces this sense of distortion, craning in towards Darcy at the same time as canting the angle. Out loud, she comments about how late it is, but internally she thinks, "I'm glad you're here: I'm stuck and I feel so alone". He offers to help: she declines; he perseveres. As they talk, she reveals that she is ill and has "basically stopped sleeping" since taking the job. This, too, is a common pattern for postfeminist representation: post-Ally McBeal, the career woman is increasingly imagined as a *fragile* figure, anxiously struggling to maintain (the facade of) success. While Darcy's self-presentation at work is capable and confident, she remains physically "delicate": blond, extremely slender, impeccably turned out in pale shades. J.C. Wiatt was a "Tiger Lady", but it seems implausible that anyone would describe Darcy as the "man-eating bitch Darth Vader of the ad world". She's just too nice, and admits defeat all too easily.

Nominally, Darcy is Nick's "superior", but he has the power for most of the film. The narrative is constructed around him – we rarely see Darcy without him, for example – and the film's subplots reinforce his importance, as he rescues his daughter from the prom, intervenes in a co-worker's possible suicide, and saves Darcy's job. To redress the balance, the film inserts a last-minute reversal: Nick is struck with the realization that, while it looks like he is there "being all heroic, trying to rescue" Darcy, he is the one that "needs to be rescued". The fairy-tale rhetoric is intensified by the couple's final embrace. Meeting in a mid-shot on the spiral staircase, Darcy wonders, "What kind of knight in shining armour would I be if the man I love needs rescuing and I just let him walk out my door?" The scene cuts to a close-up as he moves around her, circling like a dance, before tipping her back slightly (so he appears taller). Sighing, he declares, "My hero", and kisses her. The dialogue's glib gender inversion is counteracted by framing and performance, both of which emphasize Nick's "natural" male dominance as he controls the embrace and kiss.

What is particularly disconcerting about this ending (from a feminist perspective, at least) is the idea that Darcy *needs* love – that, as Nick puts it, she does not feel "complete" or a "winner" without it (in marked contrast to Judy Benjamin's final triumph). This rehabilitation of het-erosexual romance is also explicitly old-fashioned in conception. While the postfeminist narrative requires that Nick's sexual prowess is brought into question, the romantic fantasy would be undermined if Darcy were the one to re-educate him sexually; instead, this function is fulfilled by Lola (Marisa Tomei), an easily manipulated (and discarded) coffee shop waitress. In contrast, Nick and Darcy's relationship is associated with the old-fashioned innocence of kissing and dancing, displacing sex with romance in a very knowing way: as they sway to a modern rendition of Cole Porter's "Night and Day", Nick points out, "So, if you had a bed, we'd be dancing on it".

I find one aspect of this romantic nostalgia particularly striking. The date scene at the Hidden Door bar reminded me of a similar scene in *Woman of the Year* (1942), where newspaper columnists Tess Harding (Katharine Hepburn) and Sam Craig (Spencer Tracy) sit in a back booth, learning about each other while having a drinking competition. The DVD extras confirmed my suspicion: the actors watched some of *Woman of the Year* before rehearsing the scene. I find the connection striking not simply because of the "old-fashioned" influence, however, but because *Woman of the Year* was part of a cycle of career woman comedies in which a successful woman falls in love, becomes more "appropriately" feminine and relinquishes some of her power in order to form a (relatively) more "equal" heterosexual couple.[8] Another film from the cycle, *Honeymoon in Bali* (1939), includes dialogue which may seem strangely familiar:

> I'm not a feminist...but the expression "it's a man's world" always irritates me. It's *any*body's world, who can live it.... I don't believe in marriage... – not for me or for any woman who has the sense to live her own life.... I earn a salary that makes most men's look sick and I'm the boss. And [I have] the most precious thing of all: absolute personal freedom.

These words are spoken by Gale Allen (Madeleine Carroll): initially married to her job as Executive Vice-President of Morrissey's Department Store, by the end of the film she has adopted a small child and married the man she is speaking to, Bill Burnett (Fred MacMurray). A film like *Baby Boom*, then, not only foreshadowed a conventional postfeminist narrative – it also resurrected one. In a sense, these postfeminist retreatist narratives are telling us the same old story, using heterosexual romance as an old-fashioned solution to the "problem" of the independent woman. But there is a paradox here: while the onscreen narratives of career woman comedies typically involve the heroine's feminization, domestication and/or retreat from power, off screen these films enable a few women to have unusually successful careers. *Woman of the Year*, for example, was part of a very deliberate strategy on Hepburn's part to revitalize her film career,[9] and *Honeymoon in Bali* was scripted by Virginia Van Upp, who later became an executive producer at Columbia

Studios. Similarly, by centring her films on topical issues affecting the lives of (white, middle-class) independent women, Meyers has been able to develop increasing control over her own career within an industry that is still heavily dominated by men. Indeed, Martha L. Lauzen's annual report on women's employment on the top-grossing 250 films at the US box office suggests that things are getting worse, not better: in every category studied – directors, writers, executive producers, producers, editors, and cinematographers – the percentage of women employed was lower in 2009 than it had been in 1998, totalling just 16 per cent of the people working on these films. Bearing in mind that in at least one case – *It's Complicated* – the director, writer, and producer would have been *one* woman, not three, Nancy Meyers's exceptional status becomes still clearer.

Some aspects of reception and consumption also warrant attention. Reviewers usually suggest Meyers's films are uneven, unoriginal, and too long, yet they also acknowledge the pleasures of the performances and the romance, before (often begrudgingly) admitting the films' affective power. Anna Smith's review is typical:

> While fitfully amusing, *The Holiday* is at its best when going all out for old-fashioned romance. True, it's overlong and peppered with corny dialogue, much like director Nancy Meyers' previous romantic comedies *Something's Gotta Give* and *What Women Want*. But with a likeable cast and credible romantic unions, it still has the power to move us as the credits roll over its shamelessly idealised closing scene. (58)

I suspect the length of these films is an important part of their commercial success. The leisurely pace of *What Women Want* (127 minutes), *Something's Gotta Give* (128 minutes), *The Holiday* (138 minutes), and *It's Complicated* (120 minutes) enables a certain self-indulgent expectation in the audience – a wallowing in postfeminist pleasures and old-fashioned romance. Self-indulgence is extremely prevalent in current discourses around chick flicks, from the popular cultural idea of the "Girls' Night In" to niche marketing and product tie-ins: Galaxy chocolate, for example, had tie-ins with *Down With Love* (2003) and the *Sex and the City* movie. In various ways, watching chick flicks has been constructed as the filmic equivalent of – and accompaniment to – comfort eating. It is not surprising, then, that recent reviewers have used food metaphors to describe Meyers's films: Justin Chang describes *The Holiday* as "a lavishly overstuffed gift basket of a movie"; the UK DVD cover quotes the *Mail on Sunday* describing *It's Complicated* as "a delicious treat"; while Peter Travers suggests, "You don't have to feel guilty for lapping up this froth. Just don't expect nourishment".

Metaphors such as these are part of a much longer history of taste formation, in which hierarchies of quality are constructed along the lines of gender and class. Genres such as romance have been culturally denigrated partly through their association with "feminine" audiences and the idea that romance "readers" are passive and lacking emotional distance. These are loaded debates for feminist study of popular culture – extending well beyond the scope of this chapter – but I want to conclude by considering how the commodification of self-indulgence relates to postfeminist and neoliberal discourses of pleasure as a way of addressing the problems that "popular feminism" might pose for feminist politics.

It was once a political necessity for feminist scholars to validate "feminine" popular culture as a strategic interrogation of the ways in gender power was structured through hierarchies of taste. This work was vitally important, but I share Stevi Jackson's concerns:

> Some recent accounts... give me the uneasy feeling that romance is being rehabilitated.... new perspectives which take women's pleasure in romance seriously... have produced more sophisticated accounts of women's readings of romance. At the same time, this shift of emphasis risks blunting the edge of feminist critique. Recognizing the pleasure gained from reading romance should not prevent our being critical of it. (262)

Much postfeminist criticism tends to do just this, however, often invoking second wave feminist analysis in order to reject it as overly severe. As Charlotte Brunsdon notes, this has led to the emergence of an "Ur feminist article" (112), in which an academic takes a popular media text centred on women, addressed to a "feminine" audience. The Ur article

> usually involves setting up... an "obvious" [second wave] feminist reading... in which the text itself – and the heroine – fail some sort of test. The heroine is not independent enough... she is always worrying about her looks, or she just wants to find a man and settle down. The author then mobilizes her own engagement with the text... to interrogate the harsh dismissal of this popular text on "feminist" grounds. The author thus reveals the complex and contradictory ways in which the text – and the heroine – negotiate the perilous path of living as a woman in a patriarchal world. (113)

I have no intention of redeeming Nancy Meyers's work in this way: her films *are* complex *and* contradictory, but they are also conservative, stereotypical, and increasingly reliant on heterosexual romance as the solution to the independent woman's problems. Looking at her films within a broader historical context reveals patterns of representation that further confirm the limitations of the texts. Nonetheless, *I enjoy watching these films*.

While Meyers's films undoubtedly bear the traces of second wave feminism in the way they foreground independent women, they are more directly influenced by neoliberal and postfeminist gender discourses. Neoliberalism and the postfeminist sensibility encourage self-indulgent pleasure to be mistaken for empowerment, as if the mere fact that a woman enjoys doing something means this pleasure is, in some sense, "feminist". To me, the pleasures these films provide are antagonistic to feminist politics. "Popular feminism" is feminism without protest, politics replaced with pleasurable self-indulgence in the personal problems of the privileged few. We need to acknowledge the limits of our fantasies and pleasures as distinct from the political struggle against sexism and inequality. Lest we forget the economic realities, the US Census Bureau estimates that, between 2006 and 2008, 14.5 per cent of women were living in poverty, compared to 11.7 per cent of men (S1701); the average median earnings for men over 25 was $41,298, compared to $29,104 for women (S2001); and the pay gap between male and female median earnings was over 33 per cent at every level of educational attainment (S2001), *including* professional careers. The success of an individual woman – onscreen or off – should never be mistaken for the achievement of feminism's goals.

Notes

1. Compare this to another writer-director, Nora Ephron, whose eight films earned $515,045,627 at the US box-office; Meyers's five films earned $549,809,187 (*Box Office Mojo*).
2. See Walkerdine and Gill.
3. See Negra 93.
4. Each film is also a key moment in Meyers's career. Her first film, *Private Benjamin*, was the first time she worked with Shyer; *Baby Boom* was the first film she produced single-handed (Shyer directed) and the first time she worked with Diane Keaton, who then co-starred in the *Father of the Bride* films (1991 and 1995) and *Something's Gotta Give*; and *What Women Want* was her first film without Shyer (and the only one she did not write).

5. This issue was explored in more depth by Yvonne Tasker in her keynote address at the FWSA's *Feminism and Popular Culture* conference (Newcastle University, 2007).
6. See *IMP Awards* for poster images.
7. Interestingly, J.C.'s change of career appears to have little bearing on her economic status. While many postfeminist fictions associate the professional woman's shift towards domesticity with various forms of financial sacrifice, *Baby Boom* presents a female protagonist who prioritizes her family but retains her affluent lifestyle and enhances her business profile.
8. See Glitre 110, 116–30.
9. See Glitre 113–15.

Works cited

Baby Boom. Dir. Charles Shyer. MGM, 1987.
Box Office Mojo. http://boxofficemojo.com/. [Accessed May 19, 2010].
Brunsdon, Charlotte. "Feminism, Postfeminism, Martha, Martha and Nigella". *Cinema Journal* 44.2 (2005): 110–16.
Chang, Justin. Rev. of *The Holiday*. *Variety* (November 30, 2006). http://www.variety.com/awardcentral_review/VE1117932231.html?nav=reviews07&categoryid=2352&cs=1. [Accessed May 19, 2010].
Gill, Rosalind. "Postfeminist Media Culture: Elements of a Sensibility". *European Journal of Cultural Studies* 10.2 (2007): 147–66.
Glitre, Kathrina. *Hollywood Romantic Comedy: States of the Union, 1934–65*. Manchester: Manchester University Press, 2006.
Gorton, Kristyn. "(Un)fashionable Feminists: The Media and *Ally McBeal*". *Third Wave Feminism: A Critical Exploration*. Ed. Stacy Gillis, Gillian Howie, and Rebecca Munford. Basingstoke: Palgrave Macmillan, 2004. 212–23.
The Holiday. Dir. Nancy Meyers. Universal, 2006.
Honeymoon in Bali. Dir. Edward H. Griffiths. Front Row Entertainment, 1939.
IMP Awards. http://www.impawards.com/. [Accessed May 19, 2010].
It's Complicated. Dir. Nancy Meyers. Universal, 2009.
Jackson, Stevi. "Love and Romance as Objects of Feminist Knowledge". *Women and Romance: A Reader*. Ed. Susan Ostrov Weisser. New York: New York University Press, 2001. 254–64.
Lauzen, Martha L. "The Celluloid Ceiling: Behind-the-Scenes Employment of Women on the Top 250 Films of 2009". http://womenintvfilm.sdsu.edu/files/2009_Celluloid_Ceiling.pdf. [Accessed May 19, 2010].
Negra, Diane. *What a Girl Wants?: Fantasizing the Reclamation of Self in Postfeminism*. London: Routledge, 2009.
Private Benjamin. Dir. Howard Zieff. Warner Bros, 1980.
Smith, Anna. "*The Holiday*". *Sight and Sound* 17.2 (February 2007), 58.
Something's Gotta Give. Dir. Nancy Meyers. Warner Bros, 2003.
Tasker, Yvonne. "I'm not a feminist, but…". *Feminism and Popular Culture*. Feminist and Women's Studies Association Annual Conference. Newcastle University, June 29–July 1, 2007. Keynote address.

Travers, Peter. *"It's Complicated"*. *Rolling Stone.* 2009. http://www.rollingstone. com/movies/reviews/%3Bkw=%5B15595,104832%5D. [Accessed May 20, 2010].

US Census Bureau. "S2001: Earnings in the Past 12 Months". American Community Survey, 2006–2008. http://factfinder.census.gov/servlet/STTable?_bm=y &-geo_id=01000US&-qr_name=ACS_2008_3YR_G00_S2001&-ds_name=ACS_ 2008_3YR_G00_. [Accessed May 21, 2010].

US Census Bureau. "S1701: Poverty Status in the Past 12 Months". American Community Survey, 2006–2008. http://www.factfinder.census.gov/servlet/ STTable?_bm=y&-geo_id=01000US&-qr_name=ACS_2008_3YR_G00_S1701&- ds_name=ACS_2008_3YR_G00_. [Accessed May 21, 2010].

Walkerdine, Valerie. "Neoliberalism, Femininity and Choice". *New Femininities: Post-feminism and Sexual Citizenship Seminar Series: Seminar 1: Theorising the Changes.* LSE. November 19, 2004.

What Women Want. Dir. Nancy Meyers. Icon, 2000.

Woman of the Year. Dir. George Stevens. MGM, 1942.

2
"I'm nothing like you!" Postfeminist Generationalism and Female Stardom in the Contemporary Chick Flick

Shelley Cobb

Since the term first accrued cultural currency in the early 1980s, "postfeminism" has been entangled with critical debates about feminist histories, the legacy of the second wave, and the tensions between different "generations" of writers, theorists, and activists.[1] Several Hollywood "chick flicks", including *Monster-in-Law* (2005), *The Devil Wears Prada* (2006), *Prime* (2005), *The Family Stone* (2005), and *Because I Said So* (2007), stage this generational conflict by pairing baby-boomer female stars, associated with the 1970s, with younger female actors. In these films, the younger star tends to perform "the tropes of freedom and choice which are now inextricably connected with the category of young women, [while] feminism is decisively aged and made to seem redundant" (McRobbie 11). Typically, then, the postfeminist woman has been presented as the envoy of an apolitical version of feminism that "has been effectively assimilated into our cultural common sense" (Tasker and Negra 2). Postfeminism maintains this assimilation by promoting a traditional view of femininity, in which "good" women are defined by their personal relationships, while "bad" women are marked out by their resistance to familial and romantic intimacy. In the postfeminist generational plot, either the younger woman or the older woman can learn the lesson of prioritizing family and relationships over her career and herself, although it is the younger woman who is prevailingly situated as the exemplar of appropriate postfeminist behaviour. By contrast, the older actor's stardom is used as shorthand for a politicized and "outdated" mode of feminism that is based around the caricature of the career-obsessed and/or neurotic woman.

This stereotype not only refuses to occupy her "proper" place within the patriarchal family unit, but is also, seemingly, incapable of maintaining "normal" or functional relationships. The figure of the aging woman is thus central to theories of postfeminist generationalism as the default symbol for a feminist lifestyle that is inconsistent with, or inappropriate to, the preoccupations and concerns of contemporary Western women. As Sadie Wearing reflects, this "scandalous presence of the inappropriate is . . . a feature of both popular representations of the aging body *and* postfeminist representations of feminist critical positions" (280). In the context of the postfeminist chick flick, then, the (in)appropriate practice of female choice and independence is mediated, in part, through the specific bodies of the film's female stars (280).

In her article "The Selfish Feminist", Imogen Tyler describes how the earliest (and most persistent) criticism directed at feminism in the 1970s was that it made women selfish – that liberation meant nothing more than a rejection of home and family in order to pursue the narcissistic goal of self-fulfilment. These accusations, Tyler argues, were founded on truths, insofar as they reflected – albeit in a very distorted manner – feminism's belief that "the institution of the family needed to be opened to scrutiny, dismantled and restructured in order for women to gain any measure of social and political equality" (179). For many conservatives, however, it was the feminist political agenda, and not the oppressive structure of the traditional nuclear family, that was encouraging women to leave their husbands and abandon their children. In this "anti-family" version of feminism, the selfish feminist is prevailingly situated as the worst perpetrator of the 1970s "narcissism of minorities that was ripping apart the social fabric of America from within" (184). In this chapter, I am interested in the extent to which Jane Fonda and Meryl Streep – two actors whose star personae were principally defined in the late 1970s and early 1980s – are each, to varying degrees, associated with the feminist narcissism that Tyler identifies with this historical moment. With special reference to *Monster-in-Law* and *The Devil Wears Prada*, I would like to show how the casting of Fonda and Streep, respectively, works to perpetuate "backlash" images of the "selfish feminist", while also taking account of the ways in which the aging female star can resist, and even subvert, the uses to which she is put in these films.

Punishing Hanoi Jane: Teaching the feminist monster a lesson

Monster-in-Law was the film which marked Jane Fonda's return to acting, 15 years after she declared her retirement in 1991. Fonda's Hollywood career had initially taken off in the early 1960s, when she was regarded primarily as a "sex-kitten".[2] Richard Dyer and Tessa Perkins have both suggested that her sex appeal became implicated in the growing feminist movement as a result of her role as the prostitute Bree Daniels in *Klute*, the 1971 film for which she won an Oscar. In 1972 she visited Hanoi, in Vietnam, and was photographed on an anti-aircraft battery that had been used against US forces. That visit, along with her other leftist political activities during the 1960s and 1970s – including her participation in the occupation of Alcatraz, her association with the Black Panthers, and her marriage to Tom Hayden (one of the Chicago Seven) – earned her regular and ongoing censure from conservatives, who nicknamed her Hanoi Jane.[3] Unsurprisingly, critics have tended to interpret Fonda's choice of films in the 1970s as a reflection of her intensifying political convictions. It was during the latter part of this decade that she took on two of her most overtly political roles, playing the left-wing writer Lillian Hellman in *Julia* in 1977, and Sally Hyde, a character who works with disabled Vietnam veterans, in *Coming Home* in 1978. In one of the defining moments of *Coming Home*, Fonda's earlier status as a titillating symbol of sexual liberation is compellingly fused with her new profile as a key representative of the progressive gender politics of the 1970s when Hyde experiences her first orgasm with a veteran with whom she falls in love while her husband is serving in Vietnam.

For Tracy Young, Fonda's box-office appeal during this decade was "a direct result of the women's movement, a movement in constant search of role models" (80). In a similar vein, Tessa Perkins situates Fonda as "the Hollywood star who, in the seventies at least, came closest to being a feminist heroine" (238). Throughout the 1980s, Fonda's star persona changed with the development of her aerobics video empire, her marriage to the media mogul Ted Turner, and her public conversion to Christianity after the breakdown of her 10-year marriage to Turner. This decade saw her berated by the Left for being a sell-out, while remaining, for a large portion of the United States, the hated Hanoi Jane. Within the context of the Hollywood star system, then, Fonda is unusually defined by the ambiguities and ambivalences by which she is encircled. As Perkins puts it, " 'Jane Fonda' functions as a sign whose meanings are still the subject of contestation"; it is within the framework of this contestation that Fonda's return to Hollywood in 2005 is, in my opinion, most productively considered (248).

Despite the contradictory reception of her star persona, Fonda's talents as an actor have been publicly acknowledged through the various awards she has received over the years, and her return to Hollywood was hotly anticipated. This anticipation was amplified by her pairing with Jennifer Lopez, a multi-sector star (pop music, fashion, and film) with previous success in romantic comedies such as *The Wedding Planner* (2001) and *Maid in Manhattan* (2002). Readings of Lopez's action films (such as *Anaconda* [1997], and *Out of Sight* [1998]) have suggested that her ethnic profile functions ambivalently in her stardom – drawing on stereotypes of tough Latina femininity that add an air of authentic urban identity to her embodiment of Hollywood beauty.[4] This tough-but-sexy image on screen coincides with the period of Lopez's life when she was in a highly public relationship with the rapper Sean "Puff Daddy" Combs. Lopez's stardom both on and off screen regularly overlaps in this way, a conflation that continues through her appearance in *Monster-in-Law*. Since the earliest days of her fame, Lopez's personal life, including two failed marriages and relationships with P. Diddy and Ben Affleck, has been a staple feature of tabloid gossip columns. While her engagement to Affleck undermined her image of authenticity – most notably when he appeared in her video for the hit song "Jenny from the Block" lounging about on a yacht and giving her diamonds – her credibility was restored, to some extent, following her marriage to her music collaborator Marc Anthony in a private ceremony in 2005. As Alan Dodd and Martin Fradley have noted, in *Monster-in-Law* Lopez brings a "more confident...tone" to her role, mirroring as it does contemporaneous press descriptions of Lopez as "a woman who has crawled through an abyss and got out the other end stronger" (204–05). The promotional materials for the film give Lopez top billing over Fonda, conceding the power of Lopez's popularity and the importance of her own return to the screen after the box-office failures of *Gigli* (2003) and *Jersey Girl* (2004). Her character's success in finding personal happiness works to reinforce the narrative of Lopez's renewed success in her personal life, creating the perfect star text for promoting the postfeminist lessons that this chapter attempts to enumerate.

In *Monster-in-Law* Lopez plays Charlie, a dog-walking temp and part-time artist who lives in Venice Beach, California. At the beginning of the film, Charlie meets and falls in love with a young, handsome doctor (Michael Vartan), who asks her to marry him during her first meeting with his mother, Viola. Viola, played by Fonda, has already been established within the film as a formidable and intimidating, if emotionally unstable, woman. Viola is initially introduced to the viewer as a woman who has carved out a long and successful career for herself as a Barbara Walters-type talk show host. This career, however, comes to an abrupt end when Viola is informed by the studio executives that she is being replaced by a younger woman. Angry and betrayed, Viola gives vent to her frustration during a live interview with Tanya Murphy, a "teen singing sensation" in the mould of Britney Spears. As the latter attempts to promote her single, which features the line "if you want to know me look in my makeup bag", Viola admonishes her for "probably having no idea of the significance of Roe versus Wade". Lending credence to Viola's suspicion, Murphy replies, "Oh, I don't support boxing as a sport. I think it's too violent". This inane comment, from a pop star who has sold five million CDs (which Viola initially refers to as "albums" – one of several signifiers of her age and "outdatedness"), causes Viola to scream in anger, before launching herself at the young girl and toppling them both to the ground. The specific reference to Roe versus Wade – the 1973 US Supreme Court abortion rights case that remains the touchstone for American feminist politics and a lightening rod for the ongoing culture wars – is, in this instance, the ultimate sign of Viola's 1970s feminism. It is also the first moment when Fonda's historical stardom is directly invoked and contained as redundant and of the past.

As Dodd and Fradley argue, "Lopez's roles in rom-coms are typically imbued with the neo-utopian discourses of post-feminist 'choice' ", meaning that Viola is positioned within the structure of the narrative as "the dysfunctional and fundamentally unhappy victim of second-wave feminism's supposedly anti-feminine imperatives" (204). The two women do perform postfeminist/feminist opposition, but rather than Fonda filling the role of feminist victim, the film seems to draw on Fonda's historical stardom to situate her as a *perpetrator* of feminist politics, one who has become emblematic of the long-running stereotype of liberal feminists as narcissistic and selfish. Certainly, the film works hard to equate Fonda to Viola, and the plot functions to punish Fonda/Viola from both sides by making jokes that contradictorily evoke and invert Fonda's political history: Viola, for example, mentions interviewing Henry Kissinger and receiving a gift from Chairman Mao, and her assistant jokes that Charlie has had fewer lovers than Viola did on "the last day of Woodstock". In this way, the particular politics of Fonda and/or Viola no longer matter; her only consistent crime is to be a successful woman of a certain age with three failed marriages and a Freudian obsession with her only son.

Viola receives her first narrative punishment for being "too old" when she is replaced by a younger woman. Viola's narcissism causes her to mistake her replacement for an intern, and she commands the young woman to get her a latte. In the following scene, the network executives tell Viola that she has had an "amazing career", but they are "trying to appeal to a younger demographic". From behind a closed dressing room door, we, and everyone on the set of her show, hear her screaming and breaking things before she interviews (and attacks) Tanya Murphy. It is at this moment when Viola becomes the "abject feminist" of the popular imagination, whom Tyler describes as having "physical and psychical...connotations [that] include the figuration of the feminist as selfish, cold, frigid, irrationally angry, confused, and perhaps more than anything a singular, lonely and unhappy figure" (185). *Monster-in-Law* works hard to make the stereotype clear when, upon release from a clinic where she has "learned to change" after her breakdown, Viola says to her assistant Ruby (Wanda Sykes), "I've figured it out. Life, I mean. It's not about how many celebrities I interview or what my ratings are; it's about relationships and family. Me and my son". In the midst of this speech, Ruby responds with sarcastic comments like "This ought to be good". Sykes's character plays on the long tradition of the "sassy" black servant, while also filling the role of the loyal and straight-talking ethnic minority friend often found in contemporary cinema – a role which predictably marginalizes the black woman, at the same time as effecting a liberal-left critique of Viola's whiteness and privilege.[5] Additionally, Ruby articulates the position of disbelief that the film expects of the audience in response to Viola's claims that she has learnt her lesson.

These doubts echo a wider cultural suspicion of Fonda – that she never really learnt her lesson – which is still registered, I would suggest, in the continual presence of Vietnam veteran protestors at major Fonda events.[6] Viola's and Fonda's images become further entangled in the film when Kevin brings Charlie to meet his mother. On the way, he tells the stories of his mother's four marriages (evoking Fonda's own three marriages), and finishes with "I'm all she's got now". Upon entering the house, Charlie peruses a side table full of pictures of Viola with various famous figures, including the Dalai Lama, Barbara Walters, Nelson Mandela, Gloria Steinem, Jon Voigt, and Oprah Winfrey – many of which are actual photos from Fonda's life. Missing, of course, is the most (in)famous photo of Fonda on the anti-aircraft gun in Vietnam. In the context of the film, these photos – some of which point to Fonda's activism – are politically neutered, as they now represent Viola's successful career. These photographs are the central symbol of Viola's grandiose, narcissistic, and selfish life, which is further signified through the film's formulation of class and race.

Throughout the entire film, Lopez's Charlie acts the carefree, good-hearted postfeminist woman: she is independent; she keeps herself afloat with odd jobs; she has ambitions in her art, but they always remain domesticated and charming. Viola's own mother-in-law may call her "an exotic Latina", but the characterization of Charlie's ethnicity in the film mostly functions to highlight her "quasi-proletarian ordinariness". This, in turn, implies "that the fight for racial equality is no longer relevant", and uses ethnic identity, instead, as a marker of class (McRobbie 69). By contrast, Viola exudes wealth. Her house is a suburban mansion: "four acres, with two swimming pools, one indoor, one out". On first seeing Charlie from the window of her upstairs bedroom, Viola references their class differences by saying to herself, "Playing dress-up are we?" Later, she even asks Charlie if she is "an illegal alien". Charlie's ethnic identity is again referenced, albeit less explicitly, at the "barbeque" Viola throws to celebrate Kevin and Charlie's engagement. Having assumed that the event will be casual, the couple are surprised and embarrassed to find Viola and all her famous friends decked out in full formal dress. Viola has laid out a vintage dress for Charlie to wear, but it is the wrong size. Lopez is famous for her posterior, which is regularly invoked as a signifier of her authentic ethnic identity. As such, Charlie's inability to get the dress over her hips performs a "refus[al] to fit into the restrictive bourgeois world symbolized by the dress" (Dodd and Fradley 205). The conflict between the two women, then, figures Viola's feminism as inextricably intertwined with a supercilious, racist, bourgeois whiteness that invokes the critiques of second wave feminism by ethnic minority activists and academics. At the same time, and very problematically, it recontextualizes that critique as being just as antiquated as Viola's feminism. It does this by representing Lopez/Charlie as the exemplar of a version of contemporary femininity that supposedly transcends racial politics, and by making her the recipient of the ultimate postfeminist fantasy: finding romantic and (hetero)sexual fulfilment with a successful and rich (white) man.

Throughout the rest of the film, the two women torture each other, each trying to gain the upper hand in their relationship triangle. Finally, at the wedding for Charlie and Kevin, Viola's own "monster-in-law" shows up for a *deus ex machina* ending. Gertrude (Elaine Stritch) mocks Viola and makes plain that she was never good enough for Kevin's father. This pattern of generational conflict convinces Charlie to call the wedding off. After an intervention by Ruby, Viola convinces Charlie not to walk out, and offers to stay out of Charlie's and her son's life. It seems that she has finally learned her lesson, but Charlie has one more lesson for her: she demands that they *do* have a relationship – one which is constructed wholly around the family unit and the projected grandchildren. Charlie says, "You must be present for every Christmas, Thanksgiving, birthday, school play, clarinet recital, and soccer game in our kids' lives. I want you to love them, and spoil them and teach them things that Kevin and I can't. I want you there, Viola. I do, up front and center". Only when the postfeminist woman articulates it does Viola accept the lesson the narrative has been trying to teach her all along. The feminist "monster" is tamed. Throughout the film the humour and satisfaction in Viola's punishment and taming depends on the stardom of Fonda and the spectacle of witnessing the domestication of Hanoi Jane on her return to Hollywood.

From Joanna Kramer to Miranda Priestly: The power of the feminist "Devil"

Since Susan Faludi's publication of *Backlash* in 1991, negative characterizations of feminism and feminists in popular culture have seemed to be symptomatic of the postfeminist era. However, Tyler argues that "by the mid-1970s the most defiant, dismissive and powerful images of feminism had been supplanted by pejorative images of the selfish feminist and her narcissistic twin, commercialised images of 'liberated women'" (185). To illustrate, she gives a detailed reading of the 1979 film *Kramer vs. Kramer*, starring Dustin Hoffman and Meryl Streep. Hoffman plays Ted Kramer, a family man who spends most of his time at his job. Streep plays his wife, a graduate of Smith College who stays at home, becoming depressed, isolated, and neurotic, before leaving him and their son. Her absence permeates the narrative of Ted's change into a loving and feminized father, which develops in contrast to his wife's selfishness, epitomized in a letter to her son explaining why she left: "Being your mommy was one thing, but there are other things and this is what I have to do". Tyler argues that the film enacts the perceived destructiveness of feminism, dramatizing the scorn of conservatives like Phyllis Schlafly: "As a homewrecker, women's liberation is far in the lead over 'the other man', 'the other woman', or 'incompatibility'" (182). After a protracted custody battle that she wins, Joanna decides to let Ted have full custody. What might appear to be Joanna's most selfless act actually condemns her for abandoning her "natural" feminine identity as a mother. In *The Devil Wears Prada*, the 2006 film directed by David Frankel, the character of the selfish feminist is not only resurrected but also updated and adapted for the twenty-first century.

Tyler notes that Streep was first identified with feminist politics as a young actor (181, n. 9).[7] Streep's political affinities and activities have never been seen as strident, but over the years she has supported feminist causes and, along with Fonda, she recently signed an open letter to

George W. Bush appealing for equal rights for Afghan women.[8] In her early film career, Streep co-starred in the Vietnam film *The Deer Hunter* (1978) and appeared as Woody Allen's lesbian ex-wife in *Manhattan* (1979), gaining a reputation, like Fonda, for portraying strong female characters. This reputation was further galvanized by her decision to play the title role in *Silkwood* (1983), which dramatized the life of Karen Silkwood, who was murdered for exposing safety violations at a nuclear plant. After her first Oscar nomination for *The Deer Hunter*, Streep was nominated for an Academy Award every 2 years. The 1980s was a period of highly regarded films, including *Sophie's Choice* (1982), *Out of Africa* (1985), and *Ironweed* (1987), and she received seven Oscar nominations during this decade. She went on to receive a further three nominations in the 1990s and five in the 2000s. Streep, with 16, has the most Academy Award nominations for any actor (and has won twice). From the very beginning, Streep's stardom was formed by, and continues to be understood in terms of, her quality as an actor. Accordingly, in *The Devil Wears Prada*, she was given top billing over Anne Hathaway and received an Academy Award nomination for Best Actress.

The Devil Wears Prada is based on the book of the same name by Lauren Weisberger, a thinly veiled exposé of her time as Anna Wintour's assistant at *Vogue* magazine. Streep plays Miranda Priestly, the tyrannical editor-in-chief at the fictional *Runway* magazine, while Hathaway is cast in the role of Andrea, Miranda's latest assistant's assistant. As Andrea, Hathaway exudes Midwestern naïveté and is initially distinguished by her lack of fashion savvy. She is, however, quickly seduced by the world of designer labels and celebrity parties and gradually begins to put her job – and Miranda – before her family, her friends, and her boyfriend. Eventually, Andrea is chosen over Emily, the other assistant, for a coveted opportunity to accompany Miranda to Paris Fashion Week. As Carina Chocano, a critic for *The Los Angeles Times*, has commented, while *The Devil Wears Prada* might "[cast] doubts as to who the actual heroine of the story is, it's very clear on who's the star of the show" (para. 1). Miranda becomes the star of the show, if not the heroine of the film, due in large part to Streep's screen presence; through her quality stardom and the sensitivity of her performance, she usefully complicates the film's representation of a character that, in the original novel, is a fairly straightforward caricature of female selfishness and narcissism.

On the whole, the film presents Miranda as a woman who puts the concerns and needs of others, and any feeling she might have for them, far behind her hard-won success and desire for control. In the climax of the film, Miranda thwarts a plan by the owners of the magazine to give her job to the younger female editor of *Paris Runway* by giving the Paris editor a job that she had promised to her loyal fashion editor Nigel (Stanley Tucci). As Nigel's friend, Andrea is disappointed by Miranda's decision, and on the way to the next fashion event she sits quietly while Miranda explains how she used her power to keep her position. This, however, is followed by another, more startling, revelation: "I never thought I would say this Andrea, but I see a great deal of myself in you.... You can see beyond what others want or think they need, and you can choose for yourself". In response, Andrea disagrees with Miranda: "I don't think I'm like that. I couldn't do what you did to Nigel", to which Miranda replies, "But you already did...to Emily". Andrea protests that she had no choice since Emily was ill, but Miranda tells her that she made the choice to get ahead. The postfeminist lesson of this scene is clear: for some time Andrea has been seduced by the success of the "selfish feminist". When Andrea says, "But what if I don't want to live the way you live?", Miranda is quick to retort: "Oh don't be ridiculous Andrea. Everybody wants this. Everybody wants to be us". Delivered by Streep, wearing designer sunglasses and a mink stole in the back seat of a chauffeur-driven limousine, the expected reaction of Andrea and the audience, that none of "this" is worth it, is difficult to accept. As Chocano concludes in her article for the *LA Times*, "What is unexpected here is that the triumph of virtue...doesn't feel entirely triumphant. It smacks of giving up" (para. 17). Yet, when they arrive at their hotel, Andrea does not follow Miranda in; she walks away. Her phone rings, and the name displayed, predictably, is "Miranda". With a smile, Andrea triumphantly throws it into a fountain, before making amends with her boyfriend, her friends, and even Emily. The female generational plot demands a moral climax in which the young postfeminist woman who expects career success learns her lesson not to become just another selfish feminist with an unsuccessful personal life. As a rising star, Hathaway fulfils this role perfectly. Only 24 when the film was released, she was previously most well-known for the "tween" film series *The Princess Diaries* (2001/2004), in which she plays Mia, an awkward teenage girl from San Francisco who learns she is meant to inherit the throne of a small European country. These films offer a postfeminist view of independence and agency (Mia chooses to accept the crown on her own, and only then does her "prince" arrive) in the midst of a girlish princess fantasy.[9] Hathaway's personal life also seemed princess-like, with her Italian millionaire boyfriend and her burgeoning professional profile.[10]

Inevitably, Streep brings to the role of Miranda Priestly the intertextual references of the selfish feminist Joanna Kramer – the role for which she won her first Oscar. It is possible to read Miranda Priestly as Joanna Kramer 25 years later: in *Kramer v. Kramer*, after all, Joanna gets a job in the fashion industry. Furthermore, an important scene links the two characters, indicating how Streep's actorly stardom complicates the contemporary caricature of the selfish feminist. When they are in Paris, Andrea finds Miranda in her hotel in a state of undress, sitting forlornly on her couch after her third husband has left her. Without make-up, hair undone, and wearing a grey robe and reading glasses, she looks much older. Abjection is written on her body, fulfilling the image of the selfish feminist as *"a singular, lonely and unhappy figure"* (Tyler 185; emphasis added). Streep's performance, however, works to complicate this interpretation. Miranda says that she is not concerned for herself but for her daughters, who will take the loss hard, and who will have to endure the gossip. Streep delivers the line without irony, and sadness infuses her face, implying that Miranda does care about more than just herself. The scene is in such contrast to what we expect of Miranda that it stands out as an "actorly" moment that is invested with Streep's "quality" stardom. At the moment when Miranda most conspicuously fills the stereotype of the selfish feminist, then, Streep intervenes and infuses her with pathos.[11]

In both the book and the film Andrea's rejection of Miranda's version of success is rewarded with a job in journalism. In the book, she sends a short story about her experiences at *Runway* to *Seventeen* magazine. The editor of *Seventeen* hates Miranda Priestly too, and says, "Someone needed to tell that woman to go fuck herself, and if it was you, well, then, hats off! That woman made my life a living hell for the year I worked there, and I never even had to exchange a single word with her" (426). She says she will take anything Andrea writes for the magazine. They are two young women bonded in postfeminist sisterhood against the old, lonely, crone-ish feminist. The film's ending is subtly, but also radically, different. Andrea has an interview with the male editor of *The New York Mirror*. He tells her that he called *Runway* for a reference and "received a fax from Miranda Priestly herself, saying that of all her assistants, you were her biggest disappointment. And, if I don't hire you, I'm an idiot". In this instance, the "selfish" feminist has acquired enough power and influence to compel a man into giving another woman a job – a triumph of selfish feminism that, to the surprise of Andrea and the audience alike, works to the benefit of the postfeminist woman.

Given the casting of Streep as Miranda, this denouement is, perhaps, not that much of a surprise. Later, Andrea makes brief eye contact with Miranda as she gets into her car, and Andrea waves. Miranda snubs her, and Andrea shakes her head in recognition laced with relief. The penultimate shot, before we see Andrea's obligatory confident walk through the streets of New York, is a close-up of Miranda in her car. Watching Andrea walk away, she appears pensive, but then a slow, wry smile appears on her face, and she lets out a small knowing laugh. Played by Streep and imbued with her star persona as a "quality" actor, the older feminist is not the young woman's enemy; Miranda seems to find some pride in Andrea's choice to go her own way. As much as it is clear that the film needs Andrea to make a decision not to be like Miranda, and to learn to prioritize relationships over ambition, it cannot help but give Miranda a final moment of respect because of Streep's star persona as the older, wiser, and more successful female actor. As the *LA Times* review suggests, the ending casts doubt on Andrea's status as the hero, and the film most definitely knows that Streep is the star. Through her quality stardom Streep subverts the image of the feminist "devil", making a fissure in the film's structuring of generational conflict and suggesting that postfeminism's insistence that women can now do whatever they want would not be possible without the selfish feminist who did whatever she wanted.

Conclusion

I hope that these initial examinations of postfeminist generationalism and female stardom might invite more scrutiny into "the ways in which we appropriate icons as they age and outgrow their initial purpose, and how icons weather changing cultural climates" (Roberts 102). Many of the female icons of 1970s Hollywood are being re-appropriated by contemporary Hollywood for postfeminist narratives that emphasize the impossibility of generating bonds amongst women outside of familial relationships, and which thus participate in the general cultural climate that understands "successful" femininity only in terms of a woman's relationships. This is particularly true in *Monster-in-Law*, in which Fonda's star persona is used to subordinate her to the example of the young postfeminist woman. I have argued, though, that Streep's performance in *The Devil Wears Prada* shows that stardom can still offer agency and authority to women in contemporary Hollywood; this, in turn, suggests that we need to further consider the ways that age, stardom, and the discourses of (post)feminism interact to confine and, on occasion, expand the roles that women play in Hollywood films.

Acknowledgements

Many thanks go to Neil Ewen and the editor of this book for their comments and suggestions.

Notes

1. See Gillis and Munford.
2. See Perkins 239–42.
3. For more on "Hanoi Jane", see Kinney.
4. See Beltrán.
5. See Hicks.
6. See Dobnik.
7. A 1979 article in *The New York Times* parenthetically remarks that as a university student Meryl Streep "wrote funny feminist dramas" (see Gussow).
8. This open letter was organized by Equality Now in 2005.
9. The "girlish princess fantasy" is a key feature of other postfeminist texts. For an analysis of the ways in which the princess fantasy is utilized in the reality makeover show, see Brenda Weber's "Imperialist Projections: Manners, Makeovers, and Models of Nationality" (in this book).
10. Hathaway's relationship with Raffaello Follieri ended in 2008 when he was arrested on charges of fraud. In court, he blamed her Hollywood lifestyle for influencing his actions (see "The Envelope").
11. Unlike Fonda, Streep has largely kept her private life private, distancing the characters she plays from herself and her personal investments in feminism.

Works cited

Beltrán, Mary. "The Hollywood Latina Body as Site of Social Struggle: Media Constructions of Stardom and Jennifer Lopez's 'cross-over butt' ". *Quarterly Review of Film and Video* 19.1 (January 2002): 71–86.

Chocano, Carina. "A comic Meryl Streep Brings a Stylishly Better-than-the-Book Allure to Prada". *The Los Angeles Times*. June 30, 2006. http://www.calendarlive.com/movies/reviews/cl-et-devil30jun30,0,7739063.story. [Accessed September 5, 2009].

The Devil Wears Prada. Dir. David Frankel. 20th Century Fox, 2006.

Dobnik, Verena. "Jane Fonda's Broadway Play Picketed by Vietnam Vets". *Huffington Post*. February 22, 2009. http://www.huffingtonpost.com/2009/02/22/jane-fondas-broadway-play_n_168897.html. [Accessed 30 August 30, 2009].

Dodd, Alan, and Martin Fradley. "Jennifer Lopez, Romantic Comedy, and Contemporary Stardom". *Falling In Love Again: Romantic Comedy in Contemporary Cinema*. Eds. Stacey Abbott and Deborah Jermyn. London: IB Tauris, 2009. 190–207.

Dyer, Richard. *Stars*. 2nd edn. London: BFI, 1998.

"The Envelope". *The Los Angeles Times*. http://latimesblogs.latimes.com/thedishrag/2008/10/raffaello-folli.html. [Accessed September 30, 2009].

Gillis, Stacy, and Rebecca Munford. "Genealogies and Generations: The Politics and Praxis of Third Wave Feminism". *Women's History Review* 13.2 (2004): 165–81.

Gussow, Mel. "The Rising Star of Meryl Streep". *The New York Times*. February 4, 1979.

Haskell, Molly. "Finding Herself: The Everlasting Prime of an Acting Powerhouse Who Gracefully Eludes Definition Yet is Every Inch a Star". *Film Comment* (March–April 2008): 33–41.

Hicks, Heather J. "Hoodoo Economics: White Men's Work and Black Men's Magic in Contemporary American Film". *Camera Obscura* 18.2 (2003): 27–55.

Kinney, Katherine. "Hanoi Jane and Other Treasons: Women and the Editing of the 1960s". *Women's Studies* 32 (2003): 371–92.

McRobbie, Angela. *The Aftermath of Feminism: Gender, Culture, and Social Change*. London: SAGE, 2009.

Monster-in-Law. Dir. Robert Luketic. New Line, 2005.

Perkins, Tessa. "The Politics of 'Jane Fonda'". *Stardom: Industry of Desire*. Ed. Christine Gledhill. London: Routledge, 1991. 239–52.

Roberts, Chadwick. "The Politics of Farrah's Body: The Female Icon as Cultural Embodiment". *The Journal of Popular Culture* 37.1 (2003): 83–104.

Tyler, Imogen. "The Selfish Feminist". *Australian Feminist Studies* 22.53 (July 2007): 173–90.

Tasker, Yvonne, and Diane Negra, eds. *Interrogating Postfeminism: Gender and the Politics of Popular Culture*. London: Duke University Press, 2007.

Wearing, Sadie. "Subject of Rejuvenation: Aging in Postfeminist Culture". *Interrogating Postfeminism: Gender and the Politics of Popular Culture*. Ed. Yvonne Tasker, and Diane Negra. London: Duke University Press, 2007. 277–310.

Weisberger, Lauren. *The Devil Wears Prada*. New York: Anchor Books, 2003.

3
Alias: Quality Television and the New Woman Professional

Rosie White

The character of Sydney Bristow in *Alias* (Warner Brothers, 2001–06) offers a compelling representation of the female spy that both reflects and illuminates contemporary debates about the role of women in the professions.[1] The cinematic production values of this spectacular series, together with its complex narrative arcs and stellar guest list, epitomize what has come to be known as American quality television.[2] As with earlier quality television series centred on female protagonists – such as *Ally McBeal* (Fox, 1997–2002) and *Buffy the Vampire Slayer* (Warner Brothers/UPN, 1997–2003) – *Alias* focuses on the uneasy relationship between women's professional ambitions and personal responsibilities. Like these earlier shows, *Alias* explores the profound inextricability of the professional and the familial/romantic, positioning the workplace as a space in which and through which the personal is worked *upon*. Exploring the ways in which emotional labour is tethered to professional employment, quality series such as *Alias* function – at one level – as etiquette guides for the (post)modern urban woman. In this respect, *Alias* does invite consideration alongside HBO's *Sex and the City* (1998–2004), in which the drama is based around the sexual practices and quandaries of four women with apparently limitless time and funds. Certainly, Carrie Bradshaw and friends have hours to spend planning, engaging in, and discussing their emotional and sexual lives. Their work lives, on the other hand, are barely visible. While in *Alias* the drama is set entirely around Sydney Bristow's career as a secret agent, the series – like *Sex and the City* – is characterized by its slick, glossy surface. Although Sydney is not overtly obsessed by fashion, the "undercover" sequences where she dresses in glamorous outfits and struts to a pumping soundtrack do mimic the fashion aesthetic which is more demonstrably operative in *Sex and the City*.[3] Both series also privilege the emotional lives of their protagonists: despite Sydney's spectacular ability to defend herself from the physical threats she encounters at work, it is the emotional trials which are shown to be most painful. As Elizabeth Barnes notes, Sydney's visible suffering "is the *raison d'être* of the show: this is a woman who takes on the pain of the world" (57). With its sustained focus on emotional drama, its continuous-serial storylines, and its exposition of familial/romantic conflicts, the show draws heavily on the heritage and conventions of soap opera. In the case of *Alias*, however, the soap opera is set within the workplace (which for Sydney includes hi-spec office space and exotic global missions), so that the narrative reflects upon shifts in the twenty-first-century workplace and women's roles within it. Sydney's emotional vulnerability thus resonates beyond the scope of the domestic or romantic narratives that have traditionally featured female protagonists on television. Angela McRobbie argues that popular accounts of the post-feminist working girl [*sic*] constitute a reconfiguration of normative femininity which is part of a wider process of gender re-stabilization in the light of recent shifts in employment and global economies:

> The post-feminist masquerade exacts then on the part of the working girl a kind of compromise, she takes up her place in the labour market and she enjoys her sense of status as a working girl without going too far. She must retain a visible fragility and the displaying of a kind of conventional feminine vulnerability will ensure she remains desirable to men. (79)

This is a particular feature of the "new woman" on television; like Ally and Buffy, Sydney must suffer visibly. In this regard these series again follow the visual and narrative traditions of soap opera; viewers are offered privileged insights into private moments where Sydney is alone and distressed. Such narrative strategies bear comparison with earlier depictions of working women in films like *Presumed Innocent* (Alan J Pakula, 1990) and *Disclosure* (Barry Levinson, 1994), where the new woman was seen as "bad news" and thus as "deserv[ing] punishment and/or annihilation by the patriarchal system she so overtly transgresses" (Jones 297). The visible distress of Ally, Buffy, and Sydney represents a different version of such "punishment", which functions both to confirm their hetero-femininity and to indicate the personal cost that they – as working women – will inevitably incur. While the alternative is seldom presented in any explicit sense, the implication is that women who follow a more traditional career route to marriage, family, and housekeeping are less "conflicted" and more fulfilled. The finale of *Alias,* for example, gave Sydney a "happy" ending where she is suddenly depicted in an idyllic nuclear family setting, far from the world of work. Invariably, the model of femininity on which these depictions draw is that of an idealized white Western middle class: "White middle-class women, historically viewed as the cultural bearers of compassion and the producers of human feeling and family, are thus not so much reimagined in these shows as recontextualised" (Barnes 58).

These strategies in popular cinematic and televisual narratives regarding working women may be understood as part of an ongoing response to second wave feminism and to perceived shifts in the number of women entering the workplace at a professional or managerial level.[4] Several critics have deployed the term "New Woman" to refer to representations of the working woman in late twentieth- and early twenty-first-century popular culture – not least because these accounts of women in the professions bear comparison with debates that took place in Britain and America a century earlier. Sarah Grand is credited with originally coining the term "New Woman" in an article for the 1894 *North American Review,* which noted "a modern discontent with the traditional stay-at-home life of marriage and motherhood deemed appropriate for middle-class women" (Gamble 283). It was taken up by journalists and authors (both pro- and anti-feminist) as part of a debate about the public role and sexual identity of middle-class white women at the *fin de siècle.* Like her sister the *femme fatale,* the New Woman marked shifts in gender roles that were taking place as the nineteenth century drew to a close and the twentieth century began; both terms, then, represent a nexus of contradictory discourses regarding gender, sexuality, race, and class. In the 1990s a number of scholars working in film studies identified comparable shifts in screen portrayals of working women. Yvonne Tasker's *Working Girls: Gender and Sexuality in Popular Cinema* (1998) reflected on the sexualization of the working woman. Amelia Jones argued that in the "new woman's films" of the 1980s and 1990s career women are caricatured and punished; she proposed that films such as *Working Girl* (Mike Nichols, 1988) and *Presumed Innocent* may be understood as "structured by what Alice Jardine has called 'male paranoia'" even as they offer apparently positive accounts of women in the workplace (297). Hilary Radner examined Sarah Connor from *Terminator 2: Judgement Day* (James Cameron, 1991) and Marge Gunderson from *Fargo* (Joel Coen, 1996) as examples of how the female body has been transformed in its cinematic representations.[5] Work such as this mapped evident changes in popular depictions of working women in the late twentieth century, while noting how such changes may be seen as the latest in a series of modifications that rarely serve women well. Inevitably, representations of new woman professionals in film and high-end Hollywood action series such as *Alias* comment on late Western capitalism and the continuing evolution of white-collar working practices, such as the demands of the New Economy.

The term "New Economy" refers to the exponential expansion of a global economic system towards the end of the twentieth century – an expansion made possible by electronic capitalism and the increasing dominance within Western economies of information, computer technologies, and telecommunications (ICT). For some, the putative work practices of the New Economy are regarded as potentially liberating, in that they enable employees to choose where and when they work, while providing a flexible and market-responsive pool of labour (Takacs 148). Certainly, the New Economy is often seen as a feminized workplace, privileging communication skills and white-collar forms of labour. In theory, ICT could allow women to work from home, to combine child-care and a professional career, to "have it all". In reality, however, it has not fulfilled its egalitarian potential: as Stanworth writes, "ICT-based work physically and contractually outside organisational boundaries is often isolated and exploitative, for women especially where skills are low, easily replaceable or undervalued" (21).[6] Sydney Bristow and her sister professionals in mainstream Hollywood cinema and television do work in computerized environments, but they are not an underprivileged, out-sourced workforce. Rather, they represent a recent variation on Hollywood representations of the American white middle classes as over-achieving professionals. The phenomenon of the over-achieving professional appeared on American television just as it surfaced in the American corporate culture of the 1990s, depicting working lives of extreme dedication, long hours, and superhuman ability:

> In the supermom fantasies of TV and the mommy track proposals of corporate America, what remains enshrined is our country's craven, hypercompetitive yuppie work ethic. Babies and parents are supposed to work around these increasingly preposterous norms of what constitutes adequate job performance.
>
> (Douglas 282)

The "mommy track" was a media term which emerged in the 1990s, referring to American corporations' proposal that "mothers should be on a separate – and unequal – career track that gives them more flexible hours in exchange for no promotions, no challenging assignments, less autonomy, and no raises" (Douglas 282). Takacs, Stanworth, Perrons, and Douglas indicate the contradictory and conflicted terrain of such white-collar work, particularly for women who choose to have children; television fictions which address the New Economy have the potential to expose that terrain in ways which fuel the narrative drama and inspire external debate.

ER (NBC, 1994–2009) has repeatedly exposed the difficulty of maintaining a career as a professional medic and raising a family, particularly through storylines involving Abby Lockhart (Maura Tierney). While *ER* may favour a more realist account of professional life – fuelling its drama with many accounts of its characters' chaotic personal lives outside the Chicago hospital – the action-adventure style of *Alias* lends a fantastic bent to the depiction of espionage as professional occupation. *Alias*'s Sydney Bristow is consequently a fantasy of the professional superwoman, and, by Season Five, a "supermom". In this way, Sydney Bristow is an extreme version of such over-achieving fantasies; the series continually reveals that she has no life outside the agencies she works for, as her friends and family are either working for secret agencies or are inadvertently swept up in the spying game. In her essay "Why Sydney has no social life", Jody Lynn Nye enumerates the commitments and training that actually *being* Sydney would involve, producing a convincing argument regarding the unfeasibility of her workload. Sydney Bristow is a mathematical and physical impossibility; her expertise in almost every field, her language skills, her physical prowess, and her infallible efficiency make her a parody of over-achievement. Sydney may thus be understood both as a fantasy of the superhuman professional and as an ironic account of the extreme demands of professional labour in the twenty-first century.

In this sense, *Alias* and series like it comment upon a failure of second wave feminism and mainstream responses to it, as they comment upon the *lack* of change in working practices across the professional sphere. What Sydney Bristow tells us is that women may have a position in the professional workplace but can sustain it only by being more driven, more unassailably efficient than their colleagues. She also tells us that the workplace remains unfailingly masculine in outlook and organization. Sydney and her sisters in quality television drama represent the privileged middle-class professional. They are separate from the masses, from the often unseen and undifferentiated "ordinary" women who exist around them (Radner 5). Slim, predominantly white, immaculately presented, and committed to their jobs, they embody professional efficiency. Female characters in ensemble dramas such as *Without a Trace* (CBS, 2002–), *CSI Miami* (CBS, 2002–), *CSI New York* (CBS, 2004–), and *Grey's Anatomy* (ABC, 2005–) are subsumed by their work, matching their male colleagues' dedication, focus, and long hours. Like their male colleagues these working women are rarely allowed successful relationships or functional family lives. Where personal lives intrude on the work of the professional team – whether familial or romantic – they are most often shown to be problematic, a cause of disruption in the workplace and thus likely to produce further drama. The conflict between personal and professional lives is sometimes a storyline for male characters, but it more often becomes a women's issue, involving problems with childcare, ex-partners, or inadvisable liaisons.

Women in the professions have had a chequered history on screen; as characters who combine femininity and authority they are always-already ambiguous figures, contradicting the traditional formation of femininity as powerless and passive. Amelia Jones describes how these women are punished in mainstream Hollywood cinema, citing examples such as *Presumed Innocent*, *Working Girl*, and *Fatal Attraction* (Adrian Lyne, 1987):

> The extraordinary lengths to which [these films] go to destroy or close down female sexuality and professional independence indicates precisely that there is a real threat perceived in the new woman – in her destabilization of patriarchal economies of labor and relations of sexual difference. (299)

Professional women on television tend to be compromised by problems in their personal life; in Sydney's case, the threat of her professional ability is also contained through hyperbole and fetishization. Sydney Bristow is one of the most exaggerated accounts of such femininity on the small screen; she is unfailingly efficient, impeccably glamorous, and largely impervious to human failings, such as envy, anger, or exhaustion. Sydney is clearly an aspirational figure, a hyperreal account of what women in the professions should be, could be, or would want to be. This idealized figure also inadvertently indicates the costs of Sydney's extraordinary life, and these costs are specifically those of a masculine economy, thus giving the lie to any notion of the New Economy as liberating or indeed feminized.

Sydney at home and at work is unfailingly caught within an economy of power, hierarchy, and exchange. As Irigaray noted in "Women on the Market", her 1977 account of the masculine economy, "The work force is always assumed to be masculine, and 'products' are objects to be used, objects of transaction among men alone" (800). *Alias* shows us that little has changed in the last 30 years. Many of the intricate plotlines centre on Sydney herself as a desirable asset; not just in professional and sexual terms but literally, as a commodity within the secret world she inhabits. In "Full Disclosure" (3.11) Sydney's eggs are harvested by acolytes of Rambaldi who think she is the "chosen one",[7] while in "There's Only One Sydney Bristow" (5.12), the enemy agency is seeking to acquire a sample of Sydney's DNA in order to replicate her appearance. Sydney's unique chemistry has become part of the trade in information which the secret agencies compete for – and despite the role of her mother, Irina Derevko (who in one storyline is symbolically referred to as "The Man") – this is an unequivocally masculine environment of trade between men, where Sydney is an asset but never a director. The Derevko sisters intervene in this masculine trade – as does CIA director Hayden Chase (Angela Bassett) – but only as, respectively, demonized or marginal figures.[8]

As in her professional life, in her personal and familial relationships Sydney is framed by masculine economies. Despite a tortured relationship with her father, Jack Bristow, he is the central figure in her life, and Arvin Sloane's claims to be her (other) father only make Sydney's identification with a masculine economy more evident. Jack Bristow is Sydney's creator as well as her father; as the manager of "Project Christmas", a secret scheme to train and develop young children as super-agents, Jack is revealed to have brought his daughter into the field as a child, without her consent.[9] A successful woman in a man's world, Sydney is an exceptional figure – her female co-stars are either less able than Sydney or are shown to be working for the wrong side – and Sydney's exceptionality is taken further than the Project Christmas revelation; the Milo Rambaldi storyline posits Sydney as part of a wider plan for the salvation or destruction of the world (Ruditus 79–94). Sydney is, quite literally, a superwoman: a chosen one, like Buffy the Vampire Slayer, who is predestined to have a significant role in events. Her abilities are, however, at the service of the CIA and are thus part of a masculine bureaucracy in which women are present but have little power. Sydney, as Project Christmas and the Rambaldi prophecies imply, is man-made.

While Sydney is framed by a masculine economy in her professional and private life, *Alias* occasionally reveals the costs that such an economy incurs. Sydney is rarely at rest. She lives to work, and the intensity of this work is repeatedly foregrounded in the depiction of her espionage assignments, characterized by rapid editing and pumping soundtracks. This is epitomized by the Season Four credit sequence, which was cut to the rhythm of the theme tune. This sequence is organized around images of Sydney in disguise and in various fetishistic costumes – costumes which she is required to wear in the course of her work. In the DVD commentary for the opening episode of the season, Jennifer Garner comments that the credit sequence is a "bit much", while JJ Abrams states that he cannot think of a better opening than this quick-cut sequence of 70 images in 30 seconds. What the new credit sequence capitalizes on is the fantasy role-play of Sydney's professional roles: this is an accomplished actor playing a professional woman playing a range of feminine clichés. The multiple images underline Sydney's *exchangeability*; she is "everywoman" and all possible fantasies: "just as a commodity has no mirror it can use to reflect itself, so woman serves as reflection, as image of and for man, but lacks specific qualities of her own. Her value-invested form amounts to what man inscribes in and on its matter: that is, her body" (Irigaray, 2004, 808–09). Yes, there are a few less sexual images in the sequence (particularly, perhaps, the beekeeper's outfit?) but as a whole the sequence reveals the economy in which both Jennifer Garner and Sydney Bristow work – one in which women are most valued as sexually visible figures.[10] None of the rapidly edited shots show Sydney in her mundane office suits or at home; the visual and aural onslaught of fetishized images and theme music compound the heightened reality of Sydney's assignments and present them as the "real" focus of the series. As if to confirm this impression, the first episode of Season Four opens with Sydney on assignment, revealingly dressed in a blonde wig and baby-doll lingerie to seduce a chemist in order to obtain an isotope. In this way, Sydney Bristow's professional labour is clearly aligned with sex work (Tasker, 1998).

Such images conform to elements of the "male gaze" as it is conceptualized by Laura Mulvey; Sydney is presented to-be-looked-at, in scopophilic terms, with fetishistic costumes and props. The aspect of Mulvey's argument Sydney confounds in these sequences is the fast editing and speed of movement; the Hollywood stars Mulvey described in her famous essay were largely static figures, composed and carefully presented for the camera. While Garner is carefully presented she is rarely static, and her fleshless, muscular physique suggests athletic movement rather than static femininity. *Alias*, like much action cinema and television, has a hyperactive aesthetic but here that aesthetic is symbolic of the organizations that employ Sydney and her peers. In its attempt to make white-collar labour sexy, *Alias* depicts office work on fast-forward.

This is most graphically embodied by Sydney's espionage assignments, during which Sydney is constantly on the move, physically and geographically. Fast-paced, high-octane action sequences are accompanied by fast-paced, high-octane music, which was played on the set during the filming to ensure that the frequent shots of Garner "strutting" towards some action were kept to a beat. Missions inevitably involve Sydney going undercover in glamorous locations, referencing the jet-set tradition of Bondian espionage and offering a narrative reason for Garner to be dressed in body-skimming outfits.[11] This hyperactive aesthetic, however, might also be read as a parody of white-collar labour in the twenty-first century.

In the first season, Sydney's exceptional work ethic is the subject of comment within the series:

WILL TIPPIN: It doesn't make sense any more. Nobody works as hard as you. I mean, it's not like you're a brain surgeon getting called in the middle of the night to save a life. I mean, these are bankruptcies. And how much are they paying you to live like this?

SYDNEY: Not enough.

WILL: I'm going to actually call them and quit for you right now.

SYDNEY: I can't quit my job.

WILL: Why? Why – because you just have to be, like, the greatest banker?

SYDNEY: Because it's my job. I want to do it well.

WILL: Okay. Congratulations. Me too. But at what cost?

SYDNEY: Look, to you my job might seem pointless and stupid, but it's not. It's far from pointless and if you knew what I dealt with every day you might *thank* me for doing my job so well.

WILL: What the hell are you talking about?

SYDNEY: Nothing. I'm going to work.

(1.10)

This dialogue makes explicit the nonsense of Sydney's cover; her alias as a college student and banker are not feasible within the terms of the series itself: Will merely voices what is self-evident. This lack of fit between the roles Sydney plays at work and in her private life offers a critique of the demands made upon professional workers; it is an account of work–life *im*balance in a postmodern workplace where the employee is constantly on call via email, mobile phone, or Blackberry. Will's reference to brain surgery makes the connection between *Alias*'s fictive account of professional employment (espionage) and other professions. Sydney has entered a workplace where a personal life is a luxury she cannot afford. Most tellingly, in the pilot episode Sydney's fiancé is assassinated by her employers, SD6, thus precipitating her discovery that SD6 is not a secret arm of the CIA but the very enemy she thought she was fighting against.

What such narrative details make evident is the cost of the new economy. By Season Four Sydney's personal life has been subsumed by her work. Sydney no longer lives in a shared graduate house in a leafy suburb, but a slick urban apartment. She invites her half-sister, Nadia, to live with her, and life outside APO is barely distinguishable from her life inside the agency, as she socializes only with colleagues. The plotlines of the series marry Sydney's family and sexual life with that of her profession: her mother, father, aunts, and sister all work in the field, and her romantic interest, Michael Vaughn, is her CIA handler when she is a double agent in SD6. Most of the major protagonists in the series have family within secret agencies and – in the case of Vaughn, Sydney, and Nadia – are fascinated by the mysteries around their parents. The internecine familial plots in *Alias* would appear to open it up to psychoanalytic interpretation, yet the extreme nature of the family relationships are, like the account of professional life, a hyperreal pastiche of emotional dysfunction. Sydney's mother Irina Derevko is first thought to be dead, then is found to be alive but working as an enemy agent who eventually takes out a contract on her daughter's life.[12] Sydney's father, Jack Bristow, has Irina killed in order to save Sydney but it later emerges that a genetic duplicate of Irina was killed in her place, so she is still alive but being kept prisoner and tortured by her sister, Elena Derevko. Towards the end of the fourth season Nadia and Sydney rescue and release their mother, Irina, with Jack Bristow's help. The family narratives of *Alias* grow ever more bizarre as the series progresses, so that by the fourth season Sydney's private and professional worlds have effectively combined.

Despite Sydney's professional abilities she is unable to function outside the workplace and this symbolic fault demonstrates the cost of the masculine economy.[13] This is not merely a masculine economy of emotion where "male power in *Alias* is associated with lack of emotion ... the ability to keep one's vulnerabilities concealed" (Wright 203). It is also a privileging of masculine forms of power, (self) control, and cultural capital. Despite the allegiance of television series such as *Alias* to the style of soap opera – by including family drama in the scenario, together with a romantic narrative – a form which has traditionally been seen as privileging feminine concerns, these dramas inevitably return to the father as a source of epistemological authority.[14] Jack Bristow is Sydney's prime source of truth and knowledge, a man who sacrifices his own life in the final episode to save his daughter and the world. Mothers, however, are shown to be untrustworthy. Irina, Katya, and Elena Derevko in *Alias* occupy ambiguous moral ground during the series, but by the finale their motives are exposed as greedy and self-serving. Yet these older women are themselves subsumed within a masculine economy; they are women who have conformed to the demands of the professional sphere rather than shifting the terms on which it operates. In this sense the Derevko sisters do not represent a postfeminist aesthetic, but instead gesture towards the continuing politics of a pre-feminist work environment. While this is a depressingly predictable binary conclusion it also exposes the limits of any egalitarian politics that fails to examine the terms of that binary. Legislative interventions for "equality" in the workplace have failed to address the basis of work itself as a gendered field: historically, "work" is what men do and women's work has tended to be denoted as separate (Irigaray, 1993, 84–86). Women's work in the home and childcare is designated as amateur and thus undeserving of financial support or reward.[15] In these terms, *Alias* offers a fractured and fragmented reflection upon battles lost following the second wave. More specifically, Sydney's mother and her aunts represent that generation, and also a potential (and feared) future for the new woman professional. These are women who have taken the "equality" agenda to its logical conclusion by assuming the most derogated aspects of masculinity and femininity. Their betrayals and manipulations are presented as a contrast to the moral and ethical figures of Sydney and Jack Bristow.[16] Because such quality television privileges a masculine economy – and a New Economy that is as damaging for men as it is for women in the workplace – older female characters reveal the limited options open to professional women when they are no longer young. If Sydney could be proposed as representing an "empowered" new woman, then her older counterparts give the lie to any assumption that power relations have significantly shifted. *Alias* thus offers its viewers an account of the new woman professional as a monstrous figure, but also represents the battles yet to be won.

Notes

1. An earlier version of this essay appeared in White, 126–46.
2. For a sustained analysis of "quality television", see Jancovich and Lyons' *Quality Popular Television* (2003).
3. One of the *Alias* fan websites features an editorial called "The Fashion Assassin", which wittily critiques Sydney Bristow's outfits episode by episode for the first two seasons of the show. See <http://www.vartanho.com/fa/1x01. html>. [Accessed May 5, 2009].

4. As sources such as the Fawcett Society website note, this perceived influx of women is not statistically proven; for example, in Britain: "Women working full-time earn, on average, 17% less an hour than men working full-time. For women working part-time the gap is 36% an hour. Two-fifths of women in employment in Britain work part-time, compared with 11% of men. 11% of directors of the UK's top 100 companies are women". See <http://www.fawcettsociety.org.uk/index.asp?PageID=459>. [Accessed April 9, 2009].
5. See Radner.
6. See also Perrons 65–93.
7. See Angelini 30–31.
8. While the five main leads in *Alias* – all male apart from Jennifer Garner – performed in 105 episodes, Lena Olin as Irina Derevko (Sydney's mother) was in 27 episodes, Isabella Rossellini and Sonia Braga, as Yekaterina (Katya) and Elena Derevko (Sydney's aunts), were in five episodes each, and Angela Bassett as CIA director Hayden Chase was in four episodes.
9. See Angelini 31–34.
10. See also Finding and MacLachlan 75–77.
11. Part of the action-espionage genre, the Bond franchise is, perhaps, a useful point of reference when analysing Sydney's status as a female action hero and spy. For an examination of the roles accorded to women in Bond films, see Lisa Funnell's "Negotiating Shifts in Feminism: The 'Bad' Girls of James Bond" (in this book).
12. The murderous mother is an increasingly frequent feature of quality television, making appearances in *The Sopranos* (1999–2007) and *Prison Break* (2005–09) See Anna Gething's " 'A Caligula-like despot': Matriarchal Tyranny in *The Sopranos*" (in this book).
13. See Irigaray "When the Goods Get Together" and "Women on the Market".
14. See Modleski 85–109 and Fiske 179–97.
15. See campaigns in the 1970s and in recent years for Wages for Housework, and also Ann Oakley's groundbreaking study *Women's Work: The Housewife, Past and Present* (1974).
16. For a resonant analysis of this intergenerational tension in the context of the postfeminist chick flick, see Shelley Cobb's chapter in this collection.

Works cited

Abbott, S., and Brown, S. (eds.) *Investigating Alias: Secrets and Spies*. London: I B Tauris, 2007.
Alias. Warner Bros, 2001–2006.

  1.10. "Spirit". Dir. Jack Bender. December 16, 2001.
  3.11. "Full Disclosure". Dir. Lawrence Trilling. January 11, 2004.
  5.12. "There's Only One Sydney Bristow". Dir. Robert M. Williams Jr. April 26, 2006.

Angelini, S. "Endoscopic Spies: Mapping the Internal Landscape of *Alias*". *Investigating Alias: Secrets and Spies*. Ed. S. Abbott, and S. Brown. London: I B Tauris, 2007. 27–39.

Barnes, E. "The New Hero: Women, Humanism and Violence in *Alias* and *Buffy the Vampire Slayer*". *Investigating Alias: Secrets and Spies*. Ed. S. Abbott, and S. Brown. London: I B Tauris, 2007. 57–72.

Douglas, S. J. *Where the Girls Are: Growing Up Female With the Mass Media*. London: Penguin, 1994.

Finding, D., and A. MacLachlan. "Aliases, Alienation and Agency: The Physical Integrity of Sydney Bristow". *Investigating Alias: Secrets and Spies*. Ed. S. Abbott, and S. Brown. London: I B Tauris, 2007. 73–86.

Fiske, J. *Television Culture*. London: Routledge, 1987.

Gamble, S., ed. *The Routledge Companion to Feminism and Postfeminism*. London: Routledge, 2001.

Irigaray, L. "When the Goods Get Together". *New French Feminisms: An Anthology*. Ed. E. Marks, and I. de Courtivron. Hemel Hempstead: Harvester, 1981. 99–110.

———. *Je, Tu, Nous: Toward a Culture of Difference*. London: Routledge, 1993.

———. "Women on the Market". *Literary Theory: An Anthology*. 2nd edn. Ed. J. Rivkin, and M. Ryan. Oxford: WileyBlackwell, 2004. 799–811.

Jancovich, M., and J. Lyons, eds. *Quality Popular Television*. London: BFI, 2003.

Jones, A. " 'She Was Bad News': Male Paranoia and the Contemporary New Woman". *Camera Obscura* 25–26 (January–May 1991): 297–320.

Ledger, S. *The New Woman: Fiction and Feminism at the Fin de Siècle*. Manchester: Manchester University Press, 1997.

McRobbie, A. *The Aftermath of Feminism: Gender, Culture and Social Change*. London: Sage, 2009.

Modleski, T. *Loving With A Vengeance: Mass-Produced Fantasies for Women*. London: Methuen, 1984.

Mulvey, L. *Visual and Other Pleasures*. London and Basingstoke: Macmillan, 1989.

Nye, J. L. "Why Sydney Has No Social Life". *Alias Assumed: Sex, Lies and SD-6*. Ed. K. Weisman with G. Yeffeth. Dallas: Benbella Books, 2005. 89–100.

Perrons, D. "The New Economy and the Work-Life Balance: Conceptual Explorations and a Case Study of New Media". *Gender, Work and Organization* 10.1 (January 2003): 65–93.

Radner, H. *Shopping Around: Feminine Culture and the Pursuit of Pleasure*. London: Routledge. 1995.

———. "New Hollywood's New Women: Murder in Mind – Sarah and Margie". *Contemporary Hollywood Cinema*. Ed. S. Neale, and M. Smith. London: Routledge, 1998. 247–61.

Ruditis, P. *Alias: Authorized Personnel Only*. New York: Simon and Schuster, 2005.

Stanworth, C. "Women and Work in the Information Age". *Gender, Work and Organization* 7.1 (January 2000): 20–32.

Takacs, S. "Speculations on a New Economy: *La Femme Nikita*, The Series". *Cultural Critique* 61 (Fall 2005): 148–85.

Tasker, Y. *Working Girls: Gender and Sexuality in Popular Cinema*. London: Routledge, 1998.

White, R. *Violent Femmes: Women as Spies in Popular Culture*. London: Routledge, 2007.

Wright, L. A. "Only Ourselves to Blame". *Alias Assumed: Sex, Lies and SD-6*. Ed. K. Weisman with G. Yeffeth. Dallas, Texas: Benbella Books, 2005. 199–212.

4
The Horrors of Home: Feminism and Femininity in the Suburban Gothic

Melanie Waters

In *The Aftermath of Feminism* (2009), Angela McRobbie draws on a constellation of imagery that has become peculiarly prevalent in recent feminist scholarship. In order to describe the variety of "postfeminist" phenomena she identifies, McRobbie takes repeated recourse to the notion of a phantasmatic feminism that haunts popular culture. While this "ghost of feminism" (22) presents itself as a "hideous spectre of what feminism once was", it bears little correspondence to any "real" feminism and instead adopts as the basis of its spectral visage the cartoonish features that are so frequently, if erroneously, ascribed to second wave feminists. In this way, explains McRobbie, feminism is fantastically and insistently (re)configured as a "monstrous ugliness" which sends "shudders of horror down the spines of young women today, as a kind of deterrent" (1). Evocative and striking, these macabre formulations of feminism's "ghostly" status have been an increasingly common point of reference in feminist discourses since the 1990s. From Avery Gordon's work on psychoanalysis to Terry Castle's critique of queer representation in *The Apparitional Lesbian* (1993), the spectral metaphor has been deployed as a means of symbolizing and interrogating women's historical (in)visibility and cultural inheritance. Given the centrality of these issues to contemporary debates about postfeminism, it is perhaps no surprise that the apparitional trope has been invoked with growing regularity in the twenty-first century. In *Female Chauvinist Pigs* (2006), for example, Ariel Levy rationalizes the perceived reluctance of young women to articulate "feminist" anxieties through reference to the phantom of 1970s radical feminism: "nobody", she proposes, "wants to be the frump at the back of the room anymore, the ghost of women past. It's just not cool" (92). Karen Boyle, likewise, points to the ways in which postfeminism has endeavoured to "banish the spectre of the radical...feminist and her analysis of patriarchy" from its accounts of popular culture (185), while Natasha Walter – in a contrary vein – advises "this generation of feminists" to work on exorcizing the second wave "spectre of political correctness" from its rhetoric in order to enhance the credibility of feminism in the new millennium (4).

For a number of scholars, then, the concept of haunting is a convenient and apposite metaphor for the state of feminist politics in the twenty-first century. Crystallizing anxieties about the legacy of feminism and its current relevance to women, it functions not only as a sign of loss, but also as a site at which losses can be acknowledged, recuperated, or worked through. As Victoria Hesford reflects:

> Haunting is intrinsic to every dominant social and political order because it is a sign of what has been forcibly expunged or evacuated from that order: the other that threatened to disrupt the emergent hegemony. (229)

As well as registering collective concerns about the relationship between power and oppression, the use of spectral metaphors in contemporary feminist discourses productively focalizes particular strategies in popular culture, and in feminist readings of it. Perhaps the most prevalent of these is the staging of tension or conflict between different generations of women. As Shelley Cobb explains elsewhere in this book, recent chick flicks like *The Devil Wears Prada* (2006) and *Monster-in-Law* (2005) often pit older career women against their younger counterparts. In such scenarios, the older woman is prevailingly situated as a figure who has made sacrifices – usually hard, personal sacrifices – in order to achieve professional success. "Learning" from this example, the younger woman, when faced with similar choices, refuses to prioritize her career ahead of her domestic obligations, seeking instead to find a compromise in which the personal and professional can exist comfortably alongside one another. This kind of postfeminist manoeuvring is equally evident in television shows like *Damages* (2007–) and *Ugly Betty* (2006–10), in which the female protagonists are frequently required to choose between their loyalty to family and friends, and the fulfilment of their career ambitions. In each of these scenarios, then, the older woman tends to "ghost" for second wave feminism – emblematizing through her professional achievements and domestic impoverishment the sacrifices by which the struggle for equality was necessarily striated.

Just as the notion of a phantasmatic feminism illuminates the ways in which postfeminist culture attempts to negotiate the complex legacy of the second wave, the concept of spectral femininity might perhaps shed new light on popular formulations of female identities and the relationship of these identities to the past. In this chapter, then, the spectral metaphor functions as a starting point for investigating the representation of feminine identities in contemporary female-centred television fictions. Focusing on texts that foreground the tensions between women, maternity, and domesticity, I analyse the extent to which mainstream representations of gender are haunted by anxieties about femininity, whether in terms of its perceived over-abundance or lack, its desirability or sustainability, its authenticity or fraudulence, or, of course, its relationship to the feminist subject. With specific reference to *The Feminine Mystique* (1963), I excavate the dark Gothicism that inflects Betty Friedan's account of the "happy housewife heroine" and show how it continues to inform contemporary representations of domestic femininity, from the nostalgic stylings of primetime shows like *Desperate Housewives* (2004–) and *Mad Men* (2007–) to the suburban supernaturalism of *Medium* (2005–) and *Ghost Whisperer* (2005–10). While I am intrigued by the persistence with which revived versions of the "happy housewife heroine" continue to haunt mainstream portrayals of feminine identity, I am more explicitly interested in how the idea of a "spectral femininity" – with all its eerie resonances – might speak to the prevailing uncanniness of domestic feminine identities, as they are rendered in contemporary American programming and twentieth-century feminist theory alike.

Uncanny femininities?

As it is identified by Freud in his 1919 essay, the uncanny, or *unheimlich*, is an order of experience that is expressly "related to what is frightening – to what arouses dread and horror". More explicitly, though, it is a special subcategory of the frightening in which "the frightening element can be shown to be something repressed which *recurs* . . . . something which is familiar and old-established in the mind and which has become alienated from it only through the process of repression". The uncanny, then, registers the defamiliarization of the familiar: it is the point at which what the individual has tried to evacuate from his or her conscious mind re-materializes, horribly, in a form that is experienced as strange and threatening. Although Freud struggles to define the uncanny in any precise or categorical sense, he does trace its threatening elements to two particular sources: the fear of repetition and the fear of castration. Castration anxiety, of course, occupies a key position in the Freudian imaginary; when the infantile male becomes aware of the anatomical differences between the sexes, he assumes that the female has already been castrated, and that he himself will suffer the same fate at the hands of the father, as a punishment for desiring his mother. Freud's tethering of the uncanny to castration anxiety – which is, necessarily, a masculine concern – might thus imply that women are unlikely to experience its full force. As Tania Modleski asks in *Loving with a Vengeance* (2008), however, if women are less attuned to the sensation of the uncanny, then how can we account for its prevalence within the *female* Gothic, specifically? In response to this question, she offers an alternative formulation of the uncanny, in which it is recast "as part[s] of a deeper fear – fear of never developing a sense of autonomy and separateness from the mother". Given the female's anatomical similarity to her mother, and the consequent difficulty of establishing an identity that is distinct from hers, the fear of being forever "lost in the mother" is one to which women are acutely sensitive. This approach to the uncanny helps to make sense of its prevalence within the female Gothic, which – in Modleski's terms – performs the reassuring function of convincing "women that they are not their mothers" (22).

While it is left to Modleski to account for women's experience of the uncanny, Freud insists on their centrality to the generation of uncanny effects. The womb, as Freud points out, is the ultimate uncanny venue, having "originally nothing terrifying about it at all", but becoming unfamiliar through the processes of repression. Indeed, as Barbara Creed reflects in *The Monstrous Feminine* (1993), what Freud refers to as "the phantasy ... of intra-uterine existence" provides the architectural blueprint for the dark, enclosed spaces that constitute the preferred venue of Gothic horror (367). As it is connected to the "feminine" space of the womb, so the uncanny is inextricably yoked to the equally feminized space of the home; indeed, amongst the many definitions that Freud cites in the etymology of *heimlich* and *unheimlich* with which he opens his essay, "homely" and "unhomely" are the most markedly recurrent. If Freudian theory sometimes blurs the boundaries between the female body and the home, then this symbolic convergence is also discernible in postfeminist discourses, where, for Negra, "new rhetorics of domestic practice symbolically extend the female body to include the home ... [redressing] the crisis over the female body, subject as it is to intense, deeply anxious, and often conflicting discourses of management, regulation, and surveillance" (130). In this way, the homemaker, with her special relationship to maternity and the home, emerges as a logical locus for the contestation of anxieties about the uncanny nature of femininity and the threats it might conceal.

From Plato to Luce Irigaray, theories of femininity have tended to intersect – though not necessarily intentionally – with elements of the uncanny. Within feminist thought in particular, scholars have often explored the artificial status of femininity in ways that imply its uncanniness. Identified by Friedan as a post-war media myth, the "happy housewife heroine" is the idealized incarnation of the suburbanite homemaker: "healthy, beautiful, educated, concerned only about her husband, her children, her home", she was imaginatively embedded as the "cherished and self-perpetuating core of... American culture" from the late 1940s to the early 1960s, though her influence is still in clear evidence today (15–16). According to Friedan, the "happy housewife heroine" is the fictional embodiment of the post-war "feminine mystique", which "makes certain concrete, finite, domestic aspects of feminine existence – as it was lived by women whose lives were confined, by necessity, to cooking, cleaning, washing, bearing children – into a religion, a pattern by which all women must now live or deny their femininity" (39). Femininity, then, is understood as a mechanical state that estranges women from themselves. The woman who seeks to conform to the impossible model of the "happy housewife heroine" is thus regarded by Friedan as turning away "from individual identity" in order to become "an anonymous biological robot in a docile mass" (267). Associated with inanimate artefacts, and imitating the awkward contours of an "unreal, fixed [and] perfect" femininity, women begin to resemble the frightening automata to which Freud makes reference in "The Uncanny"; denied independence, women appear as "living dolls" who look as if they are "real" and autonomous, while they are really only agents through which a fiction of femininity is transmitted (547).

With its unrelenting equation of "perfect" femininity to the fulfilment of domestic and familial accomplishments, the feminine mystique aggressively restricts women's sphere of influence to the home and its inhabitants. In this way, Friedan argues, it generates a situation in which the housewife is valorized as the expert guardian of the home, but is simultaneously recognized as a danger within that home. Narrowly focused on her role as domestic custodian, the housewife is endowed with the potential to damage or destabilize the family unit through her "excessive" attempts to supervise, dominate, protect, and maintain it (167–79). This apparent antithesis continues to inform representations of women and the domestic, and is key to understanding the ways in which the relationship between femininity, agency, and threat is configured within the terms of popular culture.

The creative configuration of domestic feminine identities as uncanny has been a long-standing, if under-theorized, strategy within popular culture. Across different historical periods, different media, and different genres, the home has functioned consistently as a site at which anxieties about women – and about their capacity to nurture and harm, to charm and deceive – have been dynamically contested. Even in the 1950s, when the ideology of the "happy housewife heroine" was at its strongest, domestic femininity was routinely configured as uncanny in popular American drama. Marked by its speculative engagement with issues relating to technology, invasion, and conformity that reflect its Cold War context, *The Twilight Zone* (1959–64) is enduringly concerned with the home and its vulnerability to malevolent forces. Women are often placed at the heart of these dramas, as both guardians of domestic stability and threats to it.[1] This is exemplified with characteristic eeriness in "Long Distance Call" (1961), an episode which takes place entirely within the space of the home. In the opening scene, a boy named Billy receives the gift of a toy telephone from his doting, widowed, grandmother. After she dies (in the family home), he continues to "talk to her" on the phone – an activity that his parents initially dismiss as a childish fantasy. When the boy throws himself in front of a moving car, however, his mother – the paradigm of protective maternity – starts to become suspicious. Suspecting the dead grandmother's (supernatural) involvement in Billy's strange behaviour, she grows angry and tries to shake an explanation out of him. Later, when she hears him "talking" on the phone, she pulls it from him, only to drop it when she hears what she thinks is breathing on the end of the line. Billy, meanwhile, runs downstairs and tries to drown himself in the fish pond. It is only after Billy's father "speaks" to his dead mother through the toy telephone, pleading with her for the life of his son, that the doctors are able to revive him.

From the outset, the grandmother's aggressive dedication to Billy is placed in the register of threat; it is repeatedly shown to disrupt the "natural" bond between the boy and his mother and causes conflict between Billy's parents. However, because the threat is wrapped up in the cuddly guise of domestic femininity, it is repeatedly mistaken for "ordinary" – if particularly intense – grandmotherly devotion. As Billy's father reassures his wife: "No matter what she did, she did it out of love". This is, perhaps, true; "Long Distance Call", after all, explores the point at which the selfless, unconditional love that we associate with, and expect from, maternal guardians reaches its logical limit, becoming selfish, suffocating, and ultimately destructive. While Billy's mother is situated as the "happy housewife heroine" of this particular fable, she is – as the mother of an only son – the natural successor to the dead grandmother. This disturbing configuration of motherhood is redolent of other Cold War approaches to maternal femininity. In particular, it recalls Philip Wylie's cult of "momism", which held bored, overprotective mothers accountable for ruining the nation's children through their excessive maternal attentions.[2] Although the concept of momism lost currency in the wake of women's entrance into the workplace, it continues to inflect contemporary representations of maternity in popular film and television. This is especially marked in shows like *Mad Men* and *Desperate Housewives*, where the figure of the "happy housewife heroine" is the agent through which the Gothic dimensions of suburban existence are most compellingly excavated.

"I Don't Know Who I Am!"

Mad Men, a critically acclaimed AMC series about the rise of advertising in the early 1960s, trades heavily on the restrictive model of the "happy housewife heroine" that Friedan describes in *The Feminine Mystique*. The character of Betty Draper, an ex-model and the wife of Don Draper – a creative director at an advertising agency in Manhattan – exemplifies the plight of the white, middle-class woman who is tethered to the private space of the suburban family home while her husband conducts his affairs – both business and romantic – in the city. As is the case with many other examples of contemporary US drama, *Mad Men* is embedded in the very cultural critiques that we might use to make sense of the show's approach to femininity; indeed, the character of Betty even shares a first name with Friedan, telegraphing the creator's knowing engagement with Friedan's epochal text.

Betty's domestic discontent, like that which Friedan ascribes to the post-war American housewife, is stressed from the outset; in the second episode of the first season she begins to see a psychiatrist after suffering from spells of numbness in her hands. This numbness initially becomes apparent when Betty is unable to open and apply her own lipstick, though it is most dramatically evidenced when she is driving her two children through the neighbourhood and loses control of the car. Speculatively diagnosed as a psychosomatic condition, Betty's episodic paralysis seems to have particular connections to the "feminine" uncanny. With historical links to hysteria, and thus to the womb, psychosomatic disorders are traditionally gendered as "feminine" maladies. In the first place, it theatricalizes the return of the repressed, in that it marks the point at which psychic fears and desires that have previously been held at bay make an unanticipated reappearance in the guise of a neurological symptom. Secondly, of course, Betty's condition generates a situation in which she experiences her own body as something which is both unfamiliar to her and – as is made clear in the car accident – potentially threatening. Significantly, Betty's bouts of numbness are each entangled with anxieties about "feminine" appearance: her inability to apply lipstick seems to register Betty's growing, if mostly unconscious, resistance to the demands of the feminine mystique, while the incident with the car functions as a catalyst for Betty's nightmarish fantasies about her daughter's future. As she explains to Don:

> I keep thinking – not that I could have killed the kids – but worse... that Sally could have survived and gone on living with this horrible scar on her face and [lived] some long, lonely, miserable life. Don... what's happening to me? Do I need to see someone?
>
> (1.2)

Here, Betty's uncanny experience of her own body is replicated in her seeming estrangement from her own mind, as she asks Don what is "happening" to her – a concern that she repeats a number of times, in various contexts and to various interlocutors, throughout the series. Certainly, repression, as it is highlighted through Betty's psychoanalysis and Don's wartime flashbacks, is a key point of reference in *Mad Men* and remains central to the way in which the show forges the relationship between femininity and the uncanny. As Freud himself reflected, psychoanalysis is itself uncanny, in that it lays bare psychological mechanisms that are otherwise obscure to the subject. Unfortunately for Betty, her psychological mechanisms are not only revealed in the course of the analysis itself, but also retrospectively, when her doctor reports back to Don about his wife's state of mind.

In the context of the psychiatrist's office, Betty's symptoms are tentatively attributed – not least by Betty herself – to her mother's recent death. Experiencing the aftershock of bereavement, Betty scarcely knows who she is, and her identity becomes ever more problematically entangled with that of her dead mother.[3] When her father has a stroke and she goes to visit him, Betty is repeatedly shown staring at, or set against, a portrait of her mother. At one point, Betty's father even mistakes her for his dead wife, groping her breast and inviting her to "go upstairs". The kind of psychical estrangement to which this statement speaks is not only implied through the show's dialogue, but is also inscribed at a visual level – both through Don's flashbacks and Betty's daydreaming. Like other recent shows, such as *Six Feet Under* (2001–05), *Mad Men* takes occasional recourse to daydream sequences in order to illuminate the unspoken (or unspeakable) desires of the housewife, while also literalizing – and simultaneously effacing – the split between fantasy and reality. In one memorable scene, shots of Betty pressing herself up against the washing machine are intercut with images of a "fantasy" seduction sequence, in which she imagines herself having sex with a male acquaintance in the family home. This is one of the ways in which the uncanny comes to inscribe itself as a formal, as well as a thematic, preoccupation. As is the case in this scenario, Betty's repressed frustrations tend to manifest themselves most forcefully in the domestic space within which they were conjured: on one occasion she is shown smashing a chair to pieces while her children watch television, and on another she slips outside to shoot the neighbour's pet birds after he threatens the family dog. In this way, Betty's femininity – her performance as the perfect wife and mother – is often represented as uncanny, functioning as a mask for her aggression and the dangers that she (potentially) poses to domestic stability.

Similar anxieties are explored through the protagonists of ABC's *Desperate Housewives*. While *Mad Men* is interested in a metaphorical spectre of femininity, and its estranging effects on women, *Desperate Housewives* is narrated by an actual spectre – the dead Mary Alice, whose suicide marks the point at which the show begins its run. This narrative device literalizes the idea of haunting. Despite its contemporary setting, the show's formulation of feminine identities is strangely nostalgic, trading heavily on the 1950s model of the "happy housewife heroine". Bree Van Der Kamp, played by Marcia Cross, conforms to the popular image of the happy housewife from her flipped-out bob to her twin set and pearls. Certainly, she is styled in ways that are not dissimilar to January Jones's Betty in *Mad Men*. In the pilot episode of the series, Bree is introduced through a montage of images that demonstrate her domestic prowess. As the accompanying voice-over states:

> Bree was known for her cooking, and for making her own clothes, and for doing her own gardening, and for re-upholstering her own furniture. Yes, Bree's many talents were known throughout the neighbourhood. And everyone on Wisteria Lane thought of Bree as the perfect housewife and mother. Everyone, that is, except her own family.

(1.1)

Bree's adept mastery of traditional domestic skills forms the pretext for her suburban status as "the perfect housewife and mother" – a status which is subsequently formalized by her public success as a professional caterer and the acclaimed author of *Mrs. Van Der Kamp's Old-Fashioned Cooking*. Over the course of the next six seasons, however, Bree's cartoonish performance of feminine perfection disguises her "secret" involvement in murder, infidelity, divorce, alcohol addiction, sexual fetishism, and various other deceits, from the incidental to the monumental. Indeed, the show's contemporary twist is in many ways reliant on the repeated exposure of the discontinuity between the seductive, wholesome appearance of suburban femininity she projects and the dark, threatening behaviours that it conceals. What is particularly interesting in the case of Bree is that the dangers she presents are often linked to her desire to fulfil her duties as the "perfect housewife and mother". In an early episode she interrupts the funeral of her first husband in order to change his tie; elsewhere, she publicly intimidates one of her daughter's friends for scooping some icing from a perfectly frosted birthday cake, and she later shoots at a spurned lover from her bedroom window, having excused herself from the dinner party she is hosting downstairs.

Although very different, *Desperate Housewives* and *Mad Men* instrumentalize the uncanny in similar ways. In each series, visual analepses, prolepses, dream sequences, and (in the case of *Desperate Housewives*) otherworldly narration are used to generate uncanny fissures in the verisimilitude of the narrative – fissures in which the repressed desires of characters are dramatically articulated or envisioned. These devices are used with particular regularity in relation to the housewife, serving to highlight the uncanny split between her controlled exterior and the threats it supposedly hides – implying, once again, the unstable and irrational status of femininity. While these devices necessarily destabilize the boundaries of fantasy and reality, these shows are not engaged, in any explicit sense, with the supernatural; they are used, rather, to give image (or voice) to repressed desires that cannot be symbolized in any other way. Even shows which are outwardly unconcerned with the relationship between femininity and domesticity *per se* tend to construct and interrogate new female identities – and the ambivalences by which they are striated – through close reference to the space of the home. In recent drama, the home is rarely a safe haven to which female characters retreat to rest or recuperate; rather it is always and already a site which is eminently vulnerable to threats that are conjured from within – and without – its architectural borders.

Domestic femininity and suburban supernaturalism

Following the success of supernatural dramas like *Buffy the Vampire Slayer* (1997–2003) and *Charmed* (1998–2006), there has been a renaissance in female-centred Gothic television. Like their popular predecessors, the majority of these shows are concerned primarily with investigating "young" femininities: *Joan of Arcadia* (2003–05) follows the exploits of a girl who converses with God; *Point Pleasant* (2005) focuses on the strange events that ensue when Satan's teenage daughter washes up on the shore of a small town in New Jersey; *Tru Calling* (2003–05) features Eliza Dushku as a psychic mortuary assistant who is able to hear the voices of the dead and "relive" the past in order to save them; and *True Blood* (2008–) centres on the life of Sookie Stackhouse, a telepathic waitress who falls in love with a vampire. Some recent examples of Gothic television do, however, use the supernatural as a means of exploring the anxieties about maternity and femininity that are addressed in *Desperate Housewives* and *Mad Men*. CBS's *Ghost Whisperer* stars Jennifer Love Hewitt as Melinda Gordon, a young wife and mother with psychic abilities. As well as owning an antiques store, Melinda helps restless spirits to cross over into "The Light" by carrying out their unfinished business on earth. *Medium* features Patricia Arquette in the role of Allison DuBois, a medium who assists law enforcement agencies in the investigation of unsolved crimes. In both series, the paranormal insight that the protagonists appear to possess is part of a dreadful maternal legacy: Melinda can trace her "ghost whispering" back through five generations of women to her great-great-great-grandmother, while it transpires in the first few seasons of *Medium* that Allison shares her psychic abilities with her three daughters. In a broad sense, the seeming inextricability of maternity and the paranormal in these dramas works to revivify long-standing cultural anxieties about the "otherness" of femininity, as well as fears about female sexuality, motherly influence, and women's special connectedness to dreams, the unconscious, and irrational (or supernatural) forms of knowledge. Certainly, the female protagonists in *Ghost Whisperer* and *Medium* are held accountable, albeit indirectly, for contaminating the purity of the bloodline and for introducing (potentially) malevolent forces into the otherwise sacrosanct space of the home.

In *Medium*, when Allison's eldest child starts dreaming about a little girl who was abducted by a child molester, it is Allison who becomes the target of her husband's anger: "There's enough death and darkness waiting out there for her when she's an adult.... [T]wo days ago she didn't know that there were really monsters. And now she does. And I hate that" (1.9). Here, Allison's husband is principally concerned with the fact that his 10-year-old daughter's apparent psychic abilities have acquainted her with the horrors – in particular the *sexual* horrors – of the adult world. This intertwining of carnal knowledge and psychic insight is interesting, in that it subverts conventional formulations of the *femme-enfant* as a figure that is granted special access to the fantastical as a result of her purity.[4] Rather, *Medium* suggests that the psychic insight of the child is to some extent concomitant with an awareness of adult sexuality and/or the onset of sexual maturity.

As Barbara Creed has commented, because of its reproductive and procreative functions, the post-pubescent female body is inherently "unstable": it grows during pregnancy to accommodate its progeny, it lactates, it menstruates, it can be "taken by force" (15). In short, the maternal body is both penetrable and porous, and in this way it works to query the borders – and thus the integrity – of individual female identity. In *Ghost Whisperer* and *Medium*, the permeability of the maternal body is replicated in the representation of the psychic mind, which confounds the notion of individual identity in similar ways. In the cases of Allison and Melinda, after all, the boundaries of the mind are perpetually breached by memories, thoughts, and experiences which are not their own. Already mothers, these women are forced to relive the experience of pregnancy at a symbolic level, being forever laden with an evolving cast of restless souls. As Allison describes it, "there's a kind of collective consciousness out there, a kind of giant filing cabinet filled with all the thoughts of everyone who has ever lived, just floating around, waiting to be received by someone" (1.11). Like children, these souls make sustained demands on the women's reserves of time and energy: the stock shot in both shows is that of the female protagonist waking up in the middle of the night, having intuited that someone needs her help. This visual trope quite clearly evokes the interrupted sleep patterns of early parenthood. *Medium*, in particular, seems to elaborate on this connection. In an episode from the first season, Allison appears to awake to her eldest daughter's insistent cries for "mommy". Moving through the home, Allison is unable to locate her daughter, though her cries remain persistent. What she finds, instead, is a strange, affectless man, who introduces himself as he steps out of the shadows: "You know me. I'm a golum. I'm the devil. I'm a monster. And your little girl? She's in the trunk of my car. And if you'll excuse me, I've come back to get the other ones". Within seconds, Allison awakes for a second time, to the same cries of "mommy". On this occasion, however, she finds her daughter asleep in bed and sources the cries to a mechanical doll on the bedroom floor (1.6). Here, and in a number of other episodes, the vulnerability of Allison's subconscious to unsolicited psychic invasions is imagined through the visual motif of the domestic intruder. This motif is similarly deployed in *Ghost Whisperer*. In the opening episode of the first season, Melinda and her husband move into a house that is literally falling apart. During the first week in their new home, Melinda wakes up during a thunderstorm to find her husband gone. Seeing him outside in the rain, trying to reattach some tarpaulin that has come loose in the wind, Melinda opens a window to shout out to him, only for the frame to break off in her hands. When she makes her way back to bed, she is confronted by the cadaverous spectre of a soldier who claims to be lost and asks for her help. Melinda agrees, but only after she has admonished him for his encroachment upon her private, domestic space: "You're not supposed to be in my home. That's not how this works" (1.1). As the architectural borders of the home are crumbling around her, the perimeters of Melinda's psyche are likewise breached. The home, then, is again understood as an extension of the female body and/or mind; both are eminently penetrable in ways that undermine their apparent status as "place[s] of peace" from which evil is absent. Such complex evocations of domestic space are typical of the Gothic genre from which shows like these draw, where "the home can never be purified once and for all [because] it is inextricably connected to 'the world', whose violence and danger must be faced, and wrestled to the ground, again and again" (Ellis 220). As psychics, Allison and Melinda are magnets for the supernatural forces that endanger the home and also the guardians of that home – guardians who are not only charged with the role of keeping evil out, but who must also ensure that those around them are forewarned about, and protected against, the forces by which they are threatened. Set in this light, the custodial responsibilities of the psychic are broadly continuous with the nurturing duties of the "happy housewife heroine". Allison and Melinda are symbolically recast as über-mothers, becoming temporary custodians to those whose consciousnesses (apparently) converge with their own.

In this way, the psychic woman becomes a powerful metaphor for feminine identity and the tensions by which it is beset. Torn between fulfilling her own needs and carrying out her responsibilities to others – both living and dead – her condition speaks to the increasingly complex negotiations that women are required to undertake as they try to balance personal, familial, domestic, and professional obligations.

While uncanny configurations of feminine identity are by no means new to American television, they have been particularly prevalent in the early years of the twenty-first century. This phenomenon is explicable, in part, through reference to the growth in programming for female viewers which has taken place over the past decade, and the related foregrounding of "women's issues" within television fictions. It might also, however, invite consideration alongside more widespread concerns about privacy rights and surveillance culture. At a time when the US government is able to monitor the activities of the individual in unprecedented ways, and to an unprecedented degree, it seems apposite that anxieties about the sanctity of domestic space and personal autonomy should loom so large in the cultural imaginary. From *The Twilight Zone* to *The Ghost Whisperer*, feminine identity remains a key venue for the inscription of these kinds of anxieties. While feminism has interrogated patriarchal formulations of femininity as masculinity's mysterious, irrational "other", such formulations are a mainstay of recent television drama, pointing to the stubborn resilience of conventional conceptions of gender within the seemingly enlightened context of postfeminist culture.

Notes

1. This demonization of the feminine is especially characteristic of the male Gothic. See Creed.
2. Wylie explains the premise of "momism" in scathing detail in the chapter on "Common Women" from *Generation of Vipers*: "Nowadays, with nothing to do, and all the tens of thousands of men ... to maintain her, every clattering prickamette in the republic survives for an incredible number of years, to stamp and jibber in the midst of man, a noisy neuter by natural default or a scientific gelding sustained by science, all tongue and teat and razzmatazz. The machine has deprived her of social usefulness; time has stripped away her biological possibilities and poured her hide full of liquid soap; and man has sealed his own soul beneath the clamorous cordillera by handing her the checkbook and going to work in the service of her caprices". See Wylie 184–96.
3. *Mad Men* is, of course, fundamentally concerned with anxieties about individual identity. In order to escape his impoverished past, "Don" (born Richard Whitman) stole the identity of an army colleague – Lieutenant Donald Draper – who was killed alongside him in the Korean War. Issues about female identity also loom large, not least in the offices of Sterling Cooper, where the identities of the women who work there are regarded as largely interchangeable. This is demonstrated in an episode from the first season when the new secretary Alison is referred to, incorrectly, as "Debbie"; when she attempts to correct the error, her objections are disregarded, as if such confusion is of little consequence: "Whatever".
4. See Creed 154–55.

Works cited

Boyle, Karen. "Feminism Without Men: Feminist Media Studies in a Post-Feminist Age". *Feminist Television Criticism: A Reader*. Ed. Charlotte Brunsdon and Lynne Spigel. Maidenhead: Open University Press, 2008. 174–90.

Castle, Terry. *The Apparitional Lesbian: Female Homosexuality and Modern Culture*. New York: Columbia University Press, 1995.

Creed, Barbara. *The Monstrous Feminine: Film, Feminism, Psychoanalysis*. London and New York: Routledge, 1993.

—— *Phallic Panic: Film, Horror and the Primal Uncanny*. Melbourne: Melbourne University Press, 2005.

De Beauvoir, Simone. *The Second Sex*. London: Vintage, 1997.

Desperate Housewives. ABC, 2004–.

1.1. "Pilot". Dir. Charles McDougall. October 3, 2004.

Ellis, Kate Ferguson. *The Contested Castle: Gothic Novels and the Subversion of Domestic Ideology*. Champaign, IL: University of Illinois Press, 1989.

Freud, Sigmund. "The Uncanny" (1919). *The Pelican Freud Library: Art and Literature*, vol. 14. Ed. Albert Dickson. Harmondsworth: Penguin, 1985. 339–68.

Friedan, Betty. *The Feminine Mystique*. London: Penguin, 1992.

Ghost Whisperer. CBS/ABC, 2005–10.

1.1. "Pilot". Dir. John Gray. September 23, 2005.

Gordon, Avery. "Feminism, Writing and Its Ghosts". *Social Problems* 37.4 (1990): 485–500.

—— *Ghostly Matters: Haunting and the Sociological Imagination*. 2nd rev. edn. Minneapolis, MN: University of Minnesota Press, 2008.

Hesford, Victoria. "Feminism and Its Ghosts: The Specter of the Feminist-as-Lesbian". *Feminist Theory* 10.1 (2009): 227–50.

Hollows, Joanne. "Can I Go Home Yet?". *Feminism in Popular Culture*. Ed. Joanne Hollows and Rachel Moseley. Oxford and New York: Berg, 2006. 97–118.

Levy, Ariel. *Female Chauvinist Pigs: Women and the Rise of Raunch Culture*. London: Pocket Books, 2006.

McRobbie, Angela. *The Aftermath of Feminism: Gender, Culture and Social Change*. London: Sage, 2009.

Mad Men. AMC, 2007–.

1.1. "Smoke Gets in Your Eyes". Dir. Alan Taylor. July 19, 2007.
1.2. "Ladies Room". Dir. Alan Taylor. July 26, 2007.

Medium. NBC/CBS, 2005–.

1.6. "Coming Soon". Dir. Vincent Misiano. February 7, 2005.
1.9. "Coded". Dir. Bill L. Norton. February 28, 2005.
1.11. "I Married a Mind Reader". Duane Clark. March 21, 2005.

Modleski, Tania. *Loving with a Vengeance: Mass-produced Fantasies for Women*. 2nd edn. London: Routledge, 2006.

Negra, Diane. *What a Girl Wants?: Fantasizing the Reclamation of Self in Postfeminism*. Oxon and New York: Routledge, 2009.

Oakely, Ann. *Housewife*. Harmondsworth: Penguin, 1974.
The Twilight Zone. CBS, 1959–64.

   2.22. "Long Distance Call". Dir. James Sheldon. March 31, 1961.

Walter, Natasha. *The New Feminism*. London: Virago, 1999.
Wylie, Philip. *Generation of Vipers*. 1942. New York: Pocket Books, 1955.

Part II
Sex and Sexuality

5
Bad Girls in Crisis: The New Teenage Femme Fatale

Katherine Farrimond

In May 1992, 17-year-old Amy Fisher confronted and shot Mary Jo Buttafuoco, the wife of Joey Buttafuoco, with whom Amy was having an affair. In the extensive tabloid coverage that followed – most of which emphasized the spicy details of the affair and the young woman's past involvement in the sex industry – Fisher was dubbed the "Long Island Lolita" and became the inspiration for three salacious made-for-television movies: *Amy Fisher: My Story* (1992; released in the United Kingdom as *Lethal Lolita*); *Casualties of Love: The Long Island Lolita Story* (1993); and *The Amy Fisher Story* (1993). As Elizabeth Wurtzel points out, "The Amy Fisher story is about an attempt to focus on one girl's special effects and pretend that no storyline preceded it. And there's a lot of that going around these days" (94). In this chapter, I argue that while this troubling dynamic has persisted in the teenage femme fatale films that have emerged in the wake of the Fisher story, recent examples of the genre have registered a shift towards a potentially more fruitful consideration of the background "storyline" that Wurtzel describes. While the focus on the fireworks caused by girls-behaving-badly remains a staple of the teen femme fatale narrative, some texts have moved away from the straightforward glorification and/or demonization of the bad girl's bad behaviour in order to examine the lived reality of her experiences.

Throughout the history of Hollywood cinema, teenage girls have been variously presented as tearaways, Lolitas, coquettes, high-school bitches, and jailbait.[1] Until the 1990s, however, these bad girls were not approximate to the sexy-but-deadly femme fatales of classic American noir. Indeed, it is only in the last two decades that the femme fatale's cruel single-mindedness and erotic allure has been transferred to the figure of the teenage girl.[2] In an acknowledgement of the advent of the teenage femme fatale, Timothy Shary notes the following:

> "Evil women" whose power arises from their sexuality and intelligence have been popular since at least the 1940s emergence of femmes fatale in films noir, and seemed to find a resurgence in the last generation as a reaction to women gaining professional power.... The fact that teen films have recently been demonstrating the supposedly corruptive effects of female intelligence and sexuality suggests that this tradition is shifting its concerns (and fascinations) to a younger generation of women. (249–50)

As Shary suggests, the teenage femme fatale has emerged from the 1980s noir revival which took the form of femme fatale-centred erotic thrillers such as *Body Heat* (1981), *Black Widow* (1987), and *Fatal Attraction* (1987). This resurgence coincided with what Catherine Driscoll has termed "a hypersuccessful genre" (216) of teen films in the 1980s, exemplified by John Hughes' *The Breakfast Club* (1985) and *Pretty in Pink* (1986), and Amy Heckerling's *Fast Times at Ridgemont High* (1982). This cinematic climate is arguably the reason that the director Katt Shea was, in her words, "hired by New Line Cinema to come up with a teenage *Fatal Attraction*", resulting in *Poison Ivy* (1992), the first major teen femme fatale film (qtd. in Williams 392). While many teenage femme fatales do feature in films made for teenagers, still more appear in erotic thrillers, as in the case of Shea's *Poison Ivy* and *Wild Things* (1998), science fiction horror films such as *The Faculty* (1998) and *Decoys* (2004), and independent productions such as *Brick* (2005) and *The Opposite of Sex* (1998). Such films register the media's growing interest in girls and girlhood during the 1990s and 2000s, out of which context the teenage femme fatale emerges as a locus for debates about the ways in which teenage girls are understood by, and represented in, Western popular culture at the beginning of the twenty-first century.[3]

Postfeminist lolitas: The evolution of the teen femme fatale

As I have indicated, the beginnings of the teenage femme fatale can be traced to the erotic thrillers of early 1990s, such as *Poison Ivy* and *The Crush* (1993), which feature teenage girls as babysitters, daughters of landlords, and high-school students. These films present scenarios that are designed to place older men in proximity to devious and nubile teenage girls who first seduce them, then wreak havoc on their lives.

Although the Amy Fisher case, and the media frenzy surrounding it, did not initiate the cycle (*Poison Ivy* was released before the murder), the particular way it was reported speaks to the same concerns as the films that were released at this time: the combination of sexuality, criminality, and youthful femininity is interpreted in a way that emphasizes the teenage girl's seductive danger, while playing down any concern for her personal wellbeing. The femme fatale in these films thus functions primarily as the object of desire: her motivations go unquestioned and the threats she poses to the family (and to adult masculinity in particular) are neutralized through her death or incarceration. This trend continues throughout the 1990s, with films like *Wicked* (1998), *Devil in the Flesh* (1998), *Teacher's Pet* (2000), and *Swimfan* (2002) presenting the teenage femme fatale as an unexamined psychotic who will stop at nothing to get what she wants. Although this trend shows no sign of abating (the latest in the *Poison Ivy* series was released in 2008), the teenage femme fatale has evolved since the mid- to late-1990s into an increasingly complicated figure, whose own desires and motivations are not only acknowledged but also foregrounded. Rather than being punished at the end of her films, then, the new teenage femme fatale is celebrated for her ability to escape justice, as in *Wild Things* and *Mini's First Time* (2006). Such films seem indebted to postfeminist valorizations of female sexuality that began to emerge in the mid-1990s. Certainly, using sex as a means to an end is presented as an empowering strategy in these "getting-away-with-it" narratives; as the patriarchal desire for younger women is mocked, so the femme fatale's sexual conquests are advanced as evidence of her agency and independence. Such an interpretation is, however, undermined by the patriarchal iconography of the films; structured around titillating images of threesomes, pseudo-lesbian sex, and the femme fatale's teenage body, these narratives exemplify what Rebecca Munford refers to as "the dangerous slippage between feminist agency and patriarchal recuperation" (148–49). While she is prevailingly presented as an icon of female empowerment, then, the teenage femme fatale – with her outwardly conventional "sexiness" and apparent sexual availability – is best understood as a figure that occupies the liminal territory between sexual empowerment and patriarchal objectification.[4] In this way, these films speak to a core myth of postfeminist ideology: "the sense that we inhabit a world which already offers us a range of ready choices and where we can play at sexy vamp with no ill-effect because we are 'in control' of the look we create" (Whelehan 178). What the teenage femme fatale narrative fails to note is that the "control" to which Whelehan refers is surrendered as soon as the "look" or image of the femme fatale becomes public. In other words, the dominating patriarchal gaze is likely to read the teenage "sexy vamp" as anything but powerful. And while the teen femme fatale does appear to control and create her "hot bad girl" persona in order to gain agency from it, this power is reliant on the unexamined assumption that the role of sexual performer is the only valid source of agency available to pretty teenage girls. Although this persona may permit her victory over patriarchal figures in the narrative's conclusion, this victory depends on a visual style which insists that – for the teen femme fatale who gets away with it – her *only* power is her highly problematic ability to look sexy.

Sympathy and punishment: The new teen femme fatale

Both *Cruel Intentions* (1999) and *Pretty Persuasion* (2005) present versions of the teenage femme fatale which, in making her a more central and sympathetic character than her Lolita-style predecessors, follow a similar pattern to the postfeminist films discussed above. However, in contrast to the unequivocal celebration of the femme fatale's victory, these films do not end happily for the teenage bad girl. Similarly, unlike the earlier "Lolita" femme fatale films, they do not culminate in the femme fatale's death or incarceration, but instead demonstrate the impact of her actions and the environment in which she lives on her emotional well-being. As Kerry Mallan and Sharyn Pearce have pointed out, contemporary Western culture promotes a "concept of the youthful body as a site of cultural inscription and objectification"; rather than offering a straightforward recapitulation of this formulation, these texts seek to interrogate it (xiv). In *Cruel Intentions* and *Pretty Persuasion*, the politics, pleasures, and problems of the teenage femme fatale bleed into one another, creating representations of agency and sexuality which are neither clear-cut condemnations nor unexamined celebrations; as such, they expand the depth and breadth of the femme fatale type. Rather than offering the unquestioning celebrations of the bad girl's deviancy found in the postfeminist femme fatale narrative, these films articulate the type of concern expressed by Whelehan in her analysis of postfeminism's rhetoric of sexual empowerment. While the teenage femme fatale may be punished at the end of films like *The Crush* and *Poison Ivy*, *Cruel Intentions* and *Pretty Persuasion* do not condemn and vilify these characters in the same way and are, instead, fraught with tensions about agency, sexuality, romance, and social acceptance that leave space for a sympathetic reading of the teenage femme fatale.

To begin with, the teen femme fatale's relationship to sex in these films is far more complex than in other examples of the genre. In Kimberly and Kathryn, their respective seductive schoolgirls, both *Pretty Persuasion* and *Cruel Intentions* present teen femme fatales who use sex predominantly as a means of achieving their various ambitions – hence the fact that it is inextricable from bribery, blackmail, and other forms of emotional manipulation. The sex scenes would thus appear to continue in the tradition of classic noir, in which the femme fatale's "lust was overwhelmingly for money rather than sexual pleasure.... Her sexuality *per se* was passive, limited to its allure. Although narratively she manoeuvred the male protagonist with her sexuality, the specifically sexual pleasure it served belonged to the male" (Straayer 152–53). This dynamic is also present in both the "Lolita" subgenre of the femme fatale film and the postfeminist bad girl films discussed above. However, *Pretty Persuasion* and *Cruel Intentions* reconfigure this conventional dynamic in their refusal to focus entirely on the pleasures of the male recipient on whom the femme fatale's sexual attentions are lavished; instead, they gesture towards the complex ways in which the femme fatale uses her sexuality as a means of achieving sexual and non-sexual objectives alike.[5] Scenes of sexual manipulation and sexualized performance are countervailed by others in which the teenage femme fatale does claim her sexuality for herself, and for its own sake, complicating a reading of Kimberly and Kathryn's use of their sexuality as purely a means to success in other areas of life. In *Cruel Intentions*, an infuriated Kathryn makes an extensive speech bemoaning the sexual double standard which prevents her from exercising her sexuality publically:

> Eat me Sebastian. It's alright for guys like you and Court to fuck everyone, but when I do it I get dumped for innocent little twits like Cecile. God forbid I exude confidence and enjoy sex. Do you think I relish the fact that I have to act like Mary Sunshine 24/7 so I can be considered a lady? I'm the Marcia fucking Brady of the Upper East Side, and sometimes I want to kill myself.

In this statement, Kathryn not only telegraphs the intensity of pressures on young women to conform to patriarchal models of virtue and disposition, but also makes claims on the very enjoyment of her sexuality that other scenes – such as one in which she stages a screamingly orgasmic sexual performance with a man in whom she has no interest just to demonstrate her power to her step-brother Sebastian – would seem to deny her. In light of Kathryn's actions throughout the rest of the film, and her apparently constant use of sex as a means to empowerment, the points she makes in this scene may be easily dismissed as an anomaly. Certainly, this is the position taken by Brigine E. Humbert:

> If Sebastian enjoys his reputation as a seducer while Kathryn does her best to appear virtuous, it seems that this opposition lies less in a difference imposed by gender as in [the original novel] – although Kathryn alludes to this – than in the different natures of their ambitions: he is happy just being the "bad apple" whereas she worries about securing her position as student body president. (281–82)

Humbert's throwaway reference to Kathryn's dissatisfaction with the constraints of her femininity belies the pivotal role that this speech plays in illuminating the intricate ways in which anxieties about social expectations, personal (female) desires, and power are woven together in the film. While Kathryn *does* worry about preserving her position as president, this is arguably because that position allows her to live the decadent and highly sexual lifestyle she finds appealing – the lifestyle that Sebastian can enjoy unencumbered by public rejection and shame – behind a smokescreen of modest and appropriate feminine behaviour. Here, sex for the teenage femme fatale is not about the binary oppositions of male pleasure and female success; rather, sex is the means through which her own desires – whether erotic, emotional, or material – might be realized.

Similarly, in an early sex scene from *Pretty Persuasion*, Kimberly is the recipient of oral sex, which she is shown as actively enjoying. This scene complicates straightforward constructions of the femme fatale's sexuality as a means to a lucrative end, as Kimberly's relationship with her boyfriend is apparently one that she entertains solely for the purposes of attaining her own sexual pleasure. She does not appear to like the boy, who is presented as ignorant and boorish, and he complains that she always tricks him into pleasuring her first, after which she makes her excuses and leaves. Although Kimberly's relationship with sex is frequently framed as one in which she performs oral sex on other people in order to achieve her ambitions, this scene disrupts the notion that the femme fatale is the sole provider of erotic stimulation. At the same time, it complicates the idea that the teenage girl is someone who does not or should not pursue her own sexual desires. If the femme fatale narrative is characterized, in part, by its tendency to identify female sexuality with manipulation, then the teen subgenre is one in which the lines between the femme fatale's use and enjoyment of her sexuality are decidedly blurred. In the final analysis, then, the teen femme fatale's sexual conquests are not only a way of getting what she really desires, but also expressions of desire itself.

Rather than following a naïve and inherently problematic "girl power" model, these two films demonstrate the complexities of trying to live as a teenage girl in a space which insists that girls' only power lies in their sexuality, and yet judges and vilifies them for utilizing it publicly. While these films are neither explicitly nor exclusively feminist, their strategy of exploring this situation is closely aligned to the "pro-woman" argument asserted by Jennifer Baumgardner and Amy Richards in *Manifesta*. With reference to second wave rhetoric, they argue that

> women weren't passively brainwashed by the patriarchy into marrying or looking as pretty as possible; they were actively making the best choice they could, given the circumstances of sexism. The reality was, and still is, that married women had some economic and societal protections that single women didn't have; and attractive women *could* get better jobs than their mousy sisters. [Ellen] Willis and the Redstockings argued that women would make different choices in a non-sexist world, but the point of a pro-woman line is to acknowledge the barriers around which women must manoeuvre rather than to blame the women themselves. (95–96)

This argument usefully acknowledges the strategies that women employ to negotiate the restrictions placed upon them, and shows how these strategies might be reframed as expressions of agency rather than passivity. Within this model, actions which may be read as implicitly antifeminist – traditional heterosexual coupling, wearing high heels and makeup, and using sex as a means to an end – can instead be viewed as aids to survival within systems that attempt to dictate how should women look, behave, and achieve power. Unlike the postfeminist and antifeminist teen femme fatale films outlined at the start of this chapter, the new teen femme fatale films uncover the usually invisible networks of constraints and requirements within which the twenty-first-century teenage girl must function, and in doing so they shed vital light on the techniques she employs in order to succeed within those systems.

In re-visioning the teenage femme fatale, these films articulate and interrogate postfeminist notions that using sex to get what one wants is a form of empowerment for young women. In both *Cruel Intentions* and *Pretty Persuasion* the teenage femme fatale is thus presented as existing in a double bind: the high premiums that Western societies place on teenage femininity allow her to use her youthful sexuality to get what she wants; however, these same societies also demonize girls who are too available, too sexual, too promiscuous, and this not only impacts on her ability to use sex to achieve her ambitions, but also on the extent to which she can explore her own personal sexual desires.

In *Pretty Persuasion*, the contradictions that swirl around the sexuality of the teenage girl are explicitly foregrounded in an incident involving Warren, a boy Kimberly was "sort of" dating who persuades her to engage in anal sex, before dumping her on the grounds that he "didn't want to go out with a girl that would let a guy do that to her". As becomes apparent, Troy, the former boyfriend over whom Kimberly pines and obsesses, broke up with her because he heard about the incident with Warren. Troy's retelling of this incident is of great significance to understanding *Pretty Persuasion*'s treatment of the femme fatale's sexuality: "I heard something, that kind of freaked me out, and to be honest with you it was kind of making me look bad. I was over at Kimberly's house one night and she came out of the bathroom and started doing this nasty little dance". The film then cuts to a flashback in which Kimberly is shown doing a dance that echoes the dance that her teacher's wife performs for him, while dressed as a schoolgirl, earlier in the film. What her teacher, Mr Anderson, finds alluring and attractive in his naive wife's performance of the sexy schoolgirl, Troy finds repellent in the apparently genuine expression of desire from a girl with a bad reputation. In this way, the film suggests that standards of appropriate sexuality for women vary enormously based on the public perception of the woman's sexual experience and identity. To return to Whelehan's comments on the problematics of public sexual performance, the film implies that women are not "in control" of the look they create, and that power is removed from them as soon as they fall under the attentions of the male gaze. Troy then stops Kimberly with the line "Warren Prescott told me what he did to you". This line again highlights a sexual double standard: Warren is presented as the active party in the relationship, as Troy attributes the incident to his ability to "do" anal sex to Kimberly, while she is the one taken to task for it. Kimberly attempts to rescue the situation by saying "If you're good I'll let you go where Warren went", to which Troy replies "no, that is not cool Kimberly, I don't take some loser's sloppy seconds, alright? And I don't want to be with some dirty little whore". Again, this scene is instrumental in acknowledging the disjunctive ways in which female agency is exercised and interpreted. While Kimberly may be active in choosing her partners and consenting to sex with them, under the heteronormative patriarchal gaze – embodied here by Troy – her attempts to attain the status she wants will never truly function as manifestations of agency, as sexual activity will always be something that is "done to her" by someone else. This dynamic is demonstrative of what Catherine Driscoll describes as a "patriarchal capitalist coding" in which feminine adolescence is positioned as both "desirable commodity and undesirable identity" (130). Kimberly knows that sexual availability is the best way to get what she wants, as evidenced by frequent scenes in which she exploits this very idea, and yet the sexual history she accumulates in doing so marks her as undesirable to partners she is interested in romantically. In this instance, the sexually available girl is as appalling as she is alluring, and so her attempts to gain agency via sex are both facilitated and vilified by the patriarchal society in which she aims to succeed. This situation is also explored in *Cruel Intentions*, in which Kathryn makes it clear that she hates the role she must maintain; if she could be as overtly promiscuous as Sebastian, she would, but she understands how the society she inhabits expects her to act and knows that she must at least *appear* to conform in order to behave in the way she wants.

While male promiscuity is persistently glorified in the film, female promiscuity is approached rather differently. When Kathryn suggests to Cecile that she ought to sleep with as many people as possible because "practice makes perfect", Cecile worries that this might make her "a slut", but Kathryn is quick to reassure her that "everybody does it; it's just that nobody talks about it". This contrast makes it clear that male promiscuity is rewarded with admiration and status, whereas women who wish to behave promiscuously must do so discreetly or be branded as sluts. What this implies, in turn, is that the teenage girl can define her image in accordance with one of two key paradigms: virgin or whore. Kathryn's desire for exciting and varied sexual experience must be hidden behind a veneer of virginal innocence, but in order to maintain this pretence and attain a social position that will allow her access to the type of men she wants to have sex with, she uses her sexuality as leverage for blackmail and bribery. As a result, the motives that underlie Kathryn's various sexual exploits are difficult to discern, and never readily locatable as either erotic or emotional or manipulative. Just as in *Pretty Persuasion*, this confusion of purpose is what ultimately causes her downfall. When Sebastian's secret diary is revealed to everyone at her school, it not only denounces Kathryn as an "alcoholic" and a "liar", but also – most tellingly – brands her as "promiscuous". Kathryn is judged and castigated for her sexual history – a history that reflects her ambition and her pursuit of pleasure within the context of a society that finds the sexually available girl both desirable and distasteful. In *Cruel Intentions* and *Pretty Persuasion* alike, the voyeuristic display of the slutty bad girl's sexual antics gives way to her punishment, thus re-enacting the very combination of sexual objectification and vilification that I have argued these films critique. However, rather than simply re-inscribing Driscoll's model of female adolescence, these narratives pose an important question about the ways in which sex and power are negotiated in relation to the figure of the teenage girl: If the only power available to teenage girls is their sexuality, and if that sexuality is temporarily sexy but ultimately unacceptable, what happens to ambitious young women?

Such a question invites consideration alongside the "girls in crisis" discourses that emerged in the 1990s. Exemplified by Mary Pipher's *Reviving Ophelia* (1994),[6] recent studies of "mean girls",[7] and a growing academic interest in Western cultural attitudes to sex and teenagers,[8] the "girls in crisis" phenomenon predates films like *Cruel Intentions* and *Pretty Persuasion* and seems to inform their ambivalent portrayals of teen femininity. As femme fatales who are both desirable and disgusting, Kathryn and Kimberly are presented as "girls in crisis": away from the eyes of their neglectful and frequently absent parents, they each (ab)use drugs, such as cocaine and prescription medication, and exhibit signs of eating disorders. That these pathological behaviours are typically perceived as the domain of rich white Western youth seems to speak to the main point of the films: while these teenage femme fatales deceive, cheat, and seduce everyone around them, they cannot be interpreted straightforwardly as evil Lolitas, but nor are they postfeminist heroines to be lauded and celebrated. Instead, they are girls suffering in environments where their bodies and actions are under constant scrutiny. In this respect, the looming presence of eating disorders is particularly revealing, in that it connects the abstract concept of "girls in crisis" with the more specific desires that are ascribed to these girls: firstly, the desire for control over a body that is seemingly incapable of creating its own meaning away from the male gaze; and secondly, the desire to remove "the social and sexual vulnerability involved in having a female body" (Bordo 179). While the suggestions of domestic instability point to a generalized sense of "femme fatales in crisis", the spectre of the eating disorder draws explicit links between the teenage girl's sexualized body, the power it supposedly gives her, and the cultural meanings it is ascribed – meanings which she is incapable of anticipating and/or manipulating.

Both *Cruel Intentions* and *Pretty Persuasion* struggle with the implications and contradictions of the bad girl identity, with each film developing a narrative strand in which the femme fatale attempts to turn her virginal love-rival into a slut so that she, too, will be rejected. In *Cruel Intentions*, Kathryn vows to make Cecile, the girl who inadvertently "stole" her boyfriend, "the premier tramp of the New York area". She then embarks on a plot to ensure that Cecile gains an enormous range of sexual experience under the expert tutelage of Sebastian so that Court, the ex-boyfriend, will no longer desire her. Similarly, at the end of *Pretty Persuasion*, Kimberly reveals her plot to make Brittany look cheap so that Troy would reject her. While this motif of good-girls-turned-slutty certainly provides further evidence for the precarious nature of the sexual girl's position in Western society, it also speaks to the "girls in crisis" sensibility that surrounds the representation of femme fatale in *Cruel Intentions* and *Pretty Persuasion* alike. In Kimberly's final scene, she explains her motivation and methods to the now-crushed Brittany: "you're not [Troy's] perfect little angel any more are you? Oh no. Now, you're a dirty little whore, just like me. I turned you into me!" In this announcement lies an inherent self-loathing which is likewise present in *Cruel Intentions*; in each film, the femme fatale's project to turn the virginal girl into herself, and to see her punished for it, is a clear indication that the teen femme fatale is not happy with her lot. The teenage girl may be able to extort status and success from her sexual availability, but these prizes are hard-won and do not, ultimately, grant her happiness.

If these films spell out the disasters that can occur when "active girlhood becom[es] too active" they also attempt to analyse the strategies that young women employ in order to succeed within the restrictive parameters of patriarchal society (Nayak and Kehily 61). That said, neither *Cruel Intentions* nor *Pretty Persuasion* is capable of expanding these parameters: while both films identify the various dilemmas by which the teenage girl is plagued, the representations of Kathryn and Kimberly do not suggest a clear means of escape from the restrictive boundaries of the desirable-but-despicable bad girl role.[9]

The femme fatale model can only, perhaps, go so far in untangling the complex intersections of gender, sex, and power that take place within and around the body of the teenage girl. Still, in reflecting on the causes and effects of the teen femme fatale's vexed behaviour, films like *Cruel Intentions* and *Pretty Persuasion* offer valuable correctives to recent cinematic representations of hot-but-dangerous girls; while they do not necessarily disrupt the teenage girl's cultural objectification, they usefully analyse her strange social currency in a world where the postfeminist rhetoric of sexual empowerment is in permanent competition with the sexual double standards that continue to prevail.

Notes

1. See, for example, *The Big Sleep*'s Carmen Sternwood (1946), Veda in *Mildred Pierce* (1945), Sue in *Pretty Poison* (1968), Delly in *Night Moves* (1975), Violet in *Pretty Baby* (1978), and the eponymous characters in *Heathers* (1988).
2. For a useful list of qualities connected with the femme fatale figure, see Tasker 120.
3. For more on girls and girlhood, see Gonick 1.
4. In *Rethinking the Femme Fatale in Film Noir*, Julie Grossman argues that critics have tended to fixate on the category of the femme fatale in ways that can undermine the complex and varied ways in which women in film noir are characterized. According to Grossman, an examination of "narrative, social psychology and the mise-en-scene in film noir ... reveal[s] that a large majority of so-called bad women in noir are not demonized in the films in which they appear and are very often shown to be victims: first, of the social rules that dictate gender roles and, second, of reading practices that overidentify with and overinvest in the idea of the 'femme fatale' " (2).
5. This is not to say that the femme fatale with sexual desires of her own exists only within teenage incarnation. The deadly women of *Basic Instinct* (1992), *The Last Seduction* (1994), and other frequently discussed neo-noirs of the 1980s and 1990s would attest to the strong presence of personal feminine desire existing alongside the femme fatale character in recent years. However, where female sexual desire is presented in such films as aggressive, dangerous, and unnatural, I argue that the teen femme fatales operate within entirely different frameworks that instead allow for a more complex interpretation of feminine sexuality and ambition.
6. For further examples of "girls in crisis" literature, see Orenstein and Sadker and Sadker.
7. This cluster of literature on "mean girls" is exemplified by Wiseman's *Queen Bees and Wannabes: Helping Your Daughter Survive Cliques, Boyfriends, Gossip, and Other Realities of Adolescence* (2003) and Gabarino's *See Jane Hit: Why Girls are Growing More Violent and What We Can Do About It* (2006).
8. See Levy, Valenti, and – from the anti-feminist right – Platt Liebau.
9. See Grossman 1–21.

Works cited

Baumgardner, Jennifer, and Amy Richards. *Manifesta: Young Women, Feminism, and the Future.* New York: Farrar, Straus and Giroux, 2000.

Bordo, Susan. *Unbearable Weight: Feminism, Western Culture, and the Body.* 10th Anniversary edn. Berkeley: University of California Press, 2003.

Driscoll, Catherine. *Girls: Feminine Adolescence in Popular Culture and Cultural Theory.* New York: Colombia University Press, 2002.

Gabarino, James. *See Jane Hit: Why Girls are Growing More Violent and What We Can Do About It.* New York: Penguin, 2006.

Gonick, Marnina. "Between 'Girl Power' and 'Reviving Ophelia': Constituting the Neoliberal Girl Subject". *NWSA Journal* 18.2 (2006): 1–23.

Grossman, Julie. *Rethinking the Femme Fatale in Film Noir: Ready for Her Close-Up*. Basingstoke: Palgrave, 2009.

Humbert, Brigine E. "*Cruel Intentions*: Adaptations, Teenage Movie or Remake". *Literature/Film Quarterly* 30.4 (2002): 279–86.

Levy, Ariel. *Female Chauvinist Pigs: Women and the Rise of Raunch Culture*. London: Pocket Books, 2006.

Mallan, Kerry, and Sharyn Pearce. "Introduction: Tales of Youth in Postmodern Culture". *Youth Cultures: Texts, Images, Identities*. Ed. Kerry Mallan, and Sharyn Pearce. Connecticut and London: Praeger, 2003. i–xix.

Munford, Rebecca. " 'Wake Up and Smell the Lipgloss': Gender, Generation and the (A)politics of Girl Power". *Third Wave Feminism: A Critical Exploration*. Ed. Stacy Gillis, Gillian Howie, and Rebecca Munford. Basingstoke: Palgrave Macmillan, 2004. 142–53.

Nayak, Anoop, and Mary Jane Kehily. *Gender, Youth and Culture: Young Masculinities and Femininities*. Basingstoke: Palgrave Macmillan, 2008.

Orenstein, Peggy. *Schoolgirls: Young Women, Self Esteem, and the Confidence Gap*. New York: Doubleday, 1994.

Pipher, Mary. *Reviving Ophelia: Saving the Selves of Adolescent Girls*. New York: Ballantine Books, 1994.

Platt, Liebau, Carol. *Prude: How the Sex-obsessed Culture Damages Girls (and America Too!)*. Nashville: Center Street, 2007.

Sadker, Myra, and David Miller Sadker. *Failing at Fairness: How America's Schools Cheat Girls*. New York: Charles Scribner, 1994.

Shary, Timothy. "The Nerdly Girl and Her Beautiful Sister". *Sugar and Spice and Everything Nice: Cinemas of Girlhood*. Ed. Frances Gateward, and Murray Pomerance. Detroit: Wayne State University Press, 2002. 235–52.

Straayer, Chris. "*Femme Fatale* or Lesbian Femme: *Bound* in Sexual *Différance*". *Women in Film Noir*. Ed. E. Ann Kaplan. rev. edn. London: British Film Institute, 1998. 151–63.

Tasker, Yvonne. *Working Girls: Gender and Sexuality in Popular Cinema*. London: Routledge, 1998.

Valenti, Jessica. *The Purity Myth: How America's Obsession With Virginity is Hurting Young Women*. Berkeley: Seal Press, 2009.

Whelehan, Imelda. *Overloaded: Popular Culture and the Future of Feminism*. London: The Women's Press, 2000.

Williams, Linda Ruth. *The Erotic Thriller in Contemporary Cinema*. Edinburgh: Edinburgh University Press, 2005.

Wiseman, Rosalind. *Queen Bees and Wannabes: Helping Your Daughter Survive Cliques, Boyfriends, Gossip, and Other Realities of Adolescence*. New York: Three Rivers Press, 2003.

Wurtzel, Elizabeth. *Bitch: In Praise of Difficult Women*. London: Quartet Books, 1999.

6
Butch Lesbians: Televising Female Masculinity

Helen Fenwick

Critical accounts of lesbian representation have been enduringly vexed by the contentious and polysemic status of the term "lesbian". As Judith Butler explains in "Imitation and Gender Insubordination", it is "permanently unclear what that sign [lesbian] signifies". While Butler embraces the freedom that this ambiguity represents, pointing to the fact that "identity categories tend to be instruments of regulatory regimes" (13–14), Elaine Marks has observed that "a *sense* of identity", however fictitious, remains essential to understanding the ways in which different identities are formed and interrogated within any given society (110; emphasis added). In exploring the nuances of lesbian representation, then, we need to establish "a sense of [lesbian] identity" in order to address key questions about on-screen images of lesbianism: How is lesbianism represented within visual culture? How, if at all, do representations of lesbians shape impressions of, and approaches to, lesbianism in wider society? Why does it matter if lesbians are represented in ways that are positive, negative, or even authentic?

The development of digital technologies has an important role to play in debates surrounding representations of lesbians on screen. The advent of systems that allow live programmes the same functionality as recorded ones and the growing popularity of online downloading and streaming has changed the way we consume television profoundly. Such developments have created a "new, demographically fragmented universe in which networks must compete" to attract audiences that are "composed of multiple minoritarian segments". According to Sasha Torres, this competitive environment can account, to some extent, for "the recent explosion of gay-themed programming" (399). As well as impacting on the content of the schedules in the way that Torres describes, the ease of access to global programming has also worked to diminish anxieties that US television is eroding and endangering British broadcasting. Paul Rixon argues that in the present technological times, "the question should not be one of an alien culture invading our screens, but [one of] how American programmes work as part of our television culture" (50). It is clear that US programmes are no longer used to fill in the gaps between the "proper" programmes; rather, "American programmes are now attractions in their own right" (55) and contribute vitally to the shaping of European identity (Morley and Robins 57).

The rise of American quality television has been led by Home Box Office (HBO), a subscription channel which provides original programming to paying customers. As Marc Leverette acknowledges in his introduction to *It's Not TV*, "other networks have begun to imitate the HBO formula in terms of style and content", producing programmes that have the "HBO effect" (1). Showtime's *The L Word* (2004–09) is one such example of the HBO formula at work. *The L Word* was even marketed by Showtime under the slogan "Same Sex Different City", alluding to HBO's hugely successful show, *Sex and the City* (1998–2004). The HBO effect or formula stands on the economic foundations of the channel; being subscription-based, the channel can afford to take risks and provide viewers with programmes that they are "not … *willing* to watch, but [which] they *want* to watch" (15). The viewers of HBO expect provocative and challenging content, and the channel has certainly delivered on its promise to be "Different and First" – its slogan from 1972 until 1978 (McCabe and Akass 88). While the popularity of HBO may have waned in recent years – most likely as result of new digital technologies – its commitment to producing provocative, original programming, such as *Sex and the City* and *The Wire* (2002–08), has percolated down to the other networks, leaving viewers with an increasing number of shows that they *want* to watch.

Before embarking on my analysis of the representation of the "butch" lesbian[1] in *The Wire*, I want to first consider the Showtime programme *The L Word* – a show that was screened in the United Kingdom in advance of *The Wire* and which actively follows the "HBO formula". In both *The L Word* and *The Wire* the portrayal of the butch lesbian is bound up with ideas about race.[2] While Samiya Bashir has referred to the black lesbian as the "big pink elephant in the middle of the room", on account of her prevailing underrepresentation in mainstream popular culture (20), the black *butch* lesbian is, perhaps, a less elusive figure. Light and dark have traditionally been used to symbolize the butch-femme dynamic: black lesbians are partnered, in the main, with lighter-skinned or white femmes. Indeed, as Anna Marie Smith observes, "it is often assumed that the black woman is, by nature, the butch" (214). On occasions when the white butch does appear within the field of visual representation, her identity is intimately linked to female-to-male transgenderism, without the tension of the "border wars . . . between these two modes of identification" (Halberstam 172). In light of this, it would appear to be easier for white heteronormative supremacy to accept transgenderism, which upholds traditional gender binaries, than to endorse the idea of white, butch lesbianism.

Following the notorious demise of the show *Ellen* (1994–98), the commercial success of an American mainstream show about lesbians seemed an unlikely prospect. In *Ellen*, both the character and the actor/comedian Ellen DeGeneres came out as lesbian and this, in turn, led to the show being cancelled. As the ABC President Roger Iger explained, *Ellen* was cancelled because it "became a programme about a character who was gay every single week, and . . . that was too much for people" (qtd. in McCarthy 596). So what has changed since Iger made this remark in 1998 to allow *The L Word* to show characters being "gay every single week" without it being "too much"? The answer can be found in the two groundbreaking shows: *Sex and the City* and *Queer as Folk* (1999). Through their innovative depictions of female agency and male homosexuality respectively, these shows created a space on mainstream television where lesbian identities could emerge. *The L Word* is, to some extent, a hybrid of *Sex and the City* and *Queer as Folk*. According to Showtime's executive, Gary Levine, however, *The L Word*'s "potential appeal" initially "rested on the understanding that lesbian sex . . . is a whole cottage industry for heterosexual men" (qtd. in Sedgwick xix). Although there are some attempts to run with a butch character, the show never escapes the demands of this heterosexual market, meaning that the bastion of white male masculinity remains secure.

In *The L Word* the butchness of the central character, Bette, is closely linked to her racial heritage. However, Bette can pass as a straight woman and as white, embodying the "social expectations of womanhood while simultaneously embodying butch ideology" (Farr and Degroult 428). *The L Word* thus implies a connection between butchness and blackness – a connection that is consolidated by the fact that Bette's partner, Tina, is a blonde femme. This strategy is reminiscent of the early lesbian film *Desert Hearts* (1985), where " 'hyperfemininity' and its 'butch' counterpart are constituted through a set of 'colour codings' which connote wider discourses of racial difference" (Stacey 105). The characters of Ivan and Moira/Max have the potential to introduce a

representation of the white butch into *The L Word*. However, the possibility of a white butch and its threat to white male masculinity vanishes
into the issue of transgender, whereby an "Ivan who is fluid in gender
identity disappears leaving a male-identified Ivan full of shame about his
female body" (Moore and Schilt 167). This change in Ivan has the wider
impact of averting a crisis in white masculinity and restoring the binary
distinction between male and female. This narrative is almost duplicated
in a later season of the show through the character of Moira/Max, who
initially presents as a white butch, but whose identity – like that of
Ivan – is more clearly defined as transgender. Although Max does not
disappear during the transitioning process in the way that Ivan does,
what does disappear – in both cases – is the representation of white
butch lesbians performing white female masculinity.

By Season Four, it is clear that the images of butch lesbians that
predominate in *The L Word* are those which pose the least threat to
white masculinity. The only stable image of the butch in *The L Word*
is that of Tasha Williams, a young, African-American GI in the US military. Throughout the series, Tasha's butchness remains consistent and
uncompromised, and this seems progressive within the context of the
show.[3] On closer consideration, however, this particular construction
of butch identity remains conservative: the fact that Tasha is black
not only means that she poses little threat to the supremacy of white
male masculinity, but also connects her to prevailing stereotypes of the
"unfeminine" black woman.[4]

As with any series, *The L Word* is bound by economic limitations
and the need to keep the heterosexual audience engaged. Although
the notion of white female masculinity is raised, then, it is simultaneously collapsed into the category of transgender – where the binary split
between male and female is actively reasserted – before it can pose any
tangible threat to the authority of white male masculinity. While it may
be pleasurable to watch a butch lesbian being portrayed in an "authentic" way, the pleasure in watching the character of Tasha Williams is
disturbed by the racist implications of show's decision to present her as
black – especially given that the show is set, predominantly, in white
America.

The Wire

The Wire is a Baltimore-based police drama that explores issues of institutional corruption within the intersecting spheres of politics, education,
law, and the media. While the show investigates the interconnectedness

of these institutions, it is equally committed to an analysis of the ways in which they impact on the day-to-day lives of the Baltimoreans, in particular those who live in poverty and deprivation.

Here, I would like to examine how the lesbian bodies of Detective Kima Greggs (Sonja Sohn) and Snoop (Felicia Pearson) are visualized in the series, and the wider impact this has in relation to lesbian representation. In her role as a detective, Kima is initially attached to the Narcotics Department, but is subsequently moved into the Homicide Unit. Snoop, on the other hand, is part of a criminal duo that engages in murder and intimidation on behalf of the drug lord Marlo. Sixteen minutes into the first episode of *The Wire*, "The Target", we are introduced to Kima's partner, Cheryl. By the end of this episode, then, Kima has been established as a black, butch police detective, with a live-in, middle-class, femme partner, who encourages Kima to study law.

If, as Ann Ciasullo attests, the "body or image that is [constantly] made invisible is the 'butch'", then the character of Kima necessarily contravenes dominant tendencies within the mainstream media through her sustained portrayal of female masculinity (578). If "we regularly punish those who fail to do their gender right", it might be supposed that Kima's subversion of gender conventions will be "corrected" through her eventual disappearance or demise (Butler 140). Kima, however, is not killed off; she not only survives for the show's five seasons, but survives as a black butch dyke who works on the side of law and order and lives with a black femme. Kima, in fact, is only ever coupled with a black femme – be it Cheryl or her nameless one-night stand. Given that Ciasullo has argued that "the femme body is... a white body", and the black lesbian "cannot be a femme" (597), *The Wire* marks itself out as progressive through its attempt to subvert and re-script of the traditional on-screen partnership of the black butch and the white femme.[5]

In "Mission Accomplished" (3.12) there are two scenes which epitomize *The Wire*'s approach to sex. The first of these takes place in the opening half of the episode and features Kima having a one-night stand with another black woman. Kima is shown sucking noisily on the breasts of her lover, who straddles her, while Kima's mobile phone rings – with a call from Cheryl – in the background. The second sex scene of the episode takes place between Cedric Daniels, a black police lieutenant attached to the Major Case Unit, and Rhonda Pearlman (or Ronnie), a white female attorney. This scene is intercut with scenes of another character, Dennis "Cutty" Wise, venting his own frustrations on a punch-bag in a gym across town. Although Kima is committing infidelity, while

Daniels and Ronnie are in a relationship, it is this second scene which is presented as illicit and erotic. Obviously speaking to the issue of miscegenation, this scene also comments on the lesbian sex scene that precedes it; in particular, it refuses to resort to the commonplace strategy – evidenced in *The L Word* – of presenting lesbian sex as titillating and instead reserves this effect for the heterosexual sex scene.

While Kima's sexuality is not the focus of the drama, she does not escape the oppression of homophobia. That said, the drama tends to use Kima's sexuality as a means of illuminating the ignorance and/or sensitivity of other characters. In an episode from the first season, Carver attempts to press Kima on the issue of her sexuality: "Kima if you don't mind me asking, when was it that you first figured that you liked women better than men?" Kima's retort – "I mind you asking" – immediately terminates the conversation, leaving the viewer in little doubt that her sexuality is not going to be the principal focus of *The Wire* (1.2). There are a few homophobic slurs in the early part of Season One, many of which are made by Kima's work colleagues behind her back, though these dissipate as her professional relationships evolve. However, when Marquis "Bird" Hilton is arrested for murder, he tells Kima to "suck my dick, dyke cunt", and refers to her as a "freak cunt eater" and an "ugly ass cunt eater". In this tirade of verbal abuse, Kima's sexuality is not only rendered visible, but is also – along with her gender – the subject of policing by Bird (1.7).

Towards the end of the first season, the institutionalized homophobia and racism of the Baltimore Police Department are signposted with increasing regularity. When Kima is shot during a covert operation, the Police Commissioner arrives on the scene and immediately assumes that the white Crime Scene Investigator is, in fact, Daniels. His apology reeks with the embarrassing insincerity that inflects his expressions of sympathy for Kima's injuries. This is evidenced further when Carver and Daniels are discussing "Kima's girl", whom Erve, Lieutenant Daniels' superior, assumes to be Kima's daughter, rather than her partner. Daniels, protecting Kima's privacy, explains to Erve that Cheryl is Kima's "room-mate". At this point, Erve approaches the Police Commissioner to request that he speak with Cheryl on behalf of the Baltimore Police. Although the viewer is not privy to this dialogue, it is clear that dealing with black lesbian lovers is not something with which the white, racist Police Commissioner is entirely comfortable and Erve comments to Daniels that he'll do it himself. In this scene, the homophobia for which Kima is a target is complexly entangled with the racism to which Daniels is subject. The ignorant attitudes of the Police Commissioner thus come to symbolize the bigotry that pervades the upper echelons of civic life, while also functioning to query the public legitimacy of the successful white male. At this point it is unclear whether Kima will live, or whether she will be "punished" for her performance of female masculinity, and the drama plays with the traditional expectation that "all dykes die".

Over the course of its five seasons, *The Wire* charts Kima's development into "true police". Kima negotiates this journey, in part, through her resistance to Cheryl's designs on her passing the bar and becoming a lawyer; not to mention through her narrow avoidance of McNulty's pathological drinking, womanizing, and professional rashness. In a scene from "The Cost" (1.10), Kima's identity as "true police" is humorously emphasized over and above her identity as a lesbian. Set in a bar, where Kima and Cheryl are socializing with their lesbian friends, this scene is plotted as a "coming out" scenario; here, however, it is Kima's status as "true police", rather than her already-established identity as a lesbian, that is subject to revelation. The only white lesbian present asks Kima how she knew she wanted to be a cop: "I mean how did you choose that? When you were little did you think about it at all?" This question echoes Carver's earlier attempts to probe Kima on the subject of her sexuality, though Kima here responds in full confessional mode. In revealing and rationalizing her identity as "true police", Kima satirizes the process of coming out as a lesbian and indirectly highlights the series' strategic eschewal of any conventional coming-out sequence.

The feminization of Kima is one of the methods by which the series simultaneously comments on and reinforces mainstream portrayals of lesbianism. In "The Cost" (1.10) Kima goes undercover as the feminine girlfriend of Orlando and comments that she is "looking the part too". Interestingly, it is when Kima performs this version of female femininity – and when her Southeast Asian looks are the subject of "traditional" eroticization – that she gets shot. In other words, it is as a feminine woman that Kima comes closest to being killed off. The only things that are killed off, however, are old stereotypes and expectations, as *The Wire* reverses the stale, if persistent, formula that "all dykes die". When Kima is funnelled into an office job after the shooting, she is routinely emasculated. She is ridiculed by Herc for being a "house cat" and "pussy whipped" (2.1), and her clothes reflect this domestication. Although this subversion of stereotypes may push boundaries, we are reminded that Kima is feminine enough to attract the heterosexual male. In one particular scene from Season Three, Kima walks away from Jay Landsman and Bunk, and they are both shown staring at her buttocks. "Man", Jay remarks, "I would murder that if she wasn't...". As Jay's reflection trails off, Bunk weighs in, finishing his colleague's sentence with the word "particular" (3.4). There is no denying the humour here, but such scenes do appear to problematize the straightforward representation of Kima as butch. The reason for this feminization becomes clearer when the murderous Snoop enters the series in "Homecoming" (3.6). Snoop, after all, operates on the border between butch lesbian and transgender, necessitating the careful repositioning of Kima as the face of heterosexually acceptable lesbianism.

The character of Snoop ticks all the predictable boxes in relation to lesbian representation: she is black, butch, and a criminal.[6] Described by Stephen King as "the most terrifying female villain to ever appear in a television series", Snoop's performance of female masculinity is monstrous yet comedic as she develops exaggeratedly "masculine" behaviours in order to compensate for her female body (para. 3). Like Kima, Snoop is not the tokenistic face of lesbianism in *The Wire*. Her character's story is not focused on sexuality; it is concerned with revealing how she has been shaped by her experiences within the institutions in Baltimore.

At first glance, Snoop's violent criminality seems to be at odds with her physical presentation as a petite, beautiful, doe-eyed young woman. Because she uses a gun to kill, her diminutive stature rarely interferes with her role as Marlo's henchwoman and over time she develops a reputation for extreme brutality. Indeed, by the end of Season Three, Snoop's notoriety is such that when she claims to be responsible for the murder of Stringer Bell – the second-in-command of the renowned Barksdale gang – she is believed readily and without question (3.12). Even the hardened criminal Hungry Man defecates in fear at the prospect of being tortured and killed at the hands of Snoop (5.4). Snoop's monstrosity takes on a distinctly gothic dimension in Season Four, when she and her partner, Chris, are rarely seen during daylight hours and are depicted, with increasing regularity, as silhouettes – easily recognizable on account of Snoop's exaggerated swagger. Indeed, in the opening credits of Season Four Snoop is shown in silhouette, sitting outside the empty houses where she entombs the victims that Chris, for the most part, murders. To Snoop, these killings are just a part of business, and are undertaken without emotion. Chris, in fact, takes a perverse care in making sure the kills are quick and clean for his victims. This theme of murder-as-a-job is highlighted through Snoop's dialogue. After liming and entombing one particular victim, she turns to Chris as they walk away from their "work", and enquires casually if he wants to "get some Chinese?" (4.8). By contrast, in "Misgivings" (4.10), Chris kills Michael's stepfather, who sexually abused Michael. This murder is extremely graphic, as Chris kicks and punches the man until he is dead, eschewing the execution-style method of killing that he and Snoop have made their signature. As she watches Chris's bare-knuckle attack, Snoop is forced to acknowledge the fact of her own "feminine" limitations. This silent acknowledgement is granted open articulation in her final scene: Snoop's last question to Michael, as she prepares for him to shoot her, is "how's my hair?" (5.9).

Snoop's status as a monster is often convergent – perhaps predictably – with her status as a woman, and in "Soft Eyes" (4.2) she is situated explicitly in relation to the institution of motherhood. In one particular sequence, Snoop is shown training young boys how to shoot a gun. While this is grossly irresponsible on a number of levels, the fact that Snoop's "lesson" takes place within the benign greenery of a local park implies its status as an act of nurture: like a mother, Snoop is equipping her charges with the skills they need to survive in the dangerous world of Baltimore's "corners" (4.8). On other occasions, Snoop's palpable monstrosity is offset by humour, much of which ensues from the discontinuity between her status as a woman and her "masculine" presentation. In order to operate effectively in the criminal world of Baltimore, after all, Snoop needs to override traditional gender stereotypes: she needs to be tougher than the men, talk more "gangsta" than the men, and have a swagger to match. When Snoop is shown buying a nail gun at a large hardware outlet in the opening episode of Season Four, for example, her comic dialogue with the salesman, as they talk at cross-purposes about the effectiveness of different products, serves to distract the viewer from the grim use to which the nail gun will doubtlessly be put (4.1). Similarly, when Chris kills Michael's stepfather with his bare hands, Snoop relieves the horror of the scene with a characteristically affectless statement: "Damn, you didn't even wait to get the mother-fucker in the house".

Throughout its five series, *The Wire* avoids representing its lesbian characters solely in terms of their sexuality. Kima's journey is not presented as a journey of sexual self-discovery, but as a journey in which she establishes her status as "true police". Snoop, on the other hand, is never even shown with a sexual partner, and only once in the series does she mention "pussy", giving a subtle nod to her sexual preference. Although, in some respects, Snoop does adhere to the conventional model of the black butch lesbian, her monstrosity is not ascribable to these aspects of her identity, but to the fact she is a product of the failing and corrupt institutions by which Baltimore is governed.[7] While *The Wire*'s treatment of same-sex desire does begin to trouble viewers' traditional expectations of what lesbian characters can be and do, it would be misleading to situate the show as a representational utopia in which these expectations are wholly subverted or reversed. On this point, it is noteworthy that the only queer to make it through the series unscathed by injury is Rawls, who we see in a flitting moment in a gay bar in "Reformation" (3.10). Ultimately, then, it is the figure of the white (closeted) male who remains at the helm of Baltimorean institutional life, leaving the standard balance of patriarchal power fundamentally unchallenged.

Conclusion

Since the late 1990s, fictional representations of lesbianism on British and American television have increased exponentially, and lesbian characters are now staple features of soap operas, sitcoms, and costume dramas. The portrayal of female masculinity – and *white* female masculinity in particular – is probably the last taboo of lesbian representation. As I have already suggested, this is largely a result of the implicit threat that the butch poses to the structures of masculine (and patriarchal) authority – a threat which is rendered particularly proximate in the figure of the white butch – who, as a white woman, already enjoys greater access to these structures than her non-white counterparts. While *The Wire* does not shy away from the representation of female masculinity, it represents *black* female masculinity, consolidating existing links between blackness and butchness. Still, given that the series is set in Baltimore, where the majority of the population is black, such representations do not emerge as being particularly stereotypical – especially in light of the fact that lesbianism is only ever represented as one facet of the characters' identities. Yet for all the progressiveness of *The Wire*, the continued supremacy of Rawls – a powerful white man – functions as a strategic reminder of the resilience of white patriarchy, and throws any powers accorded to Kima or Snoop into stark relief. In redefining the parameters of lesbian representation, then, *The Wire* also telegraphs the persistence of discrimination, stressing the need for an ongoing interrogation of existing power structures and underlining the continued role that feminism has to play in accounting for the complex renderings of female identity in contemporary culture.

Notes

1. Butch-femme identities have often been understood as imitating the perceived dynamics of heterosexual relationships. Attempts to define butch-femme identity positions against this dominant construction emerged in the late 1980s and early 1990s. Judith Butler acknowledges a level of heterosexual imitation within butch-femme roles, but this derivativeness is used to displace heterosexual norms through subversion and illuminate the mechanics of gender constructions. See "Imitation and Gender Insubordination" (1991).
2. In *Female Masculinity* Judith Halberstam is consistently attentive to the complex ways in which racial stereotypes inform cultural representations of the butch lesbian. For Halberstam, images of the black butch are "particularly complicated locations" that "may all too easily resonate with racial stereotyping in which white forms of femininity represent a cultural norm and nonwhite femininities are measured as excessive or inadequate in relation to that norm". In line with my own argument, however, Halberstam also contends that the "butch of color" might also possess "the power to defamiliarize white masculinity and make visible a potent fusion of alternative masculinity and alternative sexuality" (180–81).
3. For a fuller discussion of Hollywood and femininity, see Dyer.
4. In Debra Wilson's 2003 documentary on black butch women, *Butch Mystique*, several of the women interviewed report feeling as though they are regularly perceived not as black women, but as black men.
5. This is evident in the 1991 film *Salmonberries* where the Native American butch is partnered with a blonde white femme. For a discussion of race, gender, and sexuality in *Salmonberries*, see Allen.
6. For a fuller analysis of blackness, butchness, and criminality, see Halberstam 114–16. See also Halberstam's discussion of Queen Latifah's "gangsta butch" in Gary Gray's *Set it Off* (1996) in *Female Masculinity* 227–29.
7. See Wiltz and HBO's biography of Snoop http://www.hbo.com/thewire/cast/actors/felicia_person.shtml. [Accessed May 10, 2009].

Works cited

Allen, Louise. "*Salmonberries*: Consuming k.d. lang". *Immortal Invisible: Lesbians and the Moving Image*. Ed. Tamsin Wilson. London: Routledge, 1995. 70–84.
Bashir, Samiya. "Fear of a Black Lesbian Planet". *Curve*. February 1, 2001. 20–22.
Butler, Judith. *Gender Trouble: Feminism and the Subversion of Identity*. New York: Routledge, 1990.
———— "Imitation and Gender Insubordination". *Inside/Out: Lesbian Theories, Gay Theories*. Ed. Diana Fuss. London: Routledge, 1991. 13–31.
Ciasullo, Ann M. "Making Her (In)Visible: Cultural Representations of Lesbianism and the Lesbian Body in the 1990s". *Feminist Studies* 27.3 (2001): 577–608.
Desert Hearts. Dir. Donna Deitch. 1985.
Dyer, Richard. *White*. London and New York: Routledge, 1997.
Fuss, Diana. *Essentially Speaking: Feminism, Nature and Difference*. New York: Routledge, 1989.

Halberstam, Judith. *Female Masculinity.* Durham, N.C.; London: Duke UP, 1998.

King, Stephen. "Setting Off a 'Wire' Alarm". *Entertainment Weekly* 894 (2006). http://www.ew.com/ew/article/0,,1333799,00.html. [Accessed May 10, 2009].

Leverette, Marc, Brian L. Ott, and Cara Louise Buckley, eds. *It's Not TV: Watching HBO in the Post-Television Era.* New York: Routledge, 2008.

Marks, Elaine. "Feminism's Wake". *Boundary 2* 12.2 (Winter 1984): 99–110.

McCabe, Janet, and Kim Akass. "It's Not TV, It's HBO's Original Programming: Producing Quality TV". *It's Not TV: Watching HBO in the Post-Television Era.* Ed. Marc Leverette, Brian L. Ott, and Cara Louise Buckley. New York: Routledge, 2008. 83–93.

McCarthy, Anna. "Ellen: Making Queer Television History". *GLQ* 7.4 (2001): 593–620.

Moore, Candace, and Kristen Schilt. "Is She Man Enough?: Female Masculinities on *The L Word*". *Reading* The L Word: *Outing Contemporary Television.* Ed. Kim Akass, and Janet McCabe. London; New York: IB Tauris, 2006. 159–71.

Morley, David, and Kevin Robins. *Spaces of Identity: Global Media, Electronic Landscapes and Cultural Boundaries.* London: Routledge, 1995.

Rich. B. Ruby. "When Difference is (more than) Skin Deep". *Queer Looks: Perspectives on Lesbian and Gay Film and Video.* Ed. Martha Gever, John Greyson, and Pratibha Parmar. London: Routledge, 1993. 318–39.

Rixon, Paul. "The Changing Face of American Television Programmes on British Screens". *Quality Popular Television.* Ed. Mark Jancovich, and James Lyons. London: British Film Institute, 2003. 48–59.

Sedgwick, Eve Kosofsky. "Foreword". *Reading The L Word: Outing Contemporary Television.* Ed. Kim Akass, and Janet McCabe. London; New York: IB Tauris, 2006. xix–xxiv.

Sinfield, Alan. *Cultural Politics – Queer Reading.* 2nd edn. New York: Routledge, 2005.

Smith, Anna Marie. "'By Women, For Women and About Women' Rules OK? The Impossibility of Visual Soliloquy". *A Queer Romance: Lesbian, Gay Men and Popular Culture.* Ed. Paul Burston, and Colin Richardson. London: Routledge, 1995.

Stacey, Jackie. "*Desert Hearts* and the Lesbian Romance Film". *Immortal Invisible: Lesbians and the Moving Image.* Ed. Tamsin Wilton. London: Routledge, 1995.

The L Word. Showtime (2004–09).

The Wire. HBO (2002–08).

1.2. "The Detail". Dir. Clark Johnson. June 9, 2002.

1.7. "One Arrest". Dir. Joe Chappelle. July 21, 2002.

1.10. "The Cost". Dir. Brad Anderson. August 11, 2002.

2.1. "Ebb Tide". Dir. Ed Bianchi. June 1, 2003.

3.4. "Hamsterdam". Dir. Ernest Dickerson. October 10, 2004.

3.6. "Homecoming". Dir. Leslie Libman. October 31, 2004.

3.10. "Reformation". Dir. Christine Moore. November 28, 2004.

3.12. "Mission Accomplished". Dir. Ernest Dickerson. December 19, 2004.

4.1. "Boys of Summer". Dir. Joe Chappelle. September 10, 2006.

4.2. "Soft Eyes". Dir. Christine Moore. September 17, 2006.

4.8. "Corner Boys". Dir. Agnieszka Holland. November 5, 2006.

4.10. "Misgivings". Dir. Ernest Dickerson. November 19, 2006.

5.4. "Transitions". Dir. Daniel Attias. January 27, 2008.
5.9. "Late Editions". Dir. Joe Chappelle. March 2, 2008.

Torres, Sasha. "Television and Race". *A Companion to Television*. Ed. Janet Wasko. Malden, MA: Blackwell, 2005. 399–408.
Wiltz, Teresa. "The Role of Her Life". *Washington Post*. March 16, 2007. http://www.washingtonpost.com/wp-dyn/content/article/2007/03/15/AR2007031501664.html. [Accessed May 10, 2009].

7
"Challenging and Alternative": Screening Queer Girls on Channel 4

Martin Zeller-Jacques

While in the early history of television, lesbians, when present at all, "were only seen as an 'issue' – a 'subject' up for analysis", the growth of digital media culture has greatly increased the quantity of televised representations of lesbians, often as recurring characters, or even as series protagonists (Collis 120–21). This mainstreaming of lesbian representations has significant implications for the discourse around lesbian visibility, which has been a major staple of feminist and queer critiques of television over the last several decades. In particular, such mainstreaming offers us the opportunity to explore some of the complex entanglements that surround lesbian visibility, many of which are neglected in critical analyses that imply the polarization of visibility and invisibility, and transgression and containment. Rather than investigating the effects of lesbian visibility "in the media" or "on television", it is imperative to examine particular trends in representation and to situate these within the wider mediated culture. For example, visibility on a subscription, quality television programme like Showtime's *The L Word* (2004–09) surely comes with different costs, and different representational freedoms, than visibility on a network sitcom like *Ellen* (1994–98). While some of these pressures will be registered in the text, others demand to be theorized on their own terms. Thus, current studies of lesbian visibility need to provide contextualized examinations of texts, which ask what costs, and what freedoms, might be incurred through representation on different media platforms.

In this chapter, I analyse recent representations of lesbians on the Channel 4 and E4 teen dramas *Sugar Rush* (2005–06) and *Skins* (2007–) through the lens of the Channel 4 Corporation's public service remit. Subject to the competing pressures of a public service obligation and an overcrowded commercial sector, Channel 4 and its subsidiaries represent a unique television ecosystem that promotes a degree of lesbian and gay visibility at the same time as it imposes particular limitations on that visibility. These Channel 4 programmes, I argue, understand lesbian visibility – especially teen lesbian visibility – as challenging content. More specifically, though, they use this content to attract a young, lucrative demographic, while also fulfilling the terms of a public service remit that implicitly regards the provision of gay and lesbian visibility as a public service, *regardless* of the qualities of that visibility. As a result, these programmes construct a "post-lesbian" environment for their characters, in which a certain type of normative lesbian is accepted and almost all sexual choices are presented as entirely valid, so long as they do nothing to disrupt the fundamental unity of the normative structures of family, friendship, and the monogamous sexual relationship.[1] In creating this safe space for the representation of lesbians, Channel 4 contributes to the "double-entanglement" of postfeminist media culture, in which

> neo-conservative values in relation to gender, sexuality and family life [are combined] with processes of liberalisation in regard to choice and diversity in domestic, sexual and kinship relations. It also encompasses the co-existence of feminism as at some level transformed into a form of Gramscian common sense.
>
> (McRobbie 255–56)

As we will see, *Sugar Rush* and *Skins* are caught firmly in this double entanglement, as they reaffirm their lesbian characters' commitment to family and friendship groups, while valorizing their personal expressions of sexuality. This emphasis on personal choice leads to "the almost total evacuation of notions of politics or cultural influence ... [as] every aspect of life is refracted through the idea of personal choice and self-determination" (Gill 260). In fact, the figure of the queer teen girl in *Sugar Rush* and *Skins* is profoundly apolitical. Rather than challenging and alternative, this figure is thoroughly contained within Channel 4's public service context, the normative structures of couples and families, and a contemporary media culture that is now comfortable with this well-defined, "common sense" vision of lesbian sexuality.

Channel 4: Public service and queer broadcasting

Channel 4 has a special place in the history of British broadcast television. Its creation, as an alternative to the broad, mainstream address provided by the BBC and ITV, helped to usher in a time of increased variety in television provision, and thus increased viewer choice. Channel 4's original remit required it to cater to tastes not catered for by other terrestrial channels, and "to encourage innovation and experiment in the form and content of programmes" ("Broadcasting Act, 1981" 11.1). Subsequent legislation has further refined this remit, requiring the corporation to address "the tastes and interests of a culturally diverse society", and to contribute "programmes of an educational nature and other programmes of educative value" ("Communications Act, 2003" 265.3). Taken together, these responsibilities have given Channel 4 what Maggie Brown refers to as "a license to be different". Dorothy Hobson, too, suggests that the "main theoretical analysis which explains both the difficulties and triumphs of Channel 4 is the concept of difference" (192). Even today, Channel 4's marketing discourse emphasizes its "challenging and alternative" programming – and its consequent appeal to younger viewers – as its chief distinguishing characteristic ("Why Advertise on Channel 4?" para. 3 of 4). In the current media climate, Channel 4's brand is also strengthened by its associated digital television channels: More4, Film4 and E4. As part of the umbrella structure of the Channel 4 Corporation, each of these contributes to Channel 4's public service remit, although the manner in which they do so is left largely to the discretion of the corporation. Originally subscription services, all three channels were changed into commercial, free-to-air digital stations as part of Chairman Andy Duncan's project to keep Channel 4's public service remit at the forefront of its activities, even in the multi-channel environment. This strategy necessarily implies that simply spreading access is seen as helping to serve the public (Brown 293–97).

However it fulfils its public service role in the contemporary digital environment, Channel 4's "license to be different" has enabled it to engage with racial, social, and sexual minorities in a way that earlier terrestrial television channels had not. If, in its early days, this commitment to diversity grew out of the channel's public service remit, it now has a sound basis in the commercial logic of contemporary television. As television bandwidth has increased over the past several decades, the intense competition for audiences has led broadcasters to pursue programming strategies which target small, but lucrative, demographics and promote easily identifiable brands.[2] Thus, Channel 4's task of distinguishing itself, already inscribed in its charter, is also encouraged by the commercial conditions in which the channel now must operate. Consequently, Channel 4 works to strengthen its established brand as a provider of "difference". Its yearly review documents highlight this aspect of its programming by publishing polls that show Channel 4 beating all of Britain's other terrestrial television channels in categories like "Covers ground other channels wouldn't" and "Caters for audiences other channels don't cater for" (Lygo, "Channel 4 Annual Review, 2007" 6). Meanwhile, its reputation for difference is maintained by the channel's willingness to showcase the lifestyles of racial, sexual, and social minorities, a programming tactic which helps Channel 4 to reach beyond these minorities and target some of their most lucrative markets. Ron Becker has charted the way that American networks have used gay and lesbian visibility in order to target a socially liberal demographic, arguing that appealing to discourses of multiculturalism and celebrating diversity became a way of reaching the "selectively affluent" consumers desired by advertisers (81–96). Channel 4's strategy of branding itself as "challenging and alternative" television is based on a similar logic: its showcasing of gay-themed programming is used to promote its reputation for difference and attract its young target audience. Brown offers an example of this dynamic at work, writing that *Queer as Folk*, Channel 4's most famously successful gay drama, was not so much marketed as "gay programming" as "anti-establishment programming": "Middle-aged women were shown the tapes, their shocked reactions recorded and used in radio commercials.... When Becks lager withdrew its sponsorship, the marketing department was jubilant: still more press coverage" (233). Both *Sugar Rush* and *Skins* rely on a similar strategy, exploiting a music-video aesthetic and foregrounding the explicit sex, drug use, and frank treatment of homosexuality in the programmes. In this way, these shows mark themselves out as "anti-establishment" and thus begin to court their young target audience.

The politics of this approach, however, need to be problematized, in terms of both public service and commercial contexts. First of all, if the representation of lesbian characters is prescribed by the channel's public service commitment to diversity and difference, then the quality of that visibility becomes, implicitly, a secondary concern. As Amy Villarejo writes, "[t]o promote portraits of lesbian lives is to promote representational presence in public cultures and therefore to heighten public authority" (14). Thus, Channel 4's requirement to represent diversity reinforces the power of the public service television channel, and the state which empowers it, to set the terms of representation, both for lesbians and for other minorities. Historically, mainstream representations of lesbians have been, in Ann Ciasullo's terms, both "heterosexualized ... via the femme body ... [and] because the representation of desire between two women is usually suppressed ... de-homosexualized" (578).

Channel 4's "license to be different" allows it to move past this older formulation and to produce texts which not only engage with lesbian desire, but centralize it. However, because these texts tend to be under-lain by the assumption that the explicit is inherently challenging, they often trade on forms of representation that are predicated upon explicit sexuality rather than challenging politics. Channel 4's programming may be unafraid to showcase lesbian desire, but the desire it showcases is limited to sexual desire. It stops short of representing the desire for equal treatment, for social status, for alternative ways of living, and implicitly equates lesbian identity to lesbian sex. Secondly, if the representation of homosexuality is deemed commercially valuable because it is considered inherently "challenging and alternative", then the programmes which take part in that representation help to reinscribe an othering of homo-sexuals. In other words, while Channel 4 identifies homosexuality as transgressive, it also, simultaneously, *contains* its transgressive potential by presenting it within the "challenging and alternative" (yet publicly sanctioned) space of Channel 4 itself.

However, as representations of queer girl sexuality, *Sugar Rush* and *Skins* are marked by more than their presentation on a public ser-vice broadcaster. Both texts feature predominantly teenaged casts and focus on the social and sexual development of their teenage charac-ters; they must also, therefore, be understood as teen texts. Davis and Dickinson point out that, whatever the investment of their audiences, "teen shows"

> are created by adults, arguably with a particular adult agenda. In the broadest sense this might be: to educate and inform while enter-taining...to set certain agendas at this delicate time just prior to the onset of a more prominent citizenship; and/or to raise crucial issues (of *adult* choosing) in a "responsible manner" that is entirely hegemonically negotiated. (3; emphasis in original)

One of the "crucial issues" so frequently raised in teen television is the thorny question of sexuality. As Ben Gove reminds us, "adult framings of pre-adult sexuality always involve an uneasy use of discursive power, for the adult show of interest immediately implicates the framer in what she/he frames" (177). The adult role in the creation of these teen texts cannot help but leave its ideological mark: the representation of queer teens is always and already caught in the crossfire of hegemonic dis-courses which frame ideas of "the teenager" and ideas of "the queer". Davis himself points this out, noting that Karen Lury's characterization of teenagers as "being opposed to a dominant or mainstream culture" (12) "could be seen as analogous to that of queers; that is as outside the mainstream, not wishing to be compromised by the representational regime of the popular medium" (Davis 130–31). However, Channel 4's representations of lesbian teens seem less concerned with the lesbian part of that identity than with the teen. In fact, Channel 4's programmes represent the lesbian teen as a profoundly *un*-remarkable sexual subject. Rather than being marked by difference due to her sexuality, she is *just like* everyone else around her as she negotiates a matrix of personal and sexual behaviours, constantly exploring and reconstructing her own subjectivity. In fact, in both *Sugar Rush* and *Skins*, she makes these negotiations somewhat more successfully than her heteronormative peers, and is thus positioned as a fulfilled and fully realized subject by the end of the narrative. Susan Driver has commented on a tendency in contemporary culture for girls in general, and queer girls in particular, to be regarded as exemplary neo-liberal subjects:

> A convergence of popular, commercial, and theoretical discourses valorizing the nonfixity of girls intersects with public representations of queer girls as not only fathomable but symbolically special and convenient in displaying the unique uncertainties of adolescent desires. (7)

In this way, the non-fixity of the lesbian teen, who is unfailingly represented as socially and sexually flexible, comes to stand for the more general non-fixity that is characteristic of contemporary subjectivity. However, in emphasizing the importance of the lesbian teen as subject, these programmes also depoliticize her. Even if the representations in question are sometimes genuinely novel, the effect of this discourse of subjectivity is all too familiar. In a broad summary of typical trends in the representation of gays and lesbians in the media, Bonnie Dow comments that they "all contribute to the conclusion that homosexuality is relevant almost exclusively for its impact on personal relationships, and moreover, that the most important personal relationships a gay or lesbian character has are those s/he has with heterosexuals" (100–01). Since Channel 4's lesbian teens exist in a more generally heterosexual milieu, their sexuality is typically represented as important only insofar as it disrupts their relationships with family and friends. Dow suggests that this kind of emphasis on the personal allows such programmes to elide the political, ignoring the real-world problems of discrimination and prejudice.

As I have mentioned above, Channel 4's lesbian teens exist in what we might call a "post-lesbian" space. Their identity as lesbians, and the questions it might raise, is sidelined in favour of the more generic valorization of personal, sexual choice. Wolfe and Roripaugh have noted popular and scholarly trends towards post-lesbian representation, observing that such perspectives "centre primarily around a perceived need to uncouple lesbian and feminist identities, as well as a desire to dismantle, usurp, and transgress against prior generations' identitarian formations of lesbian identity" (213). This tendency, amply evidenced in both *Sugar Rush* and *Skins*, has the benefit of breaking down stereotypical representations of lesbians, but still elides questions around identity politics. Ultimately, it often manifests in the form of lesbian characters who are indistinguishable from their heterosexual peers, except when they are in the act of desiring, or having sex with, other women. As a result, all that is left which might be transgressive in these texts is the presence of lesbian sex itself; as I have argued above, however, this content is also rendered safe through its confinement to the publicly sanctioned, commercially lucrative, and "challenging and alternative" Channel 4.

Lesbian teens on Channel 4: *Sugar Rush* and *Skins*

I have argued that Channel 4's public service remit and commercial imperatives will direct its representations of lesbian lives in particular, apolitical directions. In the following analyses of *Sugar Rush* and *Skins*, I hope to demonstrate some of the parameters of those representations, which typically validate a singular, relatively conservative form of lesbian subjectivity – one which is entirely compatible with other forms of orthodox, neo-liberal subjectivity. Both of these programmes value personal choice above personal identity, and thus portray the problems of their characters' sexuality as personal or family problems. Significantly, this is no different to the treatment of any other character in the narrative. Being a lesbian, these texts imply, is morally and practically equivalent to being black, or poor, or having divorced parents, or living with a mental illness. In their attempts to avoid all of the potential restrictions of these categories of identity, both *Sugar Rush* and *Skins* risk a dangerous levelling in their representations – rendering all difference as the same kind of obstacle to the free, subjective choice which is represented as ideal.

Sugar Rush follows the late teenage years of Kim, a self-identified "15-year-old queer virgin", as she explores her burgeoning "sexual obsession" with Maria "Sugar" Sweet. Set in Brighton, where Kim and her family have just moved, the programme chronicles the way the family is tested and redefined as a result of its proximity to Brighton's culture of relatively free (queer) sexual morality. Throughout the show's run, the family struggles to cohere, briefly breaks apart, and is ultimately reconstituted in order to make room for the wide variety of non-normative sexual practices of its various members. During this time Kim eventually comes out, develops a brief sexual relationship with Sugar, and ultimately enters into a committed relationship with Saint, the owner of a local sex-shop. Kim's experiences are aligned to the equally tortuous sexual journeys of her parents, Nathan and Stella, her brother Matt, and the eponymous Sugar. These journeys involve infidelity, bondage, swinging, abstinence, cross-dressing, date-rape, anal sex, and more, prompting Kim to ask herself, "Why is everyone so fucked up about sex?" (1.1).[3] It is this question that the rest of the series sets itself to answering.

In its representation of lesbian teens, *Sugar Rush* employs two strategies, both of which valorize the independence and subjectivity of the lesbian teen, while simultaneously setting boundaries around her choices. The first and most consistent strategy is best described as "normalization-through-juxtaposition". Amidst the vast variety of sexual practices engaged in by the characters in *Sugar Rush*, lesbian sexuality is presented as something ordinary and unsurprising. Next to Stella's infidelity, or Sugar's penchant for allowing herself to be taken advantage of, Kim's lesbianism is consistently shown to be both relatively "normal" and entirely consistent with the healthy functioning of the nuclear family. The second strategy is perhaps more familiar, involving another juxtaposition – this time of "good" lesbians against "bad" ones. Here, Kim and Saint's model of lesbian subjectivity, which is white, middle-class, femme, and monogamous, is opposed to alternative models of lesbian subjectivity, sometimes characterized as frumpy, sometimes as predatory, but always as ultimately unhealthy or undesirable. Through this combination of representational strategies, *Sugar Rush* constructs a post-lesbian space in which Kim is free to explore and express her sexuality, but where the hegemony of the nuclear family and the monogamous couple is never really in doubt.

The strategy of normalization through juxtaposition is best exemplified by an episode late in the second season (2.8). By this time Kim has come out to her parents and is involved in a committed relationship with the sex-shop owner, Saint. Although her parents are (relatively) comfortable with her sexuality, they are also pushing their children to exhibit more traditional family values, and for this reason Kim remains reluctant to tell them that Saint owns a sex shop. Unbeknownst to Kim, however, Nathan's recent penchant for "family" activities stems from the fact that, while he and Stella claim to be attending marriage counselling, they are actually visiting swingers' parties. He thus over-compensates, first by inviting Kim and Saint to a wholesome family dinner, and then, paradoxically, by chastising his teenage son, Matt, for cross-dressing. All of this sets in motion a farcical chain of events; of course, Nathan and Stella's parties are supplied by Saint's sex shop, and through a series of coincidences, both Kim and Saint arrive at one of the parties just in time to see Nathan and Stella collapse in a heap beneath a shoddily assembled sex-swing. During the later family lunch, the power dynamic shifts so that it is not Kim and Saint who feel interrogated, but Nathan and Stella. All of a sudden, sex has invaded the family home. It is present during lunch when Nathan asks Saint if she would like "breast or thigh", and in the fact that Matt now openly wears a pair of metallic gold pumps at the dinner table. As a result of the revelation that Kim's parents are attending a swingers' party, then, the discovery that Saint is running the party, and works in a sex shop, becomes normalized. In fact, Saint, as the party organizer, becomes analogous to the fictional marriage counsellor that Nathan and Stella claimed to be seeing, a figure of wisdom and a source of support for the nuclear family.

Perhaps the most marked example of *Sugar Rush*'s strategy of normalization-through-juxtaposition is evidenced by an event which does not appear in the programme at all. Despite being one of the few television programmes to focus explicitly and unremittingly on the development of a single lesbian character, *Sugar Rush* features no scene of Kim's "coming out" to her family. The first season ends without Kim telling any major character, other than Sugar, about her sexuality, and the second begins with Kim openly gay and with her parents largely, if awkwardly, supportive.

If the coming-out scene has been a staple of lesbian film narratives from *Personal Best* (1982) and *Desert Hearts* (1985) to *Kissing Jessica Stein* (2001), then its role in television is, perhaps, less clearly established. Within film, the coming-out scene is often used as a narrative crux; it is a way of organizing narratives about lesbian identity and a means of signalling a character's final realization of that identity. Still, as a number of critics have noted, the heavy stress that filmmakers have placed on coming out – and its presentation as a "positive and healthy action" – can work to "[reduce] the importance, and even the imperative, of the action of coming out" (Bronski 23). In contrast to film, with its obvious time constraints, the serial nature of television shows like *Sugar Rush*,

Skins, and *The L Word* would seem to present programme makers with an opportunity to look beyond "the action of coming out" in order to examine the lives of lesbian characters in more complex, sustained, and groundbreaking ways.

The elision of Kim's coming out seems to occur because it happened at the same time as a number of other events that were more integral to the progression of the narrative. In the final episode of the first season of *Sugar Rush* (1.10), Sugar and Kim flee from Brighton in order to hide Sugar from the police and to get Kim away from her parents' deteriorating marriage. During their escape to London, Sugar and Kim become partners in crime, stealing credit cards and staying together at an expensive hotel, where they drink champagne in the penthouse suite and make love for the first and only time. Thus, Kim's first consummated sexual experience has its transgressive force normalized by the many other, much more transgressive activities in which she is involved when it occurs. When her parents come to pick her up, Kim's involvement in a stabbing, several thefts, and running away are foremost in their minds; her sexuality is secondary. The only reason we know that it must have been discussed is that, when we first see her in Season Two, Kim is out and proud. More than any actual event in the narrative, the absence of a coming-out scene works to portray Kim's lesbian sexuality as important only in regard to its potential to disrupt the nuclear family; since the rest of the narrative attempts to demonstrate the polymorphous perversity of that same nuclear family, Kim's lesbianism is drained of its transgressive potential.

In addition to comparing Kim to her family, *Sugar Rush* juxtaposes Kim's performance of lesbian sexuality with those of other lesbians, creating a neat binary of "good" and "bad" lesbians. This comparison is not accomplished, as might be expected, through the well-worn categories of butch and femme; without exception, *Sugar Rush*'s lesbians are femme.[4] In fact, *Sugar Rush* judges its lesbians based upon their performance of normative femininity and monogamous sexuality, representing Kim and Saint as superior to other lesbians by virtue of their conventional appearance and committed relationship. This is accomplished chiefly through the pair's interactions with several other lesbian characters during the second season of *Sugar Rush*. The most significant of these are Anna, a predatory older woman who picks up teenage girls, and Melissa, a bookish, young lesbian who is politically aware, but sexually inexperienced. Whereas Kim and Saint are presented as ideal, normative lesbians, capable of moving easily within heterosexual society, Anna and Melissa are stigmatized through their failure to satisfactorily perform, respectively, monogamy and femininity. Thus, while *Sugar Rush* celebrates the sanctioned, monogamous sexual desire of Kim and Saint, the desires of Anna and Melissa are mocked, or pathologized, and serve as obstacles to the central characters.

Anna, the first woman with whom Kim has sex as an adult, is the most openly vilified character in *Sugar Rush*. An attractive, middle-aged femme, her encounter with Kim comes after a dizzying night at a local lesbian club. The sex scene is treated briefly, with a pumping pop song insisting "I've fallen in love again", as Kim looks out upon the lights of Brighton. Anna then treats Kim to a bout of cocaine-fuelled cunnilingus, and the next morning dresses Kim in her school uniform in order to enact a predictable S&M fantasy. Although this is initially played for laughs, especially when Kim's parents catch them in the act, the audience's potential discomfort with the scene is given voice by Sugar. Siding with Kim's angry father, on hearing the story she denounces Anna as "some filthy old perv". It is not the association with casual drug use or paedophilia, however, which condemns Anna in the show's diegesis; in fact, she is only confirmed as a villain when she makes it clear to Kim that she was only interested in a one-night stand. Kim is devastated, and Anna, now referred to as the "psycho-bitch", becomes Kim's touchstone for everything undesirable in a sexual partner. In pointed contrast to Anna's villainy, the most obviously comic of the lesbian characters in *Sugar Rush* is Melissa, Kim's college classmate. Referred to in the voiceover as an "uber-geek", she shares some superficial physical similarities with Kim, but is socially awkward and makes no effort to appear conventionally attractive. Melissa is the only character in *Sugar Rush* to even gesture towards a wider discourse around lesbian identity, and even this is couched as a joke, as she invites Kim around to see "her Jeanette Wintersons" (2.2). Due to her frumpy appearance, Melissa is portrayed as chronically undesirable, and her advances towards Kim are framed as ridiculous. Finally, she is dismissed as more prey for Anna, as *Sugar Rush* unites both of its models of the undesirable lesbian, the more easily to dismiss them.

Meanwhile, *Sugar Rush* offers an exemplar of its approved performance of lesbianism in the form of Saint. Slightly tomboyish, but still unmistakably femme, Saint is portrayed, from the moment of her introduction, as a confident woman in full control of her own sexuality. When she first bumps into Kim on the Brighton promenade, the crate she is carrying spills its contents: an assortment of multi-coloured dildos and other sex-toys. In a programme which often seems to equate sexuality solely with sexual activity, Saint's puissance with sex paraphernalia is the ultimate sign of her secure sexual identity. At the same time, though, Saint's life experience is portrayed as being even more important than her sexual experience. Early in their relationship (2.3), Kim and Saint take a lunch date at Saint's apartment just above the Munch Box. Assuming that the date's purpose is sexual, Kim worries: "What if she had accessories I'd never seen? What if I couldn't strap them on right? What if I put the wrong end in the wrong place?" We are offered just a glimpse of the imaginary scene, with Saint dressed in bondage gear and a black veil, brandishing a riding crop and ordering Kim to use a variety of arcane sex-toys, which is then contrasted with the actuality of Saint, casually dressed, making sandwiches and tea. When the pair do make love, Saint sets Kim at ease by explicitly opposing their soft, consensual lovemaking to Kim's previous experience with Anna. Reassuring Kim that "We don't have to *do* anything", Saint exhibits a less aggressive mode of lesbian sexuality, allowing Kim gently to take the lead. In contrast to the earlier scene of Kim's night with Anna, this scene is suffused with soft music and the camera remains relatively still, focusing on the faces of both girls as Kim runs her fingers along Saint's thigh, then strokes her hand and face. Instead of the cuts and dissolves that characterized the scene with Anna, we have simple hand-cam shots which pan or zoom to capture small moments: Saint running her finger along the edge of Kim's bra, or staring in wonder at her bare stomach. As Saint kisses Kim's torso, the shot dissolves and reverses the girls' positions, with Saint lying on her back and Kim kissing her way up Saint's body and into shot, creating the sense of *mutual* sexual experience. The scene is altogether quieter and gentler, and finishes with Kim's relieved exhalation: "That wasn't half as scary as I thought it was gonna be". Given the context in which *Sugar Rush* was broadcast, it is difficult not to read Kim's remark as indicative of the attitude of Channel 4 itself: satisfied that it has provided a public service in the form of lesbian visibility, yet relieved that nothing too transgressive has taken place.

Taken together, these two strategies help to construct the post-lesbian space of *Sugar Rush*. Coupled with the permissive atmosphere of the programme's Brighton setting and the outright stigmatization of alternative modes of lesbian identity, the juxtaposition of Kim and Saint's monogamous, apolitical sexuality with the hedonistic (and equally apolitical) sexuality of Kim's family promotes an atmosphere in which sex and sexuality are one and the same. For Kim and Saint, being a lesbian means nothing more than sexually desiring women – but rather than moving them towards a transgressive, queer disavowal of homo-normativity, this leads them towards the adoption of the entirely conventional model of normative monogamy.

In contrast to *Sugar Rush, Skins,* as an ensemble drama, presents lesbian teens as a small part of a wider narrative, but still partakes of a similar dynamic, which on the one hand normalizes them through comparison with other teens, and on the other valorizes their sexuality as a product of personal choice rather than identitarian discourses. Focusing on the lives of a group of British sixth-formers, *Skins* unapologetically celebrates teenage sex, drug-use, and alcohol abuse as aspects of a universal teen culture that cuts across the boundaries of race, gender, and sexuality. Thus, unlike *Sugar Rush,* it does not merely ignore identity politics; rather, it actively sets itself against them, asserting "teen" as an identity category capable of superseding Queer, Asian, Muslim, or any other. In its third season, *Skins* returned to its setting but followed a new group of sixth-form students. Among the new cohort of characters introduced by the show are the quiet Emily (identical twin of the more popular, and seemingly much less intelligent, Katie) and the indie-outcast, Naomi. Throughout the course of the third season of *Skins,* Emily and Naomi develop a tentative romance. Although Naomi enters sixth form stigmatized as a lesbian, having supposedly made a pass at Emily years before, it quickly becomes clear that Emily not only initiated that contact, but is the more certain of the two about her own sexual feelings for girls. Naomi, on the other hand, is harder to read, and certainly more cautious. Although clearly attracted to Emily, it takes several episodes and a plate of drugged brownies before Naomi and Emily kiss again. This sparks a series of tense exchanges, first between the two would-be lovers, and later involving Emily's family, who are concerned that Naomi's influence will shatter the (supposedly) close relationship between Emily and her twin sister, Katie.

The first significant example of normalization through juxtaposition occurs in relation to Emily and Naomi when they finally do consummate their romance (3.6). Despite a central narrative conceit in which each episode of *Skins* is focalized through a different character, the sex scenes in the third season are almost exclusive in their representation of hard, fast, unsentimental, heterosexual sex. In contrast, Emily and Naomi's coupling focuses on slow, small details, such as holding hands, or removing an article of clothing. The first quasi-sexual contact is made through "blow-backs", the sharing of the smoke from a joint. This offers the viewer a coy image of the girls kissing behind their hands, which are held up to keep in the smoke and to mask this private moment. As their passions escalate the camera focuses solely on Naomi as she reaches her climax. This emphasis on the softness, slowness, and pleasure of sex is in marked contrast to the rough and ready sexual encounters of other episodes, which are often constructed as moments of desolation, especially for the girls involved. As in *Sugar Rush*, then, a tender, monogamous mode of lesbian sexuality is valorized. Here, however, it is not set in contrast to other modes of lesbian sexuality, but to the coarse, loveless heterosexual sexuality of *Skins'* other teens.

Throughout the series, Emily's sexuality is not only defined in relation to the sexual practices of other characters, but in relation to more broadly defined personal practices as well. In the episode following her sexual encounter with Naomi, Emily visits a local psychiatrist (3.7). There she runs into JJ, a character with an unspecified mental illness which causes him to become "locked on" when upset. Both Emily and JJ have been prescribed the same pills (Sitro-Tesic-Ulbaceous-Neoprenes [STUN]) for their "conditions", and both express their contempt for the treatment. Yet even while disavowing the adult world's treatment of Emily, *Skins* reaffirms it, allowing her insight into the way JJ thinks and feels, and explicitly linking her abnormal sexuality to his abnormal personality. Emily seems immediately to understand JJ, and is able to stop his emotional outbursts, something previously managed only by his best friend, Freddy. Ultimately, this connection allows Emily the opportunity to demonstrate to JJ the power of subjectivity over identity when she offers to make love to him. When he is suspicious of the offer, because he knows she is gay, she retorts, "I'm lots of things, JJ, and I really like you". This highlights the performativity of both Emily's sexuality and JJ's disability, implying that, if Emily can choose whether or not to act gay, JJ can choose whether or not to act "autistic". This comes perilously close to the advice of JJ's uncaring doctor, who tells him, when he begins to worry or feel upset, "Just don't". In its valorization of personal choice and interpersonal equality, then, *Skins* is happy to explode identity categories indiscriminately, regarding them as uniformly constrictive and hierarchical.

Skins unites the strategy of normalization through juxtaposition with the rejection of narrow identitarian categories in the exchanges between Katie and Emily. Throughout the series they are contrasted to one another, with Katie dressing in revealing, "trashy" clothes and aggressively pursuing social success, while Emily is quiet and academically successful. The opposition between the twins is brought to a head in the penultimate episode of the third season when Emily, frustrated with Naomi's refusal to acknowledge their relationship, outs herself to her family (3.9). Appearing at the dinner table, bedraggled and upset, Emily responds to her family's insistent questioning with the truth: "I've been making love to a girl. Okay? Everybody satisfied?... Her name's Naomi. She's rather beautiful. So I was nailing her". So shocked are Emily's family by her declaration, and her appropriation of the coarse, masculine word, "nailing", that they react as if she's joking. Even Katie, who has previously seen Emily and Naomi kissing (3.4), later accuses Emily of having concocted a relationship with Naomi because she is jealous of the attention Katie gets from boys. Emily, however, attacks the consequences of Katie's supposedly normal behaviour, reminding her sister of the beating she recently received at the hands of her boyfriend's ex-girlfriend: "I'm stupid because I don't let anyone fuck me when they're in love with somebody else.... That's a normal relationship, isn't it? She fucked you up good, didn't she? Nobody hits me over the head with a rock" (3.9). By questioning the foundation of Katie's self-image, her skilful performance of normative femininity, Emily explicitly restates the critique already posed by her sexuality. If Katie's femininity no longer provides her with success and happiness, and Emily's lesbianism no longer stigmatizes her, or leads to unhappiness, the foundation of the twins' mutual identity is called into question. Moreover, since the twins effectively form a kind of controlled pairing, in which the single factor which truly separates them is their sexuality, Emily's superiority to her sister implicitly queries the value of normative femininity itself.

Ultimately, however, *Skins* shies away from such a broad interpretation, instead remaining on the safe ground of personal choice. The final episode of Season Three sees Katie carrying the incestuous suggestion of her rivalry with Naomi to its logical conclusion as she coerces Emily into accompanying her to the end-of-year "Love Ball". Wearing matching dresses with coordinated hair and makeup, the twins' attire loudly proclaims a unity which is quickly shattered by Naomi's arrival. This opposition – between an identity so innate that it marks Emily from birth and a sexual preference so particular that it may extend little farther than Naomi – is fully articulated in the final scene of the episode. Here, Emily and Katie literally wrestle out their differences in the middle of the ballroom, with Emily defeating her sister, but still helping her to her feet. Emily then tears off the matching dress and explains to her sister that: "I love you, and I'll never really leave you. And I can't fix us. I like girls. No, I like a girl. No, I love her... ok? I love (pointing at Naomi) her. Okay?" Emily thus avoids any explicit avowal of sexuality, transferring her desire from girls in general to Naomi in particular. She constructs her love for Naomi as a personal choice, and one that should not come into conflict with her identity as Katie's twin. This micro-personal treatment of Emily's sexuality is emblematic of *Skins'* general approach to subjectivity, and, more specifically, its whole-sale rejection of identity categories in favour of the related ideals of self-determination and individuality.

As the visibility of lesbians in the mainstream media becomes ever more regularized, it remains important for us to continue interrogating the costs of that visibility, while acknowledging the powers and the pressures at work in different media outlets. In both *Sugar Rush* and *Skins*, then, the lesbian teen is presented first and foremost as a teen like any other, though in her negotiation of the difficult terrain of personal subjectivity, she leads the way for others who seem less certain of what they want. Her sexual choices are celebrated, but she is careful not to transgress against the hegemonic structures of family and friendship, within which she remains bound. Moreover, this type of representation is encouraged, if not mandated, by the complex network of competing discourses at work in Channel 4 as a broadcaster, as it seeks to attract an audience, fulfil a public service remit, and educate its teenage audience. Thus, even while Channel 4 encourages the expansion of lesbian visibility, its nature as a channel limits the quality of that representation, circumscribing any discussion of lesbian identity within a carefully constructed post-lesbian environment and confining its potentially transgressive images of lesbian sexuality to a publicly sanctioned forum for "challenging and alternative" content.

Notes

1. See Wolfe and Roripaugh.
2. See Rogers et al.
3. For full episode details, see "Works Cited".
4. Helen Fenwick discusses the conventions of butch/femme representation on television in "Butch Lesbians: Televising Female Masculinity" (in this book).

Works cited

Becker, R. *Gay TV and Straight America*. New Brunswick, NJ and London: Rutgers University Press, 2006.
"Broadcasting Act, 1981". Office of Public Sector Information. http://www.england-legislation.hmso.gov.uk/RevisedStatutes/Acts/ukpga/1981/cukpga_19810068_en_1. [Accessed June 15, 2009].
Bronski, M. "Positive Images and the Coming Out Film: The Art and Politics of Lesbian and Gay Cinema". *Cineaste* 26.1 (2000): 20–26.

Brown, M. *A Licence to be Different: The Story of Channel 4*. London: BFI Publishing, 2007.

Brunsdon, C., and L. Spigel, eds. *Feminist Television Criticism: A Reader*. 2nd edn. Maidenhead, UK: Open University Press, 2008.

Ciasullo, Ann M. "Making Her (In)Visible: Cultural Representations of Lesbianism and the Lesbian Body in the 1990s". *Feminist Studies* 27.3 (2001): 577–608.

Collis, Rose. "Screened Out: Lesbians and Television". *Daring to Dissent: Lesbian Culture From Margin to Mainstream*. Ed. Liz Gibbs. London: Cassell, 1994. 120–46.

"Communications Act, 2003". Office of Public Sector Information. http://www.opsi.gov.uk/acts/acts2003/ukpga_20030021_en_1. [Accessed June 15, 2009].

Davis, G. "Saying it Out Loud: Revealing Television's Queer Teens". *Teen TV: Genre, Consumption and Identity*. Ed. G. Davis, and K. Dickinson. London: BFI Publishing, 2004.

Davis, G., and K. Dickinson, eds. *Teen TV: Genre, Consumption and Identity*. London: BFI Publishing, 2004. 127–40.

Dow, B. "*Ellen*, Television and the Politics of Gay and Lesbian Visibility". *Feminist Television Criticism: A Reader*. 2nd edn. Ed. C. Brunsdon, and L. Spigel. Maidenhead, UK: Open University Press, 2008. 93–110.

Driver, S. *Queer Girls and Popular Culture: Reading, Resisting, and Creating Media*. New York: Peter Lang, 2007.

Ellen (1994–98). ABC.

Gill, R. *Gender and the Media*. Cambridge, Polity, 2007.

Gove, B. "Framing Gay Youth". *Screen* 37.2 (1996): 174–92.

Hobson, D. *Channel 4: The Early Years and the Jeremy Isaacs Legacy*. IB Tauris: London and New York, 2008.

The L Word (2004–09). Showtime.

Lury, K. *British Youth Television: Cynicism and Enchantment*. Oxford: Clarendon Press, 2001.

Lygo, K. "Channel 4 Annual Review, 2007". http://www.channel4.com/about4/programmepolicy.html. [Accessed June 15, 2009].

——. "Channel 4 Statement of Promises, 2008". http://www.channel4.com/about4/programmepolicy.html. [Accessed June 15, 2009].

McRobbie, A. "Post-feminism and Popular Culture". *Feminist Media Studies* 4.3 (2004): 255–64.

Rogers, M., et al. "*The Sopranos* as HBO Brand Equity: The Art of Commerce in the Age of Digital Reproduction". Ed. D. Lavery. *This Thing of Ours: Investigating the Sopranos*. Columbia University Press: New York, 2002. 42–57.

Skins. E4 and Channel 4 (2007–).

3.4. "Pandora". Dir. Simon Massey. February 12, 2009.
3.6. "Naomi". Dir. Simon Massey. February 28, 2009.
3.7. "JJ". Dir. Charles Martin. March 5, 2009.
3.9. "Katie and Emily". Dir. Charles Martin. March 19, 2009.

Sugar Rush. Channel 4 (2005–06).

1.1. Dir. Sean Grundy. June 7, 2005.
1.10. Dir. Harry Bradbeer. August 2, 2005.
2.2. Dir. Harry Bradbeer. June 15, 2006.

2.3. Dir. Harry Bradbeer. June 22, 2006.
2.8. Dir. Philip John. July 20, 2006.

Villarejo, A. *Lesbian Rule: Cultural Criticism and the Value of Desire*. Durham: Duke University Press, 2003.

"Why Advertise on Channel 4?" *Channel 4 Sales*. http://www.channel4sales.com/platforms/Channel + 4. [Accessed June 15, 2009].

Wolfe, S., and L. Roripaugh "The (In)visible Lesbian: Anxieties of Representation in *The L Word*". Ed. C. Brunsdon, and L. Spigel. *Feminist Television Criticism: A Reader*. 2nd edn. Maidenhead, UK: Open University Press, 2008. 211–18.

Part III
Makeovers

8

Under the Knife: Feminism and Cosmetic Surgery in Contemporary Culture

Stéphanie Genz

"There are no ugly women, just lazy ones", Helena Rubinstein once said, highlighting that beauty is essentially women's work and responsibility. Indeed, the seemingly intrinsic links between womanhood and the desire for beauty have long been upheld by patriarchal discourses that seek to characterize women in relation to their looks, thereby consigning them to the status of objects, to be looked at, displayed, and bought. At the same time as beauty has been championed by patriarchy as a route to female, or rather feminine, success, it has also been criticized by waves of feminist writers who unmask its manipulative, constraining, and mutilating aspects. From Mary Wollstonecraft's feminist classic *The Vindication of the Rights of Woman* (1792) to Naomi Wolf's bestselling *The Beauty Myth* (1991), feminists have called out for female enlightenment and liberation from the "gilt cage" of beauty, denouncing whatever pleasure and power women believe that beauty accords them (Wollstonecraft 113). In effect, one of the most iconic events that brought (second wave) feminism to public attention – the demonstration that the New York Radical Women's group staged at the Miss America beauty pageant in Atlantic City in 1968 – was conceived as a direct attack on the beauty industry and an attempt at collective consciousness-raising, designed to engender a feminist-inspired realization of oppressive standards for (feminine) appearance.[1] In this sense, feminist activism and consciousness-raising were meant to bring forth a more enlightened, emancipated and "authentic" femaleness that defines itself in opposition to male-identified femininity and beauty.[2]

What makes beauty – and women's involvement therein – so treacherous and precarious in feminists' eyes is precisely that it does not come without its benefits and seductions; historically, beauty has functioned as a "patriarchal invitation to power" that confers onto (mostly white, heterosexual, middle-class) women a number of social privileges and economic gains (Lorde 118). Liberal feminist critics like Betty Friedan refer to this as "the pretty lie of the feminine mystique" or femininity's "protective shade" (180, 208), while radical feminists like Mary Daly maintain that patriarchy has colonized women's (even feminists') heads to such an extent that it "prepossesses" them and inspires them with "false selves" (322). To combat this stealthy colonization ("the pig in the head"), Daly urges her readers to free "the Hag within" and become "wild women" – a process she describes in terms of a radical defeminization and exorcism, an undoing of femininity and an "unravelling of the hood of patriarchal woman-hood" (343, 15, 409). For these feminist writers, women are oppressed not only from the outside by institutional, political, societal, and cultural directives and norms, but also, more insidiously, they are victims of their personal beliefs and self-understanding, caught in "the prison of their own minds" (Friedan 265). In these accounts, a woman's feminist awakening is intimately connected to an acceptance of victimization, a growing awareness of alienation, and a willingness to wage war against those parts of society and her self that have undermined her attempts at freedom. Consciousness-raising is thus predicated on a differentiation between "real" femaleness and "false" femininity whereby women are encouraged to relinquish those harmful and "inauthentic" elements and practices that bind them to feminine beauty and adopt a state of self-division and suspicion, of "being radically alienated from her world and often divided against herself" (Bartky 21).

This feminist mode of argument is unequivocal in its outlook and message: beauty is depicted as a culturally and socially constructed lure, whose perpetrator is patriarchy and whose victims are women. It is a sexualized form of dehumanization that is institutionalized and systematic, a "form of obedience to patriarchy" that reduces women to mere bodily beings who are cut off from a fully human existence, from autonomy, agency, and independent thought (80). Everything that helps to perpetuate or facilitate this objectification of women – that reinstates and regulates norms of female embodiment and comportment – is similarly condemned, from the so-called "instruments of female torture" (bras, curlers, false eyelashes, wigs) that were thrown into the "freedom trash can" at the Miss America protest in 1968 to more modern and progressively high-tech beauty practices. The feminist focus on the risks and oppression inherent in beauty routines has given rise to a now widely held belief that feminists are "enemies of the stiletto heel" who, in a gesture of political activism, discard the mask of femininity in an attempt to refuse patriarchy's gaze (41).

In this chapter, I suggest that this line of reasoning has become increasingly problematic and difficult to sustain, particularly since the advent of postfeminism and its celebration of femininity as a source of empowerment. Postfeminism stands feminism's critique of beauty on its head by claiming femininity as a route to female power and – in contrast to earlier liberal and radical feminist analyses – authenticity. In postfeminist rhetoric, the feminine body is no longer envisioned as a site of manipulation and feminist "disidentification", whereby women who adopt beauty regimes are necessarily understood as victims or – even worse – as co-conspirators of patriarchy (McRobbie 255). The postfeminist feminine body questions the causal link between beauty, oppression, and inauthenticity by highlighting a paradoxical form of female/feminine embodiment that is experienced as "authentic" while being (self) created. In effect, authenticity emerges as a new discursive ideal in postfeminist media culture that stresses the possibility of self-realization in the absence of essentialist conceptualizations of the self. This is especially apparent in contemporary forms of "lifestyle television" and surgical makeover shows that are premised around the notions of transformation and renewal.[3] In this case, authenticity comes to acquire a range of different meanings, being at once an indicator of individual agency and choice while also becoming linked to consumerist ideologies and a postmodern visuality that privileges surface over interiority. As I will go on to argue, the construction of a "real" self in cosmetic surgery makeover shows is now fully incorporated in a postmodern, consumer-orientated world in which self-image is inextricably bound to physical appearance, and where authenticity is converted into a saleable commodity. Moreover, I will investigate how the paradox of the makeover genre allows us to shed light on what Young has identified as a crucial contradiction inherent in feminine embodiment and its surgical reconstructions: the tension between the female subject as embodied agent and the female body as object. The surgical makeover show thus provides us with a new medium and lens through which the long-standing question "Is beauty good or bad for women?" can be re-evaluated, while also offering an opportunity to complicate existing feminist approaches to cosmetic surgery.

To begin, I would like to revisit some of the ideas that have structured the debates on cosmetic surgery and feminist responses to it. Cosmetic surgery has witnessed an unprecedented boom in recent years with a growing number of people opting to change their bodies surgically; in

Britain alone, £1 billion was spent on cosmetic surgery and treatments in 2008 (Williams 7). The term "cosmetic surgery" (instead of "aesthetic" or "plastic surgery") already firmly establishes this field of medicine as a predominantly feminine or feminized site. Indeed, women in particular are drawn to the modern culture of *chirurgia decoratoria* that instructs the individual to remake herself in the pursuit of social success, desirability, and, above all, "happiness". According to the rates of inflation published by the British Association of Aesthetic Plastic Surgeons (BAAPS), the majority of cosmetic surgery is carried out on women (91%), with breast augmentation remaining the most popular "job" among the 34,000 procedures in 2008.[4] One clinic was even reported to offer one-hour breast implant operations that can be performed in the patient's lunch hour. The procedure (which costs £4500 and is done under local anaesthetic) was hailed by the owner of the clinic (Medispa in Cheshire) as a revolutionary development in breast enlargement surgery: "You walk into hospital and within hours you are walking out. Professional women haven't got time to spend lying in hospital.... In years to come the lunch time boob job will be happening across the industry" (qtd. in Kumi). Cosmetic surgery is normalized and "domesticated" in this way as a "perfectly natural, affordable, routine procedure", which women especially are encouraged to embrace as an expression of individual pleasure and consumer sovereignty (Tait 119; Douglas 266). As Sue Tait notes, this is part of a "post-feminist surgical imaginary" that values individual consumption as a means to empower the gendered body (124, 120).

Cosmetic surgery's popularity and normalization are not only the result of increased availability and surgical developments but also of sustained media coverage. From newspaper articles to televisual makeover shows (including *Nip/Tuck* [2003–10], *The Swan* [2004], *Extreme Makeover* [2002–07], and *Ten Years Younger* [2004–], to name but a few), cosmetic surgery has been popularized as a new "lifestyle" option available to seemingly everyone in a postfeminist, neo-liberal society.[5] Nowadays, it seems that achieving a *Brand New You* (2005) (the title of another makeover show broadcast on British television) has become a feasible possibility and choice, achievable through the magic of modern-day fairy godmothers who appear to participants in the form of cosmetic surgeons, dentists, nutritionists, fitness gurus, beauticians, and fashion stylists. In recent years, these televised makeovers have become increasingly more radical, invasive, and time-consuming – from Trinny and Susannah's infamous breast-grabbing and fashion advice on *What Not to Wear* (BBC 2001–07) to more extensive life and body transformations that can take months, and even years, to accomplish. The makeover paradigm thus emerges as a crucial feature of postfeminist media culture whereby the "idiom of reinvention" can be applied to every aspect of our social world, from homes and gardens to clothing, cleanliness, and raising children (Gill 262; Lewis 441). As Tania Lewis summarizes, the classic personal makeover format often starts with a surprise visit to the home or workplace of the participant; the "makeoveree's" deficiencies – whether in the areas of taste, health, appearance, or broader life management issues – are then diagnosed by the show's experts before s/he undergoes a series of procedures and a lifestyle regime (442). The climax of each episode consists of the "reveal" – a narrative moment employed by almost all televisual makeover shows that is reminiscent of a fairytale trope[6] – when the transformed candidate is shown his/her new self and restored to family and friends.

In the cosmetic surgery variant of the makeover paradigm, the focus on (mostly female) bodies underlines the gendered nature of this medical field, as the majority of these shows circle around the construction of a particular norm of feminine beauty which is, as Brenda Weber observes, white, heterosexual, and middle class.[7] In Sarah Banet-Weiser's and Laura Portwood-Stacer's eyes, the end result of such cosmetic surgery programmes is a flawless, idealized kind of femininity that is inherently racist, sexist, and classist: "makeover shows continue to reinforce a certain dominant beauty ideal when they literally cut away physical features that deviate from this ideal" (264). They insist that the outcome of these shows constitutes a kind of "mainstreaming", as the new, improved self conforms "even more readily to dominant norms". This leads Banet-Weiser and Portwood-Stacer to the conclusion that the " 'celebration' of the body, the pleasure of transformation and individual empowerment function as a justification for a renewed objectification" and a "more intense policing" of female bodies (267, 257, 263). While I do not deny that most candidates emerge from their makeover process more feminine or feminized, for me the vital ingredient and key to the makeover shows' continuing appeal and success is the articulation not just of a normatively beautiful body but of a more authentic feminine self that understands empowerment as an effect of consumption and firmly binds (self-) identity to representation. The makeover genre constructs a version of femininity that – while still dependent on the body as a site of female power – severs its former associations with inauthenticity/falseness and reframes appearance as a location of individual choice and agency. In this sense, the (female) body is no longer conceived merely as a two-dimensional image that simply reflects back patriarchal meanings and norms; contrastingly, the corporeal surface acquires a centrality in makeover shows whereby authenticity – itself a crucial theme and component of reality television[8] – is expressed through (feminine) embodiment and – in the course of becoming feminized and televised – is turned into a marketable commodity. The emphasis on feminine authenticity, rather than physical beauty, also helps to account for recent scheduling changes on British television that see shows based around fashion advice, such as *What Not to Wear*, being cancelled in favour of more psychologically orientated programmes like *How to Look Good Naked* (Channel 4 2006–) in which presenter Gok Wan tells the makeoverees that fashion can be "life-changing", that being better dressed can make you into "a happier, more fulfilled, better person".[9]

Similarly, in the documentary-style *Brand New You*, participants do not just experience a superficial makeover and fashion fix; rather, they are carving into their own flesh to overcome past traumas, kick-start a new, more rewarding, life, and discover a more authentic identity that has been hiding inside their bodies and can only be brought to light by the surgeon's scalpel. In one episode (broadcast on 12 June 2007), the viewer is introduced to 48-year-old Penny Wilkinson from Winchester who, we are told, looks 20 years older: "Smoking, childbirth and bad genes have ravaged her face and body". The solution is extreme but effective: Penny is whisked off to Los Angeles for a $200,000 makeover that includes facial and dental surgery, a marathon 10-hour operation, oxygen therapy, a diet and exercise regime, a tummy tuck, and a couture dress. Penny continues to remind the viewing public how grateful she is for her 4-month transformation: "I feel guilty that I am getting everything I asked for", she declares at the beginning of her journey. Throughout her painful surgical interventions, she keeps reiterating how "absolutely ecstatic" she is "about being able to do this". Her surgeons also confirm that she has made the right decision: "When you go home, people won't even know who you are", her dentist tells her after he has reshaped and whitened her teeth. At her "reveal" party, we are presented with a "brand new" Penny: dressed in a couture gown, with a new face and body, she is greeted by her surgeons' and instructors' exclamations of how "amazing" and "beautiful" she is. Penny herself cannot believe her luck and concludes by saying how "deliriously happy" she is.

What are we to make of the surgical makeover that produces a seemingly more confident, content, and self-assured individual? Does cosmetic surgery have the potential to bring about such a state of delirious happiness, as we are led to believe by the programme, or is this a case of self-induced delirium? The show itself leaves no room for doubt, depicting the participant's transformation as the creation of a better self, a more proactive, determined, and courageous identity. The opening sequence conveys this message of increased freedom, using the almost-biblical image of two hands releasing a white dove, supposedly representative of the new self that is set free by the hands of the surgeons. As Cressida Heyes has argued, "in this context, cosmetic surgery is less about becoming *beautiful*, and more about becoming *oneself*" (21; emphasis in original). The makeover show sidesteps the notion of beauty, then, by focusing on the patient's "inner truth" – an "inner truth" that is not, at the outset, aligned with her bodily appearance. While feminine beauty is still visibly achieved in these programmes, it is not acknowledged as the driving force that motivates these transformations. Instead, cosmetic surgery is seen as a strategy to bring a deviant and unrepresentative body into line with the inner beauty and strength that hide behind its unshapely contours. Accordingly, as Sadie Wearing suggests, the logic of cosmetic surgery makeover shows is predicated on "the assumption of a psychic split between the 'inner self' and the body, which can be rectified by expert...intervention" (289). The goal of these programmes, then, becomes not so much the creation of a beautiful body but "the externalisation of a supposedly more authentic inner self": as Gareth Palmer puts it, "you are what 'you appear to be' " (qtd. in Roberts 242). Rather than just being vain, the women seeking cosmetic surgery are portrayed as "enterprising" selves who are engaged in a project of self-realization and actively use their determination to change their bodies and improve their lives.[10]

Not surprisingly, feminist writers have been wary of readings of cosmetic surgery that present appearance as the basis of identity and have thus identified a number of motives for women going "under the knife". Equally, the question of authenticity has produced a range of different interpretations and raised a series of questions, most specifically with regard to its undeniable connections to commodification: feminists who are critical of femininity/beauty have attacked the idea that the post-operative body can be the site of an "authentic" female self. The surgically refashioned face and body have been read as patriarchal inscriptions that signal an oppressed subjectivity that also bears the hallmark of individualist, consumerist capitalism. As Anne Balsamo notes, this presupposes "romantic conceptions of the 'natural' body", a pre-inscriptive body that is uncontaminated by cultural, patriarchal, and economic scripts (79). Holliday and Sanchez Taylor agree, noting that "feminists have come to celebrate the 'natural' body: beauty is associated with decoration and adornment, and the natural body strips these accoutrements away", leading to a "rejection by feminism of the enhanced body" (185). The discourse of surgically constructed, feminine authenticity is similarly discarded as the profitable creation of a capitalist market economy that sells the idea of an authentic female self in its effort to interpellate women in their capacity as consumers.[11]

Other critics working within postmodern and performative frameworks have highlighted the liberating and democratic possibilities of viewing the body as text. In her study of the body in Western culture, Susan Bordo notes that "the postmodern body is no body at all" and she invokes "plasticity" as a postmodern paradigm, celebrating a newly imagined condition of human freedom from bodily determination (229). Following postmodernism's deconstruction of the humanist self, the status of the body as a fixed, unitary, and natural given has been transformed into a malleable construct, an object of work to be fixed and improved. The "natural" body (if we can still use this term) is presented as nothing more than the starting point of a person's "identity project", which potentially leads to an intriguing distinction between the naturally defective body and its authentic, textually mediated counterpart. Some critics, such as John Fiske, have extended the idea of bodily construction to a radical suggestion that thoroughly "textualizes" the body and thereby eradicates its historicity and materiality. The notion of the body as pure text has been criticized for the way in which it masks the body's historical, social, and cultural links. Teresa Ebert, for example, argues that "to engage in the textual play of postmodernism, taking the body (as an inscriptive surface) as the text to play with is 'romantic'" (34) – a view which is in direct contrast with Balsamo's previous identification of a feminist nostalgia for a "natural", pre-inscriptive body. Ebert goes on to locate textual play within a masculinist tradition, implicating it in the power structures which reinforce patriarchy and capitalism. Instead of plastic multiplicity, the body operates in a highly restricted realm of cultural plasticity that reconstructs the bodily frame according to eminently ideological standards of physical appearance.

As might be evident from these diverse theoretical positions on the body, cosmetic surgery has been the subject of an equally complex and varied critical history. While Banet-Weiser and Portwood-Stacer insist that "it is difficult for feminists *not* to theorize the cultural practice of cosmetic surgery – and especially its televisual expression – as anything short of objectifying and alienating" (262), others have highlighted that this is a modern democratic (albeit capitalist) solution to a most undemocratic problem. In *Flesh Wounds* (2003), Virginia Blum makes the point that once beauty turns out to be surgical, "something any of us can have for the purchase, then we are no longer in thrall" (259). In this context, we can vaguely distinguish between two main critical strands that can be grouped, rather presumptively, into the "yes, but" and "no, but" camps. On the one hand, we have critics like Kathy Davis and Sander Gilman who focus on the potentially liberating aspects of cosmetic surgery, exploring how patients use it as a resource to protest against the constraints of the "given" in their embodied existence. As Davis suggests, "cosmetic surgery may be, first and foremost about... taking one's life into one's hands, and determining how much suffering is fair" (23). These commentators do not deny the existence of cultural and social restrictions but they advocate a pragmatic, consumer-oriented approach to the constraints that their bodies impose on their lives.

By contrast, critics who adopt a "no, but" approach are generally more sceptical about the benefits of cosmetic surgery, while still seeking to attribute some degree of agency to this medical practice. This is mainly the position of writers who adopt a Foucauldian framework to analyse cosmetic surgery as a form of normalization, characterized by a paradoxical effect whereby it acts in both constraining and enabling ways. In *Discipline and Punish* (1977), Foucault describes the "power of the norm" in terms of its two functions: "In a sense", he writes, "the power of normalization imposes homogeneity; but it [also] individualizes" (184). The concept of normalization can be usefully employed to explain the disciplinary powers inherent in cosmetic surgery and the televisual makeover. *Brand New You* provides an example of the homogenizing aspects of normalization, as the participants' bodies are measured for their deviation from the norms of heterosexual desirability. In the episode previously mentioned, the makeoveree is told that "she is not a perfect 10", and the purpose of her extensive transformation is to narrow the gap between the perceived inadequacy of her old self and the more feminine sphere into which she aspires to move. At the same time, normalization also provides an opportunity for individualization as it promises the eradication of self-loathing and the release of a more authentic identity. As the *Brand New You* contestant asserts at the end of the programme, she is "finding it much easier to look in the mirror" and her makeover "will allow [her] to lead a more normal life". Ultimately, however, writers in this camp remain highly critical of the amount of agency and choice enabled by cosmetic surgery. Kathryn Morgan voices these concerns, noting that "while the technology of cosmetic surgery could clearly be used to create and celebrate idiosyncrasy, eccentricity, and uniqueness, it is obvious that this is not how it is presently being used" (35). In effect, "choice" could be nothing more than "necessity", whereby "elective cosmetic surgery... *is becoming the norm*" and those "women who contemplate *not using* cosmetic surgery will increasingly be stigmatized and seen as deviant" (28; emphasis in original). This is one of the challenges posed by the rhetoric of choice: what looks like individual empowerment, agency, and self-determination can also signal conformity and docility. Rosemary Gillespie refers to this as "the paradox of choice": "The decision whether or not to undergo cosmetic surgery clearly involves individual choice, yet the concept of choice is itself enmeshed in social and cultural norms" (79).

Similarly, I propose that critics seeking to come to terms with this contradictory medical practice – and its expression on reality television – face equally paradoxical choices: Do we keep our intellectual and feminist authority intact, but thereby risk victimizing cosmetic surgery patients by subjecting them to what has come to be known as "the cultural dope approach"? Or, do we accept their agency and maybe endanger our feminist beliefs and any attendant critique of beauty norms? Moreover, how do we account for the commodified version of femininity that is produced through the makeover genre – with its explicit blurring of surface and depth, appearance and identity – once and for all? Rather than interpreting this development despairingly as a postfeminist elision of critique and a displacement of feminism (Tait 123), I maintain that the surgical makeover show provides an opportunity to confront the contradictions and possibilities inherent in commodity culture and its construction of femininity and authenticity. The cosmetic surgery makeover presents us with a rich site for examining the shifting dynamics of selfhood and the conjunction of "citizen" and "consumer" in late modern societies (Roberts 228). What this amounts to is a call for a more nuanced and comprehensive understanding of postfeminist agency that addresses citizens' choices of/and identities within the context of neo-liberal consumer cultures that value individualist conceptions of empowerment and depict authenticity as an effect of representation and consumption.[12] Perhaps, then, the challenge of our "paradox of choice" as feminist critics is to interrogate the usefulness of our own theoretical and ideological paradigms, the preconceptions that ultimately determine how we interpret cosmetic surgery and makeover shows. In this sense, "choice" stands for an ongoing debate which acknowledges that simple divisions between feminism and femininity, embodiment and authenticity, consumption and critique are just as likely to limit our enquiries as to enhance them.

Notes

1. For a detailed analysis of the Miss America protest, see Genz, *Postfemininities in Popular Culture*, chapter 2.
2. Mary Daly expresses this idea clearly in *Gyn/Ecology* (1978), stating that "femininity is a man-made construct, having essentially nothing to do with femaleness" (68).
3. See Bell and Hollows.
4. In the largest-ever survey of breast augmentation, BAAPS announced that there has been a 275 per cent increase in the number of operations since 2002, with almost 8500 procedures carried out in 2008 (www.baaps.org.uk). These already remarkable figures for the United Kingdom seem modest when compared to American statistics: Of the 1.7 million cosmetic surgical procedures carried out in 2008, breast augmentation was also a favourite among American women (with over 307,000 operations). This was closely followed by liposuction, nose reshaping, eyelid surgery, and tummy tucks. Overall, far more women than men underwent cosmetic surgery, with 1.4 million female patients compared to 220,000 male patients (www.plasticsurgery.org).
5. In *Ordinary Lifestyles* (2005), David Bell and Joanne Hollows highlight the importance of the concept of lifestyle for our contemporary existence and self-understanding. The idea of lifestyle is underpinned by a description of the self that foregrounds personal choice and flexibility. This line of thought is common in sociological examinations of self-identity and is particularly associated with the work of Anthony Giddens who formulates a flexible notion of "post-traditional" selves that are able to (re)invent their own biographies. *See Modernity and Self-Identity.*
6. For a more sustained consideration of fairytale tropes in the makeover show, see Brenda Weber's analysis of the *American Princess* and *Australian Princess* franchises in "Imperialist Projections: Manners, Makeovers, and Models of Nationality" (in this collection).
7. See Weber.
8. See Holmes and Redmond.
9. When it was announced in 2008 that Trinny Woodall and Susannah Constantine were not having their ITV contracts renewed after their *Undress the Nation* programme lost viewers, British newspapers blamed "the Gok factor" (Freeman, "Why Britain fell out of love with Trinny and Susannah"). In contrast to "a gorgon-headed beast of matronly, imperious bossiness", Gok Wan – who as news reports never fail to recount used to be a "21-stone, mixed-race, gay teenager" who was bullied at school – is "much nicer than T & S" and teaches the female participants to love their "gorgeous curves" and "bangers" (breasts in Gok Speak) (Freeman, "We are all beautiful!"). As Wan notes in an interview, "clothes aren't just this superficial thread you put on your body. There's a massive psychology behind dressing and I think that [the programmes] have enabled people to see that" (qtd. in Freeman "We are all beautiful!").
10. See Rose.
11. A similar charge has been raised in many critiques of postfeminism in relation to the rhetoric of "choice". As Sadie Wearing points out, feminist television criticism has to be vigilant to the notion of choice as it has "a

sinister edge of compulsion, where the celebration of 'choice' and the upbeat reliance on a rhetoric of possibility to become your own 'best self' exist alongside a concomitant edge of responsibility" (292). This amounts to a paradoxical kind of "compulsory freedom" where subjects are encouraged to freely choose an image of themselves within prescribed guidelines (Roberts 241). As John Storey aptly summarizes, "there are choices, but not choices over choices – the power to set the cultural agenda" (229).

12. See Genz and Brabon 166–72.

Works cited

Balsamo, Anne. *Technologies of the Gendered Body: Reading Cyborg Women.* Durham and London: Duke University Press, 1996.

Banet-Weiser, Sarah, and Laura Portwood-Stacer. " 'I Just Want to be Me Again!': Beauty Pageants, Reality Television and Post-feminism". *Feminist Theory* 7.2 (2006): 255–72.

Bartky, Sandra Lee. *Femininity and Domination: Studies in the Phenomenology of Oppression.* London and New York: Routledge, 1990.

Bell, David, and Joanne Hollows, eds. *Ordinary Lifestyles: Popular Media, Consumption and Taste.* Maidenhead: Open University Press, 2005.

Blum, Virginia L. *Flesh Wounds: The Culture of Cosmetic Surgery.* Berkeley, CA: University of California Press, 2003.

Bordo, Susan. *Unbearable Weight: Feminism, Western Culture and the Body.* Berkeley: University of California Press, 1993.

Daly, Mary. *Gyn/Ecology: The Metaethics of Radical Feminism.* 1978. London: The Women's Press, 1995.

Davis, Kathy. "Remaking the She-Devil: A Critical Look at Feminist Approaches to Beauty". *Hypatia* 6.2 (1991): 21–43.

Douglas, Susan. *Where the Girls Are: Growing Up Female with the Mass Media.* New York: Times Books, 1995.

Ebert, Teresa. "Ludic Feminism, the Body, Performance, and Labor: Bringing Materialism Back into Feminist Cultural Studies". *Cultural Critique* 23 (1992–93): 5–50.

Fiske, John. *Understanding Popular Culture.* London and New York: Routledge, 1989.

Freeman, Hadley. "Why Britain Fell Out of Love with Trinny and Susannah". *The Guardian.* August 20, 2008. http://www.guardian.co.uk/lifeandstyle/2008/aug/20/fashion.beauty/print. [Accessed May 13, 2009].

Freeman, Hadley. "We are All beautiful!". *The Guardian.* October 21, 2008. http://www.guardian.co.uk/lifeandstyle/2008/oct/21/women-television/print. [Accessed May 13, 2009].

Friedan, Betty. *The Feminine Mystique.* 1963. London: Penguin, 1992.

Foucault, Michel. *Discipline and Punish: The Birth of the Prison.* London: Penguin, 1977.

Genz, Stéphanie. *Postfemininities in Popular Culture.* Houndmills, Basingstoke: Palgrave Macmillan, 2009.

Genz, Stéphanie, and Benjamin A. Brabon. *Postfeminism: Cultural Texts and Theories.* Edinburgh: Edinburgh University Press, 2009.

Giddens, Anthony. *Modernity and Self-Identity: Self and Society in the Late Modern Age*. 1991. Cambridge: Polity, 2008.

Gill, Rosalind. *Gender and the Media*. Cambridge: Polity, 2007.

Gillespie, Rosemary. "Women, the Body and Brand Extension in Medicine: Cosmetic Surgery and the Paradox of Choice". *Women and Health* 24.4 (1996): 69–85.

Gilman, Sander L. *Making the Body Beautiful: A Cultural History of Aesthetic Surgery*. Princeton, New Jersey: Princeton University Press, 1999.

Heyes, Cressida, J. "Cosmetic Surgery and the Televisual Makeover". *Feminist Media Studies* 7.1 (2007): 17–32.

Holliday, Ruth, and Jacqueline Sanchez Taylor. "Aesthetic Surgery as False Beauty". *Feminist Theory* 7.2 (2006): 179–95.

Holmes, Su, and Sean Redmond, eds. *Framing Celebrity: New Directions in Celebrity Culture*. London and New York: Routledge, 2006.

Kumi, Alex. "One-Hour Breast Implant Operations Raise Concerns". *The Guardian* February 11, 2006. http://www.guardian.co.uk/print/0„5397361-110418,00.html. [Accessed May 2, 2006].

Lewis, Tania. "Introduction: Revealing the Makeover Show". *Continuum: Journal of Media & Cultural Studies* 22.4 (2008): 441–46.

Lorde, Audre. *Sister Outsider: Essays and Speeches by Audre Lorde*. Freedom, CA: The Crossing Press, 1984.

McRobbie, Angela. "Post-Feminism and Popular Culture". *Feminist Media Studies* 4.3 (2004): 255–64.

Morgan, Kathryn Pauly. "Women and the Knife: Cosmetic Surgery and the Colonization of Women's Bodies". *Hypatia* 6.3 (1991): 25–53.

Roberts, Martin. "The Fashion Police: Governing the Self in *What Not To Wear*". *Interrogating Postfeminism: Gender and the Politics of Popular Culture*. Ed. Yvonne Tasker, and Diane Negra. Durham and London: Duke University Press, 2007. 227–48.

Rose, Nikolas. "Governing the Enterprising Self". *The Values of the Enterprise Culture*. Ed. Paul Heelas and Paul Morris. London: Routledge, 1992. 141–64.

Storey, John. *Cultural Theory and Popular Culture: An Introduction*. Harlow, England: Pearson Longman, 2009.

Tait, Sue. "Television and the Domestication of Cosmetic Surgery". *Feminist Media Studies* 7.2 (2007): 119–35.

Wearing, Sadie. "Subjects of Rejuvenation: Aging in Postfeminist Culture". *Interrogating Postfeminism: Gender and the Politics of Popular Culture*. Ed. Yvonne Tasker, and Diane Negra. Durham and London: Duke University Press, 2007. 277–310.

Weber, Brenda. *Makeover TV: Selfhood, Citizenship, and Celebrity*. Durham, NC: Duke University Press, 2010.

Williams, Rachel. "Cosmetic Surgery and Treatments Set to Hit £1bn a Year". *The Guardian* December 19, 2007: 7.

Wollstonecraft, Mary. *A Vindication of the Rights of Woman*. 1792. Vol. 5 of *The Works of Mary Wollstonecraft*. Ed. J. Todd, and M. Butler. London: Pickering and Chatto, 1958.

Young, Iris Marion. *Justice and the Politics of Difference*. Princeton, NJ: Princeton University Press, 1990.

9

Imperialist Projections: Manners, Makeovers, and Models of Nationality

Brenda R. Weber

In 2000 the media scholar Rachel Moseley identified a "makeover takeover" in lifestyle programming; as of this writing in 2009, that takeover has flourished to such a degree that we might more vividly describe the television lifestyle mediascape as colonialized, the takeover having given way to complete occupation. Colonialism, with its particular connotations of the overbearing and imperious British Empire, is a rather apt metaphor, for in the context of a diversified set of television texts that teach viewers how to pimp a ride, spice up a wardrobe, prune back household clutter, and discipline a diet comes a modified form of the makeover that attends to manners and etiquette in its attempts to enact image-based and class- and race-specific transformation goals.[1] Each of these shows corrals a group of "hopeless", "unruly", "incorrigible", and largely working-class participants (what could well be taken as the "ignorant" natives) and subjects them to the ministrations and demands of English expertise (to close the metaphor, such experts here handily stand in as foreign agents of domination and control). Even so, these makeover texts are not so straightforward or so one-dimensional that we can read them only as uncomplicated popular culture tracts that simply re-enact colonialist oppression. Makeovers, after all, contain a complex ideology that covers a theoretical spectrum ranging from neoliberalism to postfeminism, and from identarian empowerment to authoritative religiosity. In saying, then, that makeovers work through a logic of imperialism, I do not mean to indicate that they do not also contain and contribute to other discourses, but in this article I want to focus my examination on the way in which transformation-themed shows are simultaneously nostalgic for an idealized past conveyed through the

specific mythos of the British Empire and critical of the very qualities
they so idealize.

These themes of endorsement and critique are all the more nuanced
when filtered through other national media outlets. In the United
States, many shows – both those imported from Great Britain and those
produced by American companies – deploy the trope of the English
expert/scold, who can save the day, open paths to enlightenment,
eliminate dirt and clutter, soothe long-standing familial tensions, and
essentially save the ignorant masses. Indeed, Englishness is pointed, for
although reality television shows with Scottish or Welsh hosts do exist
and are broadcast in the United States, they are rare. More common are
the English experts, who stand in for a class-based form of knowledge,
superiority, and instruction, even when the hosts themselves speak in
accents or behave in ways that do not suggest Oxbridge educations,
toney addresses, or cultivated behaviours (as, for instance, when the
notorious Trinny Woodall and Susannah Constantine of *What Not to
Wear, Trinny and Susannah Undress, The Great British Body*, or *Making Over
America with Trinny and Susannah* pull down their own trousers so as to
show a seemingly universal trait of womanhood: cellulite). Such shows
where English experts dominate American subjects include *Supernanny,
Nanny 911, Clean House, Hell's Kitchen, Wedding SOS*, and, of course, *Making Over America with Trinny and Susannah*.[2] Thanks to BBC America,
Americans are also given access to the toxic brew of Gillian McKeith's
You Are What You Eat, although thus far she has exclusively targeted
corpulent Brits, not daring to venture into the unchartered adipose of
America. One must still travel to the United Kingdom or trawl the Inter-
net to see examples of McKeith's other television fare, which includes
Three Fat Brides One Thin Dress, Supersize vs. Superskinny, or *Gillian Moves
In*, each show seemingly fascinated with the mandatory "poo samples"
that McKeith so regularly demands.

On the manners makeover shows that I will analyse in this article, new
hairstyles and refined fashion codes are insufficient to these programmes
that put both female and male participants through a series of tests and
challenges designed to build the social infrastructure necessary to support the refinement accorded to the terms "lady" and "gentleman". In
each case, the class-specific designation of "lady" or "gentleman" – or in
particular of "princess" – is *a priori* understood as a recognizable, desirable, and achievable identity location. An underlying logic suggests that
it is the participants' internalized desire to change – rather than the
mandates imposed by the style gurus and etiquette coaches – that brings
this rag-a-muffin crew to the transformation domain of Makeover TV.

In this way, these shows underscore a tacit mandate of colonialism that justifies incursions into others' lands, politics, governments, and society through an argument that natives wish to be "saved" by the knowledge the imperializing force wields. Those shows airing on US expanded cable that make use of the English style expert or the surrounding trappings of butlers, charm schools, and British cultural capital include *Australian Princess*, *Ladette to Lady*, *Mind Your Manners*, *Girls of Hedford Hall*, *American Princess*, *Style by Jury*, *Mo'Nique's Flavor of Love Girls: Charm School*, *Rock of Love Charm School*, *Ricki Lake's Charm School*, *Groomed*, *Tool Academy*, and *From G's to Gents*.

These behaviour and image modification shows air across the globe and are produced either in Great Britain or in Anglophone countries, including the United States, Canada, and Australia. Together, they speak to and help to create the myth of a performance and appearance-based model of identity that simultaneously reifies and critiques the classed codes of British Empire. These tensions are expressed through an agonistics between elitism vs. egalitarianism, aristocracy vs. meritocracy, blood-entitlements vs. social privilege, and royalty vs. commoners. Although made by different production companies, aired on competing networks, and targeted to a diverse viewership, each of these shows gives narrative space to the complicated raced and classed tensions and power dynamics that reproduce notions of class hierarchies, style etiquette, and social status. In short, these programmes reproduce the colonialist norms that sustain the conceptual significance of the British Empire. Yet, their construction of the "princess" or the aristocratic "lady" or "gentleman" is often enigmatic, as participants are typically coached in such lessons as, on one episode of *Groomed*, how to do the dishes or iron a shirt properly, or, on an episode of *Charm School*, how to assemble an outdoor play set for children – both labour-intensive activities far outside the ken of the upper-class denizen.

Colonialist makeover ideologies are less enigmatic and more depressingly regressive in relation to gender. As I have already noted, men are frequently referenced in this genre of programming, but the attention focused on women's behaviours, bodies, and appearance is fierce. Rigid gender imperatives prevail on shows such as the US-based *Mind Your Manners*, where a "scary feminist" must learn to be less intimidating, or on *Ladette to Lady*, where "Britain's worst women" are quarantined in a finishing school and taught to enact more normative iterations of femininity. As so depicted, television programming that is consumed with the *Pygmalion*-inspired idea of "making the lady" offers an interesting gendered commentary on the shifting meanings of class. Such

hermeneutic slipperiness is particularly evident on the two shows I analyse in this article, *American Princess* (2005–07) and *Australian Princess*
(2005–07), since residents of both America and Australia pride themselves on national identities grounded in independence and autonomy,
even as citizens of each country are fascinated by the exploits of the
English royals. Indeed, in both countries a sentiment prevails that the
English crown may have begun things, but a larger ethos of democratic
meritocracy far outweighs any obligations to the British motherland.
In this case, *American Princess* and *Australian Princess* equally and auda-
ciously suggest that it is possible to achieve princess status – technically
a position claimable only by birth and sometimes by marriage – through
hard work, training, and competition.

Revealed in these fantasies where "ordinary girls" compete to become
"actual royalty" is the very pointed idea that when women are allowed
to participate in a competitive democratic meritocracy where they can
achieve whatever they desire, they will desire precisely what meritocracy is unable to offer: the privileges of aristocracy. In both of the
programmes I will examine, the dominant rhetoric encourages subjects
to adopt a neoliberal regard for the self, whereby women learn to regulate their bodies and behaviours, ostensibly for the new confidence and
self-esteem such discipline will afford. Yet, in the midst of such arguments about individual identity in the neoliberal global marketplace,
questions emerge about the possibility of shaping the docile body into
a willing colonial subject. If makeover television shows more broadly
communicate a logic of Americanness in their reliance on notions of
egalitarianism, meritocracy, and volition,[3] then this article seeks to
determine if manners-based lifestyle television offers a counter-model
to the American Dream that simultaneously undermines and endorses
colonialist projects.

Empire of the imaginary

Although the British Empire was a real and historically verifiable phenomenon, my interest here lies in the *idea* of the Empire rather than
in its actual ascent or decline. Political theorists Michael Hardt and
Antonio Negri have argued in this regard that an "informal empire",
constituted by cultural practices and codes, is just as powerful as the
"formal empire", on which geopolitical formations are based. Thus,
multinational corporations, systems of monetary hegemony such as the
International Monetary Fund and the World Bank, and cultural ideology exercise a comparable degree of influence to the soldiers and agents

of the British state that enforced the pax Britannica. Hardt and Negri consequently argue that "Empire dictates its laws and maintains the peace...through mobile, fluid, and localized procedures" (354). This is particularly so, explains Ketu H. Katrak, in the geographies of the affective – in the homes, schools, and other interior places where ideology takes hold: "Colonial power was consolidated with the chalk and blackboard, more crucial ideological tools than military might" (92). In our current historical moment, where the might of the British Empire is more historical memory than political reality, it is the public iteration (and constant reiteration) of former glory that keeps the Empire of the imaginary alive.

It is presently not so much in the schoolroom where the significance of Empire finds its pedagogical meaning and perpetuation, but in the mediated spaces of television. Accordingly, Empire as a culturally resonant category is alive and well and airing each day through reality TV, offering those of us who consume reality fare sound-bite lessons in the shape and stature of the British Empire. A bit of a personal confession in this regard is perhaps telling. Although I lived in the United Kingdom for a year and have visited there frequently, it was not until I began studying *American Princess* and *Australian Princess* that I actually discovered that there was a Loyal Toast offered at formal social occasions in obeisance to the Queen of England, much less heard the words (admittedly, I lived in a particularly independent-minded part of Scotland, but I attended plenty of formal dinners throughout the UK). I have also, perhaps not surprisingly, never heard a toast made in honour of the Queen of England on my trips to Australia or Canada. Yet, due to the *Princess* programmes, I now have not only heard the toast upwards of 25 times, I seem to have memorized part of it. Thanks to Ally, the winner of the first *Australian Princess* competition, here is the toast in full: "To her most Excellent Majesty, Elizabeth the Second, by the Grace of God, the United Kingdom of Great Britain and Northern Ireland, and all of her other Realms and Territories Queen, Head of the Commonwealth, Defender of the Faith, the Queen". Even when said in jest as a lugubrious tongue-twister test for the "princesses in training", if these words and their constant repetition do not remind the viewer of the ubiquitous reach of Empire, then television surely cannot be blamed for a lack of trying.

In choosing *American Princess* and *Australian Princess* as my case studies in this chapter, I necessarily privilege a trope of British imperialist colonialization that stresses the opposition between a white foreign body and an indigenous land inhabited by darkened peoples. While the phenomenon I am examining here is not necessarily anomalous, in that many shows work through this model, it is also not the most common trope through which the power dynamics of makeover shows exert themselves. Most television makeovers, after all, feature Americans attending to sloppy Americans or Brits making over other hopeless Brits. Still, the logic of colonialism is equally pervasive in these shows, as style gurus, designers, and "experts" invade the homes of their fellow country people, those who are deemed dowdy and down-on-their luck. The principle that allows for "intervention" and "salvation" – words the makeover throws around with abandon – is clearly one predicated on class and race, where the working classes are labelled as "a race apart", what nineteenth-century British Prime Minister Benjamin Disraeli called "The Two Nations".[4] In the mediated spaces of postmodernity, where image functions as an index to identity, one need not actually be working class or coded as non-white to cause concern. Indeed, one need only *appear* working class or non-white to be thought of as the "worst" of the two nations, and thus to draw the eyes of the reality TV makeover squads roaming across America and Britain in the name of enforcing positive self-esteem and empowerment through the image. *American Princess* and *Australian Princess* take the imperative for style beyond the usual mandates established by Makeover TV, however, since they seek to create the edifice not just of style, nor even of the class-coded "lady", but of royalty.

Producing the princesses

Both *American Princess* and *Australian Princess* are made by Granada Entertainment, a media company based in London that not only sells primarily to Britain's ITV1 and ITV2 channels but also produces and distributes widely in Germany, Australia, and the United States. In fact, Granada's website boasts that it is one of the "largest international producers for the US market and a major force in acquiring, developing and producing reality and scripted programming for US networks". Granada is global in its reality TV imagination, covering a wide range of programming that includes cooking shows such as *Hell's Kitchen, The Chopping Block*, and *Ramsay's Kitchen Nightmares*, more conventional makeovers such as *Celebrity Fit Club, Nanny 911*, and *Room Raiders*, and docu-tainment programming such as *Animal Extractors: Polar Bears in Peril* and *Cracker: An American Dream*. Both *American Princess* and *Australian Princess* premiered in their respective countries in 2005. *American Princess* aired for two seasons in the United States, the first in 2005, the second in 2007. *Australian Princess* aired for two seasons in Australia, also in 2005 and 2007. Since then, both shows have been broadcast in England, Canada, Australia, and across Europe and the Middle East. They are in continual rotation and air regularly in the United States on the WE (Women's Entertainment) network.

Australian Princess and *American Princess* adhere equally to a reality competition format, where advisors admonish and inspire "average" young women, who are then judged as they compete to win what the show offers, in this case a "$100,000 prize package" including a "real diamond tiara", a "real British title", $50,000 in cash, and other princessly baubles. The winner of each respective competition also becomes the guest of honour at a lavish grand coronation ceremony, where she is escorted by "a real prince". As is evident even in this small description, the prize package itself sets up a contrast between categories of the real and artificial that works to service an aspirational fantasy for young women. As the title princess might indicate, it is significant that participants be youthful (ages range between 19 and 29) and unmarried, although several of the subjects are mothers of young children. Most women are white, although there are some Indian and African American participants. The women are coded as uneducated – although not necessarily working class – and their naiveté is situated as a factor of age as well as upbringing.

Central to the Princess competition format are the key advisors and *de facto* television presenters, Paul Burrell, former butler to Princess Diana and self-proclaimed "authority on all things regal", and Jean Broke-Smith, an English etiquette teacher and former principal of the Lucie Clayton House, a ladies school specializing in grooming, modelling, and deportment.[5] Burrell and Broke-Smith anchor each programme and are typically joined by a third judge: for the Australian competition this role was filled by Lady Jane Ferguson, sister to the (former) Duchess of York, Sarah Ferguson (aka Fergie); for the American competition the third judge was often Catherine Oxenberg, an American actress who has notably played such roles as Princess Diana in the made-for-television drama, *The Royal Romance of Charles and Diana* (1982). As the eldest daughter of Princess Elizabeth of Yugoslavia, Oxenberg has royal blood coursing through her veins. In the contradictory logic of Makeover TV, where revealing the "authentic" self requires that one overwrite the natural body, Oxenberg's bonafides as a princess make her the perfect person to participate in a show about commoners who aspire to royalty. The shows are hosted by good-looking television personalities, whose celebrity and attractiveness are meant to indicate some standing in the world of glamour, if not royalty. On *Australian Princess*, the radio host, television presenter, and Barbie look-a-like Jackie O assumed this role – her name ironically referencing Jacqueline Kennedy Onassis, arguably the exemplar of American-style royalty. On *American Princess*, hosting duties fell to Mark Durden-Smith, whose website claims he is "one of Britain's most versatile presenters", having worked on such reality television shows as *I'm a Celebrity Get Me Out of Here Now* and *Millionaire Manor*.

In all of this illustrious assortment of celebrities and expertise, it is the butler and the charm school doyenne who govern the shows. Burrell and Broke-Smith have made a post-career career of their days in service through the various manners modification outlets offered by reality TV and other media sites. Burrell is a veritable media phenomenon, having turned his service to the royal family into several tell-all memoirs (and having survived a scandal in which he was accused of stealing Princess Diana's personal possessions. As rumour has it, he managed to broker a deal directly with Queen Elizabeth in which charges against him were dropped in exchange for a promise that he would not reveal damaging information about the royal family). Broke-Smith has appeared across a broad swathe of television programming far beyond the *Princess* franchises, including *Ladette to Lady*,[6] *Britain's Next Top Model*, and *Snobs*. By her own reckoning, it is no longer Britain's high-society girls, but those from more working-class backgrounds, that keep her so busy, particularly since this clientele accesses her wisdom through the pedagogical reach of television. As she told *The Guardian*, "There aren't any finishing schools now, sadly. I suppose people thought it was a bit naff. But I'm working more than ever, and with people from all kinds of backgrounds, from girls who work in TV to girls from council estates who want to better themselves."

Although self-improvement is a key trope of Americanness, to better oneself has never been designated as important, or even relevant, to the upper classes – and far less to royalty (finishing schools notwithstanding). Indeed, self-improvement stands as an oxymoron to an aristocratic and royal elite which believes itself to be naturally superior and thus in no need of making over: the aristocracy simply is. As Pierre Bourdieu has argued in *Distinction* (1984), a critical element of aristocracy is the belief in its own naturalness. In short, the aristocrat belies his or her own construction, which, in turn, ratifies the perceived naturalness of class distinction as a matter of perpetual status quo regeneration. Gareth Palmer and other media scholars have argued that Bourdieu's work is crucial to understanding the class dynamics of lifestyle television, particularly the notion that " 'Good taste' and discrimination may seem (and must seem) 'effortless' and 'natural', but they are in fact not easily acquired" (177). As Palmer argues, "The mystique around the tasteful is...crucial in keeping them in positions of cultural superiority" (177). That said, to crib a line from *South Pacific*, class must be carefully taught. The aristocrat learns from what Bourdieu terms the "habitus", or the tacit system of rules and expectations that structure classed conventions. As just one example, Prince Charles may have needed training when he was a boy in how to actually ride a polo pony, but he never needed to be told that an interest in polo is itself critical to his distinction. At one level, it makes sense that if all actors within a classed field must learn codes of distinction, it might be possible to ascend the class hierarchy through specific forms of deliberately acquired knowledge. Indeed, such is the promise of the *Princess* narratives (and many American literary classics like *The Great Gatsby*), since these shows traffic in the allure of elite skills and concepts and suggest that a woman must learn in order to achieve. To their credit, in their message of meritorious advancement, *American Princess* and *Australian Princess* are a far cry from the more ubiquitous Princess myths we have inherited from fairytales and folklore, where a Cinderella or Sleeping Beauty ascends to princess heights because her beauty and/or natural docility attracts the eye of a Prince Charming. While the shadowy figure of Prince Charming is referenced throughout both of these series, it is worthy of note that he does not get screen time until the final episode of each season. Despite the obvious insistence that the skills in deportment and etiquette that the women learn are ostensibly the necessary credentials that will suit her for the marriage market, the shows also suggest that these qualities of poise and self-presentation are valuable qualities in their own right. The majority of the narrative time and interest is devoted to the lessons in labour and learning afforded to the young women, and this instruction is nuanced by a competing set of logics about work, authenticity, and the image.

"It's a hard job"

Although *American Princess* and *Australian Princess* are structured by their adherence to fairytale outcomes that are punctuated by glittery tiaras, designer clothes, fancy parties, and handsome princes, the narratives they offer are more Cinderella-as-the-scullery-maid than Cinderella-at-the-ball. In some ways, this fascination with the labour behind the image puts the *Princess* shows in good company, since they join with other reality television texts, such as *America's Next Top Model* or *Project Runway*, that focus on the professional work required to produce beauty. These "making of the princess" narratives also bear a strong resemblance to feature films that have filled the Cineplex of late, including *The Princess Diaries* (2001), *The Princess Diaries 2: Royal Engagement* (2004), *The Prince & Me* (2004), *The Prince & Me 2: The Royal Wedding* (2006), and *The Prince & Me 3: The Royal Honeymoon* (2008), all of which play on the trope of an "all-American girl" who is plucked from obscurity, refashioned, and coached so that she might awkwardly fulfil the princess role.[7]

Bearing in mind their generic coding as elimination-style reality shows, *American Princess* and *Australian Princess* build several "princess challenges" into each episode, and it is on the basis of such challenges that the participants' future ascendency is determined. Labour is critical to these outcomes: it is a mark of discredit if a "princess in training" acts like a guest rather than a hostess at a social event, and she can be faulted for "not doing a lick of work". Burrell incessantly scolds the participants, reinforcing the rigour of being a princess in terms that are suited to the business world: "Do you really want to be a princess? It's a hard job. To give up your life, for a life of duty and protocols. Timetables, strict routines". In light of this, some of the princess challenges are probably quite predictable, such as having to mingle at an elite social event or learning to walk in high heels and a ball gown. Other challenges (or punishments for those who do not do well in competition) are, however, downright bizarre. Consider, for instance, the archery challenge that features in *Australian Princess*. The girl who hits the bull's eye is allowed to have an elite dinner in a Sydney hotel with one of the other participants, and with their authoritative expert, Paul Burrell, standing in waiting as the champagne-serving butler. Back at the princess compound, those who did not win the challenge are sent to the barn where they are put to the task of cleaning shoes, which requires that they scrub and polish a pile of mud-covered brown boots that have been thrown into an indiscriminate pile (an activity that I doubt was ever required of either Cinderella or Princess Diana). The advisors justify such labour by saying "the girls must learn to look after themselves before others look after [them]". Jean Broke-Smith recognizes that "of course a princess doesn't clean her own tack", but such activities, she argues, are meant to enforce discipline. What such discipline will produce is difficult to determine, since outcomes are often conflated. Zena, one of the *Australian Princess* participants, says, for instance, that she hopes to "find the discipline of becoming a female", here collapsing idealized codes of sex and gender into equally idealized conceptions of class and rank.

The mandatory tea-making lessons serve a comparable sex/gender and class/rank function. These lessons, held interchangeably on both programmes by Broke-Smith and Burrell, are meant to enforce the austerity of rank and tradition. "Every single tea cup has its handle at 5:00", instructs Burrell to the *Australian Princess* contestants. "Every single day of the year, the Queen of England sits down at 5:00 and has a cup of tea". Burrell admonishes the princess acolytes for their shoddy skills at making a cup of tea. He rebukes one subject, Karusha (of southeastern Indian descent), who has put milk in her cup before pouring the hot water: "You did the thing that is never done. You committed the cardinal sin of tea time etiquette. The milk never, never, never goes in the tea cup first. That's what the common people do". Demonstrating the proper form for serving tea, Burrell intones, "It's a fine routine; it's a strict discipline. If it's good enough for the Queen, it's good enough for you". The diegesis delights in showing resistance to Burrell's fastidiousness. Wendy, who is labelled a "tomboy from the Outback", says in a moment of reflection intercut into the tea-making lesson, "I know I want to be a princess, but bloody hell, getting a lesson on how to make a cuppah? I'd like to get him out there and show him how to make billy tea. [Wendy gestures as if she is swinging a pot around her head]. You swing it around, mate, to settle the leaves". Another participant, "surfer girl" Ally, mocks Burrell's instructions, offering a decisive critique of the class-based behaviours he endorses: "How important can tea be? It's tea, y'know? Do I have to be serious about tea?"

Such moments of resistance, however, are powerfully shut down when other subjects continue to fail at mandatory lessons of tea-making, elocution, and painting, their tears and dismay attesting to the value of the challenges and the hard work of becoming a princess. Whether princess aspirants verbally mock or model the behaviours taught by their etiquette experts, these shows make a different kind of colonialist imperative more obliquely known: in support of the ideology or in opposition, one's sex-based identity requires coherence with gender's prevalent operating codes. Accordingly, while one woman might bemoan her lack of tea-making skills, dismissively telling the camera "That's what makes the English the English", she later acknowledges gratefully, "I became a female today". We see demonstrated here that she cannot think of herself as a woman unless she also upholds the mandates of being a lady. The teleology is one way, as Mark Durden-Smith makes clear to both viewers and princess wannabes: "Before you can become an American princess, you first have to become a lady". Critical to becoming either lady or princess is satisfying the colonializing English experts.

The video-cinematic logic that governs the editing of the *Princess* shows relentlessly poses Burrell and Broke-Smith in positions of dominance to their "princess apprentices", as if to situate the experts as not only royalty themselves, but as persons of greater prestige and authority. They often speak to the contestants from brightly-lit elevated platforms that require both the women and the at-home viewer to squint up at them. Quite often, when small vignettes feature private interviews with the reality TV participants, these moments are interrupted by intercut critical remarks from the experts, as if to suggest that even in privacy the dominating rule-maker is present, which is to say there is no represented privacy in these mediated spaces, all zones – whether public and private – fall into the domain of the colonizer's power. These sorts of depictions cohere with what Anne McClintock has identified in *Imperial Leather* (1995), her important analysis of colonialism and cultural imagery, regarding the way in which mediated messages fulfil and reify larger colonialist narratives about race, gender, and oppression. Although only a few of the women competing for the title of princess are coded as non-Caucasian, the division of labour represented here effectively darkens the women, requiring that they look up to more enlightened (literally) expertise.

Even so, the shows' female participants are depicted as not only colonized subjects to the experts' royal rule and subalterns in thrall to their superiors, but as clerks or apprentices, since becoming a princess factors as a matter of learned skills and behavioural regulation. Given that the objective at hand is to take a group of "useless [Yankee and Ozzie] girls" and transform one of them into an English princess, there is a bit of a troubling contradiction at play, since an aristocrat is meant to possess wealth but not to labour for that wealth; such imperatives, of course, are even more implacable for royalty. Accordingly, one of the first rules the aristocrat would know is that those of the servant classes are not in a position to confer upper-class status on others, particularly when the subtle domain of the habitus becomes the overt instruction of the reality TV classroom. Thus, any princess made by Burrell and Broke-Smith's combined efforts in the mediated public spaces of television is, by definition, no princess at all. For Burrell and Broke-Smith their purported titles as experts is all the more problematic since it is their learned knowledge in combination with their celebrity – rather than their birth or station – that confers authority and arguably equips them to "make" princesses. Indeed, Burrell's notorious scandal-ridden past with the British royal family and Broke-Smith's on-call media expertise function more as appeals of ethos within an economic framework where celebrity and learned skills are Americanized currencies that evidence hard work, luck, and popularity.

The coded logic of the text offers a hodge-podge of ideologically contradictory possibilities, since tropes of meritocratic advancement are liberally interspersed with mandates for neoliberal marketplace competition, accentuated by a colonialist reverence for old-world power, privilege, and rank. We begin to see, then, that the elite values which are seemingly underscored in the making of the princesses are undone by the show's mandates of instruction and competition. The way the shows manage these contradictions is perhaps best revealed in the repeated references made to the categories of the natural and the artificial.

"All eyes are on her"

Given the way in which the *Princess* shows enforce neoliberal goals of market appeal and situate the creation of a gendered self as woman's most valuable commodity, it is plain to see that these programmes are as much about career development as they are fantasies of romance and royal ascendency. Or perhaps we might argue that the shows up the ante on what it means for an "average girl" to find Prince Charming: it is not apparently sufficient that she be in the right place at the right time; she must also be coiffed, dressed, refined, anointed, and crowned so that her "inner princess" will emerge and draw the eye of Mr. Right. Significantly, the male love object gets very little camera time, so in this respect the *Princess* shows perform a rather remarkable bait and switch, replacing the hoped-for male suitor with the ever-present male gaze, as it is located in and magnified by the camera. Not surprisingly, the shift from an actual viewer to an abstract sense that one is always being watched heightens the power of perceived image, and the *Princess* shows relentlessly impress upon the women that the first visual impression they give is imperative to their potential success as princesses.

Of course, whenever first impressions are at stake, mandatory style, make-up, and hair makeovers ensue. As with other iterations of Makeover TV, the "princesses in training" undergo what I have elsewhere described as affective domination, or a process of indoctrination that begins with shaming and humiliation and results in hugs and gratitude. When style and beauty experts are brought in, then, the *Princess* participants must be told that their hair looks like spaghetti, their tattoos and piercings are "tarty", or that the "chubby girls" should really "go for a run every once in a while". Burrell reinforces this tough love as a mandatory element in being a princess during a mini-lecture directed at the women: "Princesses have to look the part. The first ten seconds are the most important time when you meet someone". To the camera, Burrell reinforces his claim: "They have to understand the way people see them. The way they present themselves impacts on a great deal of people". In so saying, Burrell reiterates a claim that runs across Makeover TV, where first impressions are seemingly the only impression available to a person (male or female, although men get a few more shots at making their mark). On reality TV, women apparently have only a ten-second envelope before they fade into obscurity, spinsterhood, and unemployment. "I'm not being sexist", pleads Burrell matter of factly. "Princesses have to look good wherever they go". Given that the stakes are so high, the participants appear not just willing but grateful for their public appraisals and consequent makeovers. As is the case across the Makeover TV genre, the makeover process is not only about appearance but engages with a deeply held sense of each participant's gendered and sexed identity. As one woman on *Australian Princess* says in response to her makeover: "I turned into a female today, as you can see".

Appearance, then, is only one element in the overall image that marks the transformation of the commoner into royalty. Princesses in training must learn not to wolf-whistle in public, not to jump up and down with raucous enthusiasm at the Royal Ascot, not to wear a hat at a polo match, not to eat a banana like a monkey, not to wear a g-string or thong when sailing, and a seemingly endless list of not-centred injunctions prohibiting behaviour. Of course, while these lessons are being offered, the camera captures the princess candidates violating the precise terms of the experts' advice, so that the overall logic of the text glorifies ruptures to the rules rather than obedience to their staid terms. A further rupture comes in the manner in which the experts themselves violate codes of propriety; while we are told that it is unseemly for a woman to show her undergarments, it cannot be appropriate for Princess Diana's former butler to yell across Sydney Harbour: "Melissa, pull your pants up!!!". Nor can Broke-Smith's pedigree as a fashionista be credible when every scene of her wearing trousers reveals the cursed VPL (visible panty line), a capital offence that would authorize Broke-Smith's immediate makeover were she ever spotted by Trinny and Susannah. These faux pas underscore all the more that there is something a bit askew about Burrell and Broke-Smith, and the narrative often delights in mocking their outmoded sense of propriety as much as it enjoys revealing the difficulties the "apprentice princesses" experience in making the grade. There are many moments that illustrate this point, but one of the best featured on *Australian Princess*, when Burrell was enumerating his criteria for success: "I want someone with spirit and guts. That's what an Australian Princess should be", he declares. He immediately defies his own terms, however, when considering Laura K, an exotic dancer: "Even though she has a personality as big as a house, she failed to set the table properly", he says smugly, as if her shoddy table-setting skills completely undermine her personality.

Although Burrell's words might be laughable, the larger argument comes through loud and clear. As Broke-Smith explains: "An American [or Australian] Princess should be someone who has presence. When she arrives in a room or at a function, everyone notices her". This mandate that a "true" princess will not only command the gaze but also bask in its intensity puts the *Princess* programmes squarely in the discourses of both Makeover TV and American celebrity culture – discourses which dictate that a woman finds consummate meaning as the object of the gaze. It also, however, requires that *American Princess* and *Australian Princess* neutralize the stigma attached to desiring celebrity. It does so by suggesting that, when it really comes down to it, a princess cannot be trained for royalty; rather, it is her innate qualities that fit her for such a station.

"I am not sure how genuine she is"

By way of conclusion, I want to address the pervading contradiction between authenticity and artifice that is embedded in both *American Princess* and *Australian Princess*; even in the context of training girls to take on the elite codes of English royalty, both shows demonize those subjects who "want it too much", need too much instruction, or "play to the cameras", and instead place a premium on what it labels as "natural" qualities. "She'd murder someone to win", scoffs Jean Broke-Smith about one contestant. Sealing that participant's doom, Broke-Smith dismisses her, "She's a megalomaniac for power". In the omniscient words of one of the shows' many experts, "To be a princess you can't pretend all the time, you have to feel it from [the heart]", thus refuting the very validity of the contest by suggesting that the game is rigged from the beginning. Multiple seasons of each show notwithstanding, only one woman can be the princess, and that woman's fate, just like Cinderella's foot fitting perfectly into the glass slipper, is foreordained: "I think what's going to determine who Australian Princess is who they are inside", says one of the experts. The hermeneutic function of the shows, then, is not to train the princess at all but to give her the forum – the ball, the carriage, and the fairy godmother – that will let her intrinsic qualities find outward expression, while all of the straggling ugly step-sisters fall by the wayside. As in Cinderella, the makeover's way out of the contradiction it poses between immanent worth and constructed value is to suggest that only the "right" girl can wear the glass slipper (or the cubic zirconia tiara), and it is Prince Charming (in the form of the camera's discerning gaze) who can sort the wheat from the chaff, the lady from the ladette, the princess from the commoner. Still, *American Princess* and *Australian Princess* are not solely derivatives of the fairytale lore that positions princess status as the desired but never achievable epitome of female fantasy; rather, they here function as aspirational texts that situate the outcome of becoming a princess – the English colonizer's place of utmost privilege – as not only attainable, but as the colonized subject's necessary credential for a stable identity and marketplace success.

Notes

1. Of course, the real United States of America is as complicit in imperialist policies as the United Kingdom, but in the logic of Makeover TV, "America" adheres to class-less, democratic fair play. In these depictions where English hosts endeavour to indoctrinate unkempt natives, we see a re-enactment that supports old-world ideologies.
2. The bumper sticker on the Airstream Camper that Trinny and Susannah drive in *Making Over America with Trinny and Susannah* stresses the colonializing dimensions of their enterprise, reading "We Came, We Saw, We Madeover!"
3. See Weber.
4. See Disraeli's 1845 novel *Sybil, or The Two Nations*. Suggesting the transatlantic appeal of the "two nations" concept, the phrase was appropriated in 2004 by the US Presidential candidate John Edwards.
5. In 2007 *The Telegraph* reported that the Lucie Clayton had been sold and turned into bachelor flats. See Tyzack.
6. For a sustained analysis of *Ladette to Lady*, see Angela Smith's "Femininity Repackaged: Postfeminism and *Ladette to Lady*" (in this book).
7. These films are distinctly different than the princess craze among young girls at the moment, who idolize the Disney Princesses line and demand princess-themed birthday parties. For more on this phenomenon, see Orenstein.

Works cited

American Princess. Granada, 2005–07. 14 episodes.
Australian Princess. Granada, 2005–07. 16 episodes.
Bourdieu, Pierre. *Distinction: A Social Critique of Judgement of Taste*. New York: Routledge, 1984.

Disraeli, Benjamin. *Sybil, or The Two Nations* (1845). Oxford World's Classics. Ed. Sheila Smith. Oxford: Oxford University Press, 1998.

Hardt, Michael, and Antonio Negri. *Empire*. Cambridge, Mass: Harvard University Press, 2000.

Katrak, Ketu H. *Politics of the Female Body: Postcolonial Women Writers of the Third World*. Piscataway, NJ: Rutgers University Press, 2006.

McClintock, Anne. *Imperial Leather: Race, Gender, and Sexuality in the Colonial Contest*. New York: Routledge, 1995.

"Mark Durden-Smith". *KBJ Management*. http://www.kbjmgt.co.uk/clients/mark_durdensmith/. [Accessed August 24, 2009].

Moseley, Rachel. "Makeover Takeover on British Television". *Screen* 44 (2000): 299–314.

Orenstein, Peggy. "What's Wrong with Cinderella?" *The New York Times Magazine*. December 24, 2006. http://www.nytimes.com/2006/12/24/magazine/24princess.t.html. [Accessed August 24, 2009].

Palmer, Gareth. "'The New You': Class and Transformation in Lifestyle Television". *Understanding Reality Television*. Ed. Su Holmes, and Deborah Jermyn. New York: Routledge, 2004. 173–90.

Tyzack, Anna. "Lucie Clayton House: A Model Lesson in Home-Making". *The Telegraph* November 24, 2007. http://www.telegraph.co.uk/property/3359952/Lucie-Clayton-House-A-model-lesson-in-home-making.html. [Accessed August 4, 2009].

Weber, Brenda R. *Makeover TV: Selfhood, Citizenship, and Celebrity*. Durham: Duke University Press, 2009.

10
Femininity Repackaged: Postfeminism and *Ladette to Lady*

Angela Smith

This chapter looks at the recent backlash against postfeminist discourses of empowerment through special reference to the commercial phenomenon of "Girl Power". Since the late 1990s, this backlash has manifested itself in the British press, which has generated and fuelled a "moral panic" about binge drinking, alcohol-induced violence, and increasing levels of sexually transmitted diseases in the young. This generally gives cause for concern about adolescent behaviour, which is persistently formulated as "out of control" – a formulation that was validated, to some extent, by the introduction of anti-social behaviour orders (ASBOs[1]) under the 1998 Crime and Disorder Act. Much of this attention has been aimed at young women, who are commonly referred to as "ladettes"[2] because of their perceived adoption of behaviours more usually associated with young British men. As Katy Day et al. have shown, many British national newspapers in the period 1998–2000 reported on studies of teenage drinking which claimed that young women were "bigger binge drinkers" than their male counterparts. Such articles trade on wider moral panics about the behaviour of young women and are used to represent women as a threat to themselves (on account of the fact that their drinking leaves them more exposed to the risks of assault and ill-health) and to patriarchy (through the challenges they pose to established norms of female passivity). Although this chapter will focus primarily on representations of young women in British media texts, the anxieties with which these texts engage are not limited to the United Kingdom and are, as Ariel Levy observes in *Female Chauvinist Pigs* (2006), equally widespread in contemporary American culture.

While such negative coverage of women's behaviour is not new, what is different about this particular media attention is the extent to which it extends into television entertainment programming.[3] Certainly, the rapid rise of reality programming since the 1990s and the contemporaneous arrival of multichannel television – with its typical bias towards "female" genres – have led to an explosion in programming based around the home and domesticity (Holmes and Jermyn 24). Such programming makes conspicuous use of "documentary" strategies, altering the parameters of "factual" television in ways that are consistent with John Corner's description of "post-documentary culture" (156). As Anna Hunt observes in her study of *Big Brother, Wife Swap*, and *How Clean is Your House?*, many of these programmes feature "domestic dystopias", in which viewers are enticed by overtly negative images of domesticity. Like the inhabitants of the domestic dystopias to which Hunt refers, the figure of the ladette has – through the media – been made available for public censure. This censure is, however, specific, in that it is inextricably linked to the role the ladette occupies in postfeminist discourse as the personification of an extreme performance of Girl Power.

The equality argued for – and, in some respects, won – by second wave feminism has been diffused by an increasingly consumerist culture. While this culture trades on the gains of the second wave, it has also produced the sense that there is still something missing in women's lives. This is writ large in the theme of "change the way you look; change your life" that guides the "narrative" of makeover programmes aimed at female participants.[4] Focusing on the reality television series *Ladette to Lady* (RDF 2005–), I argue that the gender and class dynamics of such makeover shows contrast sharply with those of quality television drama – a genre that is increasingly preoccupied with "the oppression of upper-middle class suburban life" and its associated containment (Richardson 158). With special reference to the second series of *Ladette to Lady*, first screened in the United Kingdom on ITV1 in autumn 2006, I explore the complex ways in which the discourses of postfeminism operate within a makeover series that aims to turn "ladettes" into "ladies", with all the assumptions about lifestyle and class that these labels imply. As will become clear in the analysis that follows, the participants' postfeminist performances as ladettes are consistently opened up to criticism – criticism that turns on the fraught issues of taste and self-control.[5] Still, as a show that combines elements of social documentary, soap opera, and disruptive comedy, *Ladette to Lady* occupies a hybrid generic space from which it invites the viewer to take up a range of positions – both critical and sympathetic – in relation to both the ladettes and their lady mentors.

Postfeminism

As Charlotte Brunsdon, Elspeth Probyn, Sarah Projansky, and Imelda Whelehan have argued, since its emergence in the 1980s postfeminism has often been viewed negatively as hailing the end of feminism. As its prefix implies, after all, the term suggests that the aims and objectives of the (white, middle-class) second wave agenda have already been addressed, achieved, and surpassed. More positively, though, the discourse of "choices" offered by postfeminism – with respect to work, family and dating – is frequently offered as a resolutely heterosexual alternative to "anti-sex" constructions of second wave feminism (Projanksy 67). As a playful, positive strand of postfeminism, however, Girl Power has a persistent tendency – signified through the term "girl" – to infantilize the women to whom it refers. Feminist scholars often point out that the freedoms won by the second wavers have allowed Western women to live the lives that they choose – lives which often have a vexed and/or unstable connection to feminist politics and to traditional gender roles. As Probyn has observed, this climate of instability is implicated in an increasingly prevalent strand of postfeminism, in which pre-feminist ideals and traditional, patriarchal models of femininity are seductively repackaged as postfeminist freedoms. This offshoot of Girl Power is, perhaps, most readily classifiable as "Lady Power", and it is, to some extent, symptomatic of Susan Faludi's "backlash" manifesto, in which the "having-it-all" single, career woman of the 1980s is returned to the patriarchal fold within the postfeminist discourse of "neo-traditional feminism".[6]

Girl Power and ladettes

In celebrating the equality and choice afforded by second wave feminism, the ladette is the personification of an extreme performance of Girl Power that started to draw media attention in the 1990s. As Whelehan states, the ladette playfully, if problematically, celebrates the male gaze (9). This is usefully demonstrated through the representation of Frances in *Ladette to Lady*, who – having received breast enhancement surgery as a gift for her eighteenth birthday – develops a tendency to flash her breasts in public. Frances's "playful" behaviour is necessarily equated to her exhibitionism; as a result, it is persistently framed as problematic within the context of the show. Through her implied courting of male attention, the ladette is rendered distinct from the longer-standing image of the "tomboy": the tomboy, after all, wants to *be* one of the boys; the ladette wants to *be attractive to* the boys. As a result, the ladette – while appropriating aspects of "laddish" male behaviour, in terms of binge drinking and sexual promiscuity – remains resolutely heterosexual, embodying an "excessive" form of heterosexuality that could be perceived as a threat to the moral order of Western civilization. As Skeggs argues, in the British context, the sexualized appearance of working-class women is routinely defined against the well-dressed, cultivated women of the middle classes (100). In *Ladette to Lady*, middle-class tastes are insistently imposed upon the appearances and behaviours of the working-class ladettes, with a view to reinstating "safer" – or more traditional – codes of sexual conduct.

A more positively received aspect of Girl Power, according to Hollows, was its attempt to envision new, assertive feminine identities, while recapitulating – and popularizing – (second wave) principles of female solidarity (181). As Whelehan observes, Girl Power also seems to "recognise the age-old strengths of women's friendships and community and is particularly positive towards mother-daughter relationships" (46). This is writ large in *Ladette to Lady*, where the "school" venue, with its shared dormitories, is used as a tacit means of encouraging the female participants to develop strong friendships with their peers. In addition, the "teachers" at the school act as both mentors and mother figures, guiding the young women as they progress through various stages of "self-improvement". While this might be the case, however, the official curriculum works to undermine the politics of Girl Power through its nostalgic evocation of femininity – a femininity that is most readily signified in the term "lady".

Traditionalizing femininity: The spread of "Lady Power"

Diane Negra argues that one of the key premises of neo-traditional femininity is the need to abandon the overly ambitious 1980s programme of "having it all" (12). In its most assertive form, McRobbie suggests, this is part of a "patriarchal attempt to undo the achievements of the women's movement" (47). In this sense, the traditionalizing discourse of female empowerment sees ladettes as misguided, and thus "appeals to a nostalgia for a pre-feminist past as an ideal that feminism has supposedly destroyed" (Projanksy 67). That the ladette is misguided in her appropriation of Girl Power is clear in the urge to reveal the "real", "ladylike" self who will conform to neo-feminist ideals.

The decline of positive images of Girl Power in the twenty-first century marks a shift towards a "safer" femininity. In makeover television, there has been a concentration on "reforming" ladettes to be more "respectable" in conduct and appearance, reverting to traditional feminine stereotypes.[7] There is a foregrounding of the performative nature of femininity, where the sense of identity that is evident elsewhere in postfeminism becomes naturalized and internalized by the young women featured. This is seen in shows such as *My Fair Kerry* (Granada 2005) and *Asbo Teen to Beauty Queen* (North One Television 2006), as well as in *Ladette to Lady*. Such shows follow on from cinematic representations in which women who pay *too much* attention to their physical appearance are coded as lacking in moral value, socially disruptive, and working class.[8]

Whelehan has observed that lifestyle politics leaves in its wake those who do not conform to its preferred images and those who cannot afford to engage in the "liberating" consumerism that would enable them to exercise "control" over their lives (178). Consumerism is therefore linked to notions of good taste and cultural capital, where "better taste" is usually aligned to upper-middle-class ideas. Glossy magazines consolidate this connection in their regular depictions of celebrities' homes, which – in Britain at least – are often designed to emulate those of the landed gentry.[9] Likewise, when it comes to personal appearance, the "style" which is most actively esteemed is rooted in consumption patterns which seek to traditionalize femininity around a performance that is (predominantly) middle class and conservative, as we shall see shortly.

Ladette to Lady: A case study

Ladette to Lady, first aired on ITV1 in September 2005, is a reality makeover show which follows eight self-identified ladettes as they undertake a 5-week intensive course in learning how to be ladies. Predominantly white and working class, the young women are described on the show's website as being "loud, foul-mouthed, uncultured and unpleasant women, who like to drink to excess and are sexually promiscuous". Each week, one ladette is "asked to leave" the show, having failed – in the opinion of the school's teachers – to engage sufficiently with the traditionalizing process around which the show is based. Over the course of the series, the young women are assessed on their performance in various trials and at particular formal events, while also being judged on their unchaperoned behaviour. At the end of the series, the remaining participants are presented, Eliza Doolittle-like, at a "society ball", where the winner is announced as being the woman whose journey from ladette to lady has been the most remarkable.

Staged in Egglestone Hall, a former finishing school in North York-shire, the institutional format is stressed by providing the ladettes with a uniform (comprising a classic tweed suit, court shoes, and a pearl neck-lace). There is an implicit valorization of upper-middle-class, white Britishness, with an emphasis on domesticity based around heritage and glamour that is also found in a more playful way in celebrity maga-zines. Like Roberts, Skeggs has observed that the middle classes are usually associated with "restraint, repression, reasonableness, modesty and denial", contrasting sharply with the excesses of working-class behaviour that are embodied by the participants in *Ladette to Lady* (99). This traditional notion of middle-classness is carried through in the kinds of lessons which are taught, such as deportment, elocution, eti-quette, flower-arranging, cookery, and dressmaking. These lessons are conducted in a less playful way, in that the participants are situated as schoolchildren who must respect and obey the teachers' authority. This forms an extreme version of the sort of governance that is found on other makeover shows, as discussed by Roberts. The teachers are addressed formally, and the participants are expected to abide by rules that are more usually imposed on much younger, school-aged pupils, particularly those at traditional boarding schools. Should any of the par-ticipants fail to abide by the rules, they risk incurring penalties; they may, for example, be confined to the school premises while their peers are "rewarded" with a trip to the local pub. In one episode, a participant who drank to excess at a weekend house party is subsequently made to wait a table at a formal party and forbidden from speaking to any of the guests. Thus, the containment of the young women is not only physical but also, as we shall see, behavioural, in line with traditional notions of femininity.

In face-to-face encounters with individual participants, the teachers are shown to be more maternal, offering advice and encouragement to any young woman who appears to be struggling. The apparent non-competitiveness of the show is emphasized through the fact that it is the teachers who decide which participant leaves at the end of each week, not some viewer phone-in vote or skills test. Instead, the teach-ers claim to look for aptitude and attitude, gathering this information through classroom and social observation in the way a mother would judge her daughter.

Sexual etiquette

Ladette to Lady implicitly upholds traditional, gendered notions of sex-ual etiquette through its aggressive endorsement of female chastity, modesty, and reserve. The "progress" of the participants in this area is tested at regular intervals when they are required to meet a group of young men who are (euphemistically) called "eligible bachelors". These bachelors are largely upper-middle-class and aristocratic men, and are promoted, in Lucy Briers' plummy-toned voiceover, as the "cream of the private school system". Interestingly, although the sexual behaviour of these men is broadly comparable to the promiscuity of ladettes, the former tend to be cast in far less judgemental terms as "cads".[10] In this way, the men's promiscuity is licensed by virtue of their gender and social class, and it is up to the young women to avoid their sexual advances. Should any of the women succumb to the allures of these "cads", she risks being expelled, though there is no such surveillance or sanction for the male protagonists.

Throughout the series, there are montages of the participants during their ladette days; most of these sequences are shot in pubs or clubs, where the participants are shown to be drinking excessively and dancing provocatively. This content is certainly typical of the montage which documents the antics of Rebecca, who is insistently situated as problematic on account of her sexual promiscuity. According to *Ladette to Lady*, Rebecca's promiscuity is facilitated by her job as a barmaid, which affords her frequent opportunities to meet men. In the following extract, this promiscuity is contrasted with Rebecca's own testimony about the benefits of celibacy, which she outlines to Liz Brewer, the sexual etiquette coach, and Jill Harboard, the (notional) principal of the school. However, this testimony has a very specific structural rationale, and this is hinted at in the opening voiceover, which anticipates Rebecca's subsequent "misbehaviour".

VOICEOVER: Now Principal Jill Harboard is rewarding the girls with a trip to the pub but Rebecca is out for more than a few pints tonight [*shots of Rebecca as barmaid making eyes at customers*] Twenty-one-year-old barmaid Rebecca Squire has a remarkable track record.

REBECCA: [*pre-Egglestone to camera*] I've probably slept with a hundred people if not a few more. I lost count quite a while ago.

VOICEOVER: [*shots of class*] In the first week of term a class in sexual etiquette struck a raw nerve.

LIZ: Make it difficult. It's a question of putting a value on yourself and being special.

REBECCA: [*to camera after the class*] It's all common sense and everything she said don't do I do. I just feel like dead really cheap and bit of a [*sic*] ... just feel like a bit of slapper.

VOICEOVER: But after three weeks of celibacy Rebecca is becoming restless [*montage of Rebecca in pub drinking pints, shots and smoking*].

REBECCA: [*to local lads in pub*]. I'm not going home yet; not a fucking chance am I going home yet [*shot of Rebecca applying lipstick*].

VOICEOVER: Rebecca soon makes an acquaintance and arranges to meet at the local club [*shot of ladettes walking to a club*]. It's now ten-thirty and ladettes should be tucked up in bed [*dancing, kissing*]. It's one-thirty in the morning when they finally make it back to Eggleston Hall. [*Next day. Rebecca is expelled. School head to camera*].

JILL (SCHOOL PRINCIPAL): There is no way you could have turned that into a lady.

REBECCA: [*Vox pop of Rebecca packing*] I like sex and there's nothing wrong with that. It's healthy and keeps you fit. I've not had any in here and look at how much weight I've put on. When I was at home I was getting regular exercise and I weren't a chunky monkey [*laughs*].

(2.3)

The "reward" of a trip to the local pub is clearly a means of evaluating the participants' behaviour once they are out of the school and back in more familiar venues, where the stern eye of the teachers is geographically and temporally distant (though their activities are still accessible to viewers via the cameras that follow the participants). Potential problems are flagged up in the focus on Rebecca's past. She condemns herself through her own testimony, with a further montage of flashbacks of her sitting attentively through a sexual etiquette lesson before a brief to-camera shot of her after the lesson, in which she indicates that she has hegemonically accepted as "common sense" the positive messages about chastity and traditional femininity that the school promotes. However, this is immediately undermined by the voiceover, in which the delicate, euphemistic references to Rebecca's "remarkable track record" give way to a description of her sexual frustration as "restlessness". When a visibly drunken Rebecca is shown applying make-up in a pub toilet, her rebelliousness is highlighted through her use of taboo language and her refusal to abide by the infantilizing rule of lights-out by half-past ten. The cameras follow Rebecca and the other participants as they proceed to another venue, where Rebecca's raucous partying is ironically reformulated in Briers' voiceover as her "meeting an acquaintance in a local club" – a narrative register that is humorously evocative of upper-middle-class refinement and restraint. Rebecca's fall from grace is completed the following day when her behaviour leads to her expulsion. Here, the headteacher derogatorily refers to Rebecca as "that", rather than "her", while Rebecca remains unrepentant, playfully recasting her promiscuous behaviour as a legitimate form of physical exercise that prevents her becoming a "chunky monkey". Rebecca is thus removed from the programme for her failure to adapt her behaviour in a sincere way, and is not regarded as worthy of further attention by the teachers.

Interestingly, Rebecca also touches on one of the less apparent aspects of traditional feminine performance: its sedate and sedentary dimensions. As the series progresses, it is clear that many of the participants are struggling to fasten their tailored jackets. Such weight gain is, perhaps, a predictable consequence of a curriculum that enforces the importance of ladylike deportment: visible evidence of an increase in weight brought about by their enforced inactivity. Perhaps this is also one of the expected consequences of a ladylike deportment: the women, after all, are severely restricted in their movements; they are required to negotiate staircases slowly and elegantly, and are forbidden from bounding around the premises as they might at home, where they are not subject to such stringent levels of self-governance.

Lessons in housewifery

The ladettes must also develop an array of domestic skills that are inextricable from traditional accounts of feminine behaviour, such as flower-arranging, dressmaking, and cookery. While such skills are, potentially, practical, they are taught in ways that render them irrelevant to the everyday lives of the young women. During the dressmaking, for example, the participants are taught how to make eveningwear, with a particular focus on the ball gowns that the finalists will wear in the concluding episode. The impracticality of such garments is only too apparent as the finalists proceed downstairs, stumbling over trailing hems and tugging awkwardly at low-cut necklines. The cooking lessons are similarly impractical, in that they focus on catering for formal dinner parties, where game is the most common main course (reflecting the culling by the shooting party seen earlier in the series).

Within this domestic fairytale, the general lack of regard for the young women's lives prior to their arrival at Egglestone Hall lives is remarkable. These lives are, in fact, dismissed as irrelevant as the teachers impose their code of behaviour on the participants. Only occasionally are the participants allowed to divulge evidence of their cultural backgrounds, and this is usually accompanied by tears of humiliation or self-pity. One such instance involves Frances, the serial exhibitionist to whom

I referred earlier. Throughout the series, Frances is seen as something of a comedy figure, and shots of her breasts are edited into every episode by the predominantly male production team, inviting us to read her playfulness as foolishness. However, after a drunken night out towards the end of the series, when she is called to account by the cookery teacher, Rosemary Shrager, Frances shows remorse. We see in this particular episode (2.4) evidence of the confessional culture that Furedi has discussed as central to a wider move towards emotionality in the popular media in recent years.

> ROSEMARY: We don't really know anything about you, not really.
> FRAN: No, you don't [*shaking head and looking tearful*].
> ROSEMARY: Exactly, so why don't you tell me?
> FRAN: I was really picked on for having no boobs and now I've got 'em just [.] I just flash 'em about a bit too much and it causes problems with me.
> ROSEMARY: Did you expose yourself last night?
> FRAN: [*shameful and quiet*] Yeh [*sniffs*].
> ROSEMARY: You did?
> FRAN: Yeh.
> ROSEMARY: But you obviously don't have self esteem.
> FRAN: I just [.] I've never had a proper boyfriend, never had a Valentine's Day card [*brightening up as RS looks shocked and sympathetic*].
> ROSEMARY: What! Really?
> FRAN: Nope.
> ROSEMARY: Does that upset you?
> FRAN: Yeh.
> ROSEMARY: I can see that [*Fran crying*]. You know this weekend you've actually got a real opportunity to try and find out who you could be and what you could be like. [*Fran nodding*] I think you should take it up and really try.
> FRAN: I promise you I'm really going to try hard now.
> ROSEMARY: Promise.
> FRAN: I promise, yeh.
> ROSEMARY: Alright.

Rosemary here compels Frances to reveal the underlying problem: her low self-esteem. By electing to have breast enhancement surgery, Frances has taken a consumerist solution to this problem, by paying to change what she perceives to be the source of her low self-esteem. This has, however, led to other problems, given that she now exposes her breasts in ways that are sexually provocative. Frances volunteers the flaw in this, illustrating Whelehan's argument that in the neo-traditional femininity strand of postfeminism, ladettes are misguided: Frances tearfully claims never to have had a "proper boyfriend", which she clearly expects her teacher to find shocking. Frances's admission also underlines the prevailing view that ladettes are not marriageable: they may have fun and flirt with men, but the likelihood of their involvement in longer-term commitment is slim. Thus, the "genuine" Frances is revealed to be a person who accepts traditional femininity, inwardly aspiring to long-term relationships that fall within its boundaries. Rosemary then attempts to expedite the liberation of this "genuine" self by suggesting that Frances's hosting of the weekend party will be a "real opportunity to try and find out who [she] could be".

Ultimately, the programme demands that participants be grateful for their makeovers, and not bitter; enthusiastic, not cynical. This is achieved structurally through the editing and voiceover. Where a ladette is shown to be conforming, this will be intercut with a shot of her cavorting drunkenly in the past, demonstrating just how far she has been "improved" by the strict regimen. The voiceover will also draw attention to the "negative" ladette behaviour, and this is routinely reinforced by the testimony of the ladette herself. Only those whose behaviour is considered worthy are allowed to reach the series finale. Any woman who fails to embrace "Lady Power" is represented as flawed, most often through the instructors' comments, which draw on reductive discourses about gender that are presented without any critical interrogation. These essentializing tendencies are crystallized in the words of the etiquette coach, Liz, as she reflects on the meanings and implications of the term "slag":

> When you understand what a slag is, and a slag is a woman of loose morals but it's also the scum that you take off, you know a coal pit, it's that scum and what we start off with are girls who are little more than that. (*End of Term Report*)

Ultimately, the programme's most successful transformations are shown to be those which involve the young women whose "real selves" conform most closely to traditional ideals of femininity, while those who fail to reform are discarded as irredeemable owing to their innate ill-breeding.[11] In this way, traditional femininity is elevated and glorified, at the same time as unconventional behaviour is denigrated and dismissed.

Conclusion

According to Moseley, postfeminist identity is a site of tension between feminism and femininity, and as such it is understands "conventional modes of femininity as *not necessarily* in conflict with female power" (419; emphasis in original). However, what I hope to have shown is that the recent backlash against Girl Power seeks to make traditional femininity more dominant within postfeminism in popular culture, although not quite as destructively as McRobbie suggests. In *Ladette to Lady*, the adoption of "Lady Power" leads to a willing acceptance of traditional feminine roles as a form of empowerment. Social attitudes towards traditional gender roles are revealed through the rules of sexual etiquette that are imparted to the young women – rules that seek to contain female desire while refusing to condemn male promiscuity. The playfulness of the performance of the ladette is curtailed and eventually rejected as misguided by the successful participants themselves. Visually, this bias is registered in the montage of images that features in every episode. This montage charts the ladettes' arrival at Egglestone Hall, where the sartorial symbols of working-class identity (namely leisurewear and conspicuous jewellery) are immediately removed and replaced by tailored suits and pearl necklaces that are constricting, traditional, and resolutely associated with the middle class. The lessons at the school are also highly marked by social class, acting as training for the management of a marital home (whether their own or someone else's). Confined to the domestic sphere, the participants are expected to host dinner parties, where the assumption is that everyone has a dining room in which to accommodate large numbers of guests. Such an earnest, grown-up lifestyle is very different from the "irresponsible" pub-crawling of the ladettes prior to their arrival at Egglestone Hall, but the show insistently valorizes this model of neo-traditional femininity as one that is worthy of adoption. Where dissident voices do come through, as with Rebecca's reaction to her expulsion, these are framed as being the voices of participants who were never going to be "ladies" anyway, and for whom there can be no salvation or redemption.

Overall, as Whelehan comments, discourses advocating pre-feminist ideals are meant to be read ironically (147); however, from this analysis of *Ladette to Lady* we can see that the participants themselves are not only shown to be internalizing these discourses of constraint, but are also rewarded for so doing. The adoption of traditional femininity by the successful participants is emphasized by the *End of Term Report* episode, in which former participants return to the school for tea with the teachers. Of those who are finalists, we learn that they have all gained confidence and self-esteem, their experience at Egglestone Hall having "changed their lives" for the better. The positive, empowering effects of "Lady Power" over Girl Power are thus recapitulated, while the more problematic aspects of the show and its invocation of neo-traditional aspects of postfeminism escape any obvious interrogation.

Notes

1. The acronym "ASBO" stands for "anti-social behaviour order", aimed at curtailing troublesome neighbours and street behaviour. Largely perceived in the media as being served on young, working-class people, it has rapidly become synonymous with the "new lad" and, of course, the more problematic ladette.
2. Widely used in British culture, the term "ladette" was first coined in the men's magazine *FHM* in 1994 to describe young women who adopt "laddish" behaviour in terms of boisterous assertiveness, heavy drinking, and sexual promiscuity. In Britain, it is frequently associated with young working-class women.
3. See Jackson and Tinkler.
4. See McRobbie.
5. See McRobbie and Roberts.
6. See Probyn and Projansky.
7. See Roberts.
8. See Brunsdon.
9. As Brenda Weber argues, the monarchy and the aristocracy are key points of reference in the reality makeover genre, functioning as models for the contestants' behaviour and appearance. See Weber (in this book).
10. While "cad" is defined in the *Oxford English Dictionary* as "a man who behaves dishonourably", one of the many female equivalents that is used elsewhere in the series is "slag", which is defined as "a prostitute or promiscuous woman". Thus, the label applied to women carries a more explicitly moral judgement that, in turn, reflects society's double standards with respect to "appropriate" sexual behaviour.
11. The potentially awkward relationship between the reality makeover show's rhetoric of authenticity (manifested in repeated references to the contestants' "inner selves") and its emphasis on the work of self-improvement is also raised by Weber (in this book).

Works cited

Brundson, C. *Screen Tastes*. London: Routledge, 1997.

Corner, J. "Documentary in a Post-Documentary Culture? A Note on Forms and their Functions" (2001). http://www.lboro.ac.uk/research/changing.media/John%Corner@20paper.htm. [Accessed August 1, 2009].

Day, K., B. Gough, and M. McFadden. " 'Warning! Alcohol can Seriously Damage Your Feminine Health': A Discourse Analysis of Recent British Newspaper

Coverage of Women and Drinking". *Feminist Media Studies* 4.2 (2004): 165–83.

Furedi, F. *Therapy Culture: Cultivating Vulnerability in an Uncertain Age.* London: Routledge, 2004.

Hollows, J. *Feminism, Femininity and Popular Culture.* Manchester: Manchester University Press, 2000.

Holmes, S., and D. Jermyn, eds. *Understanding Reality Television.* Abingdon: Routledge, 2004.

Hunt, A. "Domestic Dystopias: *Big Brother, Wife Swap and How Clean is Your House?" Feminism, Domesticity and Popular Culture.* Ed. S. Gillis, and J. Hollows. Abingdon: Routledge, 2009. 123–34.

Jackson, C., and P. Tinkler. " 'Ladettes' and 'Modern Girls': 'Troublesome' Young Femininities". *The Sociological Review* 55.2 (May 2007): 251–72.

Ladette to Lady. ITV. Series 1. June 2, 2005–June 30, 2005. 5 episodes.

——— ITV. Series 2. September 28, 2006–October 26, 2006. 5 episodes.

——— *End of Term Report.* ITV. December 14, 2006.

Levy, A. *Female Chauvinist Pigs: Women and the Rise of Raunch Culture.* New York: Free Press, 2006.

McRobbie, A. *The Aftermath of Feminism: Gender, Culture and Social Change.* London: Sage, 2009.

Moseley, R. "Glamorous Witchcraft: Gender and Magic in Teen Film and Television". *Screen* 43.4 (2002): 403–22.

Moseley, R., and J. Read. " 'Having it *Ally*': Popular Television (Post-)Feminism". *Feminist Media Studies* 2.2 (2002): 231–49.

Negra, D. " 'Quality Postfeminism?' Sex and the Single Girl in HBO". *Genders OnLine Journal* 39 (2004): 1–23.

Probyn, E. "New Traditionalism and Postfeminism: TV Does the Home". *Feminist Television Criticism: A Reader.* Ed. C. Brunsdon et al. Oxford: Blackwell, 1997.

Projansky, S. *Watching Rape: Film and Television in Postfeminist Culture.* New York: New York University Press, 2001.

Richardson, N. "As Kamp as Bree: The Politics of Camp Reconsidered by *Desperate Housewives". Feminist Media Studies* 6.3 (2006): 157–74.

Roberts, M. "The Fashion Police: Governing the Self in *What Not To Wear". Interrogating Postfeminism.* Ed. D. Negra, and Y. Tasker. Durham: Duke University Press, 2007.

Skeggs, B. *Class, Self, Culture.* London: Routledge, 2004.

Tasker, Y. *Working Girls: Gender and Sexuality in Popular Culture.* London: Routledge, 1998.

Tasker, Y., and D. Negra "In Focus: Postfeminism and Contemporary Media Studies". *Cinema Journal* 44.2 (2005): 107–10.

Whelehan, I. *Overloaded: Popular Culture and the Future of Feminism.* London: The Woman's Press, 2000.

11
Performing Postfeminist Identities: Gender, Costume, and Transformation in Teen Cinema

Sarah Gilligan

From Hollywood classics such as *Now Voyager* (1942), *My Fair Lady* (1964), and *Pretty Woman* (1990) to TV lifestyle programming such as *What Not to Wear* (2001–07), *10 Years Younger* (2004–08), and *Gok's Fashion Fix* (2008–09), the makeover narrative is an endlessly repeated and eagerly consumed staple of popular culture. Prevailingly structured around three key components – namely the make-under, the makeover, and the final revelation/affirmation[1] – the makeover narrative implies that through the processes of consumption and feminization, the female protagonist will achieve social mobility, popularity, and the "prize" of (a new or rekindled) heterosexual romance. Through their formulaic structure, such texts work to establish the parameters of acceptable feminine appearance, while also offering viewers the vicarious visual pleasure of witnessing the protagonist's transformation from frump to bombshell.

By perpetuating class-based ideals of taste and appearance that are aggressively enforced through strategies of humiliation and intimidation, recent makeover franchises like *What Not to Wear* (2001–07) and *10 Years Younger* (2004–) have been interpreted as a form of "symbolic violence" against women (McRobbie 128). However, given these shows' reliance on a performative approach to gender – in which clothing, appearance, gestures, and utterances are rendered central to the construction and transformation of gendered identity – it is also possible to view the makeover narrative in more subversive terms.[2] As Judith Butler explains in *Gender Trouble*, after all, gender is not tethered in any straightforward sense to the biological configuration of a sexed body, but is, rather, only as real as its performance. Butler's approach, as Stella Bruzzi observes, emphasizes "the fluidity of identity and the construction of that identity simply at the moment of performance" (167).

In postfeminist transformation narratives such as *Pretty Woman*, the female protagonist is neither trapped in, nor rejecting of, her femininity. Instead, she uses it in order to gain control over her own life (Brunsdon 86). Thus, as a "series of enactments upon characters' bodies", garments and accessories can work to enhance female agency and facilitate fluidity between different versions of feminine identity (Bruzzi 167).

Unlike films such as *Pretty Woman, Clueless* (1995), and *Sex and the City: The Movie* (2008), or TV texts like *Gok's Fashion Fix* and *What Not to Wear*, teen films such as *Pretty in Pink* (1986), *Ghost World* (2001), *Save the Last Dance* (2001), and *She's All That* (1999) offer a space within which female protagonists can fashion feminine identities in ways that eschew the processes of conspicuous consumption. Rather than montages of shopping sequences and characters revelling in the pleasures of extortionately expensive designer items, teen films tend to fetishize vintage clothing, hand-me-downs, dressmaking, and stylistic experimentation as the means by which postfeminist subjectivities can be productively re-envisioned and performed. To use Bruzzi's terminology, these texts look "at", rather than "through", clothes, in order to refashion the makeover narrative for a postfeminist teen market (36).

This chapter analyses and interrogates the roles accorded to costume in the Hollywood teen film *She's All That*. Combining "traditional" theoretical approaches with more recent methodologies, I will show how the film uses costume to develop a visual discourse that not only functions as an important "storytelling" element of the mise-en-scene,[3] but also as an independent source of meaning and pleasure.[4] The film is essentially the story of a "plain Jane" named Laney Boggs, played by Rachel Leigh Cook, who believes she needs a makeover to become beautiful, popular, and to win the "prize" of a heterosexual relationship.[5] As Zack, the high-school prom king, accepts a bet that he can transform Laney from "scary and inaccessible" to prom queen material in 6 weeks, *She's All That* presents itself as an "amalgam of makeover giants" like *Now Voyager, Cinderella* (1950), and *My Fair Lady*, interweaving and reconfiguring features of the paradigmatic Pygmalion and Cinderella narratives for a contemporary audience (Ford and Mitchell 72).

Over the course of this chapter, I will argue that Laney is transformed from an outdated, anti-fashion, feminist stereotype into an image of the retro, pre-feminist[6] woman that recalls the iconic style of Audrey Hepburn. However, while *She's All That* seems to follow the arc of the Pygmalion narrative[7] – charting Laney's transformation into a fairly conventional sexual stereotype and the object of Zack's desires – her image is never fully stabilized. Instead, Laney is granted agency over her own image and has the ability to move between different "styles" of femininity. The final prom scene is not preceded by any straightforward "makeover" sequence, nor is her look determined by Zack's instructions or desires. Like the heroines of other postfeminist makeover narratives, then, Laney is never confined to a single, monolithic version of femininity; rather, exemplifying the playful approach to style that marks the postfeminist phenomenon of "Girl Power"[8] (with which the film's release was contemporaneous), Laney has access to a multiplicity of interchangeable feminine identities that are characterized by play, experimentation, transformation, and performance.

The make-under

In the context of the makeover narrative, the "make-under" plays an essential role in establishing the signifiers of dowdy and aberrant femininity. Since *Now Voyager*, these signifiers – namely poorly-fitting, unstylish, "unfeminine" clothing, unkempt hair, heavy brows, glasses, and a prevailing disinterest in cosmetics – have all functioned as clichéd indicators of a woman who needs a physical makeover in order to become attractive and achieve social acceptance. There are, in fact, two types of make-under: in the first, the subject starts out as "natural" or "made-under" and is subsequently "improved" through the processes of the makeover; in the second, conversely, the subject begins as "made-up", before being "made-under" to appear more "natural" (and thus desirable). The first use of the "make-under" is the most conventional and can be seen in films such as *Now Voyager, Sabrina* (1954), *Funny Face* (1957), *She's All That, Maid in Manhattan* (2002), and *A Cinderella Story* (2004), as well as in television programmes like *What Not to Wear, How to Look Good Naked* (2006–08), and *Gok's Fashion Fix*. In these texts, the woman undergoes a transformation from scruffy and dowdy (or carefree and childlike) to "made-up" through the acquisition of the accoutrements of "grown-up" femininity. The second type of make-under is far less common, but is exemplified to some extent by *Pretty Woman* and *Mean Girls* (2004), as well as by television programmes like BBC3's *Shag, Marry or Avoid* (2008–09), in which the participants' layers of cosmetics and revealing attire are traded in for clothes and make-up that speak to more "natural", understated versions of feminine style. Although these two kinds of make-under seem to operate in contrary directions, they are actually both about the same thing: attributing ultimate value to the beauty of the "real" woman. In both cases, however, the seemingly authentic beauty of the "real" woman reveals itself as a performative construction that is contingent upon specialist knowledge, strategic consumption, and sustained effort. Regardless of the work that lies behind it, this beauty – in order to be accepted as "real" – must be performed seamlessly, as an authentic, effortless, and thoroughly uncontrived expression of the subject's self. In the context of the make-under, then, "real" beauty is simply that which best disguises its artifice.

While acting as a prelude to the climactic moment of the reveal, the make-under also functions to build spectator identification by conjuring the illusion of ordinariness. If, in films such as *Now Voyager, Sabrina, Pretty Woman*, and *Maid in Manhattan*, glamour provides the key to social mobility, then one can argue that the functionality of clothing and the illusion of ordinariness is also class-specific. In *She's All That*, Laney is signalled as a Cinderella figure whose time outside school is dominated by housework, caring for her father and brother, or working part-time in a fast-food restaurant. This is best illustrated in the film's early scenes, when Laney's wardrobe of t-shirts, paint-splattered dungarees, Dr Marten boots, and thick-framed glasses is used to foreground the practical demands of her day-to-day life and signify her prioritization of functionality over fashion.

Questions about clothing, embodiment, and personal adornment have long been central to feminist debates about the relationship between patriarchy and women's oppression.[9] In the early scenes of *She's All That*, Laney's utilitarian costuming seems to feed into such debates through its indebtedness to dominant media stereotypes of the "masculinized" feminist woman. If Laney's additional penchant for 70s-style tie-dyed fabrics and batik detailing does imply her status as an artist, it is used more conspicuously to signify her lack of interest in contemporary trends. In the context of the postfeminist makeover narrative, then, Laney's clothes position her as a teen in need of a transformation. Laney's modest, retro-feminist costuming, her outsider status, her lack of interest in feminine dress, and her seeming reluctance to explore her (hetero)sexuality are enigmatic and threatening, signalling her difference from the other female characters, particularly the most popular girl in school (and Zack's ex-girlfriend), Taylor Vaughn.[10] Taylor sashays along the school corridors as though on a catwalk, dressed in an array of short, clingy, brightly coloured outfits. While Taylor conforms to a fairly traditional image of objectified femininity, Laney's baggy dungarees and Dr Martens testify to her rejection of this image, and although she is never explicitly identified as a "feminist", her appearance works to imply her status as such.[11]

Although the cinematic cliché of the transformation from "unflatteringly ridiculous to respected" is problematic in the sense that it diminishes the girl's "intellectual authority", the actual processes of transformation and the surrounding discourses of femininity remain worthy of investigation (Shary 243). After all, the narrative tensions between intellect and image are not only integral to the discourses of transformation and conformity, but also occupy a central role in ongoing debates about feminism, femininity, and postfeminist identity.

Makeover potential

In the makeover film, the female protagonist's makeover "potential" is most usually identified by a male character. In the case of *She's All That*, it is Zack who recognizes Laney's potential when she removes her glasses at the end of their first date. This implies that feminine beauty, though hidden, can be detected and subsequently revealed by the discerning male. As Mary Ann Doane discusses in her analysis of *Now Voyager*, glasses simultaneously signify "intellectuality and undesirability". It is only when her glasses are removed that a woman can become a "spectacle, the very picture of desire", in what Doane argues is "one of the most intense visual clichés of the cinema" (139). Functioning as a key, transformative moment, the "glasses scene" is knowingly represented and subverted in *She's All That* as an eagerly anticipated, yet humorous, cliché. As Laney and Zack stand at the traffic lights, Zack pauses, looks at Laney, and asks: "Do you always wear those glasses?" While Laney initially averts her gaze, she internalizes the makeover "moment", turns to face Zack and briefly removes her glasses. The moment is fleeting and it is only when Laney puts her glasses back on that she makes direct and lingering eye contact with Zack, who raises his hands to her face and declares, "Because your eyes are really... beautiful". Rather than playing to audience expectations and removing Laney's glasses to reveal her beauty once again, Zack pushes them further up her nose. The contradiction between Zack's words and his actions work to subvert the spectator's expectations of the revelatory "glasses moment" in Hollywood cinema. With her glasses still firmly in place, Laney is able to see and analyse the moment; she is not, then, reduced to the position of erotic spectacle. The camera cuts back to reveal a mid-shot of Laney, her face aghast as she realizes Zack's intentions:

LANEY: Oh please.
ZACK: What?
LANEY: Your eyes are really beautiful. You really broke out the guns with that one didn't you?

ZACK: Laney I was...
LANEY: No. I had an instinct, I went against it. This is my fault.

As Doane explains, glasses in film tend to signify an "active looking" rather than a deficiency in sight. Through the woman's possession of the look and "in usurping the gaze she poses a threat to the entire system of representation" (140). Laney's active status is also made manifest in her physical gestures; during her confrontation with Zack she first strides away from him, then turns back to admonish him further:

> You want to know about art? When the class president starts touching my face on darkened street corners and talks about my eyes, there's a word for it. There's entire movement devoted to it in the 20s: it's called surreal [*sic*].

By undermining narrative expectations, this scene destabilizes the power of the male protagonist; Zack is left standing motionless, alone and silenced, while Laney is established as the locus of identification in the scene.[12]

The makeover

The parallels between *She's All That* and the Cinderella/Pygmalion narrative are writ large throughout the film. While Zack differs from Henry Higgins, his Pygamalion counterpart, in the sense that he neither tutors nor supervises Laney's makeover (Ford and Mitchell 75), he does instigate her transformation by providing the dress, the "mice" (in the form of the soccer team), and the fairy godmother (his sister Mac). As Linda Mizejewski has discussed elsewhere, makeover narratives promise a "miraculous transformation" through the combination of "expert instruction" and the "use of specific cosmetics" (168). Glamour is signified by the red, silk, spaghetti-strapped dress that Zack gives to Laney. In *Pretty Woman*, when Vivien is "allowed" to shop and indulge in conspicuous consumption, her natural beauty enables her to pass as Edward's girlfriend (Wartenberg 319). Conversely, in *She's All That*, Laney expresses her concern at not possessing enough natural beauty to conform to Zack's ideal version of feminine glamour, and when she sees her red dress she exclaims, "Oh my God! I'm such a mess".

The scene that follows closely patterns Vivien's shopping sequence in *Pretty Woman*. Rather than a montage of pleasurable "dressing up" and conspicuous consumption, however, the transformation sequence in

She's All That implies that changing one's appearance is hard work: eye-brows are plucked, cosmetics are applied, and hair is restyled as Laney endeavours to cultivate a contemporary feminine appearance. Laney's new haircut is, perhaps, the key element of her transformation. The cut-ting of Laney's long, dark hair not only serves to update her "retro" look, but also signals a moment of transition within the narrative, charting her movement from adolescence to a performance of adult femininity. The cutting or restyling of hair is a recurring motif in makeover films, and is a pivotal feature of *Roman Holiday* (1953), *Funny Face*, and *Slid-ing Doors* (1998). Laney's new hairstyle – a centre-parted bob – is not as short as Audrey Hepburn's hair in *Roman Holiday* and *Funny Face*, or Gwyneth Paltrow's cut in *Sliding Doors*, but it still marks a clear shift to a less fussy and freer style, which, in turn, indicates her conformity to contemporary ideals of pretty (but not overtly sexual) femininity.

Laney's transformation is also self-consciously remarked upon, as Mac announces her entrance: "Gentlemen, may I present the new, not improved, but different Laney Boggs". Here, the spectator, along-side Zack, waits at the foot of the staircase for the new Laney to be revealed; in a knowing allusion to earlier films like *Now Voyager* or *Rebecca* (1940), Laney's careful descent signals her passage into woman-hood. As Deborah Cartmell et al. reflect, the staircase here functions as a "symbolic bridge" between the private space of girlhood and the world of "social womanhood", as stairs lead to the foyer and to the front door, which is the threshold between the familial home and "the world" (36–37). Zack looks through the spindles of the staircase (much as Claude Raines does in *Now Voyager*) to reveal a close up of Laney's feet and legs. Laney's Dr Marten boots, with all their connotations of mas-culinity, androgyny, and butch-dyke lesbianism, have been substituted by a pair of red high-heeled sandals; as modern day "ruby slippers", they promise to transport Laney into another world – that of popularity and heterosexual romance. The shoes mark a radical change in style, from functionalism to eroticism. The block heel, open toe, thick sole, and ankle strap establish Laney's fashionable status, while simultaneously situating her as an object of erotic spectacle. The block heel, in partic-ular, gives Laney power and authority, and though it is not as overtly fetishistic as an elongated, stiletto heel, it does draw attention to the shape and flesh of her newly exposed legs. The open-toe design of the strappy sandals makes the foot the focus of erotic attention by drawing attention to Laney's painted toenails. Similarly, the visible enslavement of the foot in the ankle straps hints at bondage; while the elevated platform soles might be interpreted as erotic, however, they can also "signify high status", as Valerie Steele has discussed in her work on fashion and fetishism (98). As the camera pans up Laney's body to reveal her tight, red dress – which, again, accentuates her previously hidden curves and cleavage – she comes to occupy, and self-consciously perform, the familiar role of the eroticized, objectified woman. As Ford and Mitchell argue, Laney now "looks like everybody else", because in order "to be seen as beautiful, you must comply with current trends" (76). This observation, in turn, recalls Moseley's argument that recent teen films, including *She's All That*, are narratives that centre on "correcting the aberrant femininity" ("Glamorous Witchcraft" 405).

As Laney pauses for effect on the staircase, it is not only Zack's approval that she gains, but also that of her brother and Mac, who convey delight through their surprised and smiling expressions. Still, just as the film appears to play out this narrative cliché, Laney – freshly invested with the power of her own glamour – takes her final steps and falls down the stairs; the music, meanwhile, screeches to a halt. The high shoes draw attention to her attempts at passing as an adult, sexual woman. Laney's fall acts as moment of slippage, her gawky, adolescent self revealed in a lapsed moment of concentration. As she stumbles and falls into Zack's arms, the illusion of both glamour and height is broken, as it becomes clear just how small and childlike she is. Yet, rather than allowing herself to be "rescued", Laney pulls away, looking embarrassed, quickly attempting to retain her composure, and with it recuperate her performance of grown-up femininity.

Performing power feminism

While I agree with Robin Wood that "Laney is so obviously attractive" that all she ever will need is a better hairdo and some makeup (10), Laney's makeover signals her transformation into an image of the postfeminist woman. As Laney descends the stairs at Preston's party, she initially enjoys her newfound relationship with fashion and glamour, adhering to the postfeminist image of the "power feminist", who uses clothing as an expression of her individuality. Natasha Walter in *The New Feminism* calls for postfeminism to "free itself from the spectre of political correctness" and bury for good the "old myth about feminists, that they all wear dungarees and are lesbians and socialists" (4–5). Arguing that "we do not all have to dress the same" (5), Walter highlights that women actually have a "wickedly enjoyable relationship" with "their clothes and their bodies". This relationship, she contends, is intrinsically sensual and is marked by fantasy, role play, transformation, and escapism (86). Following Walter's argument, the made-over Laney luxuriates in the admiring male gazes she attracts, and also wins female approval. Having been ridiculed previously by Taylor's friends, Alex and Katie, they suddenly want to talk to her and be seen with her. As Walter goes on to explain, while clothing can be read as the means by which women become the passive objects of the masculine gaze, it can also be seen as enabling a productive discourse of appreciation, pleasure, respect, admiration, and shared knowledge between women (89–90).

A seemingly problematic outcome for the postfeminist woman with an interest in fashion is the potential for competition with other women. A battle ensues in which the "waspy, wealthy, young and beautiful" exist at the top of the pyramid (Douglas 224). Instead of a collective "sisterhood" binding women together "across ethnic, class, generational and regional lines", individualism and competition have the negative effect of dividing women (Douglas qtd. in Heywood and Drake 43). As a consequence of Laney's acceptance by some of the "in-crowd", Taylor's position as the most popular girl in school is placed under direct threat. When Laney bumps into Taylor, she is met with disdain and scorn as the girls mirror each other's costuming with their red dresses. Towering over Laney, Taylor attacks her by pouring a drink down Laney's dress. As a clone of Taylor Vaughn, Laney has seemingly lost her individuality and is reduced to a snivelling wreck as she stumbles outside the house. On one hand, then, the dress functions to propose conformity, rather than individuality, as the path to acceptance and popularity. Yet, although the scene can be read as negative, there is the possibility of casting it in more positive terms: by approaching clothes as props, Laney is able to cast off items and styles which do not work, choosing instead to develop and adapt her own, original look. Laney's "old" confidence and "new" interest in her appearance are jointly reflected in her coupling of familiar, trademark garments, such as dungarees, with her refashioned hair and makeup, as she (like Taylor) sashays down the corridors of the school and revels in her newfound popularity.

Performing the retro pre-Feminist

For Laney, the climatic prom scene provides a space in which the difficult balancing act between adolescent transformation and self-acceptance is achieved. The prom is not simply a moment of "becoming", but a space in which – through clothing – teens make sense of what it means to be young and "solidify their social identities" (Best 2). One would expect, therefore, as a culturally determined, pivotal moment in the transition between adolescence and adulthood, that narrative time in *She's All That* would be dedicated to representing Laney's anticipation and preparations for the prom. In *Pretty in Pink*, Andie's inability to buy a new dress for the prom becomes a marker of her class status and provides a narrative space for the expression of individuality, as she is forced to create her own dress through a combination of old dresses. In *She's All That*, there are no scenes of Laney's preparations, dressmaking, consumption, or the work of femininity. For the girls in Amy Best's ethnographic study, the preparations for the prom were "as important as the end product", whereas Laney seemingly goes from scruffy clothes to prom dress without any effort (40).

Rather than making a grand entrance at the prom (like Sam in *A Cinderella Story*), Laney is revealed already on the dance floor. Despite dancing with the other students, Laney's difference is marked through her costuming. She adopts the epitome of understated, chic, sophisticated attire: a black ankle-length, spaghetti-strapped shift dress, with her hair swept up into a French chignon. Even when Laney dances, she is not shown to be overly sexual (like Taylor in her showy, clingy, gold dress); instead, attention is drawn to what she is wearing and to her face. Laney's prom outfit can therefore be read as the outcome of a second makeover, where instead of shifting from "natural" or "made-under" to made-up (as she does in her first makeover, with the red dress), Laney moves from the made-up version of femininity represented by the red dress to a more "natural" look. Laney's understated elegance conveys a similar image to that of Audrey Hepburn – an image of "natural" femininity which is regarded as both authentic and appealing.

Sensible, yet sensual, a black dress neither talks too much nor "enters the room before its wearer" (Holman Eldeman 142). As Hepburn demonstrated in *Breakfast at Tiffany's*, with a classic little black dress and a string of pearls you can go anywhere, making the dress the ultimate transformative garment for women, the perfect masquerade. Laney's look, while alluding to Hepburn (especially through the casting of Rachel Leigh Cook), does not explicitly copy the iconic Hepburn image. It is even more pared down, without sunglasses, pearls, or props. The only ornamentation is the black sequinned beading on the dress, which gently catches the light as Laney moves, without being overtly flashy. The cut of the dress makes it appear fluid; the sequins reflect the light, making it appear hard like armour. Through the absence of scenes of consumption, one could speculate that the dress originally belonged to Laney's mother. Like the ring that Laney wears around her neck, the dress connects her to her mother by creating a protective (maternal) shield; through the literal and symbolic safety of the black dress,[13] then, Laney is able to remain a child while still performing adult femininity. Laney's unspectacular clothes actually draw our gaze in, leading her to appear far more beautiful than the extravagant, showy Taylor. In drawing attention to her face, Laney's look both further alludes to Hepburn's understated style and embodies Chanel's notion that a dress is well designed if people say, "what a beautiful woman".[14]

The allusion to Hepburn's style in the costuming of Laney is interesting in terms of what the adoption of such a pre-second wave image signifies for the postfeminist woman. According to Elizabeth Wilson, the 1950s of our collective imagination has been transformed "into a world of lost innocence" that "anticipated a different and freer kind of 60s innocence" (1993, 36). For the postfeminist woman, then, Hepburn embodies an idealized "have it all" state in which she is both intelligent and beautiful, independent yet still desired by a man. The free, bohemian image of Hepburn in capri pants, ballet pumps, and black sweaters (represented in films like *Funny Face*) signifies a playful, youthful image of femininity, which is coupled with the performance of "grown-up" femininity where Hepburn wears a collection of elegant designer dresses.[15]

The central pleasures of Hepburn's look (and its re-appropriation within *She's All That*) lie in the duality of the image, together with Hepburn's existence in a transitional space in which (as in the iconic, endlessly reproduced shot from *Breakfast at Tiffany's*) grown-up clothes tend to signify a playful attempt at "dressing up". Glamorous femininity thus becomes one of many possible images that can be played at. It is not that Laney "becomes" the pre-second wave image that Hepburn embodies, but rather that she uses the space of the prom to dress as a grown-up woman before entering adulthood. The prom "provides an occasion to shed one's school identity and become someone else, even if only for one night" (Best 18). It operates, therefore, as an illusionary space between the imagination and reality, which enables the performance of gendered identity in the pursuit of heterosexual romance. Despite her attempts to perform an idealized, pre-second wave image of normative femininity, Laney is not willing to "do gender" enough to pass and win the title of Prom Queen. She performs the look without substance or meaning. As she kisses her handsome prince under the fairy lights by the pool, Laney declares: "I feel like Julia Roberts in *Pretty Woman* – except without the whole hooker thing". Through the prize of heterosexual romance, Laney is saved from her outsider status and might even be regarded as upholding a pre-feminist model of femininity through her seeming desire for a fairytale ending. Still, through its position as a teen transformation film, Laney's position is more fluid than Vivien's in *Pretty Woman*, and in this way she marks another shift in postfeminist representations of women. As a postfeminist teenager, Laney adheres in part to Brunsdon's category of the "post-feminist girlie" who "has ideas about her life and being in control which clearly come from feminism" (86). Yet unlike Cher and Dionne in *Clueless*, Laney is interested in more than surface appearances; equally, however, she does not end up becoming another "tough" postfeminist character such as Buffy. Laney therefore forms part of a shift in teen representations that includes characters such as Sara and Chenille (*Save the Last Dance* [2001]), Enid and Rebecca (*Ghost World* [2001]), Sam in *A Cinderella Story* and Cady in *Mean Girls* (2004) who each, in their differing ways, possess independence, intelligence, resilience, and often a desire to progress academically. It is not that the girls reject normative femininity, but that by the end of the narrative they each want social and geographic mobility, good looks, and a perfect heterosexual romance. Cady in *Mean Girls*, for instance, rejects the vacuous "plastics", repents, regains her friendships, wins the maths contest, and still gets the guy.[16]

Yet the acquisition of the heterosexual romance does not mark the happy ever after, as it occurs at a moment of change: the girls are, after all, on the cusp of adulthood, nearing the end of their time at High School. With their adult futures ahead of them, these girls get to escape and move on, without being represented and punished as career-orientated, power-hungry Superwomen, like those in 1980s postfeminist backlash films such as *Fatal Attraction* (1987) and *Working Girl* (1988). For Laney, being Zack's girlfriend is just another identity that she tries on before going to away to college. The spectator in such teen films is thus given the pleasure of a feel-good, escapist happy ending, without being required to witness the confinement of the young women to any fixed (and thus potentially problematic) identity. As fictional postfeminist figures they get to have it all: the narrative ends before the complications of the future commence.

Notes

1. For further discussion of cinematic makeovers, see Ford and Mitchell. See also Moseley, "Glamorous Witchcraft". For a more thorough analysis of television makeovers, see Heller and McRobbie. Also see the chapters by Weber, Smith, and Genz in this book.

2. For a discussion of performative approaches to gender, see Butler. For analysis of the ways in which costume functions in contemporary cinema to support the construction of identity, see Bruzzi.
3. See Gaines.
4. See Bruzzi and Church Gibson.
5. The allusions to Pygmalion and Cinderella were a recurring feature of the film's reviews in the press. See Macnab, Ellas, Collins, Fisher, Preston, and Cliff.
6. I use the term "pre-feminist" to refer to models of feminine identity that predate the advent of second wave feminism, in particular. Elsewhere in the chapter, I use the term "pre-second wave".
7. Originating from the Greek myth of Ovid's Metamorphosis, the figure of Pygmalion is a sculptor who carves a statue of his ideal woman (Galatea). Falling in love with his representation, the goddess Aphrodite takes pity on him and brings the statue to life.
8. "Girl Power" is a media phenomenon that emerged in the 1990s and which is largely associated with the success of the Spice Girls. As Stéphanie Genz observes, the term is typically used as "a media-friendly way of articulating a playful, sexualised subjectivity and agency that resist more passive, compliant versions of femininity" (87).
9. For examples and discussion of second wave feminist activism and debates surrounding clothes, appearance, and women, see Brownmiller, Thornham, Church Gibson ("Dressing the Balance"), and Wilson (*Adorned in Dreams*).
10. The representation of Taylor self-consciously parodies the teen film stereotype of the vapid, vacuous popular girl. Spoilt and self-obsessed, she lacks the warmth of Cher in *Clueless* and instead is more like the cliquey popular girls in films such as *Heathers* (1988) and *Mean Girls*.
11. Through her portrayal as the artistic feminist, Laney exists as a permissible, creative force, using media images to explore the victims of riots and the position of silenced women in sweatshops.
12. A second such moment occurs when Zack and his friends see Laney strip off her dungarees to reveal a classic black swimsuit. Dean declares "Check out the bobos on superfreak".
13. This need for protection is made explicit when Dean attempts to date rape Laney.
14. See Bruzzi and Holdman Edelman for a discussion of Chanel and style.
15. See *Funny Face* (1957), *Sabrina* (1954), *Breakfast at Tiffany's* (1961). Also see Moseley, *Growing Up with Audrey Hepburn*.
16. See Church Gibson, "Where Feminists Fear to Tread".

Works cited

Baum, Rob. "After the Ball is Over: Bringing Cinderella Home". *Cultural Analysis: An Interdisciplinary Forum on Folklore and Popular Culture* 1 (2000). The University of California. http://socrates.berkeley.edu/~caforum/volume1/pdf/baum.pdf. [Accessed January 18, 2009].

Best, Amy. *Prom Night: Youth, Schools and Popular Culture*. London and New York: Routledge, 2000.

Brownmiller Susan. *Femininity*. London: H. Hamilton, 1984.

Brunsdon, Charlotte. *Screen Tastes*. London and New York: Routledge, 1997.

Bruzzi, Stella. *Undressing Cinema: Clothing and Identity in the Movies*. London and New York: Routledge, 1997.

Butler, Judith. *Gender Trouble: Feminism and the Subversion of Identity*. 10th Anniversary edn. London and New York: Routledge, 1999.

Cartmell, Deborah, Imelda Whelehan, and Heidi Kaye, eds. *Sisterhoods: Feminists in Film and Fiction*. London: Pluto Press, 1998.

Church Gibson, Pamela. "Where Feminists Might Fear to Tread: Radical Shifts within Contemporary Popular Culture". Keynote address at the *Feminism and Popular Culture Conference*. Newcastle University (July 2007).

———— "Dressing the Balance: Patriarchy, Post Modernism and Feminism". *Fashion Cultures*. Ed. Stella Bruzzi, and Pamela Church Gibson. London and New York: Routledge, 2000. 349–62.

———— "Film Costume". *The Oxford Guide to Film Studies*. Ed. Pamela Church Gibson, and John Hill. Oxford and New York: Oxford University Press, 1998.

Cliff, Nigel. "*She's All That*". Film Rev. *The Times*. May 20, 1999.

Collins, Andrew. "The Best Days of Your Life? No Way". *The Observer* May 2, 1999.

Doane, Mary Ann. "Film and the Masquerade: Theorising the Female Spectator" (1982). Reprinted in *Feminist Film Theory: A Reader*. Ed. Sue Thornham. Edinburgh: Edinburgh University Press, 1999. 131–45.

Douglas, Susan. *Where the Girls Are*. London: Penguin Books, 1995.

Ellas, Justine. "*She's All That*". Film Rev. *The Village Voice*. 9 February 1999.

Fisher, Nick. "*She's All That*". Film Rev. *The Sun*. May 25, 1999.

Ford, Elizabeth, and Deborah Mitchell. *The Makeover in the Movies*. Jefferson and London: McFarland, 2004.

Gaines, Jane. "Costume and Narrative: How Dress Tells the Woman's Story". *Fabrications: Costume and the Female Body*. Ed. Jane Gaines, and Charlotte Herzog. New York and London: AFI and Routledge, 1990. 192–96.

Genz, Stéphanie. *Postfemininities in Popular Culture*. Basingstoke: Palgrave, 2009.

Heller, Dana Alice, ed. *Makeover Television: Realities Remodelled*. London: I B Tauris, 2007.

Heywood, Leslie, and Jennifer Drake. *Third Wave Agenda*. Manchester: University of Manchester Press, 1997.

Holman Edelman, Amy. *The Little Black Dress*. London: Aurum Press, 1997.

Macnab, Geoffrey. "*She's All That*". Film Rev. *Sight and Sound*. July 1999.

McRobbie, Angela. *The Aftermath of Feminism*. London: Sage, 2009.

Mizejewski, Linda. *Hardboiled & High Heeled*. London and New York: Routledge, 2004.

Moseley, Rachel. *Growing Up with Audrey Hepburn*. Manchester: Manchester University Press, 2002.

———— "Glamorous Witchcraft: Gender and Magic in Teen Film and Television". *Screen* 43.4 (2002): 403–22.

Preston, Peter. "*She's All That*". Film Rev. *The Observer*. May 23, 1999.

Roberts, Martin. "The Fashion Police: Governing the Self in *What Not to Wear*". *Interrogating Postfeminism: Gender and the Politics of Popular Culture*. Ed. Yvonne Tasker, and Diane Negra. Durham and London: Duke University Press, 2007. 227–77.

Shary, Timothy. "The Nerdly Girl and Her Beautiful Sister". *Sugar and Spice and All Things Nice*. Ed. Frances K. Gateward, and Murray Pomerance. Detroit: Wayne State University Press, 2002. 235–53.

She's All That. Dir. Robert Izcove. Miramax, 1999.

Steele, Valerie. *Fetish: Fashion, Sex and Power*. Oxford: Oxford University Press, 1996.

Thornham, Sue. *Passionate Detachments*. Edinburgh: Arnold, 1997.

Walter, Natasha. *The New Feminism*. London: Virago, 1999.

Wartenberg, Thomas E. "Shopping Esprit: *Pretty Woman*'s Deflection of Social Criticism". *Hollywood Goes Shopping*. Ed. David Desser, and Garth S. Jowett. Minneapolis: University of Minnesota Press, 2000. 309–30.

Wilson, Elizabeth. *Adorned in Dreams* (1985). London: IB Tauris, 2005.

——— "Audrey Hepburn: Fashion, Film and the 50s". *Women and Film*. Ed. Pam Cook, and Philip Dodds. London: Scarlet Press, 1993. 36–40.

Wood, Robin. "Party Time, or Can't Hardly Wait for That *American Pie:* Hollywood High School Movies of the 90s". *Cineaction* 58 (June 2002): 2–10.

Part IV
Violence

12

Return of the "Angry Woman": Authenticating Female Physical Action in Contemporary Cinema

Lisa Purse

A woman lies on her back in lush grass, eyes half-closed, panting gently – hair slightly mussed, but make-up perfect. This assemblage of signifiers speaks more of conventional cinematic representations of female sexual abandon than other kinds of physical activity. And yet this is a shot from the end of a busy action sequence in *Aeon Flux* (2005), in which the woman in question – after a running shoot-out in which she incapacitates scores of enemy guards – has just blown up a zeppelin, then been swept hundreds of metres through the air suspended from the exploding structure, finally throwing herself at the ground as the zeppelin ditches into a wall in front of her. The woman is Aeon (Charlize Theron), the heroine of the title, and this is the final action sequence of the film. Despite this, Aeon does not display any biological traces of her recent dramatic and extended physical exertion, such as a flushed face, perspiration, heavily laboured breathing, or the facial scrapes and dirt she might be expected to have picked up in the circumstances. The physical work of action has been elided, and leaves no traces on the body of the actor.

Here, and throughout the film, Aeon's face remains undamaged, undirtied, and carefully made-up; where injuries do happen they are minor and occur on other parts of the body, such as a shoulder or arm. An earlier action sequence plays on this facial untouchability; she and colleague Sithandra (Sophie Okonedo) are trying to cross a hostile garden territory in which grass metamorphoses into real blades. Sithandra lands on her hands, incurring multiple angry puncture wounds, and as Aeon tumbles headfirst towards another cluster of blades, the risk of her features being similarly punctured looms large. She prevents impact by using her legs to steady herself, but for a moment the blades wave malevolently in close-up just millimetres from her face. The film is invested in "protecting" Aeon's face and make-up from harm because, in this way, a key conventional marker of her femininity can be maintained. Another conventional marker of this femininity is her costuming, tightly fitted to emphasize her curves and the graceful lines of balletic movement she achieves in the action sequences (it is still the case that attributes such as grace and fluidity are often associated with femininity in dominant discourses about gender). Such strategies in the presentation of female physical action are also observable in a range of other films since the millennium, such as *The Mummy* (1999, 2001, 2008), *X-Men* (2000, 2003, 2006), *Lara Croft: Tomb Raider* (2001, 2003), the *Charlie's Angels* films (2000, 2003), *Underworld* (2003, 2006, 2009), *Blade: Trinity* (2004), *Elektra* (2005), *Sin City* (2005), *Fantastic Four* (2005, 2007), *Ultraviolet* (2006), the *Pirates of the Caribbean* franchise (2003, 2006, 2007), and *Watchmen* (2009).

The prevalence and homogeneity of such representations bears further scrutiny, but so too does a dichotomous development that has emerged in the same period that these popular representations have predominated in mainstream US cinema. The active women in films like *Monster* (2003), *Hard Candy* (2005), and *The Brave One* (2007) are angry transgressors, their behaviours and actions locating them outside of dominant social norms, as well as outside mainstream codes of cinematic female representation. What is clear is that this is a contemporary moment in which conflicting representational impulses are at work. Set in opposition to dominant, "sanctioned" depictions of active femininity – of which *Aeon Flux* is a useful example – are alternative images of the active woman that are developed, primarily, within films that hover on the margins of the mainstream. This chapter investigates the co-presence and polarization of these different modes in the same cultural period, as well as asking what is at stake in these versions of the active female body: under what terms *is* contemporary mainstream cinema prepared to show active female physicality?

One of the explanations for Aeon Flux's superior physical agility and strength is the future world in which she exists, where technological advances make "upgrading" the body's capacities commonplace.[1] Notably, these are *invisible* upgrades, meaning that her conventional femininity does not have to be disrupted by naturalistic evidence of exertion or strength. This is quite a different presentational strategy to the one at work in the female action hero films of the 1980s and early 1990s, such as *Aliens* (1986) and *Terminator 2: Judgment Day* (1991), in which visibly pronounced musculature authenticated – that is, made more credible – the heroines' feats of physical action. Yvonne Tasker suggests that this muscular and physically assertive heroine posed "a challenge to gendered binaries through her very existence" (1998, 69). While her biological sex "fixed" her as female – setting up expectations of behaviour, dress, and appearance that are based on dominant constructions of femininity – "her qualities of strength and determination and, most particularly, her labour and the body that enacted it, marked her out as 'unfeminine' ".[2] Tasker argues that such films sought to resolve this challenge by attempting to offer a narrative explanation for the woman's actions, "to define her as exceptional" (69). In both *Terminator 2* and *Aliens*, for example, the heroine is defined by a maternal drive that is so strong it presses her into extreme action. The science fiction context is another qualifying frame: placing the women into alternative and future realities respectively, the films distance the protagonists from the spectator's own real-world reality, in which their actions might seem unduly threatening to dominant social hierarchies and behavioural norms. *Thelma and Louise* (1991) provides an instructive counter-example: its two female protagonists, driven to manslaughter and armed robbery by an attempted rape, are depicted in a naturalistic, contemporary, everyday setting; in the resulting media furore, journalists worried that thousands of women across the United States would copy the onscreen pair's actions.[3]

Mainstream cinema's project is typically to explain away, qualify, and often to actively "undermine...female potency as it becomes threatening", usually containing the threat by reinstating "archetypal femininity" (Bruzzi 180). While the muscular heroines of the 1980s and early 1990s problematized this containment strategy in the realm of the visual, by the later 1990s and the 2000s the reinstatement of archetypal femininity was much more carefully and systematically enforced. The popularity of small-screen action heroines in series like *Xena: Warrior Princess* (1995–2001), *Buffy the Vampire Slayer* (1997–2003), and *Alias* (2001–06) had inspired a fresh influx of active women in cinema, but these women's displays of strength were qualified by particular narrative, aesthetic, and representational strategies. I want to briefly consider these strategies in the context of contemporary notions of postfeminism.[4]

In films like *Charlie's Angels, Lara Croft: Tomb Raider, Blade: Trinity, Mr & Mrs Smith, Wanted* (2008), and the *Resident Evil* films (2002, 2004, 2007), female heroes combine their readily apparent strength and skill with a more traditionally feminine, and often emphatically sexualized, physique. Tasker has called these action heroines "post-feminist", and they seem to encapsulate the "have-it-all" claims of certain strands of postfeminist discourse (2004, 9). Strong, intelligent, and resourceful, they are also highly feminine in their appearance and costume. Marc O'Day has suggested that such movies break apart the binary logic that underlies traditional conceptions of gendered behaviour because they *"assume that women are powerful"* without resorting to the conventional negative narrative explanations for female aggression – maternal instinct, rape-revenge, terrorization by a serial killer (216; emphasis in original). Nevertheless, O'Day's catchall term for these films is "action babe cinema", a phrase that revealingly resonates with connotations of objectification, visual assessment, and gender stereotyping. The contemporary action heroine enacts a sexualized femininity to which display is central; while these women are physically active, independent agents, then, there is no doubt that their bodies are also being eroticized within the terms of a conventionally objectified femininity. Sporting a range of conventionally gendered, close-fitting, and revealing outfits, they appear uncannily similar to the semi-naked gun-toting girls of 1970s exploitation flicks like *Caged Heat* (1974) and *Big Bad Mama* (1974). Pam Cook noted at the time that these earlier movies presented "serious problems" for second wave feminists, popularizing (with exploitation audiences) "an overtly coded, fetishized image of woman as sexual object" that counteracted her status as an active subject (123). Taking this into account, then, is the contemporary action heroine's status as active subject and sexualized object any less problematic?

In a postfeminist cultural context, sexualized display is often characterized as an active choice made by women who have already benefited from second wave feminism's campaigns for gender equality. Robert Goldman, Deborah Heath, and Sharon L. Smith note how "[m]eanings of choice and individual freedom become wed to images of sexuality in which women apparently choose to be seen as sexual objects because it suits their liberated interests" (338). As Sarah Projansky has pointed out, however, this position – predicated on the assumption that feminism is somehow no longer necessary – reveals its own white, middle-class bias: only women in particular economic and social positions can afford the luxury of choice (70). In this context, it is significant that the majority of current mainstream action heroines resemble white middle-class women. From luxury apartments and the uncanny ease of instantaneous international travel to top-of-the-range cars and bespoke outfits, the women of films like *Charlie's Angels*, *Underworld*, and *Wanted* signal their independence in terms of high-paying jobs and the resulting signifiers of wealth. Such movies offer not only fantasies of physical empowerment, but also fantasies of *economic* empowerment.[5] Still, if these heroines' revealing outfits and often sexually assertive behaviour are markers of their "liberation" in the fictional world of the film, their resulting status as sexual objects within the film text seems to com- modify that independence and agency, draining such representations of any radical thrust. Action heroism thus becomes another brand of "commodity feminism" (Goldman et al. 347). At the same time, it is notable that white women's empowerment is often achieved at the expense of women of other ethnicities: in *Resident Evil* the gutsy female Puerto Rican marine Rain (Michelle Rodriguez) becomes a sidekick for the white heroine Alice (Milla Jovovich), and dies before the film's end; in *Aeon Flux* Sithandra, played by an actress of part-Nigerian descent, also dies protecting the Caucasian Aeon. Such representations perpetu- ate and naturalize hierarchies of power and influence that are active in the wider society, complicating attempts to read them as progressive.

Sexual objectification and the perpetuation of dominant class and ethnic hierarchies are just some of the representational tropes that are regularly present when depictions of female physical empowerment are "permitted". Other common containment strategies are operational at the levels of narrative and/or cinematography. Each film locates the action within a generic context that is distanced from contemporary reality: many are ostensibly "present-day" settings, but in genres where the fantastic or supernatural are possible (*Elektra, Resident Evil*). Comedy is also a popular compensatory tactic, removing the need to "take these women seriously" (as exemplified by *Charlie's Angels*, the rather obvi- ous *My Super Ex-Girlfriend* [2006], and *Hancock* [2008]). Likewise, both narrative context and narrative closure often function to re-inscribe traditional feminine roles. Active women thus tend to be constructed as daughters – groomed for action by influential father figures,[6] as in *Elektra*, the *Charlie's Angels* films, *Lara Croft: Tomb Raider*, and the *Res- ident Evil* franchise – or as wives, in *Mr & Mrs Smith* and the *Fantastic Four* films. They are also, quite often, transformed into wives and/or mother figures at the narrative's close, as is the case in *Kill Bill: Vol 2* (2003), *Elektra, Aeon Flux*, and *Hancock*. Where the active woman co-exists alongside and coaches a central male protagonist into becom- ing powerful, she is most likely to have to "make way" for him, often through death: in the *Matrix* franchise Trinity (Carrie-Ann Moss) is rele- gated to the position of sidekick and love interest to Neo (Keanu Reeves), and in *Matrix Revolutions* is removed from the cinematic frame entirely when she killed in a crash. In *Wanted* the highly skilled assassin Fox (Angelina Jolie), who has helped recruit and train newcomer Wesley

(James McAvoy), commits suicide to save Wesley's life and to free him from the grip of a rogue assassins' organization. Also significant is the inclusion in such narratives of villains who signal the danger of "too much" female agency, power, or independence: *Charlie's Angels: Full Throttle* (2003) pits the heroines against an ex-Angel who is characterized as a revenge-obsessed loner. Skilled and independent, she has forsaken the group and Charlie's paternalistic leadership; notably, she is pathologized through her "masculine" love of guns, rather than the more "ladylike" martial arts combat style of the Angels. In *X-Men: The Last Stand* (2006), the timid Jean Grey is driven mad by telepathic and telekinetic powers that she is unable to control, becoming a divided – if primarily monstrous and murderous – figure who must be killed off.

As the examples above demonstrate, the physically active female protagonist is, for the most part, a figure whose "unladylike" bouts of violence are framed in ways that locate her at a distance from real life. In light of this, the re-inscription of traditional femininity has a further "off-setting" function, reasserting conservative behavioural "norms" that disconnect the feminine from the perpetration of physical aggression. The female heroine's physical potency is most damagingly qualified by the way in which her actions are not authenticated by reference to real-world laws of physics and physiology. In action sequences, the consequences of bodily momentum, weight, and collision that would be present in a more realistic rendering of the action are not conveyed. Moreover, physical markers of exertion and injury are virtually absent; recent films featuring female action heroes have tended to significantly downplay the physical pain and impact involved in action and combat sequences. Blood and other physical evidence of bodily impact are minimal: minor cuts are much more likely than more major, appearance-warping injuries such as swellings or broken bones. Moments of physical activity do not, then, intersect with realistic notions of the bodily consequences of violence, as this would unbalance the marketable hybrid formula of active hero and erotic object that the so-called "action babe" represents. Implicitly rejecting the sweat-drenched muscular exertions of earlier figures like Ripley, Sarah Connor, and Navy SEAL Jordan O'Neill in *GI Jane* (1997) as "inappropriate", these newer representations re-imagine the traditional heroic qualities of toughness and determination in ways that uphold conventional notions of gender, emphasizing the female action hero's "feminine" grace, dignity, and (well-maintained) appearance.

In a contemporary Western culture frequently characterized as postfeminist, then, these women seem to represent the "acceptable

face" – and body – of female empowerment: predominantly white, heterosexual, frequently scantily clad, and enjoying the trappings of a
middle-class lifestyle. But in this homogenous and rather "safe" set of
mainstream depictions, particular kinds of spectacles are suppressed in
relation to the active female body: images of physical stress and extension; the biological consequences of exertion and violence; and the
dangerous motivations that drive aggressive acts. However, the untidy
female exertions refused in popular "action babe" representations are
now erupting into view in a number of other contemporaneous movies.
These movies might be understood as constituting a cinematic "return
of the repressed",[7] as through their visceral and realistic portrayals of
female physicality they represent, precisely, what has been subdued
within (or entirely cast out of) mainstream accounts of female action.
In the second half of this chapter I want to turn my attention to the
small number of films which – despite occupying different generic and
production contexts – offer depictions of a female physicality that has
been rendered invisible in most quarters of contemporary mainstream
US cinema.

Patty Jenkins' *Monster* (2003) is a film based on the life of Aileen
Wuornos, a Michigan prostitute who was put to death in Florida in 2002
for the murder of several men. The film's opening montage sequence
proposes the factors contributing to her present state as an unhappy,
alienated, aggressive alcoholic and destitute prostitute, which include
(but are probably not limited to) child abuse, domestic violence, and
sexualization at an early age. From the outset, then, Aileen is firmly
established as an outsider. Despite Aileen's verbalized wish to "be beautiful and rich like the women on TV", the film – through a complex
performance (from Charlize Theron) and make-up effects – emphasizes
the range of ways in which her body does not "fit". Lank hair, pock-
marked, puffy features, a large frame, and an awkward gait distance her
from conventional conceptions of femininity. In addition, her failed or
half-hearted attempts to perform a commodified femininity – for example when she attempts to talk dirty to johns, or says the wrong thing
at a job interview – jarringly foreground both the rules of gendered
behaviour and her non-compliance. Still, it is the depiction of Aileen's
first murder that both narrativizes her aggression and offers a spectacle
of authentic physical action, mobilizing elements emphatically denied
in mainstream representations.

Aileen needs money for a date with her new girlfriend Selby (Christina
Ricci), and, soliciting at night on a busy road, she gets picked up by
Vincent Corey (Lee Tergesen), who brings the car to a halt in secluded

woodland. After some awkward small talk Aileen expresses reluctance to perform fellatio on Corey, and in response he beats her unconscious. Waking up bloodied and groggy, Aileen finds herself face down on plastic sheeting inside the car, her wrists tied; as she struggles to free herself, Corey asks her if she wants to die, brutally rapes her with a tyre iron, kicks her and douses her with bleach. In the brief moment it takes Corey to stow the bleach bottle back in the car boot Aileen struggles and screams so violently that she manages to free her wrists from their bindings. She quickly pulls a gun from her handbag and starts firing at Corey, not stopping until her ammunition is spent and he lies dying on the ground.

The rape scene is presented in medium close-up, a shallow depth of field bringing Aileen's dazed and blood-smeared face into sharp focus closest to the camera in an image that contrasts sharply with representations of the perfectly made-up, untouchable female face in *Aeon Flux*. Shallow staging foreshortens the space of the car, intensifying the claustrophobic effect of the shot, so that Corey's vicious attacks feel "too close", like an invasion of one's personal space. The staging prevents a clear view of what is being done to Aileen's body: we access the violence not through its spectacle (which risks sensationalizing or eroticizing the event) but through glimpses of Corey's instruments of torture and, much more importantly, Aileen's facial reactions; her struggle for comprehension; her silent cry as she experiences the physical and mental agony of the rape; and her shocked, agitated screams as the bleach burns into her skin. Her will to resist this horrific attack is expressed in the moment when she finds her "voice", the silent scream becoming an audible shriek of rage. Significantly, Aileen's howls mark her passage from victim to perpetrator; they begin towards the end of Corey's attack, continue during the series of gunshots she fires while propelling herself out of the car, and recur sporadically until long after Corey is dead. The vocal delivery, pitch, and persistence of these howls not only convey Aileen's rage but also her frustration at having been first compelled to endure the attack and then forced to lethally retaliate. As the gun is fired, two shots from the rapist's point of view frame the bloodied, brutalized female body as it projects itself into forceful retaliation. Out of the dark car interior Aileen moves towards the camera, wild-eyed, still screaming, still firing; her face is only fleetingly in focus in these shots, as if her angry reaction cannot be contained by the cinematic frame. The claustrophobic, static framing during the rape gives way here to the open space outside the car, Aileen freeing herself and the spectator from the confined space of physical trauma.

In its naturalistic but carefully designed presentation, this scene forces the spectator into uncomfortably close proximity with the female body as a site of violence and rage, emphasizing the visceral consequences of Corey's attack, the physical efforts of Aileen's straining, resisting body as it frees itself, and its corporeal force as she fights back. Such a representation of female agency, so markedly different from the sanitized and contained depictions described earlier in this chapter, is underpinned by an explicit return to the kind of rape-revenge narrative structure that generated early depictions of female physical agency in the exploitation movies of the 1970s and early 1980s. Films like *I Spit On Your Grave* (1978) and *Ms 45* (1981) show raped women so traumatized and angered by their experiences that they are driven to kill their rapist (and/or other men), establishing what Pam Cook called "the stereotype of the aggressive positive heroine obsessed with revenge" (124). Female anger born of a very personal, gendered suffering became an explanation for female violence and aggression – the implication being that women would not do "this kind of thing" except in response to a devastating and physically invasive assault, a hypothesis that does nothing to dismantle dominant binary conceptions of gendered behaviour. These films seemed to exemplify the problem Cook identified in the exploitation movie: depictions of female agency came at a price, frequently including titillating nudity, sexualized rape victims, and pre-vengeance "seduction" scenes. However, in a 1970s cinematic landscape in which women were not conventionally shown as physically active or aggressive beings, the rape-revenge narrative troubled representational norms by carving out a space in which female physical action *could* – at least and at last – be depicted.

In a similar way, *Monster*'s invocation of the rape-revenge narrative results in a representation of female violence that "interrupts" a contemporary landscape of sanitized images of active women. However, this time it is not the fact of female violence that is interruptive, but the realism, the credibility, of its depiction. Here the rape-revenge narrative does not precipitate titillating, sexualizing spectacles, and nor does it insist on the re-inscription of traditional femininity; rather, it produces the circumstances in which a naturalistic portrayal of female physical exertion can be advanced. Class does operate as a distancing factor – Aileen's poverty and profession locate her, initially, at a potentially reassuring distance from the majority of the audience for the film, which was distributed on the art cinema circuit – but the film encourages the audience to interrogate that distance. The film's title is crucial in this regard; it appears as we see Aileen huddled under a flyover, sheltering from the rain. Even though the situation itself is likely to elicit some sympathy for the character's predicament, the image invites the audience to associate the title with the character in the frame. As the film progresses, however, the title's connection to Aileen is undermined. Theron's performance communicates not simply her belligerent attitude but the low self-esteem and anxiety that drives it, while the designation of "monster" becomes more applicable to those who surround Aileen, from the seething, misogynist rapist Vincent Corey to the pathologically manipulative girlfriend Shelby, who pressures Aileen to continue to prostitute herself, despite knowing that this is driving Aileen to kill again. Straightforward qualifications and sanitized depictions of female violence are replaced by aesthetic strategies that challenge the spectator to rethink notions of appropriate behaviour and justified action. More broadly, they urge a reconsideration of the ways in which disenfranchised persons are framed – by the media, in films, and in society – in relation to gender and class.[8]

The process of highlighting the corporeal signs of exertion and anger is at work at the moment of initial attack (as in *Monster*'s rape scene), but also helps to authenticate the process of retribution – namely, the violence that is subsequently enacted by the female protagonist. In *Hard Candy*, Hayley (Ellen Page), a 14-year-old girl who may or may not have been a victim of sexual assault herself, is highly organized in her entrapment and punishment of suspected paedophile Jeff (Patrick Wilson), who she thinks has abused and killed a school friend. Much of her assault on Jeff is verbal, but the articulate teenager physicalizes her retribution in ways that are both premeditated (a mock castration, an electrocution) and unplanned. Despite being restrained to an office chair by electrical tape, Jeff momentarily disrupts Hayley's carefully orchestrated kidnapping and torture campaign, knocking her unconscious with a kick as she kneels in front of him, before managing to arm himself with his own gun (the "punishment" is taking place in his own house). Hayley is forced to use all her physical force to disarm him, desperately wrapping cling film around his head to cut off his airways while he uses the office chair to slam her violently into the wall behind them. An unstable handheld camera communicates this physically precarious struggle for power. Close-ups highlight sweat and Hayley's pained expression, and guttural grunts register each impact of her body against the wall. Despite this, she manages to keep Jeff restrained until he loses consciousness. Hayley extracts herself and, bent double, emits anguished groans and retches through tears as she forces herself to overcome the stomach injuries he has inflicted. Anger, a motivator for all her actions in the film, peaks here as she scolds herself for letting down her guard: there are no words, just screams, as she slams her own body back against the wall in self-punishment. Staging and presentation, sound and image, not only work to emphasize Hayley's physical resilience and the corporeal force she is able to sustain, but also the determined emotional basis of her actions.[9]

In *Monster* and *Hard Candy* proximity is a crucial tool in allowing the film to pick out naturalistic detail in the image: sweat, blood, involuntary body convulsions, appearance-warping injuries that are far-removed from mainstream conventions of presentation. Sound design is also very important: ambient sounds are reduced to a minimum, pared away in order to focus attention on the instinctive, non-verbal noises emanating from these traumatized but struggling bodies. Wails, shrieks, guttural groans, and screams do not conform to the stylized phrasing of female screams that have a long tradition in the horror genre, but are untidy, uncontrolled, unpredictable, and communicative of the physical exertions being undertaken and/or endured. Even where verbal communication is possible, the vocalization of rage warps the pitch, timbre, and volume of expression. In *The Brave One*, for example, when a sympathetic police detective (Terrence Howard) tries to stop Erica Bain (Jodie Foster) from executing the remaining member of a gang that killed her fiancé and left her for dead, he appeals to her with the phrase "You do not have the right". She responds with a cry of "YES I DO!" in a shout that modulates into a frustrated wail, which conveys both her deep anguish and her conviction that this physical violence is the correct form of retribution. These naturalistic elements of presentation, particularly the strategic use of proximate camera positions and sound, construct the female body as a site of violence, but not in a titillating or sexualized way.[10] They thus assist in creating the circumstances in which the female body can harness traumatic experiences in order to become credibly violent. The central catalyst in this transformation from victim to perpetrator is not victimhood but anger. Carol Clover's "angry woman" of 1970s horror – a woman "so angry that she can be imagined as a credible perpetrator ... of the kind of violence on which, in the low-mythic universe, the status of full protagonist rests" – returns in these films, still in the service of authenticating female physicality and aggression (17).

Of course, the assimilation of this angry woman trope into the mainstream is already being attempted. From *Kill Bill* and the *Resident Evil* franchise to *Mr & Mrs Smith* and *Hancock*, popular cinema is struggling to incorporate this figure of the angry woman into its narratives.

Even so, as I signalled earlier in relation to some of these very films, the process of assimilation means the reinstatement of well-practised containment strategies. The anomaly in this group is *Kill Bill*, which is almost schizophrenic in its oscillation between a sanitized, highly stylized mode of non-authenticated female action, and a mode which offers visceral, raw, and naturalistic depictions of violent female exertions – using, as it does, sound design, static framing, and camera proximity in similar ways to *Monster* and *Hard Candy*. The extreme tension between these two representational modes in a single movie project (the oscillation continues across both volumes of *Kill Bill*) is a testament to the extent that representations of female action and physical exertion have become polarized – between the poles of "acceptable" and "unacceptable" – in contemporary media culture.

However, the portrayals of female action in films like *Monster* and *Hard Candy* still retain an aesthetic and affective distinctness that the mainstream cannot yet quite incorporate. What these films offer is an active body that can be experienced by the spectator, its bodily stresses and pain presented in close-up. This heroine is often untidily angry, bloody, and sweaty, and we are compelled to witness her determination and physical effort "up close", rather than at a comfortable distance. Such instances do not just contravene dominant conservative conceptions of what kinds of female physicality can be shown. Rather, the persistent use of close-ups at moments of extreme exertion creates a spectatorial proximity to the female body in action, subverting socially defined notions of appropriate spatial proximity to another person's exertions and suffering. Returning this particular "angry woman" to the cinematic frame offers a valuable corrective to the relatively well-behaved and unconvincingly physical heroines of mainstream film. Films like *Monster* and *Hard Candy* communicate convincingly, credibly, and in impactful ways that the female body can be active, physically effective, aggressive, and masterful through its projection of its own force. In this way, they challenge mainstream cinema's ideological project to repeat and confirm conventional conceptions of appropriate gendered behaviours. For all their problematic aspects, then, it is these representations of female physicality and agency that retain a radical intensity in the current context of mainstream, sanitized representations of active gendered bodies.

Notes

1. In addition to her strength Aeon has a secret magnifying lens built into one eye; her colleague Sithandra has a more visible upgrade, replacing her feet with hands.

2. Such dominant cultural constructions of gender have their basis in "psychoanalytic accounts which theorize sexual difference within the framework of linked binary oppositions (active male/passive female)" that "necessarily position normative female subjectivity as passive or in terms of lack" – a perspective that positioned these muscular women as phallic, "unnatural" or "figuratively male" (Hills 39).
3. See Cook and Sturken.
4. Lindsay Steenberg illustrates some of the ways in which postfeminism and containment strategies interrelate in her analysis of the figure of the female investigator (in this book).
5. These fantasies of physical and economic empowerment are likewise central to recent female-focused television fictions. For a compelling analysis of the ways in which these modes of empowerment operate in relation to small-screen portrayals of the "new woman professional", see Rosie White's chapter in this collection.
6. The influential father figure is similarly central to understanding representations of female action in television series like *Buffy the Vampire Slayer* (1997–2003), *Alias* (2001–06), *Veronica Mars* (2004–07), and *Heroes* (2006–10). For more on the role accorded to father figures in *Alias*, see White (in this book).
7. While Freud coin this term, Robin Wood uses it explicitly in relation to the ideological operations of 1970s horror films in "The American Nightmare: Horror in the 1970s".
8. As the rape sequence analysis illustrates, through editing and camera position the film forces the spectator to access and share Aileen's perspective at key moments. The job interview sequence is extremely effective in confronting the spectator with class prejudice, writ large in the patronizing, condescending behaviours of the interviewers; this scene also speaks to the institutional failings that caused Aileen to become disenfranchised in the first place.
9. It is probably worth saying that we are not used to seeing teenagers as young as Hayley using physical force in mainstream cinema, certainly not in an abuse-revenge or rape-revenge narrative framework. In this way, both *Monster* and *Hard Candy* challenge normative expectations of gendered behaviour and physicality, one in women, the other in mid-teen girls.
10. This invites consideration alongside the visual strategies of "torture porn".

Works cited

Aeon Flux. Dir. Karyn Kusama. MTV Films/Lakeshore Entertainment, 2005.
The Brave One. Dir. Neil Jordan. Village Roadshow Pictures/Silver Pictures, 2007.
Bruzzi, Stella. *Undressing Cinema: Clothing and Identity in the Movies*. London & New York: Routledge, 1997.
Clover, Carol. *Men, Women and Chainsaws*. London: BFI Publishing, 1992.
Cook, Pam. " 'Exploitation' Films and Feminism". *Screen* 17.2 (1976): 122–27.
Goldman, Robert, Deborah Heath, and Sharon L. Smith. "Commodity Feminism". *Critical Studies in Mass Communication* 8 (1991): 333–51.
Hard Candy. Dir. David Slade. Vulcan Productions, 2005.
Hills, Elizabeth. "From 'Figurative Males' to Action Heroines: Further Thoughts on Active Women in the Cinema". *Screen* 40.1 (1999): 38–50.

Monster. Dir. Patty Jenkins. Newmarket Gilms/Media 8. 2003.

O'Day, Marc. "Beauty in Motion: Gender, Spectacle and Action Babe Cinema". *Action and Adventure Cinema.* Ed. Yvonne Tasker. London & New York: Routledge, 2004. 201–18.

Projansky, Sarah. *Watching Rape: Film and Television in Postfeminist Culture.* New York: New York University Press, 2001.

Sturken, Marita. *Thelma and Louise* (BFI Modern Classics Series). London: BFI, 2000.

Tasker, Yvonne. *Working Girls: Gender and Sexuality in Popular Cinema.* New York & London: Routledge, 1998.

———— "Introduction: Action and Adventure Cinema". *Action and Adventure Cinema.* Ed. Yvonne Tasker. London & New York: Routledge, 2004. 1–13.

Wood, Robin. "The American Nightmare: Horror in the 1970s". *Hollywood from Vietnam to Reagan.* Ed. Robin Wood. New York: Columbia University Press, 1986. 70–94.

13
Negotiating Shifts in Feminism: The "Bad" Girls of James Bond

Lisa Funnell

As the longest running film series in history, the James Bond franchise currently includes 22 films released across 48 years. Armed with a licence to kill, title character James Bond is routinely placed in situations which necessitate his use of deadly force. In order to obtain audience approval for these violent exploits, Bond functions within a clearly defined political space. Historically, then, the franchise has relied on gendered, racial, and sexual stereotypes in order to differentiate Bond's "normative" heroic identity from the deviant attitudes and behaviours of his male adversaries (Black 96–97). Operating within a British heroic tradition that links masculinity with (heterosexual) romantic conquest, Bond's serial seduction of women offers a "visual guarantee of the maleness of the Secret Service" and functions as a "tipping point" in the plot (107–09). By indiscriminately bedding "good" and "bad" women, Bond attempts to ensure the success of his missions by aligning his sexual conquests with his moral plight.

Since the start of the franchise, Bond's phallic masculinity has been challenged by an array of villainous women. Each generation of female antagonists takes stock of contemporaneous attitudes towards feminism. More specifically, through the characterization and narrative treatment of "bad" women, the Bond series endeavours to register the political impact of the women's movement and reflect popular attitudes to the evolving feminist agenda. In the 1960s, then, the Bond franchise uses the figure of the sexually liberated female villain to illuminate the new freedoms that feminism has accorded to women; while it does this, however, it also positions this woman as a locus for social anxieties about these freedoms – anxieties which are invariably borne out in her violent punishment and death. If the films of the 1970s and 1980s continue to operate in this "backlash" mode – marked, in particular, by the gradual elimination of female villains from the series – then the 1990s augurs in a new generation of adversarial women who invite consideration alongside the fraught discourses of postfeminism. In this chapter, I conduct a close, critical examination of shifting representations of female villainy in the Bond films.[1] Through detailed reference to the ways in which violence is enacted by, and upon, the female body, I show how the Bond franchise has both registered and interrogated the feminist gains that have taken place since the initial release of *Dr. No* in 1962.

Establishing the female villain

Established during the "swinging sixties", the Bond franchise initially engaged with the politics of the sexual revolution through its representation of "modernized" sexual identities, and a related querying of persistent gender stereotypes. According to Tony Bennett and Janet Woollacott, James Bond and his Bond Girl functioned as "key sites for the elaboration of a (relatively) new set of gender identities". Bond embodied a male identity freed from the sexual restrictions of chivalry that had limited the traditional aristocratic hero, while the Bond Girl was depicted as "the subject of a free and independent sexuality liberated from the constraints of family, marriage and domesticity". Still, although she appears to embody the liberal sexuality of the emerging women's movement, the 1960s Bond Girl is, perhaps, more accurately described as a "model of adjustment", a dependent and derivative character that is tailored to fulfil the sexual needs of Bond (24).

Certainly, the Bond film consistently links sexual pleasure with powerful notions of duty and punishment. Examining female characterization in the James Bond novels, Christine Bold writes that women's bodies are "designed to pleasure others: notably, James Bond". In this way, they function within a wider trope which draws connections between "lines of national affiliation and [those of] sexual attachment" (172). Bold's argument can be applied to the depiction of "good" and "bad" women in the Bond film. Throughout the 1960s, the franchise both engaged with and recapitulated historical approaches to gender that situated female sexuality as suspect and dangerous when articulated outside the confines of heterosexual marriage. When women act as independent agents expressing sexual desire, they are typically considered threatening, deviant, and "bad". According to Deborah Tolman and Tracy Higgins, "Women who wish to avoid the consequences of being labelled 'bad' are expected to define the boundaries of sexual behaviour, outlined by men's desire, and to ignore or deny their own sexual desire as a guide to their choices" (205). Thus, in order to be presented as a "good" character, the Bond Girl is expected to submit to the will and libido of James Bond, forfeiting her own liberated sexual identity for a domesticated one. By comparison, women who embrace their liberal sexualities and refuse to adhere to the "Bondian" standard of normative femininity are presented as "bad" and are violently punished.

Interestingly, the first decade of the franchise (1962–69) featured the highest concentration of female villains in leading and supportive roles, and the films produced during these years relied on particular iconography to designate villainous and heroic embodiments of female identity. The image of the Bond Girl strongly adhered to the character template outlined by Ian Fleming in the James Bond novels. In the novels, for instance, Bond Girls are described as having either blonde or dark brown/black hair with no intermediate shades, and this trait is carried through into the cinematic imaging of the 1960s Bond Girl (Amis 55).[2] On the other hand, the most dangerous female villains of the decade – including Rosa Klebb (Lotte Lenya) in *From Russia with Love* (1963), Fiona Volpe (Luciana Paluzzi) in *Thunderball* (1965), Helga Brandt (Karin Dor) in *You Only Live Twice* (1967), and Irma Bunt (Ilse Steppat) in *On Her Majesty's Secret Service* (1969) – are depicted with red hair and placed in stark visual contrast to the Bond Girl. In his novels, Fleming reserved the use of red hair for Bond's most dangerous male adversaries: he employed the colour literally and metaphorically in order to express the sinister nature of the villain. As Kingsley Amis suggests, "The one sure way of spotting him is to watch his eyes. If you see a red blaze or even a glint of red in them, you know your man" (65). This convention was adapted into the imaging of villainous women (and not men) within the first decade of the cinematic franchise. Drawing on stereotypes relating to red-haired women, Bond's early female adversaries were figured variously as hot-tempered, weird, clownish, wild, and/or oversexed (Heckert and Best 365). While these women were always positioned as social and/or sexual deviants, the franchise did distinguish between them through reference to the key factors of age and sexual availability. This, as I will go on to discuss, gave rise to two distinct categories of female villain: the oversexed siren (represented by Volpe and Brandt) and the middle-aged sexual deviant (exemplified by Klebb and Bunt).

All the Bond villains of the 1960s are affiliated with SPECTRE,[3] an international terrorist organization that is presided over by the megalomaniacal Starvo Blofeld. Consisting of 11 committee members and a variety of henchmen/henchwomen and spies, SPECTRE is a fairly contained operation, and one in which women are accorded a certain measure of authority. Fiona Volpe is the trusted advisor and primary henchwoman of Emilio Largo (Adolfo Celi), second-in-command at SPECTRE, while Helga Brant is an official member of SPECTRE, ranked eleventh in the hierarchy. Although both red-haired women are intelligent, competent with weaponry, and willing to use violence to achieve their objectives, they are not presented as physical threats to Bond; instead, it is their liberal sexual identities which work to endanger Bond's phallic masculinity. Volpe, for instance, is a "black widow" assassin who uses her body to seduce and murder her prey. When she has sex with Bond in *Thunderball*, Volpe not only dominates him in bed, but also ridicules his phallic masculinity: "But of course, I forgot your ego, Mr. Bond. James Bond, who only has to make love to a woman and she starts to hear heavenly choirs singing. She repents and then immediately returns to the side of right and virtue. But not this one!" All at once, Volpe rejects domestication, challenges the notion of ideological repositioning, and unrepentantly proclaims her status as a "bad girl" in the film.

At the end of each film, Bond's adversaries are expected to die. Bond typically engages in hand-to-hand combat with his male opponents and eliminates them in the film's climax. Bond, however, does not use lethal force against villainous women in the first three decades (16 films) of the franchise. Bond's restricted use of his "licence to kill" highlights the social and generic codes that govern the "proper" (and gendered) use of deadly retaliation in the series. In spite of the feminist struggle for equal opportunities, the Bond film creates a double standard that allows women to enact violence on the male body and then removes them from the arena of violent combat. Inevitably, this works to undermine the efficacy of women's aggressive actions, which, in turn, results in the prevailing depiction of women as inferior adversaries.

The manner in which the deviant female body is disciplined in these Bond films draws attention to the franchise's precarious attempts to balance patriarchal and commercial interests. Early in the series, Bond producers were concerned that audiences would experience an aversion towards Bond if he used his "licence to kill" against his female enemies. According to Ellen Willis, violence enacted on the female body is typically linked with notions of female victimization and only becomes palatable when it "can be blamed on deviant individuals rather than systematic male power. Most people, even antifeminists... condemn the perpetrators in principle" (47). In order to maintain a positive rapport with audiences, Bond producers shifted the responsibility of violence against women onto SPECTRE: Volpe is shot in the back by one of her henchmen and Blofeld drops Brandt into a pool of hungry piranhas. Both women are killed without warning and without the opportunity to defend themselves. The burden of their dishonourable deaths is placed on the shoulders of SPECTRE and works to further vilify Bond's long-time rival Blofeld. Volpe and Brandt are thus depicted as disposable subjects whose violent deaths strengthen the heroism of Bond, while enhancing the villainy of Blofeld.

As well as the "oversexed siren" paradigm, the Bond franchise offered another model of female villainy in the 1960s. Rosa Klebb and Irma Bunt are highly influential members of SPECTRE: Klebb is designated third-in-command of the organization, while Bunt is the trusted advisor of Blofeld. Both of these women share a remarkably consistent image: they are short, stocky, middle-aged white women who are conservatively dressed and appear androgynous in their films. However, their strongest physical link is their red hair, cut short to emphasize age over aesthetics. Too old and too unattractive to pique or satisfy Bond's libido, Klebb and Bunt retain a sexual currency in *From Russia With Love* and *You Only Live Twice* respectively through their erotic interest in the Bond Girl. Characterized as masculine lesbians, Klebb and Bunt pose an overt challenge to Bond's (hetero)sexual potency and are thus condemned as symbols of an "aberrant" (homo)sexuality that threatens to destabilize the status quo.[4]

Presented as sexually unavailable as a result of age and orientation, these middle-aged "deviants" deny Bond his plot "tipping points" and offer unbridled challenges to his phallic masculinity. Subject to the ideology of the franchise, which sanctions the disciplining of women who reject (hetero)normative gender roles, Klebb is killed in the final scenes of *From Russia With Love*. Pinned against the wall by Bond, an incapacitated Klebb is shot and killed by Bond Girl Romanova, who chooses her lover, James Bond, over her lesbian suitor. At once, Klebb is punished for her deviant sexuality while "normative" female heterosexuality prevails. As Christine Bold notes, "the equation never fails: beauty, heterosexuality, and patriotism go together", and are, in turn, pitted against "ugliness, sexual 'deviance', and criminality" (174). Bunt's fate, however, is markedly different from that of Klebb. The final scenes of *On Her Majesty's Secret Service* feature the marriage between Bond and his Bond Girl Tracy DiVincenzo (Diana Rigg). Moments later, DiVincenzo is murdered in a drive-by shooting. Interestingly, it is Blofeld who drives the car while Bunt does the killing. Although both villains flee the scene and survive the film, Bond eventually exacts revenge on the elusive Blofeld in *For Your Eyes Only* (1981). Bunt, on the other hand, is never killed, captured, or punished. She is the only villain in the history of the film series to escape the violent retribution of James Bond. One of the reasons for this is that Ilse Steppat, the actor who played Bunt, died shortly after the film's release. Considered irreplaceable, producers elected to honour Steppat's memory rather than recast the role.[5] At another level, though, Bunt's evasion of "Bondian" justice might also be understood in terms of the franchise's shift of narrative focus in the 1970s – a shift which corresponds to broader changes in the portrayal and treatment of female characters. Focusing more intently on the relationship between Bond and his Bond Girl(s), films of the 1970s relegate female antagonists to secondary and supportive roles in the franchise. In spite of these explanations, Bunt still remains the only female villain to survive the film, unpunished for the crimes she perpetrated against Bond and the social/sexual taboos she breaks.

Mayday! disappearing women

While the first decade of Bond films centred on the conflict between the protagonist and his adversaries, the films of the 1970s focused more closely on the relationship between Bond and his Bond Girl. This narrative adjustment coincides with what Susan Faludi refers to as a media-driven "backlash" against the feminist advances of the 1970s (50–54).[6] According to Bennett and Woollacott, the Bond films of the 1970s pivoted on the "putting-back-into-place" of women who were perceived as having taken their independence and liberation too far: "This shift in narrative organization clearly constituted a response – in truth, somewhat nervous and uncertain – to the Women's Liberation movement, fictiously rolling-back the advances of feminism to restore an imaginarily more secure phallocentric conception of gender relations" (28). As a result, female villains of the 1970s played relatively minor roles in the franchise and spent limited time on screen. Instead of portraying SPECTRE agents and henchwomen, these female antagonists were typically cast as incompetent spies (see Gloria Hendry's portrayal of Rosie Carver in *Live and Let Die* [1973]), tragic mistresses (like Andrea Anders [Maud Adams] in *The Man with the Golden Gun* [1974]), and sexy secretaries (Caroline Munro's "Naomi" in *The Spy Who Loved Me* [1977]). By the 1980s, the number of villainous women in the Bond franchise had contracted radically, and such roles were excised entirely from *Moonraker* (1979), *For Your Eyes Only*, and *The Living Daylights* (1987). Over a two-decade period, then, the Bond films gradually phased out any images of "bad" women that might detract attention away from the franchise's new focus on female domestication.

May Day (Grace Jones) is the only female villain of the 1980s and is prominently featured in *A View to a Kill* (1985) as the girlfriend of villain Max Zorin (Christopher Walken). Not only does May Day outshine the rest of cast, but she is also privileged in the film's promotion, standing back-to-back with Bond in movie posters that asked, "Has James Bond finally met his match?" (Black 226). In spite of Jones's charismatic performance, May Day is considered an enigma by film critics, who struggle to read her character through the ideology of the film series. According to Black, May Day presents a challenge to Bond's masculinity that is never resolved. Like Volpe, she poses a tangible threat to Bond's physical safety and challenges his libido by dominating him in bed. While the film anticipates a showdown between Bond and May Day, this confrontation never occurs. Given that Bond does not use fatal force against women, the showdown between the charismatic enemies is perhaps eschewed on account of the likelihood that May Day would defeat Bond in a hand-to-hand combat scenario. Instead, the film skirts the issue by having Zorin betray May Day, who then commits suicide. In this way, the film conveniently forecloses any opportunity there might have been for Bond to assert the supremacy of his phallic masculinity (227).

Through the character of May Day – who seems to be influenced, in part, by the emerging discourses of third wave feminism – *A View to a Kill* offers a moment of feminist possibility at the height of the franchise's feminist backlash. As a critical movement, the third wave is broadly defined by its prioritization of individuality, its rejection of essentialist notions of womanhood, and its sustained celebration of difference and contradiction (Tong 258). Critical of the "exclusive tendencies" of the feminist discourses that emerged in the 1970s and 1980s, many third wave feminists take issue with the essentialist notion that all women share certain common characteristics which unify them as a group, preferring to investigate the role played by specific social and/or political factors in defining women's individual experiences of oppression (Stone 85–87). "[S]haped by the racial and ethnic diversity of post-boomer generations" (Heywood and Drake 15), the third wave emphasizes racial, ethnic, cultural, and national difference, while pushing for the breakdown of ideological barriers, including gender binaries (Tong 288). This is most notable in the casting of Grace Jones as the first and only black female actor to portray a leading role in the Bond franchise. In addition, May Day's body performance subverts gender binaries by conflating the strength and muscularity expected of masculinity with the aesthetic beauty associated with femininity. Bond is at once fearful of and attracted to her body, and his competing feelings create confusion in a usually clear-cut narrative.

In order to generate this image of a female identity that cannot be easily understood, categorized, and/or contained, the makers of *A View to a Kill* treaded heavily on the established star image of Grace Jones. Jones is part of the Brigitte Nielsen-era of action women and is best known for her "hypermasculine"[7] performance of femininity. While feminist critics typically position *Aliens* (1986) and *Terminator 2* (1991) as inaugurating the age of the Hollywood hard woman, the muscular women who feature in the action-fantasies of the early 1980s – such as Sandahl Bergman in *Conan the Barbarian* (1982), Grace Jones in *Conan the Destroyer* (1984), and Brigitte Neilsen in *Red Sonja* (1985) – are typically overlooked.[8] In fact, Jones's characterization as Zulu in *Conan the Destroyer* appears to be transplanted wholesale into *A View to a Kill*. In the process, Jones's iconic image and celebrity status became embedded within the Bond tradition. Certainly, the makers of the film struggled to adjust Jones's star image to meet the gendered expectations of the franchise while still satisfying her fan base; as a consequence, the film does not establish any definite boundaries for her character. She is initially presented as an "other" in the film: she is wild, animalistic, hypermasculine, hyperviolent, oversexed, and amoral. Portrayed as a sadist, May Day obtains sexual pleasure by inflicting physical pain on her male victims. Her narrative treatment, however, changes when she is betrayed by Zorin. Granted the opportunity to explain her personal history to Bond, May Day reveals her motivations for employing excessive violent force and is, in the process, humanized. May Day then chooses to team up with Bond in order to exact revenge upon Zorin. When the trolley carrying Zorin's bomb malfunctions, Bond abandons the revenge mission in order to find shelter from the impending explosion; May Day, meanwhile, remains to complete the task alone, offering a competing image of heroic competency in the course of her noble death. Although all Bond villains are expected to die, May Day is the only female adversary to determine her own fate, and her character is never contained or punished for her violent and sexual exploits. In the political world of Bond, where codes and conventions clearly demarcate good and evil, May Day is a symbol of transgressive female identity that both upholds and subverts the sexist ideology of the franchise.

Postfeminist villainy

After a 6-year hiatus, the Bond film returned in the mid-1990s, having renegotiated many of its sexist codes. In order to maintain the generic integrity of the series, while still updating its identity politics, Bond producers chose "not to alter Bond's attitude towards women, but rather [altered] the attitude of the women around him" (Chapman 256). Beginning with *GoldenEye* (1995), the franchise began to incorporate postfeminist sentiments into its characterization of violent women.

Although difficult to define in any categorical sense, postfeminism is a cultural phenomena that speaks primarily to the experiences of a white, middle-class "affluent elite" which has benefited substantially from the social and political gains made by second wave feminism in the 1960s and 1970s (Tasker and Negra 2). Distinct from the third wave, postfeminism dismisses the need for continued political activism and tends to gloss over, rather than spotlight, social differences. As Jessica K. Taft observes in relation to "Girl Power", postfeminist declarations of gender equality and female empowerment can work to distract young women from the realities of oppression, ignoring the extent to which forces like racism, classism, and homophobia continue to inform the current social order (73). In this (depoliticized) context, women can lay active claim to their sexuality, and "sexiness" – as we see in the case of the postfeminist Bond villain – can be portrayed without moral judgement (Owen et al. 10–11).

The Bond films of the 1990s feature the collision of Bond's old-fashioned masculinity with the new sexual politics of the late twentieth century. By placing a deliberate focus on gender, the Bond franchise opens up a space for the emergence of new "postfeminist" female villains. These villainous women are invariably played by white American or European actors with pale complexions, shoulder-length brown/black hair, brown eyes, and petite, slender frames. As wealthy characters, their privileged backgrounds are notable through the quality and styling of their clothes, their ownership of consumer goods (like expensive cars and jewellery), and their participation in a variety of exotic leisure activities. In addition, these villains are presented as sexually empowered women who rely on duplicitous means to gain power and mastery over Bond. Recognizing his combined desire for sexual conquest and domestication, they use their bodies to develop emotional connections with Bond that render him vulnerable to attack. In *GoldenEye*, Bond is intrigued by the dangerous lifestyle and sensuality of Xenia Onatopp (Famke Janssen). She seduces Bond and then attempts to asphyxiate him between her legs during sex, bringing a new and violent meaning to the term "foreplay". In *The World is Not Enough* (1999), Elektra King (Sophie Marceau) wins the affections of Bond by masquerading as a helpless Bond Girl in need of his protection. She sleeps with Bond and enters into a romantic relationship with him, using their intimate connection to cover up her multiple attempts to kill him. Finally, in *Die Another Day* (2002) double agent Miranda Frost (Rosamund Pike) attracts Bond with her frosty and standoffish demeanour. She seduces Bond in order to disarm him by literally stealing the clip out of his gun while they are making love. By retaining his old-fashioned notions of masculinity and conquest, Bond becomes a target for "empowered" 1990s women, who systematically use their bodies to seduce him, render him vulnerable, and then attack him.

If May Day exemplified a species of third wave feminism that prohibited Bond from validating his masculinity, then the "postfeminism" of Onatopp, King, and Frost seems to offer Bond the opportunity for phallic reclamation. This, in turn, opens up space for the reestablishment of the franchise's sexist ideology and the re-subordination of female sexuality. Informed by "postfeminist" claims of gender equality, the franchise no longer restricts Bond from using lethal retaliation against villainous women: he engages in a violent fight sequence with Onatopp – which results, ironically, in her asphyxiation by a rope – and he also enters into a deadly confrontation with King, whom he shoots in the heart at point blank range in order to resist her attempts at sexual manipulation. On both occasions, the film permits Bond's employment of fatal force in self-defence. Although the Bond films of the 1990s explore competing gender politics, then, Bond's old-fashioned masculinity is presented as once again triumphing over dangerous women with liberal sexual identities.

The release of *Casino Royale* (2005) marks a new direction for the Bond franchise. The film reworks many of the conventions that define the genre, not least the heroic model that governs the series. No longer affiliated with the British lover tradition, James Bond is presented through the visual conventions and ideology of Hollywood masculinity. Bond's body, rather than his libido, is the new locus of masculinity, and his heroic competency is now established through the body's success within the space of physical action.[9] By changing the parameters of heroic identity, the franchise has also adjusted the method through which Bond's heroism is tested. Valenka (Ivana Milicevic) is the only female villain to be cast since 2006, and her characterization offers important insights into the gender politics at work in the current phase of the franchise.

In *Casino Royale*, Valenka is the girlfriend of the duplicitous LeChiffre (Mads Mikkelsen), and her identity is inextricably bound up with his: she is never featured on screen without him, she has little dialogue of her own, and she only acts upon his orders. Over the course of the film, she is paraded around in revealing costumes and her semi-nude body is placed on display in order to distract LeChiffre's poker opponents. While alluring, Valenka does not interact sexually with Bond; because she is part of a monogamous relationship, she is already "domesticated" and as such does not represent an adequate sexual challenge to the British agent. When read through the original/presumed ideology of the franchise, Valenka is underestimated as a threat. And yet, she is arguably one of Bond's most threatening adversaries and the only villain to succeed in (temporarily) killing him when she poisons his martini; indeed, Bond only survives this attack because he is resuscitated by Vesper Lynd.[10]

While sexy and dangerous (two characteristics typically associated with female villainy), Valenka is prevailingly disempowered: she is presented as a functionary of, rather than partner to, LeChiffre. Unlike the villainous women of the 1960s who made autonomous decisions while working under the megalomaniacal Blofled, Valenka is defined exclusively in terms of her (hetero)sexual relationship with LeChiffre. Her role in the film represents the trappings of postfeminism, which preferences reclaimed femininity and "sexiness" while overlooking residual gender, race, and class inequalities. This reading is supported by a consideration of Valenka's death in the *Casino Royale*. While LeChiffre is killed during the climax of the film, Valenka's death occurs off-screen and is only mentioned *en passant* during a conversation between Bond and M. Her death in the film is presented as a by-product of LeChiffre's failed business transaction with Mr. White (Jesper Christensen) – another male villain of the film – rather than a punishment for her attempt on Bond's life. Characterized as a sexy appendage to LeChiffre, Valenka is dislocated from the film's narrative conflict in a way that facilitates the re-centring of male villainy within the series.

In the late 2000s, the franchise continues to renegotiate the gendered codes of villainy and violent conflict. Although *Quantum of Solace* (2008) exclusively features male villains, the film anticipates the emergence of a new generation of female antagonists. Midway through the film, Bond infiltrates a meeting of Quantum, a secret international organization resembling SPECTRE, which appears to be made up of various members seeking world domination. Although Bond does not uncover the identities of all the key players, he observes two female Quantum members (played by Alexandra Prussa and Uygar Tamer, respectively). Presented as wealthy, powerful, and attractive middle-aged women, these characters gesture towards a potential new direction for the formulation of female villainy in the series. Motivated by personal ambition, these Quantum members have the capacity to project images of female transgression that are not contingent upon "aberrant" sexual behaviours.

Within the conventions of the Bond franchise, female villainy not only serves to strengthen Bond's heroic masculinity but also offers a perfect opportunity to demonize feminism as lesbian, deviant, threatening, monstrous, excessive, and other. As I have established over the course of this chapter, female villains are often punished for refusing to exchange their liberal sexual identities for domesticated ones, and their bodies are regularly situated as sites at which hegemonic masculinity can be reaffirmed. If the red-haired villains of the 1960s (and Grace Jones's May Day) asserted feminist possibilities that were unpopular and/or underrepresented at the time, they also projected images of individuality, liberal sexuality, female empowerment, and embodied resistance that are far less pronounced in current "postfeminist" constructions of female villainy. In order to recast female villains as strong, challenging, and competent adversaries for Bond, the franchise needs to take urgent account of the ways in which the discourses of postfeminism might work to limit, rather than enhance, women's agency. In this way, the Bond film might continue to engage with the politics of its context by responding to the increasingly complicated intersections of gender and power in the twenty-first century.

Notes

1. The Bond franchise is defined by its own, highly specific system of narrative codes and stock characters. While this chapter analyses the Bond film (and its representation of female villainy) as action cinema, its female characters might be further illuminated through reference to the conventions of the spy genre. See Rosie White's *Violent Femmes: Women as Spies in Popular Culture* (2007) and *"Alias*: Quality Television and the New Woman Professional" (in this book).

2. Elsewhere I have explored the characterization of cinematic Bond Girls and noted the transcription of Fleming's character template from novel to film. See "From English Partner" (2008).

3. SPECTRE stands for Special Executive for Counter-Intelligence, Terror, Revenge and Extortion.

4. Relying on an outdated attitude to homosexuality, the Bond franchise frequently contrasted Bond's "healthy" (hetero)normative libido with the "aberrant" and "dysfunctional" (homo)sexuality of his male adversaries. See Black.

5. Blofeld is portrayed by Anthony Dawson (1963, 1965), Donald Pleasence (1967), Telly Savalas (1969), Charles Gray (1971), and John Hollis (1981). With respect to Blofeld, the character, and not the actor(s), is considered irreplaceable.
6. According to Faludi, the antifeminist backlash was a pre-emptive strike against the increased possibility that women might achieve their goal of social equality (xviii).
7. According to Erica Scharrer, hypermasculinity is "characterized by the idealization of stereotypically masculine or macho traits and the rejection of traits perceived as the antithesis of machismo" (160). Manifesting itself, most usually, as sexual and/or physical aggression, hypermasculinity acts as an apt framework for analysing the Grace Jones persona and the representation of May Day in *A View to a Kill*.
8. While these films have not been subjected to sustained analysis by feminist scholars, their influence is noted by both Tasker and Inness. The influence of the 1980s "tough woman" is also a point of reference for Purse in her delineation of the "angry woman" in contemporary cinema (in this book).
9. As I have argued elsewhere, in 2006 the Bond franchise changed the heroic model on which it turns and thus altered the iconography through which Bond's heroism is envisaged. See "I Know Where You Keep Your Gun" (2011).
10. Vesper Lynd is a foreign liaison agent who is dispatched by HM Treasury to monitor Bond's use of the funds allocated to him by MI6. It later transpires that she is actually a double agent working for Quantum.

Works cited

Amis, Kingsley. *The James Bond Dossier*. London: Cape, 1965.
Bennett, Tony, and Janet Woollacott. "The Moments of Bond". *The James Bond Phenomenon: A Critical Reader*. Ed. Christopher Lindner. Manchester: Manchester University Press, 2003. 13–33.
Black, Jeremy. *The Politics of James Bond: From Fleming's Novels to the Big Screen*. Lincoln: The University of Nebraska Press, 2005.
Bold, Christine. " 'Under the Very Skirts of Britannia': Re-Reading Women in the James Bond Novels". *The James Bond Phenomenon: A Critical Reader*. Ed. Christopher Lindner. Manchester: Manchester University Press, 2003. 169–83.
Casino Royale. Dir. Martin Campbell. Columbia/MGM, 2006.
Chapman, James. *Licence to Thrill: A Cultural History of the James Bond Films*. New York: Columbia University Press, 2000.
Die Another Day. Dir. Lee Tamahori. MGM/Sony Entertainment, 2002.
Faludi, Susan. *Backlash: The Undeclared War Against American Women*. New York: Anchor, 1991.
For Your Eyes Only. Dir. John Glen. United Artists, 1981.
From Russia with Love. Dir. Terence Young. United Artists, 1963.
Funnell, Lisa. "From English Partner to American Action Hero: The Heroic identity and Transnational Appeal of the Bond Girl". *Heroines and Heroes: Symbolism, Embodiment, Narratives and Identities*. Ed. Christopher Hart. Kingswinford, West Midlands: IISE and Midrash, 2008. 61–80.

———— " 'I Know Where You Keep Your Gun': Daniel Craig as the Bond-Bond Girl Hybrid in *Casino Royale*". *Journal of Popular Culture* (forthcoming; 2011).

GoldenEye. Dir. Martin Campbell. United Artists, 1995.

Heckert, Druann Maria, and Amy Best. "Ugly Duckling to Swan: Labeling Theory and the Stigmatization of Red Hair". *Symbolic Interaction* 20.4 (1997): 365–84.

Heywood, Leslie, and Jennifer Drake. " 'It's All About the Benjamins': Economic Determinants of Third Wave Feminism in the United States". *Third Wave Feminism: A Critical Exploration.* Ed. Stacy Gillis, Gillian Howie, and Rebecca Munford. New York: Palgrave MacMillan, 2004. 13–23.

Inness, Sherrie A. *Action Chicks: New Images of Tough Women in Popular Culture.* Basingstoke: Palgrave, 2004.

On Her Majesty's Secret Service. Dir. Peter R. Hunt. United Artists, 1969.

Owen, A. Susan, Sarah R. Stein, and Leah R. Vande Berg. "Introduction: Why We Write". *Bad Girls: Cultural Politics and Media Representations of Transgressive Women.* New York: Peter Lang Publishing, 2007. 1–19.

Quantum of Solace. Dir. Marc Forster. MGM/Columbia Pictures, 2008.

Scharrer, E. "Tough Guys: The Portrayal of Hypermasculinity and Aggression in Televised Police Dramas". *Journal of Broadcasting and Electronic Media* 45 (2001): 613–34.

Stone, Alison. "On the Genealogy of Women: A Defence of Anti-Essentialism". *Third Wave Feminism: A Critical Exploration.* Ed. Stacy Gillis, Gillian Howie, and Rebecca Munford. New York: Palgrave MacMillan, 2004. 85–96.

Taft, Jessica K. "Girl Power Politics: Pop-Cultural Barriers and Organizational Resistance". *All About the Girl: Culture, Power, and Identity.* Ed. Anita Harris. New York: Routledge, 2004. 69–78.

Tasker, Yvonne. *Spectacular Bodies: Gender, Genre and the Action Cinema.* London and New York: Routledge, 1993.

Tasker, Yvonne, and Diane Negra. "Feminist Politics and Postfeminist Culture". *Interrogating Postfeminism: Gender and the Politics of Popular Culture.* Ed. Yvonne Tasker, and Diane Negra. Durham, NC: Duke University Press, 2007. 1–25.

Thunderball. Dir. Terence Young. United Artists, 1965.

Tolman, Deborah L., and Tracy E. Higgins. "How Being a Good Girl Can Be Bad for Girls". *"Bad Girls"/"Good Girls": Women, Sex and Power in the Nineties.* Ed. Nan Bauer Maglin, and Donna Perry. New Brunswick, NJ: Rutgers University Press, 1994. 205–25.

Tong, Rosemarie Putnam. *Feminist Thought: A Comprehensive Introduction.* 3rd edn. Colorado: Westview Press, 2008.

White, Rosie. *Violent Femmes: Women as Spies in Popular Culture.* London and New York: Routledge, 2007.

Willis, Ellen. "Villains and Victims: 'Sexual Correctness' and the Repression of Feminism". *"Bad Girls"/"Good Girls": Women, Sex and Power in the Nineties.* Ed. Nan Bauer Maglin, and Donna Perry. New Brunswick, NJ: Rutgers University Press, 1994. 44–53.

A View to a Kill. Dir. John Glen. MGM/UA Entertainment, 1985.

The World is Not Enough. Dir. Michael Apted. MGM, 1999.

You Only Live Twice. Dir Lewis Gilbert. United Artists, 1967.

14

"A Caligula-like despot": Matriarchal Tyranny in *The Sopranos*

Anna Gething

"Everybody thought Dad was ruthless", says Tony Soprano in the opening episode of *The Sopranos*, "but I gotta hand it to you: if you'd been born after those feminists, you would've been the real gangster" (1.1). Livia Soprano, the "real gangster" of the above statement, represents a new kind of violent woman in visual culture. The "formidable maternal presence"[1] of David Chase's HBO mafia series *The Sopranos* (1999–2007) is mother to Tony Soprano (James Gandolfini): mob boss, protagonist, and usual subject of critical readings of the show. The focus in this chapter, though, will be on the character and influence of Livia (Nancy Marchand), whose position as an elderly, widowed grandmother carries far greater power than the archetype might suggest. She is in fact a "Caligula-like despot" (Holden 38); "a demon-possessed matriarch" (Simon 4–5) whose authority pervades the violence that underpins *The Sopranos*.

"[W]hat really seems to have attracted feminist critics in recent years", writes Jacinda Read, "is the violent woman or action heroine", a figure whose very representation of femininity is defined by the embodiment of traditionally masculine traits (205). Such films as *Charlie's Angels* (2000), *Crouching Tiger, Hidden Dragon* (2000), *Lara Croft: Tomb Raider* (2001), and *Kill Bill* (2003 and 2004) are marked, says Lisa Coulthard, "by popular appeal, narrational centrality of active female characters, genre hybridity, and sophisticated fight choreography", placing the female at the centre of "genres usually associated with male characters, actors, and audiences" (154). Arguably, these violent women are, to borrow Elizabeth Hills' words, "figurative males", appropriating the macho behaviour of the male action hero (205). Crucially, however, and as both Barbara Creed and Jane Usher have identified, such female

213

characters combine the threat of violence with one of seduction: these violent heroines are "simultaneously deadly and desirable", offering a "coalescence of female sexuality and malevolence" that fuses the sweeping cultural division of angel/whore into an alluring mix (Usher 2). The likes of Lara Croft, with her impossible vital statistics, present a titillating performance of gender play: an exaggerated physical femininity edged with overtly masculine aggression that hints, too, at the promise of sexual domination.

In Livia Soprano we see a departure from this now-caricatured on-screen woman of violence. Rejecting the comic-book conventions of the fantasy-fuelled action heroine, Chase crafts in Livia a violence that is far more insidious, sly, and grittily realistic. This is, largely, psychological rather than physical violence, bedded in manipulation and exploitation; it is a violence that, in a postfeminist re-rendering of the angry action heroine, actively exploits the archetype of passive, weak femininity as a smokescreen for vengeful malevolence. The move to such psychological, emotional violence seems not unconnected to the condition of old age. Livia, in her seventies, subverts the popular image of the nubile, fertile, eroticized heroine that defines the films mentioned above to project, instead, an image of ageing, asexual womanhood: jaded, resentful, and ascetic, she is the text's anti-heroine, and one who unsettles any gender conventions of desirable, maternal, domestic femininity.[2] *The Sopranos* does, however, position its violent woman within a genre that is – like action cinema – "associated with male characters, actors, and audiences", in this case the gangster genre. The first section of this chapter will consider the female appropriation of a traditionally masculine screen genre, examining how *The Sopranos* works to update and feminize the "explosive virility" of the gangster narrative (Nochimson 2). I will then take a closer look at Livia's strategies of violence and her apparent omnipotence as matriarch, before considering the significance of the active/passive body in the narrative of *The Sopranos*, with particular reference to the ageing female body.

Feminizing the gangster genre

Martha Nochimson describes the gangster genre as "hypermasculine fare"; a "muscularized" narrative that "displac[es] emotion onto the tumult associated with violence", in contrast to the "feminized and openly emotional" perspective of "what is ordinarily identified as family melodrama" (2, 4). *The Sopranos* overtly aligns itself with this masculinized gangster genre: drugs, sex, gambling, and death loom large and episodes are peppered with allusions to a rich filmic tradition of mob movies, most explicitly to *The Godfather* trilogy (1972, 1974, 1990). Chase – an Italian-American born in New Jersey – has expressed his long-held enthusiasm for the genre, locating its audience appeal in "a big wish fulfilment" of power, respect, and fear (McCarty 7–8). The allegiance of *The Sopranos* to the inherent "muscularity" of the mafia story is immediately evident in its opening title sequence which, as Nochimson acknowledges, "contains a mass of aggressively virile resonances" (8). The soundtrack's phallic refrain of "got yourself a gun"[3] accompanies Tony Soprano on his drive from New York City to his luxurious New Jersey home (itself a comment on upward mobility), and points to the further phallic references made by Tony's cigar and the prominent architectural backdrop. The close-up camera view and Tony's concentrated gaze suggest his all-seeing omniscience as mafia boss, while the soundtrack's recurring final lines and closing pistol shot hint at a sexual crescendo. This undercurrent of sexual assertion continues throughout the series, evident in Tony's and others' extra-marital conquests, as well as in the backdrop of naked women provided by the Bada Bing strip club.

Importantly, however, while explicitly fulfilling this archetypal masculinity, *The Sopranos* seems also to step into that "feminized and openly emotional" perspective of Nochimson's family melodrama. Its very form, as television series rather than film, allows for an arguably more subtle development of character and plot, while the often shocking violence is set against the everyday domesticity of Tony's family life. Those opening credits, while undoubtedly wielding their phallic props, work also to relocate Tony from the testosterone-filled bars and mean streets of New York – the traditional haunts of the cinematic gangster – to the suburban safety of his New Jersey home. Indeed, the melodrama of Tony's family frequently dominates the plot, and their opulent home – most often, the gleaming kitchen – provides an immaculate stage set of idyllic domesticity, one that jars with the bloody mess of Tony's criminal activities. Certainly, if the feminized realm of the domestic is used as an aesthetic screen for the masculinized gangster action, then this screening often takes place at a very literal level, with the polished floors and ornate ceilings of the Soprano home concealing stashes of weapons and cash.

The Sopranos also updates and feminizes the mafia story through its portrayal of women who, as Clare Longrigg notes, "are by no means marginal to the series" (238). In fact, the Soprano women – Tony's wife Carmela, daughter Meadow, sister Janice, and mother Livia – comprise a matriarchy to positively rival the established patriarchy of the gangster genre. In many ways, Carmela Soprano (Edie Falco) fulfils the traditional role of housewife and mother, yet she also maintains an unblinkered perspective on her husband's lifestyle, aware of both his adulterous and criminal affairs. Hers is not a resigned surrender to the position of sub-missive, silenced wife, but an informed decision to stay in her marriage – a relationship that she, rather than Tony, directs. Livia, for her part, was always sceptical about the stability of Carmela and Tony's partner-ship, allegedly warning Carmela on her wedding day that her son would quickly grow bored with her. In response, Carmela presents a resilient front, performing her daughter-in-law duties faultlessly, while recogniz-ing Livia as manipulative, insincere, and "terribly dysfunctional" (3.2). Far from marginal, then, Carmela provides a central, stabilizing touch-stone for Tony, a secure point of refuge: "Carm, you're not just *in* my life", he tells her, "you *are* my life" (1.6). Tony and Carmela's eldest child, Meadow (Jamie-Lynn Sigler), mimics her mother's independence, presenting another model of strong femininity and assuming status as Tony's greatest source of fatherly pride. Smart and shrewd, "Meadow can take care of herself", determines Tony confidently, while directing his concerns towards his meandering son, Anthony Junior (Robert Iler): "I'm supposed to get a vasectomy when this is my male heir?" (2.9). Tony's sister Janice (Aida Turturro) plays a less consistent – if equally compelling – role in the feminized narrative of *The Sopranos*. Desper-ate to make a success of her relationship with old flame and former racketeer, Richie Aprile, Janice allows Richie to indulge his fetish of hold-ing a gun to her head during sex – a revelation that shocks Carmela: "I thought you were a feminist?" (2.12), she demands. With a capacity for violence and manipulation which recalls that of her mother, Janice is soon spurred to action by Richie's misogyny: "Put my fucking dinner on the table, and keep your mouth shut", Richie raves, punching her in the mouth when she suggests that his ballroom-dancing son might be gay (2.12). Once recovered, Janice follows up her initial (perceived) assault on Richie's masculinity with another: she coolly shoots her husband-to-be in the chest, killing him outright and fully appropriating the violence of the male gangster.

If *The Sopranos* works to feminize the gangster genre, then it does so most conspicuously, perhaps, through the "openly emotional" narra-tive of psychoanalysis. This separates *The Sopranos* from its predecessors and achieves what Longrigg calls "the successful updating of the mafia image: the boss in therapy" (238). Tony Soprano is introduced to the viewer in the first episode by the voice of psychiatrist Dr Jennifer Melfi

(Lorraine Bracco), as she calls Tony into her office. Set within this psychoanalytic context, Tony's character is mediated, or even interpreted, for the viewer by the character of Dr Melfi. Arguably, then, it is a feminized narrative that governs the characterization of the show's protagonist, extending the gangster narrative's traditional appeal (to male-dominated audiences) out towards the female viewer. Here, also, there is an inversion of the traditional relationship between the male therapist and the female patient: *The Sopranos* places Tony, exuding masculinity, in the place of scrutinized subject, while locating the discourse of diagnosis – historically the domain of men – in the character of Jennifer Melfi, another educated, assertive female. This relationship between therapist and patient is further nuanced by the conflicting desires – sexual, maternal, moral – that shape it; the desire aroused in Tony by Melfi's sharp suits and intellect is at odds with the raw, base appeal of the Bada Bing strippers, while Melfi, in an interesting aside to the (non-)maternal narrative prompted by the character of Livia, wrestles with the desire to mother, judge, and lust after her patient. In short, Tony's sessions with the psychiatrist introduce an authoritative female perspective into the generically masculine realm of the gangster genre, providing a forum in which to expose and critique the behaviour and influence of the text's most dominant female character, Livia Soprano.

Power of the mother

The Italian mother "remains a quasi-mythical figure who looms larger than life in the New World, overshadowing the Martha Stewart-type domestic goddess who rules modern America" (Longrigg 241–42). Yet in the character of Livia Soprano, writes Maria Laurino, "David Chase is trying to turn the stereotype of the Italian mother on its head" (41). Upsetting traditional assumptions about maternal or domestic femininity, Livia shatters the myth of the Italian matriarch with a performance of striking emotional coldness. "Your mother", observes Dr Melfi in a session with Tony, "is always talking about infanticide" (1.12). Indeed, the first two seasons of *The Sopranos* are spiked with Livia's frequent references to acts of maternal violence: "Some woman in Pennsylvania shot her three children ...", she reports with relish over dinner (1.12). Her fascination with such tragic episodes is further darkened by a resentment of her own children: "I gave my life to my children on a silver platter", she spits more than once. This statement, however, is inconsistent with Tony's repressed memories of a childhood marked by Livia's angry outbursts: "You're driving me crazy!" she

screams at a schoolboy-aged Tony, "I could stick this fork in your eye!".
On another occasion she threatens to "smother" her children "with a
pillow", rather than agree to her husband's plans for a move to Nevada
(1.7). Any grandmotherly instincts are similarly absent: in Season Three
we learn that Livia's *Granny Remembers* books – memory journals given
to Livia by Carmela on the birth of Meadow and then Anthony Junior –
have remained stubbornly empty (3.2). Her conclusion that "babies are
animals...no different from dogs" neatly epitomizes her unmotherly
stance (2.12).[4]

Despite these incidents, Tony's resolute denial of his mother's capacity for malevolence protects her from retribution for some time: she
remains on her pedestal as revered Soprano matriarch and maintains
her status as "a quasi-mythical figure". To Tony, Livia is a harmless "little old lady", an illusion that he defends fiercely to Dr Melfi, whose own
character analysis of Tony's mother is rather more accurate:

> DR MELFI: Your mother is clearly someone who has great difficulty
> maintaining a relationship with anyone.
> TONY: But she's my mother. You're supposed to take care of your
> mother. She's a little old lady.
> DR MELFI: Not to you. She's very powerful.
> TONY: Bullshit.
> DR MELFI: You accord this "little old lady" an almost mystical abil-
> ity to wreak havoc.... There are some people who are not ideal
> candidates for parenthood.
> TONY: Come on! She's an old sweetie pie!
>
> (1.2)

Tony's insistence that his mother is a frail old lady and innocent
"sweetie pie" works to underline Livia's successful exploitation of that
very archetype of ageing, fragile femininity. Livia's is a performance that
embraces the image of victim and trades on the supposedly vulnerable status of the elderly woman: she feigns forgetfulness, denies making
spiteful comments, and becomes tearful at will. "I wish the Lord would
take me now" is her self-pitying refrain (1.4). Tony, initially, feels only
guilt in response to his mother's seemingly helpless demise and suffers
the panic attacks that result in his visits to Dr Melfi. Yet, the power
that Dr Melfi identifies in Livia is similarly recognized by Tony's wife,
Carmela, who confronts her mother-in-law:

> CARMELA: I want you to cut the drama...this "poor mother, nobody
> loves me" victim crap. It is textbook manipulation...and I hate

seeing Tony so upset over it.... You know your power, and you use it like a pro.

LIVIA: Power! What power? I don't have power....

CARMELA: You are bigger than life! You are his mother!

(1.11)

Such a striking image of the omnipotent, "bigger than life" mother is presented to the viewer from the very first image of the first episode, which sees Tony sitting in the office of Dr Melfi, "completely framed by the legs of a female nude sculpture (recalling his origins in the birth canal and the power of the mother). His curious gaze upward at the nude sculpture is a radical reversal of the conventionally possessive male gaze" (Nochimson 5). From this moment onwards, the power of the mother continues to frame, if not stifle, the plot development of *The Sopranos*. It comes to dictate not only Tony's personal life, but also the more sinister actions of the New Jersey mob. Occupying "the position of a sort of dowager boss", Livia exerts significant influence over Junior Soprano, brother to Livia's late husband and one-time acting boss of the crime family (Longrigg 241). Junior, Livia believes, is one of the few who treat her with the respect she merits; he pays his sister-in-law frequent visits and seeks her advice on how to deal with traitorous mob members. Preferring to issue her (often life or death) judgements obliquely – with mere assenting silence or trenchant stare – Livia wields considerable authority as the true harbinger of violence. And yet, concurrently, she upholds her unyielding claim to ignorance and a position outside of the gangster narrative: "I'm a babbling idiot", she insists in answer to Junior's comment that she's "got a lot of sense for an old gal" (1.3), while continuing to protest her innocence to Tony: "I don't know that world.... I don't want to get involved" (1.6).

Evidence of Livia's capacity for hostility and violence begins to gather momentum, however, with her racist abuse of the housekeeper whom Tony hires to help her remain in her own home, and the not-quite-clearly-unintentional hospitalization of her best friend, after Livia runs her down on her own driveway. Such incidents escalate, culminating in Livia's ultimate act of violence against her own son. Despite deep feelings of guilt, Tony, concerned about his mother's ability to cope at home alone, proceeds with his plan to place her in the luxurious Green Grove retirement community. For Livia, this is akin to being "abandoned" and her brewing bitterness fuels her decision to condone (and even encourage) Junior's decision to kill off Tony. As Nochimson notes, "Junior and Livia give each other permission to rid themselves of

Tony with such minimalism that the audience is not sure what has transpired between them until the plans to kill Tony are put into action" (4). Livia's chillingly calm endorsement of Junior's hints at violence towards her son marks the understated but pivotal moment at which she severs all associations with the figure of nurturing mother and realizes her fantasies of infanticide. That the attempt on Tony's life is unsuccessful only heightens the politics of their relationship: reluctant to admit his mother's accountability, Tony is struck with confusion and anger when it is proved beyond doubt. Wrestling with emotions of shock and sorrow, he plots revenge in the form of murder, only to bow out in the final moments. He resigns himself instead to the ideological death of the mother he never had: "She's the devil.... She's dead to me" (2.1). And yet, even in the face of such unambiguous iniquity, Tony is unable to relinquish himself of responsibility; the power of the mother holds fast: "What sort of person must I be when my mother wants me dead?" (1.13).

Bodies

The viewer's first introduction to Livia Soprano comes early in the first episode, when Tony enters her house, wafts the air with his hand and mutters, "Jeez, Ma. Get some air in here" (1.1). This, combined with Livia's unkempt hair, shapeless mis-buttoned dressing gown, and distracted grumblings, gives the immediate impression of stale old age. Following this early whiff of senility, however, Livia's physicality receives little narrative attention, and it is this absence, this lack of emphasis on her physicality, that itself takes on significance in a discussion of her violence. As mentioned above, the violent heroine of popular culture conventionally combines danger with desirability; the synthesis of physical aggression with sexuality is a recurring trait in contemporary representations of the violent woman. In contrast, Livia Soprano presents an image of faded, desiccated femaleness. Notwithstanding unconvincing hints at something more than a platonic relationship between Livia and Junior, Livia's is a character of almost androgynous greyness. "In Western society", says Usher, "the ageing reproductive body is the epitome of the abject – with none of the redeeming features of youth or maternal femininity.... Older women", she continues, "are all but invisible within both high and popular culture – with the post-menopausal woman represented as the crone, the hag, or the dried-up grandmother figure, her body covered, and her sexuality long left behind" (126). The character of Livia seems both to fulfil and test this archetype: she is the dried-up grandmother figure of forgotten femininity and yet, almost by her very impression of innocuous invisibility, she remains a dominant, ever-present force within *The Sopranos'* narrative. Arguably, her very lack of physical presence – her ominous consenting silences, tacit stares, and absence from any of the violent acts she condones – is in itself more unsettling than the overt violence of the traditional action heroine. Hers is a private, pervasive violence, a considered disguise that conceals an "explosive virility" all of her own.

Corporeality is, however, central to the traditional gangster narrative, where "almost all the action is written onto the bodies of the gangsters in a subgenre that places great emphasis on physical touch in general, on drinking, and sometimes on food" (Nochimson 6). Food, certainly, plays a major role in *The Sopranos*: the kitchen and dining table provide the focal points for family dramas, while frequent references to traditional Italian dishes are effective reminders of the family's heritage. Food and copious cups of coffee facilitate many of Tony's "business" meetings and, significantly, Tony's first panic attack occurs as he prepares a family barbecue (an association that we later learn harks back to a violent incident he witnessed as a child involving a meat cleaver). Against this gastronomical abundance, however, is Livia's stock rejection of food offerings, most conspicuously those brought to her in the retirement home by Tony. Nochimson suggests that Tony "expresses affection with food in a way that also expresses his power" (60); in turn, Livia's refusal of his food offerings implies an unwillingness to relinquish any authority to her son. Similarly, Livia acts to withhold food on several occasions. In the first episode of the series she declines, sulkily, to attend Anthony Junior's birthday party in an act of premeditated emotional blackmail. Her absence is most visibly marked by the consequent lack of her "baked ziti", a dish that Tony specifically requested she bring. As an object of exchange, then, food in *The Sopranos* carries symbolic resonances of control, and Livia's reluctance both to receive and to give food reflects her quest for power, as well as her physical and emotional coldness. In contrast to Carmela's well-stocked fridge and investment in family mealtimes, Livia's meagre attitude to food further accentuates her lack of maternal warmth.

Emphasis on the body is instead transferred to Tony, whose "rich physicality is a particularly important part of his characterization" (Nochimson 6). In contrast to Livia's lack of physical presence, Tony oozes excess, solidity, and charisma. While Livia shakes off her son's demonstrative attempts to dance with her (1.1), Tony himself receives and imparts physical affection readily, unreservedly kissing and embracing his men – although, like his food offerings, these displays of warmth and affection are arguably expressions of power. His sexual escapades also carry their own mix of passion and detachment: the naked dancers of the Bada Bing strip club, for example, seem desexualized, losing any notes of desire as they fade to the familiar wallpaper of mob meetings. Likewise, Tony's extra-marital affairs are conducted with almost mechanical aloofness. Reinforced by acts of callous violence, Tony's image of robust, self-possessed physicality is threatened only, in fact, by events that are traceable – directly or indirectly – to Livia. The panic attacks, triggered by anxiety about his mother, strike Tony down; trembling and sweating, he loses his all-seeing authority as his vision blurs and he collapses to the ground: Livia literally, if temporarily, disables her son's claim to status. She also endeavours to fell Tony's authority in a more permanent way: the attempt on his life hospitalizes Tony, exposing his vulnerability and drawing attention to his mortality. It is, then, Tony's body, and not his mother's, that is most subject to medicalization. Livia once again flouts the archetype of the ageing, ailing female, seemingly exploiting the opportunity of medical diagnoses only when it suits, while her son struggles with anxiety, cries at ducks, and collects prescriptions for anti-depressants. Such medicalization extends, indeed, to the other male characters of *The Sopranos*. It is the men who are the most frequent victims of violent behaviour and bloodshed, but it is also the male bodies that are the most pathologized – with depression, suicide, cancer, and chronic illness running rife amongst the gangster fraternity. Here, the discourse of diagnosis that has historically contained and classified femaleness within the patriarchal language of medicine – that, in Foucault's terms, "integrated" the female body "into the sphere of medical practices, by reason of a pathology intrinsic to it" (104) – is subverted. In *The Sopranos* it is the male body that is exposed and made medical, and which is, moreover, contained and classified by the feminized discourse of diagnosis represented by Dr Melfi.

Conclusion

Livia Soprano's reign continues until her death, from "a massive stroke", in Season Three of *The Sopranos*. Tellingly, her character's finale was originally planned for the end of the first series but was delayed, in part, because Marchand "made her hatefulness so indelible" (Rosenberg 2). Tony's response to his mother's belated death seems to be overwhelmingly one of relief. His visceral reaction – registered at a visual level in his sweating and bewilderment – is akin to the onset of a panic attack, yet

it subsides into a state of calm composure. He confesses this sense of liberation in his next session with Dr Melfi: "All right, here's the thing. I'm
glad she's dead. Not just glad. I wished she'd die. *Wished*". Any shame at
these feelings is fleeting: "Is that right, wishing her dead? Is that being a
good son?... You're right. Why the fuck should I be a good son to that
fucking demented old bat – that fucking selfish, miserable cunt?" (3.2).
The dramatic transformation of Livia in Tony's eyes from "little old lady"
and "sweetie pie" to "demented old bat" – from revered matriarch to
reviled monster – carries fairytale connotations: the wicked (step)mother
exposed and revenged; the wolf in granny's clothing. Livia, then, is the
storybook villain. She is a woman "who spread no cheer at all", an anti-
heroine whose significance in a discussion of women and violence is
defined by her sheer denial of that violence, as well as her discord with
contemporary representations of female aggression (3.2). Rather than
assuming the overt and masculine aggression of the popular action heroine, Chase's violent woman adopts the passivity traditionally associated
with meek and mild femininity and contorts it into something far more
sinister: a considered disguise of falsified vulnerability. In contrast to
the comic-book carnage of the mainstream action film, the matriarch
of *The Sopranos* confronts the ultimate taboo act of violence: filicide.
Rewriting the narratives of motherhood, of ageing femaleness, and of
the male-dominated gangster genre, Livia Soprano questions what it is
to be "feminine" and offers a striking antidote to the now homogeneous
model of the violent woman that circulates in visual culture.

Notes

1. Dr Melfi, *The Sopranos* (1.1).
2. Livia's rejection of the domestic, maternal femininity that is so abundantly
   embodied by her daughter-in-law, Carmela, invites consideration alongside
   the forms of intergenerational conflict that Shelley Cobb examines in " 'I'm
   nothing like you!': Postfeminist Generationalism and Female Stardom in the
   Contemporary Chick Flick" (in this book).
3. From "Woke Up This Morning" (1997) by the British band Alabama 3.
4. The malevolent (and potentially murderous) mother is a feature of other quality television series, such as *Prison Break* (2005–09) and *Alias* (2001–06). See
   Rosie White "*Alias*: Quality Television and the New Woman Professional" (in
   this book).

Works cited

Coulthard, Lisa. "Killing Bill: Rethinking Feminism and Film Violence". *Interrogating Postfeminism: Gender and the Politics of Popular Culture*. Ed. Yvonne Tasker,
and Diane Negra. Durham and London: Duke University Press, 2007. 153–75.

Creed, Barbara. *The Monstrous Feminine: Film, Feminism, Psychoanalysis*. London, New York: Routledge, 1993.

Foucault, Michel. *The Will to Knowledge: The History of Sexuality: Volume 1*. Trans. Robert Hurley. London: Penguin, 1998. Trans. of *La Volonté de Savoir*. 1976.

Hills, Elizabeth. "From 'Figurative Males' to Action Heroines: Further Thoughts on Active Women in the Cinema". *Screen* 40.1 (1999): 38–50.

Holden, Stephen. "The Sopranos: An Introduction". *The New York Times on The Sopranos*. New York: ibooks, 2000. 37–45.

Laurino, Maria. *Were You Always an Italian?* New York: Norton, 2000.

Longrigg, Clare. "Women in Organized Crime in the United States". *Women and the Mafia*. Ed. Giovanni Fiandaca. Trans. Stephen Jackson. New York: Springer, 2007. 235–82.

McCarty, John. *Bullets Over Hollywood*. Cambridge, MA: Da Capo, 2004.

Nochimson, Martha P. "Waddaya Lookin' At? Re-Reading the Gangster Genre through *The Sopranos*". *Film Quarterly* 56.2 (Winter 2002–03): 2–13.

Read, Jacinda. " 'Once Upon a Time There Were Three Little Girls...': Girls, Violence, and *Charlie's Angels*". *New Hollywood Violence*. Ed. Steven Jay Schnelder. Manchester: Manchester University Press, 2004. 205–29.

Rosenberg, Howard. "Excellence, From 'Marty' to the Mafia". *Los Angeles Times* June 21, 2000 http://articles.latimes.com/2000/jun/21/entertainment/ca-43052. [Accessed January 20, 2010].

Simon, David. *Tony Soprano's America: The Criminal Side of the American Dream*. Oxford: Westview, 2004.

The Sopranos. HBO, 1999–2007.

1.1. "Pilot". Dir. David Chase. January 10, 1999.

1.2. "46 Long". Dir. Dan Attias. January 17, 1999.

1.3. "Denial, Anger, Acceptance". Dir. Nick Gomez. January 24, 1999.

1.4. "Meadowlands". Dir. John Patterson. January 31, 1999.

1.6. "Pax Soprana". Dir. Alan Taylor. February 14, 1999.

1.7. "Down Neck". Dir. Lorraine Senna Ferrara. February 21, 1999.

1.11. "Nobody Knows Anything". Dir. Henry J. Bronchtein. March 21, 1999.

1.12. "Isabella". Dir. Allen Coulter. March 28, 1999.

1.13. "I Dream of Jeannie Cusamano". Dir. John Patterson. April 4, 1999.

2.1. "Guy Walks Into A Psychiatrist's Office". Dir. Allen Coulter. January 16, 2000.

2.9. "From Where to Eternity". Dir. Henry J. Bronchtein. March 12, 2000.

2.12. "A Knight in White Satin Armor". Dir. Allen Coulter. April 2, 2000.

3.2. "Proshai, Livushka". Dir. Tim Van Patten. March 4, 2001.

Usher, Jane M. *Managing the Monstrous Feminine: Regulating the Reproductive Body*. London and New York: Routledge, 2006.

15

A Pathological Romance: Authority, Expert Knowledge and the Postfeminist Profiler

Lindsay Steenberg

Since the late 1980s, behavioural science has become a key element in telling stories about crime. The pseudo-scientific system of profiling, in which the crime scene and personal history of the suspect are used to hypothesize violent behaviour, is so ubiquitous that it has become a cultural commonplace. Profiling's cultural currency depends on truths which are formulated and gendered in ways that might be described as "postfeminist", and this is rendered especially apparent in the characterization of the female criminal profiler. This figure, after all, embodies an expert knowledge that she uses to combat an archetypal postmodern villain: the serial killer.[1] This chapter examines the gender politics of the now-conventional relationship between the postfeminist female investigator and the male serial killer – two figures who are inextricably connected in the popular imaginary. This sexualized and romanticized coupling simultaneously constructs and challenges the female investigator's expertise, making wider pathological observations about female experts whose professional struggles are effectively and implicitly reduced to a tension between their female bodies and their ability to do their jobs.

While the number of women in law enforcement remains small, and most celebrity FBI profilers are men, a large percentage of profilers on film and television are female.[2] Moreover, female profilers have been part of some of the more financially successful and critically acclaimed stories about murder and serial killers. Agent Clarice Starling (Jodie Foster) in *The Silence of the Lambs* (1991) is the most famous cinematic incarnation of this iconic expert. In a testimony to her popular status, the portrayal of the female profiler is significantly consistent: she is as much a type as the serial killer she pursues. This chapter focuses on

Special Agent Illeana Scott (Angelina Jolie), the central character of the 2004 thriller, *Taking Lives*. The film follows her as she travels to Montréal to consult on a case where a serial killer is killing men and stealing their identities. In the process she becomes romantically involved with a key witness who is later revealed to be the serial killer, Martin Asher. As a consequence, Illeana is professionally humiliated. We later learn that her dismissal is a ruse that, along with a faked pregnancy, Illeana uses to lure the killer into the open. The film is typical in its preoccupation with the profiler's sexuality and in imagining a female expert who is white, middle class, educated, and incapable of forming healthy personal relationships because of her dedication to her profession.

In postfeminist fashion, the female profiler's career successes take the opportunities won by second wave feminism as a given. Likewise, these narratives invest heavily in the concept of choice: one can choose to be a victim, or choose to be a gun-wielding FBI profiler. These women's stories celebrate an "empowered", informed individualism and are noticeably suspicious of the concept of the "victim", as well as the feminist analyses that such a designation demands. On the other hand, these characters' severe psychic trauma and lack of a healthy "work/life balance" (so key to postfeminist therapeutic culture) imply that feminism has done damage to women, as well as good. This circular logic is manifest in profiler-led fictions wherein female profilers, like Illeana, start out as deeply unhappy women; indeed, this is usually what leads them to a career in law enforcement. Furthermore, their careers *keep* them unhappy, because they are constantly investigating horrific sexualized violence. Thus, the characterization of the female investigator and the stories in which she appears are marked by a version of what Angela McRobbie terms postfeminist culture's "double entanglement" with second wave feminism (28). The profiler's career successes, authority, and expertise are made possible by the politicized efforts of second wave feminism, yet such positive gains are mediated by the fact that she remains unhappy because of her extreme dedication to a job which constantly exposes her to the serial killer's misogynist violence.

Despite the crime film's equal investment in stable gender roles, postfeminist popular culture is usually discussed in terms of more traditionally "feminine" genres, such as the romantic comedy or the melodrama. These genres share some of the same context and concerns as crime films, but the stakes are very different. As Linda Mizejewski insists,

> [t]he crime film is a genre in which violence is the central trope of relationships between the sexes and in which the transgressive

woman...has long served as a register for anxieties about female sexuality and power. It is the genre most likely to expose both the limitations of the postfeminist heroine and the nasty sex and gender issues that her presence supposedly precludes. (2005, 125)

Almost all of these "nasty sex and gender issues" are played out through the relationship between the female profiler and the serial killer – a relationship that stems from a disturbing combination of mutual trauma, a similar expertise (based on shared experiences of violence), a grudging professional admiration, and, most directly, a sexualized and romanticized attraction. With *Taking Lives* as its representative example, this chapter questions the unstable ways in which postfeminist visual culture informs the crime film and its representation of female power, expertise, and authority.

A profile of the profiler

In *Taking Lives*, Special Agent Illeana Scott is a respected profiler, well-established in her career. She has no personal life, does not date, and wears a fake wedding ring to discourage sexual attention in the workplace. Her work is framed as the most important part of her life and she is deeply dedicated to her job: her every spare moment is spent looking at crime scene photographs. She shares this intensity with the serial killer she hunts and with other cinematic and televisual profilers. This commitment to profiling is a distinctly gendered phenomenon. Male profilers, such as Will Graham in *Manhunter* (1986), Jack Crawford in *The Silence of the Lambs*, or the protagonists of the CBS series *Criminal Minds* (2005–), are framed as dangerously similar to the killers themselves. By projecting themselves into the killer's mindset in order to catch him, they risk being psychologically damaged, as happens to Will Graham. Where the male profiler is doubled with the killer and in danger of becoming *like* him, the female profiler is positioned as being dangerously attracted *to* the killer. Profilers like Clarice Starling in the Hannibal Lecter series, Agent Sara Moore in *Mindhunters* (2004), and Illeana Scott in *Taking Lives* are in danger of losing their critical distance, their professional standing, and even their lives because of their inextricable entanglement with the serial killer.

The expertise of the female profiler is founded on the assumption that the serial killer is a mobile sexual predator, unlike any others that have come before. This definition originated in the Behavioural Science Unit of the FBI, and was first brought to public attention in a 1983 Justice Department Press Conference (Schmid 77). This conference simultaneously constructed the serial killer as an immediate and real predator and championed the FBI as the source of experts best suited to capturing him. According to David Schmid, the press conference, and the flurry of popular press that followed, emphasized certain significant elements in their definition. They focused on the mobility of the serial killer, skewed the scope of his crimes, and – perhaps most significantly – considered serial killing to be essentially *sexual* in nature.[3] These three elements, taken up at the expense of all others, remain the basis for the expertise of behavioural scientists such as Illeana. Her relationship to the serial killer, Martin Asher, depends upon his ubiquitous, threatening nature and his sexual obsession with her. As part of the Behavioural Science Unit, Illeana's expertise, like that of all profilers in popular visual culture, is dependent on a perception of the serial killer as a dangerous sexual predator; her ability and willingness to stand against such a predator gives her credibility and further sexualizes her criminal investigations.

Sharing trauma and expertise

Despite her heroic and authoritative position in the film, Illeana is a deeply traumatized individual. This is clear in her pathological dedication to her work, and in her confession that she accidentally killed a prowler when she was a child. The film frames this formative moment as the reason why she chose law enforcement as a career. Illeana channels these traumatic experiences into her professional performance, and they allow her to identify other traumatized and traumatizing individuals. The mutual experience of trauma ties the serial killer to the female profiler. Serial killer Martin Asher struggles to deal with the legacy of a troubled childhood in which he was hated by his mother and overshadowed by his twin brother (whose death he witnessed and may have accidentally caused). Where Illeana deals with her experience of violence by becoming a profiler, Martin distances himself from his trauma by violently assuming other men's identities. It is, then, Illeana's psychological damage that not only drives her to excel at work but also offers her an insight into the troubled world of the serial killer.

Illeana and Martin's shared experience of childhoods marked by violence contributes to their remarkably similar knowledge base – a database built up around an eclectic collection of facts and disciplines. The expertise of the profiler (like that of the serial killer) draws on multiple and disparate sources, including psychology, forensics, and intuition. The feedback loop of cliché (Seltzer 126) that informs the serial killer is equally important to the profiler and her expertise. Both profiler and killer are experts in the subject of mediated violence, having equal experience of violence and the mediated translation of psychological pain into pathological action. They are both able to read, reproduce, and reflect on patterns of violence and trauma, and this shared referencing system is the primary method of interaction between them. It is at the crime scene that this communication takes place – through the killer's staging and the profiler's semiotic analysis. In her ability to read the mise-en-scene of the crime scene, and because of the scope of her knowledge, Illeana's insight into the killer's mind is unmatched, enhancing her status in the eyes of her colleagues and the eyes of the killer.

As soon as Martin meets Illeana he begins to communicate with her in his disguise as a murder witness, and also through his violent acts and the clues he leaves at the crime scenes. Once Illeana discovers his true identity, Martin tries to persuade her that she has been attracted to the killer in him all along; that in him she has found a true equal partner. Pointing to her habit of posting crime scene photographs all over her room and her ability to internalize her crime scene analysis, Martin demands that Illeana recognize their shared experiences of violence and thus their deep (romantic) connection and comparable worldview. He insists, as do many profiler-led fictions, that their growing relationship is one characterized by a mutual and grudging respect for each other's expertise in violence – a reciprocal recognition of each other's intelligence and panache. The "perfect partnership" established in profiler fictions highlights not only the similarities between two conventional character types, but also the fact that both rely equally on violence for their careers, authority, and even celebrity.

The grudgingly respectful partnership between profiler and serial killer is common to many serial killer narratives, regardless of the investigator's gender. However, the *female* profiler's relationship to the killer is sexualized, and the parameters of her expert knowledge are defined explicitly by her embodied experience of the world. In the novel *The Bone Collector*,[4] which tells the story of a young woman's induction into forensics, the expert investigator is described as "a renaissance man":

He's got to know botany, ballistics, medicine, chemistry, literature, engineering. If he knows facts – that ash with high strontium content probably came from a highway flare, that *faca* is Portuguese for

"knife", that Ethiopian diners use no utensils... [then] he may just
make the connection that places an unsub at the crime scene. (132)

Like the "renaissance man" of *The Bone Collector*, the female expert's
authority as a profiler is augmented by her mastery of other kinds of specialized knowledge; in particular, she possesses a "woman's intuition"
that allows her to make unique connections. These connections tend to
hinge on her experience as a woman (and thus her insider knowledge of
the genre's predominantly female victims), as well as her comprehensive
understanding of postfeminist culture and its central preoccupations:
fashion, celebrity, and self-help rhetoric.

Clarice Starling, for example, is able to tell that a woman wearing glittery nail varnish is not from the small town in which her body was
found, and Illeana is able to communicate with (and profile) Martin
Asher's mother much more successfully than the French-Canadian
police officers with whom she is partnered. Like other postfeminist
investigators, such as criminalist Catherine Willows in *CSI: Crime Scene
Investigation* (2000–) and Samantha Waters in *The Profiler* (1996–2000),
Illeana is familiar with traditionally feminine areas of expertise: fashion
and consumer culture. The female investigator notices these overlooked
details, particularly in relation to female victims, and applies this unof-
ficial knowledge where her male counterparts would not. Similarly,
the serial killer does not consider the factor of "women's intuition"
when he is staging the crime scene, despite the knowledge base he
shares with the female expert. Often, then, the female profiler's awareness of postfeminist culture allows her to get ahead of the killer she
hunts.

"That's my Girl!": Investigating the serial killer romance

As a woman, Illeana is singularly able to identify the sexual charge of the
male killer's violence. She tells her colleagues, "there's a sexual element
to all this... the strangling from behind, cutting off the hands, smashing in the face. It's tactile. It's immediate. It's what turns him on". Thus,
the communication via the crime scene is something that the female
profiler is able to read with a greater degree of accuracy than the male
profiler. Because she reads with such accuracy, especially with regard to
the sexual nature of the crime, Illeana's relationship to the serial killer
is both sexualized and romanticized. These terms are not interchangeable. Crime narratives focus on violent sexualized acts committed by the

serial killer, and he is framed as sexually (and compulsively) attracted to the female profiler. But their relationship is also framed as romantic. This is, for the most part, down to the high cultural status that characterizes many representations of the serial killer (from Hannibal Lector to Martin Asher). His knowledge of art, history, and poetry frequently signals and taps into (postfeminist) notions of romance and chivalry. Furthermore, serial killers, like Martin Asher, consider the female profiler as an equal/partner, as the one person who can read his violent acts and decipher their deeper significance. This is certainly true of the profiler/serial killer relationships in *The Silence of the Lambs*, *Mindhunters*, and the television series *The Profiler*. The serial killer Jack (Dennis Christopher) in *The Profiler* leaves red roses at crime scenes to communicate with profiler Samantha Waters. Like Illeana Scott, Agent Sara Moore is in love with the (then unknown) serial killer in *Mindhunters*. In *Hannibal* (2001) Lector kidnaps Clarice Starling. He drugs her and, in the process of trying to convince her to join him in a cannibalistic feast, gives her a makeover. When Clarice resists him and fights him at every step, he responds with admiration, at one point commenting, "that's my girl". This statement of both approval and ownership is representative of the eroticized and romanticized relationship that exists between the female profiler and the male serial killer. However, where the intimate nature of this connection is only implied in a film like *Hannibal*, it is rendered deliberately explicit in the sexual relationship that develops between Martin Asher and Illeana in *Taking Lives*.

Despite contributing to the female profiler's authority, her relationship to the serial killer also delegitimizes her professionalism. Illeana's inability to identify her sexual/romantic partner as the killer puts her in physical danger and undermines her professional authority. After Martin's true identity is revealed, Illeana faints. Later Joseph Paquette (Olivier Martinez), one of her fellow officers, publicly slaps her and she is fired from the job to which she is so dedicated. Here, Illeana's credibility and expertise are not only questioned as a result of her sexual(ized) relationship with the serial killer, but also as a result of her sexuality itself. The film implies that Illeana brings sex into the workplace simply because she is an attractive woman. She creates problems for fellow officers, especially Paquette, who regards Illeana as alternately attractive and suspicious. Expending his energies on flirting with and/or berating Illeana, Paquette is incapable of focusing fully on his job; he chooses, moreover, to blame Illeana for his feelings, and for the professional inefficiency they produce.

This sexualized disruption extends to the crime scene. Our first view of Agent Scott has her lying in a victim's grave. She is framed in close-up via a slow tracking shot along her body and is lit with soft low-key lighting more appropriate to a love scene. She gazes at the crime scene photographs pasted in her hotel room in a shot/reverse shot pattern – with the photographs taking the place of an interlocutor. Placed in the bedroom, the bathtub, and at the dinner table, the photograph-person appears to assume the position of a lover.

The sexualization of violent serial crime, especially given the FBI's pervasive definition, remains a key factor in most stories about crime. The female profiler brings another layer of sexuality to the crime scene, connecting the sexual nature of the violent act to the sexual characterization of the female investigator. This is made clear in Illeana's sexual reading of the killer's violence at the crime scene. Illeana brings sex into a place where it is inseparable from violence. This, by extension, pathologizes her sexuality. Illeana's co-workers, and the film itself, insinuate that she sexualizes violence simply because she is investigating it. Taken a step further, through the pathological romance between serial killer and female profiler, these films suggest that there is something fundamentally unsettling about a woman investigating serial crime.

Philip L. Simpson has suggested that the serial killer is often sent as punishment for the "original sin" of the profiler (24) – almost as punishment for the profiler's faults and shortcomings. This is germane given the characterization of male profilers as isolated, antisocial, compulsive, and often traumatized (for example, Will Graham in *Manhunter* and Detective Somerset in *Se7en* [1995]). This is more sinister when considering female profilers such as Illeana Scott, since she is not being punished for inappropriate behaviour exclusively, but for her gender as well. In this sense, the female profiler becomes defined and marked by the "original sin" of her body. She is unable to escape her gendered body or the pathological sexual relationship to which it commits her. The female profiler must build her authority *despite* her body, rather than through it. Consequently, Illeana faces violence, humiliation, and professional discredit to an extent that male profilers, such as Will Graham, do not.

Yet, undoubtedly, there is spectatorial pleasure to be had from these fictions. One of the key pleasures offered by crime films is the construction of the female investigator as a scientific expert and veteran professional. This plays out through her relationship to the unambiguously evil killer. While this relationship necessarily foregrounds the nuances of the investigative role, this role is always and already complex, as Ronald Thomas observes in his history of forensic science's relationship to the detective:

> At stake is not just the identification of a dead victim or an unknown suspect, but the demonstration of the power invested in certain forensic devices embodied in the figure of the ... detective. (2)

The relationship between the serial killer and the female expert allows the latter to dazzle audiences and co-workers with her command of technology, her mental database, and her familiarity with violence and trauma. Still, the pleasure in these texts is ultimately short-lived, as the female investigator is simultaneously discredited and victimized.

In his book on serial killers, Mark Seltzer describes violence primarily as an identity-building tool:

> In cases of serial sexual homicide, the withering of self-distinction is channelled in the direction of a distinctly gendered violence: as if the violent reaffirmation of sexual difference were one way, in our culture the most emphatic way, of securing or reaffirming self-difference as such. (144)

Seltzer further discusses this violence as a literal battle of the sexes. He describes the identity-tension of postmodernity (and post-industrial alienation, in particular) as "find[ing] its path of least resistance along the lines of sexual difference" (146). At first glance such a consideration of sexualized violence recalls feminist criminology's linkages of patriarchal structures with serial sexual murder – linkages which inform feminist descriptions of serial crime as "femicide" (Jenkins 139). Criminologists such as Deborah Cameron and Elizabeth Frazer have suggested that serial sexual murder (and arguably the more general sexualized nature of violence in crime fiction) can be placed on a continuum, with seemingly innocuous sexism – such as sexist jokes – on one side, and serial sexual murder as the terminal end point (164). Seltzer and Philip Jenkins dismiss such feminist interpretations of serial murder and its representations.[5] Seltzer describes feminist arguments as "self-evident, even tautological" (143), and Jenkins believes them to be exaggerations (141–42). Imagining masculinity as essentially (and psychically) sadistic, violent, and misogynist cannot adequately or fully account for the romanticized partnership between the expert female investigator and the male serial killer. However, it would also be an oversight not to acknowledge what postfeminist culture stands to gain by dramatizing a romance between a profiler and a serial killer – a disciplinary tactic that pathologizes female expertise and professional women who are unable to reconcile that expertise with their femininity.

In as much as the figure of the serial killer can be read as symptomatic of postmodernity, as Seltzer claims, I argue that both he and the female profiler by whom he is hunted speak to the concerns and preoccupations of postfeminist culture. Their pathological romance champions many of the same principles as the more traditionally feminine products of postfeminist media culture, such as the romantic comedy. Like the romantic comedy, profiler/serial killer fictions, such as *Taking Lives*, present a cautionary tale of a professional woman who fails to combine a career with "appropriate" femininity. Still, the violent nature of her profession differentiates the investigator from other postfeminist career women; she is, after all, punished violently for her involvement with the serial killer and for her criminal profiling, even as this showcases her authority.

It is tempting to read the relationship between the serial killer and the female investigator as a literal embodiment of the 1980s backlash against second wave feminism, given that it is historically continuous with the FBI's definition of, and popular culture's fascination with, the serial killer. The serial killer is a sexual predator who hunts victims – predominantly women – in public places with no obvious motivation, other than the fact that he confuses violence for sex. Just as the Gothic monster has been theorized as the product of fears about modernization, the serial killer could be read as a representative of a punitive and anxious postfeminist masculinity. The serial killer/profiler relationship is much more complex than a simple embodiment of backlash.[6] It registers anxieties about female professionalism and authority, about shifting perceptions of risk in postmodernity, about the construction of expertise, and about the violent articulation of sexuality. Linnie Blake argues that in the "improbable union of Hannibal Lecter and Clarice Starling we can…see a range of popular cultural discourses coming together in a deliciously satisfying synthesis" (208). There is, unfortunately, nothing "improbable" about the union between male serial killer and female profiler. Given contemporary postfeminist culture's suspicion of female authority and sexualization of violence, it is disturbingly inevitable.

Notes

1. With very few exemptions, the serial killer is represented as a man. While exceptional figures, such as Aileen Wuornos, are certainly significant, this article looks to the much more typical male killers. For a more detailed analysis of the female serial killer (and Aileen Wuornos's representation in *Monster* [2003]), see Lisa Purse's "Return of the 'Angry Woman': Authenticating Female Physical Action in Contemporary Cinema" (in this collection).
2. Linda Mizejewski puts the number of women working in law enforcement at approximately 10 per cent as of 2005 (123).
3. David Schmid concludes that "since 1983, the assumption that serial murder can be unproblematically equated solely with sexual homicide can be found in more or less explicit form in practically any discussion of serial murder, whether in the mass media, an academic treatise, a public policy document, or a psychological study of an individual offender" (78).
4. The film of The *Bone Collector* was made in 1999. Like *Taking Lives*, it features Angelina Jolie in the role of an expert investigator.
5. See Seltzer 142–44 and Jenkins 139–50.
6. It is likewise tempting to read the serial killer as the embodiment of the much-discussed crisis in masculinity. Still, such allegorical readings cannot account for the complexity of these representations, or for the consistency with which the serial killer/profiler relationship is implicated in the construction of an "empowered" postfeminist femininity.

Works cited

Blake, Linnie. "Whoever Fights Monsters: Serial Killers, the FBI and America's Last Frontier". *The Devil Himself: Villain in Detective Fiction and Film*. Ed. Stacy Gillis, and Philippa Gates. Westport: Greenwood Press, 2002. 196–210.

Cameron, Deborah, and Elizabeth Frazer. *The Lust to Kill: A Feminist Investigation of Sexual Murder*. Cambridge: Polity Basil Blackwell, 1987.

Deaver, Jeffrey. *The Bone Collector*. London: Hodder & Stoughton Ltd., 2006.

Hannibal. Dir. Ridley Scott. MGM/Universal, 2001.

Jenkins, Philip. *Using Murder: The Social Construction of Serial Homicide*. Hawthorne: Aldine de Gruyter, 1994.

McRobbie, Angela. "Postfeminism and Popular Culture: Bridget Jones and the New Gender Regime". *Interrogating Postfeminism: Gender and the Politics of Popular Culture*. Ed. Yvonne Tasker, and Diane Negra. Durham: Duke University Press, 2007. 27–39.

Mizejewski, Linda. "Dressed to Kill: Postfeminist Noir". *Cinema Journal* 44.2 (2005): 121–27.

Schmid, David. *Natural Born Celebrities: Serial Killers in American Culture*. Chicago: University of Chicago Press, 2005.

Seltzer, Mark. *Serial Killers: Life and Death in America's Wound Culture*. New York: Routledge, 1998.

The Silence of the Lambs. Dir. Jonathan Demme. Orion, 1991.

Simpson, Philip L. *Psycho Paths: Tracking the Serial Killer Through Contemporary American Film and Fiction*. Carbondale: Southern Illinois University Press, 2000.

Taking Lives. Dir. D. J. Caruso. Warner Bros, 2004.

Thomas, Ronald R. *Detective Fiction and the Rise of Forensic Science*. Cambridge: Cambridge University Press, 2003.

Index

ABC, 50, 66, 92
action cinema, 185–98
action television, 45–57
Aeon Flux, 185–6, 189, 192
Akass, Kim, 91
Alias, 45–8, 51–5, 187
Aliens, 186, 187, 206
Ally McBeal, 45
AMC, 64
American Princess, 138–51
America's Next Top Model, 145
"angry women," 185–96
Annie Hall, 20
anti-social behaviour orders
    (ASBOs), 153
Australian Princess, 138–51

Baby Boom, 17, 18–9, 20–1, 25
backlash against feminism, 3, 38, 199
Balsamo, Anne, 129–30
Banet-Weiser, Sarah, 127, 130
Barnes, Elizabeth, 46–7
Bartky, Sandra Lee, 124
Bashir, Samiya, 91
Baumgardner, Jennifer., 83
BBC, 105, 137, 169
Becker, Ron, 106
Bell, David, 133n
Bennett, Tony, 200, 204
Best, Amy, 201
black women, 36, 91–100, 205–6, 208,
    210–1
Black, Jeremy, 199, 205, 210
Black Widow, 78
Blade: Trinity, 186, 187
Blake, Linnie, 234
Blum, Virginia L., 130–1
Body Heat, 78
Bold, Christine, 200, 203
Bond, (James), franchise, 199–212
Bone Collector, The, 229–30
Bordo, Susan, 86, 130

Bourdieu, Pierre, 143–4
Boyle, Karen, 58–9
Brand New You, 126, 128, 131
Brave One, The, 186, 195
Breakfast at Tiffany's, 176
Breakfast Club, The, 78
Brick, 78
Britain's Next Top Model, 143
Broke-Smith, Jean, 142, 145–50
Brown, Maggie, 105–6
Brunsdon, Charlotte, 2, 27, 155, 165,
    168, 178
Bruzzi, Stella, 167
Buffy the Vampire Slayer, 45, 68, 187
Burrell, Paul, 142, 145–50
Butler, J., 90, 94, 100, 142–3, 145,
    167, 179
Buttafuoco, J., 77

Caged Heat, 188
Cagney and Lacey, 20
Cameron, Deborah, 233
Cartmell, Deborah, 173
Casino Royale, 208–9
Castle, Terry, 58
CBS, 50, 68, 227
Celebrity Fit Club, 141
Channel 4 Corporation, 103–18
    lesbian teens on, 109–18
    public service and queer
        broadcasting on, 104–9
Charlie's Angels, 186, 187, 188, 189,
    190, 213
Chase, David, 213, 217
"chick flicks," 31–42
Ciasullo, Ann M., 94, 106
Cinderella narrative, 172
Cinderella Story, A, 169, 178
class, 7, 13, 47, 48, 124, 127, 136–8,
    141, 143, 144–7, 154, 156–60,
    164, 165n, 170, 175, 176, 188,
    189, 191, 193

Clover, Carol, 195
Clueless, 178
Collis, Rose, 103
colonialism, 136, 138–9, 140, 147
Coming Home, 33
consumerism, 125–6, 129–32, 154–5,
    157, 162
Cook, Pam, 168, 176, 188, 193, 197
cosmetic surgery, 123–32
Coulthard, Lisa, 213
Creed, Barbara, 61, 69, 71, 213
crime narratives, 226–7, 230–1
criminality, 79, 153
Criminal Minds, 227
Cruel Intentions, 80–7
Crush, The, 78, 80
CSI: Crime Scene Investigations, 50, 230

Daly, Mary, 124, 133
Damages, 59
Davis, Glyn, 107–8
Davis, Kathy, 131
Day, Katy, 153
de Beauvoir, Simone, 6, 14
Deer Hunter, The, 39
Desert Hearts, 92, 111
Desperate Housewives, 60, 64, 66–7, 68
Devil in the Flesh, 79
Devil Wears Prada, The, 31, 32, 38,
    39, 59
Dickinson, Kay, 107
Die Another Day, 208
Disclosure, 46
Doane, Mary Ann, 171–2
Dr. No, 200
documentary, 128, 141, 154
Dodd, Alan, 34, 35
domesticity, 6, 9, 11, 21–3, 25, 29n,
    36, 38, 58–71, 154, 158, 161,
    214–5, 217, 223n
Douglas, Susan J., 48–9, 126, 175
Dow, Bonnie, 108
Down With Love, 26
Drake, Jennifer, 175, 205
Driscoll, Catherine, 78, 85–6
Driver, Susan, 108
Durden-Smith, Mark, 143, 146
Dyer, Richard, 33, 100

Ebert, Teresa, 130
E4, 105
Elektra, 186, 189
Ellen, 92, 103
Ellis, Kate Ferguson, 70
ER, 49
exploitation films, 188
Extreme Makeover, 126

Faculty, The, 78
Faludi, Susan, 3, 38, 155, 204, 211
family, 8, 10, 21, 29n, 31, 32, 46–7,
    54, 59, 62, 64–70, 79, 109–12, 200
Fantastic Four, 186, 189
Fatal Attraction, 50, 78, 178
Father of the Bride, 20
femininity, 2–13, 19, 21, 25, 38, 46,
    54–5, 201
  active, 52, 186–91, 193, 206, 213–4
  ageing, 217–8, 220, 221, 223
  appearance and, 123–32
  as commodity, 22, 132, 191, 230
  authenticity and, 124–5, 127–8,
      130, 132
  domestic, 58–76
  empowerment and, 125, 216
  ethnicity and, 34
  heterosexuality and, 46
  "hyper", 18, 92
  neotraditional, 155–64
  performance of, 96, 112–3, 117,
      138, 168–79, 206
  popular culture and, 27
  postfeminism and, 22, 31, 42, 125,
      155–6, 209, 226, 234
  race and, 37, 47, 93, 100n, 127
  second wave feminism and, 35
  teen, 79, 81–2, 84–6, 88
  work and, 46, 50, 234
feminism
  accounts of, 3–4, 62, 123
  as commodity, 78
  backlash against, 3, 38, 155, 204–5,
      211n
  caricatures of, 31–2, 35–6, 38–42,
      138, 168, 170, 174, 210
  empowerment and, 79, 174,
      178, 226

femininity and, 1–3, 7, 9, 21, 35, 60, 62, 123–5, 129–30, 132, 164, 171
    generational conflict and, 7–9, 31–43, 58, 123–4
    popular, 4, 17–9, 27–8
    popular culture and, 4–7, 33, 99, 103–4, 109, 133n, 199, 206, 213, 216
    second wave, 3, 5–6, 8–9, 11, 18, 20, 27–8, 31, 35, 37, 47, 49, 58–9, 83, 123, 154–5, 179n, 188, 207, 226, 234
    third wave, 205, 208
femme fatale, 77–88
Film4, 105
Fisher, Amy, 77, 79
Fiske, John, 130
Flesh Wounds, 130–1
Fonda, Jane, 8, 32–9, 42–3
Forces of Nature, 20
Ford, Elizabeth, 168, 172, 174, 178
For Your Eyes Only, 204
Foucault, Michel, 131
Fradley, Martin, 34, 35
Frazer, Deborah, 233
Freud, Sigmund, 23, 60–2, 65, 197
Friedan, Betty, 6, 60–4, 66, 70, 124
From Russia with Love, 201, 203
Funny Face, 169, 173, 177
Furedi, Frank, 162

gangster genre, 214–7
Garner, Jennifer, 52–3
gay programming, 106
Ghost Whisperer, 60, 68–70, 71
Ghost World, 168
Gill, Rosalind, 22, 28, 104, 127
Gillespie, Rosemary, 10, 132
Gillis, Stacy, 7, 43
"Girl Power," 4, 10, 11, 83, 153–6, 163–5, 169, 207
girls
    as femme fatales, 77–87
    as ladettes, 153–64, 165n
    as lesbians, 108–18
    as "Lolitas", 77–8, 80–1, 86
    "in crisis", 86–8
    identity of, 171, 173, 176, 178, 179n
    violence and, 194–5, 197n

Gok's Fashion Fix, 167, 168, 169
GoldenEye, 207
Goldman, Robert, 188–9
Gordon, Avery, 58
Gorton, Kristyn, 18
Gove, Ben, 107
Granada Entertainment, 141, 157
Grand, Sarah, 47
Greer, Germaine, 6, 14
Grossman, Julie, 88n
Guardian, The, 3, 143

Halberstam, Judith, 92, 100
Hancock, 189, 195, 196
Hannibal, 231
Hard Candy, 186, 194–5
Hardt, Michael, 139–40
Hathaway, Anne, 39–40
HBO, 45, 91, 213
Heckerling, Amy, 78
Heckert, Druann. M., 201
Hell's Kitchen, 137, 141
Hepburn, Audrey, 168, 173, 176–7, 179
Hesford, Victoria, 59
heterosexuality, 18–22, 24–5, 28, 37, 92–3, 94, 95, 106, 108, 110–1, 124, 127, 160, 164, 167–8, 173, 177, 178, 191, 199, 203, 209
Heyes, Cressida, 129
Heywood, Leslie, 175, 205
Hobson, Dorothy, 105
Holden, Stephen, 213
Holiday, The, 17, 26
Holliday, Ruth, 129
Hollows, Joanne, 1, 5–6, 133, 156
Holmes, Su, 133, 154
homosexuality, 92, 94–9, 104, 106–18, 203, 210, 210n
Honeymoon in Bali, 25
Hope Floats, 21
How to Look Good Naked, 128, 169
Humbert, Brigine E., 82
Hunt, Helen, 19

information, computer technologies, and telecommunications (ICT), 48
Irigaray, Luce, 50–52, 55–6, 62
Ironwood, 39

I Spit On Your Grave, 193
It's Complicated, 17, 26–7
ITV, 105, 141, 154, 157

Jackson, Stevi, 27
Jancovich, Mark, 55
Jardine, Alice, 47
Jenkins, Patty, 191, 233, 235
Jermyn, Deborah, 154
Jersey Girl, 34
Joan of Arcadia, 68
Jolie, Angelina, 189, 226
Jones, Amelia, 46–7, 50
Jones, Grace, 205–6, 208, 210

Katrak, Ketu H., 140
Keaton, Diane, 18–9
Kehily, Mary Jane, 87
Kill Bill, 189, 195–6, 213
Kissing Jessica Stein, 111
Klute, 33
Kramer vs. Kramer, 38, 41

ladettes, 155–6
Ladette to Lady, 138, 143, 153–65
"Lady Power," 155, 156–7
Lara Croft: Tomb Raider, 186, 187,
    189, 213
Laurino, Maria, 217
Lauzen, Martha L., 26
lesbianism, 90–102, 103–20
    black lesbians, 91–5, 97–100
    butch/femme, 91–4, 97–100, 112,
        118n
    teen lesbians, 109–18
    visibility, 103–4, 106
Lethal Lolita, 77
Leverette, Marc, 91
Levy, Ariel, 5, 58, 88, 153
Live and Let Die, 204
Living Daylights, The, 204
Longrigg, Clare, 215–17, 219
Lopez, Jennifer, 34, 35
Los Angeles Times, The, 39, 40, 42
Love with a Vengeance, 61
Lury, Karen, 107
L Word, The, 91, 92–3, 95, 103, 112
Lyons, James, 55

Mad Men, 60, 64–6, 67, 68
Maid in Manhattan, 34, 169, 170
makeovers, 123–34, 136–51, 153–63,
    165n, 167–78
male gaze, 52
male-identified beauty, 123
male promiscuity, 85
Mallan, Kerry, 80
Manhattan, 39
Manhunter, 227, 232
Man with the Golden Gun, The, 204
marriage, 19–20, 25, 35–6, 46–7, 139,
    144, 163
Matrix, 189
McCabe, Janet, 91
McCarty, John, 215
McClintock, Anne, 147
McRobbie, Angela, 1, 31, 37, 46, 58,
    104, 125, 156, 164–5, 167,
    178, 226
Mean Girls, 169, 178
Medium, 60, 68–70
Meyers. Nancy, 8, 17–29
Millett, Kate, 6, 14
Mindhunters, 227, 231
Miss America beauty pageant, 123,
    124
Mitchell, Deborah, 168, 172, 174, 178
Mr. and Mrs. Smith, 187, 189, 195
Mizejewski, Linda, 172, 226, 235
Modleski, Tania, 56, 61
"mommy track," 48–9
Monster, 186, 191–6
Monster-in-Law, 31, 32–3, 34–8, 59
Moonraker, 204
Morgan, Kathryn P., 131
Moseley, Rachel, 5–6, 136, 164, 174,
    178–9
mothers, 21, 22, 34, 36, 38, 47–8, 51,
    61, 63–4, 176–7, 189, 213–23, 228
Mulvey, Laura, 5, 52
Mummy, The, 186
Munford, Rebecca, 7, 43, 79
My Fair Lady, 167, 168

Nanny 911, 137, 141
Nayak, Anoop, 87
NBC, 49

Negra, Diane, 1, 4, 7, 21, 28, 31, 61,
    156, 207
Negri, Antonio, 139–40
neoliberalism, 28
"New Economy," 48–9, 50
"new woman professional", 45–56
New York Radical Women's group,
    123
Nochimson, Martha P., 214–15,
    219, 221
Now Voyager, 167–71, 173

objectification, 188
O'Day, Marc, 188
On Her Majesty's Secret Service,
    201, 203
Opposite of Sex, The, 78
Orenstein, Peggy, 88, 151
Out of Africa, 39
Out of Sight, 34
Owen, Susan, A., 207

Page, Ellen, 194
Palmer, Gareth, 129, 143–4
Pearce, Sharyn, 80
Perkins, Tessa, 33, 43
Perrons, Diane, 49, 56n
Point Pleasant, 68
Poison Ivy, 78, 79, 80
popular feminism, 17–28
Portwood-Stacer, Laura, 127, 130
post-documentary culture, 154
postfeminism, 1, 3–14, 17–29, 31–2,
    34–8, 40–2, 46, 55, 58–62, 71,
    78–81, 83, 86–7, 104, 125–7, 129,
    132, 136, 153–5, 157, 163–5,
    167–71, 174–5, 177–8, 187–90,
    197, 200, 207–10, 214, 225–7,
    230, 231, 234, 235
post-lesbian space, 104, 109
Presumed Innocent, 46, 47, 50
Pretty in Pink, 78, 168
Pretty Persuasion, 80–7
Pretty Woman, 167, 168, 169, 170, 172,
    177–8
Prime, 31
Prince Charming, 144, 148, 151
Prince & Me, The, 145
Princess Diana, 142, 143

Princess Diaries, The, 40, 145
Princess Elizabeth, 142
princesses, 138, 140–5, 147–50
Princess shows, 144–5, 148–9
Private Benjamin, 17, 18, 19–20, 21
Probyn, Elspeth, 155, 165
Profiler, The, 230, 231
Projansky, Sarah, 155, 165, 188
Project Runway, 145
Pygmalion narrative, 168, 172

Quantum of Solace, 209
Queer as Folk, 92, 106

race, 7, 9, 37, 47, 48, 49, 91–5, 96,
    97–100, 136, 138, 140–2, 188–9,
    191, 205, 207
Radner, Hilary, 47, 49, 56
rape-revenge narratives, 187–8, 192–4,
    197n
Read, Jacinda, 213
reality TV, 128, 132, 137, 140–3, 145,
    147, 149, 154, 157, 165n
Rebecca, 173
Red Sonja, 206
Resident Evil, 187, 189, 195
Richards, Amy, 83
Richardson, Niall, 154
Rixon, Paul, 91
Roberts, Chadwick, 42
Roberts, Martin, 129, 132, 134, 158,
    165
Robins, Kevin, 91
Roe v. Wade, 35
Roripaugh, Lee, 109, 118
Rosenberg, Howard, 222
royalty, 138, 139, 143–3, 145–6
Runaway Bride, 20

Save the Last Dance, 168, 178
Schilt, Kristen, 93
Schlafly, Phyllis, 38
Schmid, David, 228, 235
Sedgwick, Eve Kosofsky, 92
Seltzer, Mark, 229, 233–5
serial killer romance, 225–34
Sex and the City, 26, 45, 91, 92, 168

sexuality, 7, 9, 47, 50, 68, 69, 75–120
  deviance and, 199–203, 210
  empowerment and, 47, 78–87, 185,
    187–9, 195, 207, 226–7
  female, 45, 50, 51, 52, 54, 66, 68,
    69, 78–87, 199–201, 207, 208,
    210, 214, 226–7
  promiscuity and, 156, 157, 159, 165n
  violence and, 193–5, 202, 206–8,
    226–34, 235n
Shary, Timothy, 78, 171
Shea, Katt, 78
She's All That, 168, 169–78
Shyer, Charles, 17, 28
Silence of the Lambs, The, 225, 227, 231
Silkwood, 39
Simon, David, 213
Simpson, Philip L., 232
Sin City, 186
Six Feet Under, 66
Skeggs, Beverley, 156, 158
Skins, 103–4, 106–18
Sliding Doors, 173
Smith, Anna Marie, 26, 91–2
Smith, Sharon L., 188
Something's Gotta Give, 17, 26
Sophie's Choice, 39
Sopranos, The, 213–23
Spy Who Loved Me, The, 204
Stacey, Jackie, 92
Stanworth, Celia, 48–49
Steele, Valerie, 174
Stone, Alison, 205
Storey, John, 134
Straayer, Chris, 81
Streep, Meryl, 32, 38–42
Sugar Rush, 103–4, 106–18
Swan, The, 126
Sweet Home Alabama, 21
Swimfan, 79

Taft, Jessica K., 207
Tait, Sue, 126, 132
Takacs, Stacy, 48–49
Taking Lives, 226, 227–8, 231
Tasker, Yvonne, 1, 7, 29, 31, 47, 52,
    88, 187, 207, 211
Taylor, Jacqueline Sanchez, 129,
    175–7, 179

Teacher's Pet, 79
10 Years Younger, 126, 167
Terminator 2: Judgment Day, 47, 186–7,
    206
Thelma and Louise, 187
Theron, Charlize, 185, 191
Thunderball, 201, 202
Tolman, Deborah L., 200
Tong, Rosemarie Putnam., 205
Torres, Sasha, 90
transgenderism, 92–3, 97
Travers, Peter, 27
Trinity, 187
Trinny and Susannah Undress, 137
Tru Calling, 68
True Blood, 68
Twilight Zone, The, 63–4, 71
Tyler, Imogen, 32, 36, 38, 41

Ugly Betty, 59
Ultraviolet, 186
Underworld, 186, 188
Usher, Jane, 213–14, 220

Valenti, Jessica, 88
View to a Kill, A, 205–6
violence, 215
  female embodiment and, 190–5
  feminism and, 199–210
  matriarchal tyranny and, 213–23
  physical action and, 185–96
  sexualized, 227, 230, 232–4
  trauma and, 228–9, 233
visual culture, 5
Vogue magazine, 39

Walter, Natasha, 5, 59, 174–5
Wanted, 187, 188, 189–90
Wearing, Sadie, 32, 129, 133
Wedding Crashers, 20
Wedding Planner, The, 34
Wedding SOS, 137
What Not to Wear, 126, 128, 137, 167,
    168, 169
What Women Want, 17, 18, 19,
    22–5, 26
Whelehan, Imelda, 1, 4, 79–80, 155,
    157, 164
Wild Things, 78, 79

Williams, Linda R., 78
Williams, Rachel, 126
Willis, Ellen, 83, 202
Wilson, Elizabeth, 177, 179
Wire, The, 91, 93–9
Without a Trace, 50
Wolfe, Susan J., 109, 118
Wolf, Naomi, 5, 123
Woman of the Year, 25
Wood, Robin, 174, 197
Woollacott, Janet, 200, 204
Working Girl, 178

World is Not Enough, The, 208
Wright, Leigh Adams, 54
Wuornos, Aileen, 191
Wurtzel, Elizabeth, 77
Wylie, Philip, 71

Xena: Warrior Princess, 187
X-Men, 186, 190

You Are What You Eat, 137
You Only Live Twice, 201, 203
Young, Iris Marion, 125

Important Author's Note

CONCLUSION

The conclusions of this book are that whilst current methods of immunization against disease do have some positive virtues, in terms of protection, to a greater or lesser degree, many carry hazards, of both a short- and long-term nature, which makes them of profoundly questionable value.

Anyone who decides to avoid immunization procedures on their own behalf, or on behalf of their children, must be fully aware of the consequences of such action.

Parents who accept responsibility for refusing to have their children immunized are also bound to accept responsibility for maintaining their children's diet and general well-being in such a state as will enhance their overall health status, thus enabling them to withstand infections in the main, and to be better able to cope with infections which might occur, without untoward problem.

It is no use simply stating that immunization is not safe, or that it does not offer the protection claimed, if responsibility is avoided for positive action. Aspects of such action are outlined in Chapter 8. This book is not stating that you should not immunize your child, but that if you do decide to go along with medical opinion on this issue, that you be aware of potential dangers. If a decision is made against immunization, it should be done whilst in possession of ALL the facts. If a decision is made to immunize, it should also be accompanied by positive action in health enhancement, via nutritional excellence etc. in order to minimize the dangers explained in the text.

Leon Chaitow

CHAPTER 1

Is there an immunization problem?

The overwhelming view presented to the public is that immunization is a safe, scientific procedure which protects and safeguards health. The truth is somewhat at variance with this official government, medical and media message. Indeed, much that is taken as obvious and beyond reasonable doubt can be shown to be less than valid on closer examination. There is evidence that much immunization is not safe in the short term; that it offers far less protection than might be imagined, and that the long-term effects of certain forms of immunization may constitute a major health hazard.

Historically the story of vaccination and immunization is one of grandiose claims, coupled with apparent successes, massive and tragic failures, and distortion of objective evidence. The motives involved touch on the best and worst of human nature, as well as on professional short-sightedness and unwillingness to question currently held 'truths'. Evidence as to the veracity of these claims will be presented; the reader must make up his own mind. Much of the thinking behind the concept of giving protection via immunization stems from a philosophical concept of disease causation which itself requires questioning, since it appears to pervert our understanding of the inate, self-regulating mechanisms of the body.

The ability of the body to protect itself against infection is of course closely linked to underlying levels of well-being. Thus, arguments which make perfect sense when related to a child of reasonable health in a developed society may be meaningless to a malnourished child in an underdeveloped country. The hazards of immunization differ in these two opposites, and it should be realized that there are all shades of variation between these extremes, in both settings. Evidence of what variations are involved will be given in subsequent chapters. The conclusion the author has arrived at is that there are better ways of achieving health and protection. The reader must reach his own conclusions.

The views that are expressed in this book are meant to call into question the practice of immunization as it is now carried out, and it will rely heavily on the evidence of many scientists and medical practitioners who have themselves come to question one or another aspect of the procedures, so vigorously employed by organized medicine, and the agencies of government, which are responsible for public health.

It will be necessary in exposing the shortcomings and dangers of immunization to look at the history of the methods involved (see Chapter 2); to examine the rationale behind the methods used (see Chapter 3); to look closely at the claims made for efficacy in a number of areas of disease (see Chapter 4); to look at the terrifying potentials for long term chronic disease which can be seen to be inherent in the methods used (see Chapter 5); to consider carefully the evidence relating to side-effects in the short term (see Chapter 6); and to question the assumptions that have been made on the basis of the ongoing propaganda relating to the supposed desirability, efficacy and safety of immunization, especially of infants, frequently by compulsion (see Chapter 9). Having engaged in the examination of these issues it will also be apposite to think in terms of safer alternative methods of protection against some of the health hazards involved (see Chapter 8). Alternatives to immunization do exist and these deserve consideration by parents as well as by individuals who are potentially destined for immunization themselves.

That great iconoclastic writer, Ivan Illich, in his major book *Medical Nemesis* (Calder and Boyers, 1975) stated:

'The study and evolution of disease patterns provides evidence that during the last century doctors have affected such patterns no more profoundly than did priests during earlier times. Epidemics came and went, imprecated by both and untouched by either. They are not modified any more profoundly by the rituals performed in medical clinics than by the exorcisms customary at religious shrines.'

He rightly points to trends in the environment as the primary determinant of the state of general health of any

2

*trends in environment
determinant of general health*

population, with food, hygiene, working conditions, housing etc. as the major contributing factors, apart from inherited tendencies.

It will be the task of this book to convince the reader of the truth of these statements and, at the very least, to provoke a questioning attitude towards the current public acceptance of immunization as offering unqualified protection to its recipients.

This will lead to consideration of safer alternatives for those who wish to protect themselves and their offspring, and who are happy to take a large measure of responsibility for their own health. It should not be construed that advice is being offered, to not immunize children or yourself, only that the validity of many of the claims made for the methods should be questioned, and that an accurate estimation should be reached of the risks involved, as well as the real likelihood of potential benefits. Thus in discussing the many aspects of immunization we will be attempting to lift the veil of half-truths, and outright propaganda, which have been so assiduously propagated over the last century. We must ask, very clearly, is immunization safe? Does it protect against disease? Are the dangers of side-effects worth the risk? What links are there between these procedures and chronic ill-health in later life? In short we must question the validity of the concepts behind the methods, as well as looking at individual procedures, their short and long-term side-effects, and their claimed benefits.

If the evidence offered is examined with an open mind then it is contended that many long held viewpoints will alter, with the hope that medical methods and ideas may alter as well. Our initial consideration will be directed towards the fascinating and chequered history of immunization.

CHAPTER 2

The Amazing History of Immunization

The story of immunization has its origins in the attempts, over many centuries, to minimize the risks of contracting smallpox. Whilst popular knowledge has accepted Edward Jenner as the father of vaccination against smallpox, the truth is that centuries before his attempts to prevent this disease, by the use of cowpox vaccination, there were in use methods from which his ideas derived. The Druid priests of ancient Britain and Germany had used isopathic diluted exudate from smallpox victims, in trying to instil protection (Lindlahr, H. *Philosophy of Natural Therapeutics*, 1918). In the Middle Ages this method of trying to cure a disease by use of its own products (pus, exudate etc.), known as isopathy, was specifically taught by the great medical genius of those times, Paracelsus. The historian le Duc tells us of similar methods being employed in Constantinople, in the year 1672, by an old Circassian woman. She would cut a cross in the flesh of the applicant and then use smallpox exudate on the wound, announcing that this was an unfailing preventive against the disease. Among the other injunctions to exposure from smallpox ooze, was ample prayer, abstinence from meat, and a period of fasting for forty days. It is likely that the fasting had a profoundly beneficial effect on the health of the individual.

It must be remembered that smallpox was widespread in Europe at this time, and similar methods of self-innoculation were practised in many regions. However, the systematic organization of smallpox vaccination resulted from the work of Edward Jenner. He was by profession a barber and a chiropodist whose sole claim to genius, according to Bernard Shaw (letter to *The Nation*, 3 February 1923) was that he acquired, from a farmer named Jesty, the idea that exposure to a disease of cows (cowpox) could protect the individual from smallpox. In fact the story is more complex than this, for having satisfied himself that milkmaids and milkmen, who were in contact with cowpox, were not in fact protected from smallpox, despite Jesty's claim, Jenner asserted that such protection could be obtained from horses, which had themselves infected cows with horsepox. He then proceeded to innoculate people directly from diseased horses. His practice caught the popular imagination of the time, and a total of £30,000 was voted to Jenner by a grateful parliament. His claims that, once successfully vaccinated, there was no chance of contracting smallpox were widely accepted despite mounting evidence to the contrary. It later became common practice in Western Europe for all infants to be vaccinated by cowpox. Ultimately there were devastating outbreaks of smallpox (in the latter half of the nineteenth century) which led to the prohibition of the methods advocated by Jenner.

As Lindlahr states:

> In the years 1870-1 smallpox was rampant in Germany. Over one million persons had the disease and 120,000 died. 96% of these had been vaccinated, and only 4% had not been so 'protected'. Most of the victims were vaccinated, once at least, shortly before they took the disease. Bismark, the Chancellor of Germany, sent an address to the Governments of the various German states, in which it was stated that numerous eczematous diseases were the result of the vaccination, and that 'the hopes placed in the efficacy of the cowpox virus as preventive of smallpox have proved entirely deceptive'.

George Bernard Shaw wrote in *The Nation* (3 February 1923) as follows:

> When its failure to protect for life could no longer be denied, it was alleged to last for seven years (seven is the characteristic number of magic), and re-vaccination was made compulsory in many cases; for instance, persons entering various public services, and, on pain of quarantine, crossing frontiers. The every seven years might have become seven months, or even days, had not vaccination received its death blow in 1871, when compulsory vaccination was at its height, from the most appalling epidemic of smallpox on record. This was followed by another great

5

epidemic in 1881 in which, by the way, I, being a vaccinated person, caught the disease. I was more lucky than my grandfather, who was inoculated, vaccinated, and had smallpox spontaneously as well.

It was after this that the authorities ceased to rely on vaccination alone and took to isolation as a method of containing outbreaks. This method had surprising success, and together with factors of improved hygiene resulted in a decline in incidence of smallpox. Compulsion was eventually repealed in the face of the appalling failure of enforced vaccination to prevent repeated outbreaks amongst the 'protected' and the unprotected population.

Despite this and other disasters, in which vaccination plainly failed to protect the population, and despite the rampant side-effects of the methods, the proponents of vaccination continued their attempt to justify the methods by claims that the disease had declined in Europe as a whole during the period of its compulsory use. If the decline could be correlated with the use of vaccination, then all else could be set aside, and the advantage between its current low incidence could be shown to outweigh the periodic failures of the method, and to favour the continued use of vaccination. However, the credit for the decline in the incidence of smallpox could not be given to vaccination. The fact is that its incidence declined in all parts of Europe, whether or not vaccination was employed. The credit, if any, should be given to the same quarter as that for the decline in many other killer diseases of that era, such as cholera, typhoid, tuberculosis and dysentery.

Ivan Illich makes the point clear when he states:

The infections which prevailed at the outset of the industrial age can illustrate how medicine came by its reputation. Tuberculosis, for instance, reached its peak over two generations. In New York the death rate was certainly very high indeed in 1812, and declined to 37 per thousand by 1892, when Koch cultured and stained the first bacillus. The rate was down to 180 per 10,000 when the first sanatorium was opened in 1910, even though 'consumption' still held second place in the mortality tables. After World War II, before antibiotics came into (general) use, it had slipped to eleventh place with a rate of 48. Cholera, dysentery and typhoid similarly peaked and dwindled outside medical control. By the time their aetiology was understood, or their therapy had become specific, they had lost much of their relevance. The combined death rate for scarlet fever, diphtheria, whooping cough and measles from 1860 to 1965, for children up to 15, shows that nearly 90% of the total decline in the death rate over this period had occurred before the introduction of antibiotics and wide-spread immunization against diphtheria.

The explanation for this decline could relate to altered virulence in the micro-organisms themselves, as well as improved sanitation, better housing, and above all in a greater resistance to disease, due to improved nutrition.

Thus the natural history of smallpox, and many of the major infectious diseases of the past, have followed similar patterns, and this has had less to do with immunization than with better environmental and nutritional factors in the human population. This gives us a clear and important guideline as to the place to concentrate in improving control of these diseases. *The host and his immune function is the central most important aspect.* It is the nature of the debate that some consider the best method of enhancing the immune function to be exposed to attenuated and modified infecting agents (i.e. immunization and vaccination) where-as others consider that the enhancement of that function must come from improved environmental and nutritional factors. Were protection available via immunization with relatively little risk, as we are led to believe is the case, then the debate would be based on such questions as could be considered dispassionately. However, since immunization can be shown to carry inherent short-term and long-term risks, and to offer only questionable protection, the need for a reappraisal of the whole edifice of mass immunization is necessary.

The method advocated by Jenner failed miserably in the nineteenth century, and led to an eventual collapse of the compulsory vaccination programme. It was the skill and public relations genius of Louis Pasteur that rekindled the ideas and methodology of immunization, via vaccination. The results achieved in public demonstrations by Pasteur highlight one of the great difficulties in attempting to evaluate the desirability or otherwise of these methods. Vaccination can be shown to stimulate some degree of protection in the individual, against particular micro-organisms (and we will look at the mechanism involved in this process more closely, later in the book). But, and it is a huge but, what are the repercussions, short-term and long-term of the procedures involved.

This is the crux of the problem; not that immunization doesn't sometimes have at least one desirable effect, but that it may do so at a cost to health that is unacceptable. The tragedy of the situation is that the costs are not recognized, for often they do not manifest themselves for many years, and when they do the connection is not always easy to make. Fortunately recent medical research has shown that the hypothesized dangers to long-term health, produced of these methods, is not fantasy, and is deserving of profound attention.

If it were established, for example, that protection against a common children's illness, such as measles, carried with it greatly increased risks of contracting a condition such as multiple sclerosis in adult life, how many parents would happily comply with the advice to immunize and thus jeopardize their loved ones? If the short-term risks of immunization against the unpleasant, but seldom serious, condition of whooping-cough could be shown to involve a serious (if small) danger of brain damage or epilepsy, how many parents would take the risk?

In both of these examples the answer is surely that, were the connection established between these horrible consequences and vaccination, the methods would soon find few takers. This would be doubly so if the risks attached to the contracting of either measles or whooping cough were shown to be minimal, if the general health status of the child was reasonable by virtue of adequate nutrition, hygiene etc. The fact is that all the untoward possibilities mentioned above are not only possible but probable, and the risks attached to contracting the diseases in childhood are minimal, if basic health measures are carried out.

Risk of severe brain damage is real in the use of whooping cough vaccine; risk of long-term chronic degenerative disease does exist in the use of vaccines, such as measles, and these facts are but the tip of the iceberg. If a severe reaction to whooping cough vaccine can be shown (see Chapter 5) to produce brain damage, what range of less severe reactions lie between this major side-effect, and the almost minimal effects in other children? In some children there might result only minor behavioural changes, in others a decline in well-being might be noted. There is no 'all or nothing' situation in such reactions. It is not so that the only side-effects will be the most severe ones. These are the ones that will be noted most dramatically, but it is the myriad minor ones that will impinge upon the health and behaviour of the child for years to come, and possibly throughout life.

In our search for a reasonable understanding of just what is at stake in this whole area of health intervention, we must keep in mind that the evidence thus far is related to the serious and obvious side-effects, and these are only a small percentage of the total effect on the population at large of assaulting the immune system of infants with highly toxic substances, with whatever good intentions. We have briefly looked at the origins of smallpox vaccination. Our next consideration should be the work of Louis Pasteur, whose figure looms large on the stage of medical science.

Pasteur and His Legacy

As with so many innovators in medical science Louis Pasteur was not a doctor but a research chemist. There is considerable evidence that his place in medical history requires re-evaluation, for doubts have been expressed as to his probity. Indeed some of his greatest 'discoveries' have been attributed to a contemporary scientist of his, Professor Antoine Béchamp. Archie Kalokerinos MD and Glen Dettman PhD have described the controversy thus (International Academy of Preventive Medicine Seminar, Phoenix Arizona August 28 1977).

> Modern medicine is based on Pasteur's germ theory of disease — a specific organism causes a specific disease and a specific vaccine gives protection. Shades of doubt concerning the validity of this dogma were seen when we observed that some Aboriginal children did not get protection and, in fact, died when vaccines were administered (see Chapter 5).

It soon became obvious that individuals became susceptible to disease for various reasons, and the germs themselves simply take advantage of the susceptible state.
Vaccinating susceptible individuals does not necessarily
render them immune; it may have the reverse effect.
Further light was shed on this problem when it was found
that Pasteur plagiarised the work of his great scientific
contemporary, Béchamp. According to this astute observer
the basis of life is not the cell but a living 'gene' that he called
a mycrozyma. Mycrozymas can evolve with changes in the
nutritional environment to become viruses or bacteria,
harmless or harmful, and although apparently specific
viruses can be reproduced as similar organisms, this is only
true if specific environmental conditions exist. Under other
conditions evolution into other viruses and bacteria can take
place.

In the same way an infection can be endogenous or
exogenous, evolving by a process of mycrozymian evolution. The fallacy of vaccines is thus explained and the
importance of the nutritional environment of the cell
understood.

However, to simply label Pasteur as a plagiarist does no
great service to our understanding of the complexities of
immunization. Our initial attention will be to Pasteur, and
those who came after him, as well as some of the
controversies which still surround the theories based on his
works, which are indelibly imprinted on the twentieth
century mind of man.

Pasteur was a chemist whose early work was in
crystallography. In his studies of the variations in crystal
structure and his efforts to isolate these, he noted that
particular micro-organisms could identify specific variations,
and could be used in his experiments. Later in his career he
was asked to attempt to discover the reasons for the
aberrant behaviour of wine, beer and other liquids. These
would, at great commercial cost, sour or ferment inappro-
priately, although on other occasions, under apparently
identical circumstances, this did not occur. His first research
in this area was related to milk, which led him to the
conclusion that specific micro-organisms were responsible
for its souring, although he was unable to separate these
from the milk.

Over the years he studied beer, wine, vinegar, butter and the phenomena of fermentation and rancidity. He concluded that the various changes in these substances were related to the activities therein of micro-organisms. Thus he showed that different microbes were present in sour milk from those in fermented wine, and when there were anomalous changes he noted that other microbes were involved. This work was extended by the British scientist Joseph Lister, who showed that sterile wounds would not become infected, and introduced carbolic acid to achieve this end in surgical procedures.

Pasteur was at this time extending his research to include a number of human and animal diseases. He had concluded that there was a specific micro-organism related to each form of infectious disease, and that by isolating this he could begin to offer protection from its effects, by using ideas which related to the earlier work of Jenner.

The micro-organisms which Pasteur was seeking were, he believed, externally related to the host, in that they lived in the environment and infected the animal, or man, from outside his body. The work of his illustrious contemporary Béchamp suggested the opposite, for he believed in the spontaneous development of micro-organisms in cells from material called mycrozymas. These minute particles were able, Béchamp maintained, under appropriate conditions, to develop into viral and bacterial entities. Thus an external source of infection was mooted by the man from whom Pasteur 'borrowed' the discovery of wine fermentation processes. Béchamp himself, in his book, *The Blood and Its Elements* (1912), stated that:

'in 1872 Pasteur attempted his boldest plagiarism; he discovered all of a sudden, eight years after my discovery thereof, that the ferments of vinous fermentations exist naturally on the grape. In this connection he discovered also that plant and animal matters contain normally the things which cause them to alter spontaneously, in their cellules, without germs.'

According the Béchamp's theories mycrozymas must be regarded as the smallest unit of life. Cells are seen as transient and are built up of mycrozymas which are physiologically imperishable. It is fascinating to realize that Béchamp described the coupling of mycrozymas to form the double helix of the genetic DNA material in the latter part of the nineteenth century without the aid of X-rays or electron microscopes. In his book *Blood and Its Elements* he notes (page 296) that the coming together of the mycrozymas forms a figure 8 (double helix formation). He used ingenious methods of enhanced visualization which enabled him to see what was not fully described until the 1960s (by Nobel prizewinners Wilkins, Watson and Crick who used X-ray refraction). Béchamp's method was to use a polarized light, produced by a nicol prism, which vibrated in one plane and which was then viewed through a second prism.

Once we accept the likelihood of the presence in the body of a vast host of basic material called mycrozymas (or DNA) we can begin to understand the origins of virus particles. As described in *Time* magazine (November 3 1986) viruses sound a great deal like Béchamp's mycrozymas. 'They (virus particles) are models of biological minimalism, consisting of simply a core of genetic material — either a DNA or RNA molecule — and a protective envelope made of proteins'. The virus lacks a cell structure common to all life as we know it. *Time* continues,

> 'Unlike true life forms it does not need and cannot metabolise nutrients, does not grow and cannot replicate without the help of its host. Put a virus in a test tube and it cannot do anything. It cannot even make copies of itself.'

Béchamp stated,

> 'The cell is not the permanent histogenetic element, its existence being transitory, it cannot be held to be the unit of life. Beyond the cell is the mycrozyma, this forms the cell and remains when the cell is destroyed. It is the primordial organised element'.

Under adverse conditions this mycrozyma (incipient virus or bacterial particle) can become pathogenic (capable of causing disease) and this is true whether its pathogenic status is generated within the body or transmitted from external sources. (See Chapter 6 for modern supporting evidence of Béchamp's theory.)

There is a continuing controversy between the believers in the external and the devotees of the internal theory, of the genesis of infection. To be sure, the former includes the majority of those working in modern medicine, but there is still a great ground swell of opinion which holds Béchamp's view to be closer to the truth. In effect this results in our having two quite different viewpoints as to the origin of the infectious organisms, which are after all the main concern of immunization. It may well be that there is a large element of truth in both the external and the internal theories of the origins of micro-organisms, for both cases are argued at length and with great force and logic by their respective proponents.

From the standpoint of those who oppose immunization methods, the work of Béchamp appears to emphasize the importance of the health of the body, the vitality of the immune system, and therefore of natural resistance to disease. This is seen as more than a philosophical notion, and a major area of divergence from those who would protect the body against attack, from this or that micro-organism, by the stimulation of the body defences using attenuated forms of the micro-organisms involved in the particular infection (or other by-products of the infectious process).

This divergence of views is fundamental to the under-standing of alternatives to standard immunization pro-cedures. Whatever the short-term and long-term drawbacks to vaccination and immunization (and there are many as we shall see), the argument against the use of these measures collapses unless there is a viable alternative to offer, and unless we can see that despite the 'scientific' rationale behind the currently accepted methods, there is indeed a fundamental objection to its use on the grounds of it being based on inadequately established methodology and reasoning.

In other words, the faults we now see emerging as the result of immunization are inevitable since they are based on a system which flies in the face of reason, and which, whilst applicable under sterile laboratory conditions, relates less to every-day life. That infection can result from externally arriving bacteria is not contested, but that it can also arise spontaneously, in a suitably compromised body, is strongly suggested by the range of viral 'infections' which exist, and the fact that these viruses, and many bacteria, can be found in obviously healthy individuals. Even the externally delivered infective agent, of whatever degree of virulency, will not produce infection as a matter of course, but only if the host is unable to contain its activities, and provides it with a suitable environment for replication.

This is being noted increasingly in relation to that modern scourge, AIDS. Dr Jay Levy, an AIDS researcher at UCLA San Francisco, is quoted in *Time* magazine (November 3 1986 p. 46) as saying that the AIDS virus will not necessarily cause a person to contract the illness. Other infections, the use of drugs, poor nutrition, stress and lack of sleep are quoted as being possible influences on the immune (defence) system which may weaken it. 'If the person's immune system is not compromised by such events', he states, 'I believe they will be able to fight off the virus and not develop the disease'. This places the situation in the correct perspective. The host, the infected individual and his immune system, decide whether or not AIDS (or any other infection) takes hold. The virus or bacteria only plays a role, if it is allowed to do so. Professor Dubos of Rockefeller University states (*Health Consciousness* October 1986) 'Viruses and Bacteria are not the sole cause of infectious disease, there is something else' or, as Drs Kalokerinos and Dettman put it, 'It's not what viruses and bacteria cause, but what causes viruses and bacteria to evolve into pathogens and to become invasive, for example the nutrition of the cell, which is responsible. It is therefore the manner in which we live that becomes important.'

The underlying causes of AIDS are therefore seen to include drug abuse, sexual promiscuity and an incoherent lifestyle, rather than the AIDS virus which is seen to be able to seriously infect only one person in ten who are exposed to it. This is the same basic truth which holds for all infections.

The unfortunate emphasis on the importance of the micro-organism as the prime factor, rather than realization that its ability to do harm hinges on the health or otherwise of the host, had led to a shedding of individual responsibility for health maintenance. We will discuss aspects of this in later chapters, but at this stage the reader is asked to keep in mind the difference of emphasis which the two schools of thought make. One says that we are subject to the whims and dangers of minute creatures which, unless we have natural or acquired protection, will make us ill. Since the naturally acquired protection is a hit and miss matter, as far as this school of thought is concerned, this requires that we be 'protected' from the infective agent, by means of artificial immunization (the process of which we will discuss later). The other school says that a prime concern of each of us should be the maintenance of optimal health.

A part of the benefit of this would be a degree of resistance and protection from ill-health that would include an adequate degree of immunity from infection, and the ability to satisfactorally cope with infection should it occur. Were it not demonstrable that the defence mechanisms of the body can indeed be positively influenced to this end, then criticism of the current methods of immunization would be seen as mere carping, and to be of no practical relevance. The core of the argument which this book aims to unfold is that, whilst there are undoubted changes which occur when immunization is used, which may confer a degree of benefit in terms of resistance being heightened against a particular micro-organism, this benefit is qualified greatly by the innate health or otherwise of the individual, and that there are major negative effects and hazards which accompany the apparent protection, which to a great extent makes the process a highly questionable one. The degree of negative influence on the individual varies with the type of immunization, as well as on the nature and health of the individual being immunized. The immediate harmful effects are well known, in certain aspects of immunization, and these will be spelled out and emphasized. The long-term dangers are less well known but deserve even greater publicity, for their implications are, if anything, more profound in terms of the amount of human suffering potentially involved.

The argument then is not that immunization does not work at all, but that it works in a hit and miss manner (many immunized individuals still contract the condition from which they are purportedly protected) and that the concomitant risks are greater than is acceptable. That there are individuals for whom the risks may be acceptable is undoubted and admitted. What is not acceptable is that there should be a Government-backed campaign to enforce immunization universally, and that the arguments against the procedures should be dismissed arbitrarily. The emphasis on preventive measures, in the true sense of the word, is urged. This should entail the recognition of the fundamental importance of enhancement of the overall health status of the individual, thus allowing him to cope adequately with exposure to infective agents, and to safely survive infection should this occur. This means that the optimal health of each man woman and child (especially the child) should be the focus of preventive medicine. The emphasis on immunization via the introduction of attentuated micro-organism, and the by-products of infection, in an attempt to stimulate the body into this protective mode, will be seen to be a poor second choice for many people in such an overview. The emphasis of hygiene and health, via optimum nutrition and concentration on those factors which support and enhance the natural defence capabilities of the body, are the most desirable objectives of preventive medicine. Pasteur's legacy can be seen to have diverted man from this objective. There is the counter argument that through poverty, ignorance, and sometimes from choice, a vast population exists which does not follow the dictates of those who can point to better nutrition and hygiene, as being more important and more desirable than immunization. This calls for awareness that in certain conditions the various methods of immunization should be available. However the drawbacks and alternatives should be known and promoted for the benefit of those who can and would make the choice.

Before we return to Pasteur and those who came after him in order to see the progression of these ideas and methods over the past century, it is worth emphasizing, that the experimental methods employed by Pasteur and the other researchers whom we will discuss, relate to conditions far removed from everyday life. The use of a particular micro-organism in a laboratory, in connection with tissue cultures or experimental animals, has little to do with the exposure of an average individual to infection in his normal environment. The dominance in medicine of the idea of specific causes for particular conditions has blinded the majority of mankind to the multicausal background to most forms of ill health, including infections. Exposure to, and the presence in the body of, virulent micro-organisms in no way makes infection certain. This is largely irrelevant to the possibility of previous infection, and the acquisition in this way of immunity. The fact is that individuals in good health (and the definition of this requires some discussion) can adequately deal with such exposure to infective agents, in the main.

As evidence of the inability of highly dangerous micro-organisms to 'cause' a disease in unnatural conditions, a number of the pioneers of immunology demonstrated this in a bizarre manner. Dr Max von Pettenkofer, a leader in the field of hygiene, consumed millions of pathogenic cholera bacilli, which had been taken from someone with the fatal disease. The great Russian pathologist Elie Metchnikoff also demonstrated his views by undertaking the same experiment, as did a number of other experimenters at the beginning of the twentieth century. The worst that occurred was a mild diarrhoea, although the active bacilli were demonstrated as being present in their stools. This highlights the vast difference between real life conditions and the belief that, by adding a particular micro-organism to a human subject, a particular disease will emerge. The writer Rene Dubos has written of this by saying that researchers, such as Koch and Pasteur, dealt with experimental artifacts rather than natural events, and that it is not possible for nature to be reproduced in a laboratory. It is the very nature of experiments that they should impose limiting conditions on natural phenomena. Since, in such circumstances, nature is being asked to provide answers to questions devised by man, these answers will largely be influenced by the nature of the questions that are being asked. Pasteur's early work on milk, beer, etc., had conditioned his thinking. He knew that a particular germ soured milk, and a particular fermenting germ turned grape juice into wine, and then into vinegar. He assumed that like a barrel of beer, the human body was at the mercy of extraneous micro-organisms which could cause disease, much as they could cause the fermentation of the liquid in the barrel, be it milk, wine or beer. In demonstrating that micro-organisms produced specific disease, Pasteur and his fellow workers did not rely upon the catching of the disease by exposure in the air to the infecting agent, but rather by injection into the body of the substances derived from diseased bodies. They failed to replicate life, and their findings were therefore of dubious import. The medical journal, *The Lancet*, in March 1909 commented, 'When a causal bacteria is infected into an animal, often it happens that it gives rise to a disease bearing no clinical resemblance to the original malady, which produce the bacteria'. The answer, stated Béchamp, was that 'disease is born of us and in us'. Thus protection against disease can be seen to depend, in this way of thinking, on those factors which promote health in the body, which would include hygienic conditions, and sound nutrition. In the words of one of the pioneers of natural healing Henry Lindlahr 'health depends on right living' that is our habits of thinking, feeling, breathing, eating, drinking, exercising, bathing, clothing, as well as our sexual and social activities, which must all be in harmonious relation to the laws of our being.' It is the interaction between the host and the micro-organism which determines the fact and the degree of infection. Emphasis on the infecting agent, with minimal attention to the body which is destined for infection, is a fault which has led to a great deal of human suffering. Dependence on the protective aspects of immunization even if valid does not of itself lead to better health. Nutrition and other aspects of the physiological and psychological nature of man are far more important considerations than the virus or microbe, which under suitable conditions for itself, can cause such devastation.

Pasteur sought his quarry with relentless zeal and dedication. He was a hard working individual with a flair for publicity and he employed both qualities to the full. His demonstrations, as to the efficacy of the vaccines he developed for the prevention of anthrax and the treatment of rabies, were public, and were well reported by the press which was present. The dramatic demonstration that he could immunize and protect sheep against the killer disease anthrax, was witnessed by hundreds of people, and the reputation of Pasteur grew apace. In these experiments it should be noted that Pasteur induced anthrax in the unfortunate animals by injecting them with virulent anthrax bacilli, which is not the way in which a normal sheep would contract the disease. The protection offered by his vaccine was real enough, for the vaccinated sheep in the trial survived, and those not so protected died a fearful death. However the protection was against the administration of bacilli into the blood stream, and not against a naturally occurring infection. It is worth noting that, in the main, wild animals live in complete accord with infectious bacteria.

There is little if any serious infection in animals in their natural habitats. It is only when animals are domesticated and kept in unnatural environments, that they become subject of infection as we know it. The relationship between a natural animal and any bacteria that might be found in its body tissues, is not one of danger to the animal, and we should pause to consider this aspects of the puzzle. The fact of course is that man too lives in unnatural situations, and is indeed subject to infectious diseases. The question is whether it is to his advantage to subject his body to the introduction of foreign, alien, biological materials, in order to offer protection which a healthy body already has.

In 1885 Pasteur treated a child for rabies and was successful in saving his life. The precision of his work in these areas shows a single-minded dedication to his belief in the specificity of the disease causation, via micro-organisms. What Pasteur had also discovered, partly by accident, was that by using a weakened or attenuated, version of the originally virulent micro-organism, it was possible to stimulate the body into being able to protect itself from exposure to the infecting agent. This is still the basis of much immunization work. Contemporary with Pasteur, and following on from his work, there were a host of scientific workers in this field, many of whom have shaped current orthodox thinking in immunology. These include the German bacteriologist Robert Koch. He studied the anthrax bacillus and was able to demonstrate, in 1878, the bacterial character of the infection of injuries. Among his major achievements was the discovery of the tubercle bacillus. His work in this area led to the production of the substance derived from this bacillus, called tuberculin. This however failed to have success in treating the condition of tuberculosis, but has remained in use as a diagnostic substance, because when injected into the skin of a person (or animal) previously exposed to the tubercle bacillus, a local inflammation is said to develop. Koch is also known for the postulate, or law, which he developed in relation to the defining of whether or not a micro-organism could be considered to be the agent in a particular disease process. This states that the micro-organism must always be associated with the disease in question, and that if it can be isolated and cultured and then inoculated into a healthy animal, it would again produce the disease. It should then be able to be again isolated and cultured from the lesions of the disease. The fault with this apparently neat formula is that is ignores the host. Professor G. T. Stewart, of the University of North Carolina, has shown that individual responses vary with the inoculation of a standard quantity of micro-organisms, and that Koch's postulate that infection and disease should follow innoculation of specific microbes, is dependent as much on the host as on the substance injected. Professor Stewart claims that these rules fail to allow for biological variations, and make no allowances for the complex conditions influencing infection in natural states (laboratory conditions may be desirable for standardization, but they do not mimic life). The rules of Koch are applicable when specific micro-organisms, in isolation from the many others with which they are usually associated in normal conditions, are artificially introduced to susceptible experimental animals, which again differ very markedly from animals (and man) in a natural environment. We can begin to see, in Professor Stewart's views, the evolution of an emphasis on the host condition, and not just on the infecting agent, and this is central to the theme of preventive medicine which would rather avoid the introduction of materials of a toxic nature into the system, in the hope of achieving a questionable degree of protection.

Another major figure in the early work of immunology, whose influence is still to be found, is the German bacteriologist Paul Ehrlich. He worked on the use of substances to combat infectious agents, as well as defining guidelines for standardizing bacterial toxins and antitoxins. It was this work which ultimately led to the development of agents in the treatment of syphilis and bacterial diseases. It was Ehrlich who proposed a theory which attempted to explain what was happening in the body when an infecting agent, or toxic material, entered the blood stream. He showed that when this happened the body of the host was stimulated into the production of a substance called an antibody or antitoxin. Once this had happened the body was able to tolerate amounts of the toxic substance which previously would have killed it. As Ehrlich explained it, this happens because the cells of the body had receptor sites, to which the toxic material could attach itself, with poisonous results. Thus combined molecules, of receptor and toxin, were then pushed into the bloodstream together with additional receptors produced by the body, in response to the toxic insult. These antibodies were then able to neutralize subsequent invasions by microbes, or toxic material, before they could harm the body. This is what was thought to occur when a vaccine or small amount of the toxin was introduced. This early theory called the 'side chain theory' has been much modified by subsequent knowledge, but was the earliest attempt to scientifically explain the idea of antigens and antibodies. This is a topic to which we will return in greater detail in the next chapter.

The early emphasis of these researchers, and those who followed their lead, was on the identification and isolation of the infecting agent, whether this was a bacterium or anything else. By using it in a weakened form, or by using by-products of the infectious process, there was then an attempt to stimulate the defences of the body against subsequent exposure to the infection proper. The immediate response of the public and the media was enthusiastic. Here at last was an explanation for the myriad ills to which man was subjected and which science could now begin to remedy. The apparent success in dealing with the problems of infectious disease, which were rampant at this time, seemed to confirm this enthusiasm as not being misplaced. But was it? A great deal of evidence has been collected which indicates that much of the success apparently achieved by the introducion of the various vaccines and immunological procedures, was co-incidental with a decline in these diseases, for a variety of other reasons, which will be enumerated.

What is the natural history of infection? It would pay us to examine more closely some of the mechanisms involved in the artificial stimulation of the defence system of the body, by vaccines etc. In doing so there will be the opportunity to look also at the examples of BCG (tuberculosis) and poliomyelitis vaccination, as examples of procedures which fail to stand close scrutiny as to claims of efficacy and safety. These aspects of immunization will be examined more closely in subsequent chapters, in relation to other specific forms of immunization.

CHAPTER 3

Explaining Immunization and Immune Function: BCG, Polio and Diphtheria Vaccination as Examples

The body has inbuilt defence systems of which we should be aware in our consideration of the methods involved in immunization. Man has lived with micro-organisms since the dawn of his existence and his defence mechanisms are in many ways tuned to a relationship which varies from the hostile to the dependent. There are micro-organisms present in the human body without which it could not survive in good health. Some such bacteria inhabit the bowel, where in return for their shelter and food they provide useful and often vital services, such as the production of certain vitamins, and the control of other less desirable microbes. The relationship is seen to be a symbiotic one, in which the host and the guest both benefit. In other cases however there are less welcome inhabitants which, although doing no service to the body, appear, under normal circumstances, to offer little threat. When the body is compromised, however, these may take advantage and spread their activities and range of habitation, causing disease and discomfort.

This is known as opportunistic infection, and is common in conditions such as AIDS (an extreme example) in which the defence mechanisms of the body have been severely weakened, allowing the spread of previously well contained micro-organisms. One such is *Candida albicans*, which is currently inhabiting the bowels and other regions of almost every man, woman and child on the planet. As a rule this does little harm, for it is kept in moderately reduced circumstances by the defence mechanisms of the body, including the more desirable bacterial inhabitants of the bowel. In AIDs cases one of the serious signs of the decline in efficiency of the immune system, is a spread of *Candida* activity in the mouth and often throughout the digestive tract. This example should help in the appreciation of the nature of the balance which exists between man and his microscopic fellow creatures. In the main, in good health, the body can tolerate and deal with most pathogens. This is evidenced by the incredible experiments in which quantities of cholera bacteria were swallowed, with no ill effect, by brave or foolhardy researchers. Of course a great many individuals, through poverty, ignorance, poor hygiene and malnutrition, are not capable of maintaining a defence capability which can cope with the assults of micro-organisms, which are forever seeking an opportunity to spread their activities. It is in such situations that an acceptable level of habitation by pathogenic micro-organisms might change to a full-blown infection.

The defences of the body include the physical barrier of the skin, which excludes bacterial and other would-be intruders. Once penetrated, the interior of the body has other defences. One of the key methods the body uses to deal with foreign material or micro-organisms, substances which are excreted by all mucous membranes. This is aided in some areas by fine microscopic hairs (cilia), such as in the respiratory mucous membrane. These help move the sticky material which traps undesirable substances and bacteria along to a point where it can be eliminated, by coughing for example. In the stomach and digestive tract the mucus is aided by natural acidity, which helps to destroy undesirable bacteria. The tonsils also act as defensive outposts of the respiratory system and the digestive tract, and are import-ant, as will be noted later, in reducing the danger of diseases such as poliomyelitis. In the deeper recesses of the intestines, and in other body areas, such as the vagina and urinary tract, there may also be additional assistance from friendly bacterial colonies. Some of these helpful organisms actually produce antibiotic secretions, which reduces the activity of unwanted bacteria, as well as maintaining the acidity at a balanced level which is supportive of the body's defence needs. Vital bacterial colonies, which make up the flora of the bowel, are largely decimated when antibiotics are used excessively, and this can play a major part in allowing opportunistic spread of harmful bacteria and fungi (*Candida* for example). Such alterations can also occur if the acidity changes, as in diabetic conditions.

A further major factor in the first-line defence system, is known as the Alternate Complement Pathway (ACP). This plays a crucial role in immunologically induced, and nonspecific, resistance to infection as well as being involved in the generation of inflammatory processes in the body. The substances which are involved in the ACP are manufactured in the lining of the intestines, the liver, spleen and by microphage cells, and are known as properdin, or alternative complement. Among the various functions are the neutralization of viruses and the destruction of bacteria, such as enteric bacteria. This system has other functions, but is a major part of the defence mechanisms of the body, as is the reticulo-endothelial system (RES). This consists of a variety of tissues concerned with the resistance to disease. This contains cells which produce specific substances which are involved in defence, such as proteases, enzymes capable of neutralizing factors harmful to the body. The RES is largely involved with the detoxification processes, but has a defensive role as well. Should bacteria breach the defences described above, they must then face a formidable array of defenders.

There are two distinct biological defence systems. The one which is the major province of immunology is called the immunological defence system, and this is considered below. There is another, much neglected, defence capability, which is known as the chemical defence system, and this should be kept well in mind as we attempt to achieve an understanding of the complexities of the body's defences. The blood itself, if healthy, is to a very great extent bacteriastatic. This means that it can immobilize and render harmless bacterial invasion, via its very chemistry. This is dependent upon adequate nutrition. Vitamin C, (in the blood) in particular, is capable of killing bacteria, and virus particles (this action is called bacteriacidal and virucidal). It is important to realize that the levels of vitamin C required to achieve this degree of protection is far above that required to produce minimal antiscurvy effect. Biochemical individuality determines that we all have unique requirements for all nutrients. Vitamin C requirements fluctuate widely at times of stress, infection, pregnancy, alcohol and tobacco use, etc. Thus a correct personal level is not something which can be deduced from advice alone, but rather from experimentation with dietary patterns, and perhaps supplementation. Dr Jeffrey Bland, of the Linus Pauling Institute for Science and Medicine, maintains that the average individual in Western Society, beset by air and water pollution (of toxic factors such as heavy metals, not bacterial pathogens as in the days gone by) as well as the largely denatured (over refined) food patterns, is in need of supplementation in the region of 400 to 600 milligrams daily. Vitamin C detoxifies heavy metals (lead etc.) and is used by the body in allergic conditions. There is, according to Dr W. Philpott (*Clinical Ecology* Chapter 57 p. 497) no antibiotic as effective. 'Serious infections such as pneumonia, or toxic states such as insect or snake bites, are effectively treated with intravenous gram doses of vitamin C', he states. Insofar as the immunological defences are concerned there is also a need for optimum nutrition. This is the last line of defence after the skin, the mucous secretions and the chemical factors of the blood have failed to check an invader. As we will see below, the first attempt by the immunological defences is to destroy invading organisms (followed by production of antibodies which neutralize them). Alertness of this immune response is said to depend upon adequate levels of pyridoxine (vitamin B6). Both this B vitamin and vitamin C require that all the many other nutrients are adequately present, in order to operate at high levels of efficiency. According to many experts, based on clinical experience, surveys and examinations, the human race is operating to a great extent on marginal, and even submarginal, levels of these and other vital nutrients. As we will see in the experience in Australia, with aboriginals (see Chapter 5), there is a critical level of Vitamin C required to allow the body to cope with insults and infections, below which death of infants can occur from immunological shock when exposed to the toxins of vaccination. This is the area of immunological enhancement which it is possible to personally influence, and in which greater levels of protection can be achieved, without danger and with accompanying wellbeing. We will return to this theme in the chapter on alternatives to immunization procedures.

When a foreign protein enters the body via the skin, the bowel or any other route, and confronts the immune system with its presence, a number of remarkable events take place. Such substances, be they poisons or bacteria, are known as *antigens*, and these comprise almost anything which is foreign to the body, even transplanted organs. A major response, by the body, is the formation of antibodies which are specific to this antigen. Once created by the body, the antibody can recognize and attempt to neutralize only the specific antigen to which it was exposed. It is not capable of recognizing or dealing with any of the thousands of other potential invaders. The mechanism whereby this takes place is thought to relate to the formation in the antibody of a specific and unique arrangement of molecules, which exactly fits the configurations on the antigen, and by which means it locks on to and neutralizes it.

The sequence of events might run something like this. A foreign protein (bacteria for example) enters the blood stream and is spotted by a cell called a *macrophage*. These come in two types, some being free and present in the blood (to some extent), and others being fixed, for example in the tissues lining a blood vessel. These cells are scavengers of dead cells, waste material, and of course undesirable bacteria. The macrophage will ingest the invading bacteria, breaking it down into small particles. This is called *phagocytosis* ('eating by a cell'). The macrophage then comes into contact with a type of white blood cell called a *lymphocyte* (see below), with which it shares the information it now has, as to the structure of the enemy. There then occurs a transformation of the lymphocyte into a veritable factory, which produces *antibodies* specifically targeted to recognize and deal with the antigen in question. This production takes place in the lymph nodes, and other lymph structures, resulting in the eventual release into the blood-stream, of antibodies which circulate freely. This process, which we will be discussing in more detail below, may take some days or weeks, and the antibodies may be found to be present many years later. A subsequent encounter with the same infecting agent, say several years later, will call forth a far more dramatic response, as the antibodies will recognize the intruder from the earlier experience. The white blood cells of the body, the *leucocytes*, are the main mediators of the whole process. They are subdivided into two main groups. These are the *granulocytes* (*neutrophils, eosinophils* and *basophils*) and the *non-granulated lymphocytes* and *monocytes*.

Neutrophils are the main type of granulocyte. Because they usually have a nucleus which contains a number of connected lobes or segments, they are called *polymorpho-nuclear leucocytes*. They operate in the blood stream where they have a remarkable ability to form barriers preventing advance of foreign particles or micro-organisms. The neutrophils contain enzymes which can be used to digest micro-organisms. They live for a short time in the blood stream (half a day or so), and then move into other tissues, where they are active for a few days, before being themselves absorbed by the body, and are then replaced.

Another type of granulocyte is the *eosinophil*, which comprises about 2% of the leucocytes in the circulation. This relates more to parasitic infection, and to allergic responses, than to micro-organisms and toxic materials. Basophils comprise a very small fraction of the total leucocytes, and have a role in allergic responses. They contain substances such as histamin and heparin. A further major group of cells are known as lymphocytes. These make up a large section of the white blood cells. Unlike the neutrophils they are not phagocytic (i.e. they do not ingest and destroy invading micro-organisms).

Lymphocytes are subdivided into *B* and *T lymphocytes*, depending upon their origin, or connection with either the bone or bursa (B), or thymus gland (T). The T-lymphocytes take part in the process which enables cells to develop specific resistance to infection by viruses, fungi and bacteria, as well as being involved in recognizing and activating defence against tumours and foreign proteins (such as transplanted tissues). Rejection of the latter is the domain of these cells. The T-lymphocytes are themselves divided into what are called helper and killer cells. It is by the activity of these that B-lymphocytes are guided as to the production of antibodies against invading materials. The ratio between helper and killer cells is important, and is one of the features of AIDS, in which the ratio is thoroughly disturbed.

The B-lymphocytes make the changes which are specifically defensive against particular antigens (bacteria etc.). When appropriately stimulated they secrete material which is called *immunoglobulin antibody*, which is protective against exposure to particular viruses or bacteria. It is estimated that the life span of these cells varies between a few weeks and many years. (See also Chapter 8, page 136.) A further form of leucocyte is the monocyte, which has also the capacity to ingest foreign particles and bacteria. These appear to be most active in such conditions as tuberculosis and fungal infection.

As mentioned the B-lymphocytes, when stimulated by the appearance of foreign invaders, manufacture *immunoglobulin* (Ig) and this has been subdivided into different types. IgM also known as *macroglobulin* is large in comparison to other immunoglobulins, and is the first of these substances noted after infection or immunization procedures. It is bacteriacidal against bacterial toxins which enter from the intestine. IgG is also known as *Gamma globulin*. These are the largest group of immunoglobulins and they appear later in the process of defence against infection. They are antibodies to viruses, bacteria and toxins, whether these be from infection or immunization. IgA is found largely in mucus and other secretions of the body (saliva, tears, breast milk, etc.). These protect the surfaces of the mucous membranes (intestinal tract, etc.). IgE is related to allergic reactions, and IgD has no clearly defined role as yet. Each B-lymphocyte has, on its surface, approximately 100,000 immunoglobulins (antibodies) which appear to relate it to a particular role. This accounts for the ability of these cells, to only recognize specific antigens or challenging micro-organisms. This means that once 'programmed', as a result of previous activity, a B-lymphocyte cell is committed to the production of a particular antibody (Ig) and it can therefore presumably only respond to a challenge from this particular organism, and no other.

In normal circumstances infection and contact with micro-organisms takes place via a series of interconnected events, which results in the activation of the sort of cell changes mentioned above. Thus prepared the B-lymphocytes recognize and deactivate (or attempt to do so) any invader which reappears. This is what takes place when, in childhood, the normal diseases of this stage of life are overcome, one by one. By adult life immunity to these diseases will have been achieved, and it is estimated that only a small portion of the immune systems capacity will have been committed and used in this defence mode, whereby B-lymphocytes can only recognize and challenge those pathogenic invaders previously responded to. The rest of the immune function remains free to deal with new challenges. When however the immune system is artifically challenged via immunization methods, in which toxic material is injected into the blood stream (NOT the way things happen in normal infection) a far larger commitment is called forth. It is estimated (*The Dangers of Immunisation*, Humanitarian Society, 1983) that as much as 70% of total immune capacity may be thus committed (as opposed to only between 3 and 7%, committed as a result of all normally acquired previous infections). This figure may well be only 30%, but the fact remains that this is far in excess of what would take place in normal situations. The consequences of this sort of over-stimulation, and excess commitment, of immune functions is unknown. The chances are that impairment of the immune system will result, leaving the individual more susceptible to infection of other sorts, more prone to allergic response, and with greater chances of disturbed immune function diseases (rheumatoid arthritis, AIDS, etc.). Modern vaccines have been suggested as a major factor in the growing tendency towards allergy, involving both mind and body. Among other diseases which have been directly related to this sort of immune system assault are Sudden Infant Death Syndrome (SIDS) and multiple sclerosis (MS). These will be discussed fully later. In normal infections (i.e. not vaccination) the immune system responds to antigens of various sorts in an ordered and efficient manner. In artificial stimulation by vaccination the response is abnormal and unnatural.

The above simplified, and brief, description of the components of the immune reactions should indicate that the idea of immunizing against a micro-organisms, via its introduction (albeit in a modified form) by vaccination, is an attempt to protect the body against further infection from this particular micro-organism. The effectiveness of this has been challenged, and is sincerely disputed. The short term and potential long term hazards of this will be presented, and it is hoped that this will lead to a questioning of the whole process. Current methods of immunization include the use of *live vaccines* (this involves the use of an inactivated form of the micro-organisms responsible for the particular disease). The diseases which are 'protected against' by the use of live vaccines include measles, rubella, BCG (tuberculosis), polio, influenza and yellow fever. The main *killed vaccines* used, relate to the following diseases: cholera, typhoid and paratyphoid (TAB vaccine), pertussis (whooping cough), influenza, anthrax and rabies. An examples of ineffectiveness and built-in hazards can be seen in the use of BCG vaccine against TB.

BCG Against TB

The confusion which exists in the medical mind relating to BCG vaccination for tuberculosis is truly amazing. It should, in normal circumstances, be the case that tests for children should be anticipated to be safe, and that the results they yield of some value. The tuberculin skin test is not in any way compatible with this expectation. Before being immunized against TB a skin test is undertaken, which has been criticized by the American Academy of Paediatrics, in a policy statement to its members who use these methods. The statement includes these words, 'Screening tests for tuberculosis are not perfect, and physicians must be aware of the possibility that some false negative as well as false positive reactions may be obtained'!

Now just what these reactions mean is also a dispute. When a child is tested for diphtheria, by injection of a toxin, a negative reaction is considered to indicate that the child is immune (i.e. has been previously exposed and therefore does not require immunization). In BCG testing, once the child has been injected with a test dose, a negative result is seen to indicate a non-immune status, and to require immunization. Now this Alice in Wonderland thinking would perhaps be acceptable were there unanimity among the medical fraternity regarding these discrepancies. Not so however. Dr Robert Mendelsohn states (*Confessions of a Medical Heretic*), 'Your child may have tuberculosis even though there is a negative reading on his tuberculin test. Or he may not have it, but display a positive skin test that says he does. With many doctors, this can lead to some devastating consequences'. These consequences could include extremely hazardous drug therapy for TB, as well as unnecessary X-rays. Mendelsohn concludes, 'I am convinced that the potential consequences of a positive tuberculin skin test are more dangerous than the threat of the disease. I believe parents should reject the test unless they have specific knowledge that their child has been in contact with someone who has the disease'.

The introduction of a specific measured dose of tuberculin is meant to establish the presence, or otherwise, of infection by the tubercle bacillus. The *Lancet* (May 16 1952 p. 935) states, 'Nowadays there is considerable disagreement, even among tuberculosis experts, as to just what a positive or negative tuberculosis reaction really is'. This was the view expressed by Dr Carrol Palmer MD, head of the Copenhagen Tuberculosis Research Team, addressing the Norwegian Medical Society in Oslo.

In a later statement he said, 'The time has come for a wider consideration of the proposition that tuberculin sensitivity, in human beings, is very often not due to tuberculosis infection'. (*American Review of Tuberculosis* 1953 vol. 68 p. 678).

As to the dangers of the procedure, consider the view of Professor Wallgren, who was largely responsible for the introduction of BCG vaccine into Sweden. He became disillusioned to some extent and, after researching the severe reactions of five cases, of whom four died, after BCG vaccination, he stated, 'We have hitherto encouraged by publicity, as many as possible to have themselves BCG vaccinated, even if there was no obvious risk of exposure. We can no longer accept the non-dangerousness of our propaganda'.

He continued by saying, 'Most of the BCG vaccinations, in countries like Sweden, never had any opportunity of exciting any protective action during childhood. In a word they were unnecessary'. Dr Carrol Palmer, referring to these comments of Professor Wallgren, says 'His suggestion that the use of BCG vaccination should be reconsidered comes at a singularly appropriate moment. The point of view that mass vaccination with BCG would not contribute to the effectiveness of the anti-tuberculosis fight in the U.S., a point of view which is now corroborated by Wallgren's proposal for Sweden, seems to me to be sound'. Some years later, at a conference on BCG vaccine held in Glasgow (reported on in *British Naturopathic Journal and Osteopathic Review*, Winter 1964, pp. 87-91) the facts mentioned above were enhanced by a statement by the Medical Officer of Health for the city, who said, 'More than a quarter of a century has elapsed since BCG vaccination was introduced, and despite the fact that more than 100 million people have been vaccinated, there is basic disagreement on its value as a preventive measure'.

And the side effects of the procedure? Among these can be the following, as described by Harold Simon MD, in his book *Attenuated Infection* (1960). 'Some strains of BCG do produce morbidity, if not actual progressive tuberculosis in man. A report from Holland indicates that a significant number of infants developed lymphadenitis, phlyctenular conjunctivitis and draining sinuses, following BCG vaccination'. The disagreement among the doctors using the method, as well as the views expressed as to its efficacy and danger, make this a singularly indesirable method.

Toxins and Antitoxins

Toxoids are also used in vaccinations. These comprise the toxins of particular infections, such as tetanus and diphtheria, which have been partially detoxified or modified, by heat or chemical treatment. Toxins are substances which are soluble in water and which are destroyed by heat, light and oxyen, and by a variety of chemicals. They are the by-products of the activity of certain bacteria, and the pure form can be extremely poisonous. It is known that one ten-thousandth part of a millilitre of the broth in which the tetanus bacillus is grown, is adequate to kill a guinea-pig, if injected into it. Toxins combine with the material inside the cells of certain tissues, forming a fixed bonding, which destroys it. An antitoxin, produced by the body or, it is claimed, administered to it, will break this bonding if it reaches the appropriate site quickly enough. Toxins are selective so that a substance that is toxic to one species is not necessarily so to another. Toxins of different bacilli act on different tissues in the human. Thus tetanus toxin acts on the nerve cells, and diphtheria toxin on the adrenal glands. Antitoxin used in humans is derived (usually) from animals. By giving a horse, for example, regular increasing amounts of a particular toxin (commonly diphtheria or tetanus) it will be made to produce antitoxins. This is removed from the animal in the form of blood and then allowed to clot. The serum which is then freed from the blood cells, is treated with antiseptic, and this is used in individuals who have diphtheria or tetanus, in order to aid their body's ability to deal with the toxins of the disease, and to promote immunity against the infection. The natural production of antitoxins, is via the plasma. Plasma is the fluid portion of the blood and lymph in which the various blood cells are found. It is made up of complex protein constituents and is a vital part of the defence mechanisms. Apart from the manufacture of antitoxins, it is also capable of agglutinating. This is a progress in which 'clumping' takes place, which reduces the ability of the invading microbes to move freely. The agglutination progress is also used in diagnostic procedures, to indicate whether infection has occurred, in the early stages of the disease (in typhoid for example).

In immunization procedures there are two distinct objectives thought to be appropriate to different circumstances. Active immunization is achieved, it is thought, by the introduction of live or dead organisms, or their toxins. This results in a slow production of immunity which may be long lasting. This is also the manner in which natural immunity occurs, via infection. Passive immunity is achieved more rapidly, by the introduction of plasma or serum from an immunized animal. This is used when infection has already occurred, and is seen to be therapeutic rather than preventive, as is the case in active immunization procedures. Passive immunization is thought to also be more appropriate in such conditions as diphtheria, where the damage to the body is caused more by the toxins of the disease process, rather than by the action of the bacteria itself. Passively acquired immunity is also the way in which a mother passes on immunity to her unborn infant, through the placenta (or through mother's milk, to the baby).

In advising on the use of toxoids (modified toxins) or vaccines, authorities stress that possible reactions to such vaccination can be categorized as side-effects or 'adverse effects'. Side effects are usually mild to moderate, and adverse effects are more serious. Side effects are in the nature of fevers and rashes, with local irritation near the site of vaccination. Adverse reactions, which occur around the time of vaccination, are not always considered to be related to the procedure, since it is pointed out by medical authorities: 'Childhood vaccination is given at a time when conditions such as convulsions are relative common, which greatly confuses the picture for the individual child or parent'. All such reactions are however required to be reported (in the UK) to the Committee on Safety of Medicines.

Polio and Diphtheria Immunization

In order to understand the importance of the complex reactions related to vaccination we will be looking in this chapter, at polio immunization, and some startling revelations regarding diphtheria. In addition to antibody formation, which is seen as a measure of the degree of response the body has made to the vaccination, there exists a further hypothetical response of the body. This is known as 'Immunological Memory' and is thought to be independent of the presence of antibodies. This purported phenomenon is at the forefront of the debate between those doctors who wish to promote the use of oral vaccines for polio (as used in the UK) and those who are in favour of the killed polio virus vaccine (as used in Holland). It is pointed out by those who favour the oral (live) vaccine that natural acquired immunity (as occurs when a disease is caught in the normal manner, not by vaccination) to polio is lifelong. It is suggested by those who favour the oral vaccine that this form is therefore safer than the killed vaccine; and that the decline frequently noted in the presence of circulating antibodies over a period of years after vaccination with killed virus, is an indication that the protection offered by it is of limited duration. Those in favour of the killed vaccine however point out that, although there may be a relative, or total, absence of antibodies to polio virus, after some years, there exists an 'Immunological Memory', which enables a rapid response on the part of the body when subsequently challenged by contact with any of the various types of polio virus. This theory is to an extent supported by animal trials, which show that fractions of virus particles can call forth a rapid response in previously vaccinated animals, even if there is an absence of circulating antibodies. This complex debate continues, although as yet a definitive explanation as to what constitutes 'Immunological Memory', has failed to be presented. (*The Lancet* Dec. 8, 1984). There is also a phenomenon which deserves mentioning, which is brought into discussion of polio immunity. It is pointed out by researchers (*Lancet*, as above), that the efficacy of oral polio vaccine has normally been assessed by determining the levels of circulating antibodies after vaccination. This, it is suggested, is only part of the picture, since it fails to show the levels of 'intestinal immunity'. 'Theoretically', it is stated, 'such intestinal immunity may be present, even in the absence of systematic antibody response, or vice versa'. This would appear to mean that after vaccination there may not be present evidence of antibody formation, sufficient to produce protection, but that this may not mean that there is no protection, since there may be 'intestinal immunity'. It also means that there may be antibody activity, without intestinal immunity.

A combination of the 'theoretical' intestinal immunity, and the idea of 'Immunological Memory' would seem to provide several useful bolt holes for the researchers to shelter in, when explanations are required for anomalies in the system they are examining. These may turn out to be valid hypotheses, but as yet they remain conjecture and useful terms to be used. (They may also prove to be one and the same thing.) The fact remains that outbreaks of polio in recent years have often involved vaccinated individuals (Nishio et al., *Jnl. of Biological Studies* 1984; 12:1-10) and that 'In 1982 and 1983 all cases of paralytic poliomyelitis in the USA were vaccine associated, and only one case caused by wild virus, has been reported since 1980'. (Note: this report is from the Center for Disease Control, Atlanta, Georgia, reported in the *Lancet* Dec. 8, 1985 pp. 1215-7.) The term 'wild virus' is used to indicate one that occurs naturally, and which is not derived from the forms used in vaccination. Of course all these researchers are in favour of one form of vaccination or another, and give full credit to the vaccination campaigns, past and present, for the decrease of this disease. An editorial in the *Lancet*, which carried this report, states: 'There is danger that these observations (that almost all poliomyelitis cases in the USA now derive from vaccine) may increase litigation against vaccine manufacturers and public health authorities, and place in jeopardy the supply of vaccines for the protection of the populations'. Rejoicing at past success is suggested, and options for the future considered. Among such options should be consideration of the words of Dr Robert Mendelsohn (author of *Confessions of a Medical Heretic*, quoted from *East-West Journal*, November 1984). 'There is ongoing debate among the immunologists regarding the relative risks of killed virus vs. live virus vaccine (in polio vaccination).'

> 'Supporters of the 'killed' virus maintain that it is the presence of live virus organisms in the other product that is responsible for the polio cases that occasionally appear. Supporters of the live virus argue that the killed virus vaccine offers inadequate protection and actually increases the susceptibility of those vaccinated. I believe that both factions are right, and that use of either of the vaccines will increase, not diminish, the possibility that your child will contract the disease. *In short it appears that the most effective way to protect your child from polio is to make sure that he doesn't get the vaccine.*'

With this the author concurs, with the addendum that good hygiene and optimum nutrition would reduce the risks even further. The current controversy should be seen in the perspective of the history of attempts to achieve immunity against this and other diseases. The following account, which has been abridged for reasons of space, was written by Dr M. Beddow Bayly MRCS LRCP, and published by the National Antivivisection Society, in 1956. This organization has campaigned for many years against the methods of vaccination described in this book. This account is illustrative of the bumbling methods used, as well as some of the perplexing discrepancies which emerged from the research which followed the early failure of polio vaccination, and investigation into diphtheria immunization in the early 1950s. The importance of the late Dr Bayly's comprehensive investigation and condemnation of vaccination procedures deserves recognition.

'A few years ago what is called gamma-globulin was introduced as a prophylactic against poliomyelitis, and is still used for this purpose among contacts of actual cases of the disease.'

'Gamma-globulin is contained in the blood of a person who has had the disease. This is injected into people who may be liable to come into contact with the disease, with the idea of protecting them from infection. Its value in this respect was investigated in America in 1952, 54,772 children being inoculated — half of them with globulin, the other half with gelatin. It was found that after the eighth week there was no protective value which could be ascribed to the globulin, and that the injection of gelatin in the controls was itself associated with an increase of paralysis in the limb injected.'

'In the following years 235,000 children were inoculated. The National Advisory Committee conducting the inquiry were of the opinion that "it had no apparent affect on the incidence of severity of paralysis developing in subsequent cases". According to Dr Geffen (*Public Health*, March, 1955), "it is expensive, uncertain, unreliable and at the best the immunity it gives is short-lived". "Probably", he says, "5-8 weeks".'

'At any rate it was unsuccessful in protecting a laboratory technician who (in November 1954) accidentally sustained an abrasion of one finger with a bone spicule from the vertebral column of a monkey that had died after repeated intramuscular inoculation with type 2 virus. He was given gamma-globulin intramuscularly on the same day, but developed symptoms of polio eight days later.' (*Lancet*, April 2, 1955, p. 702).

'Nor did it prevent the occurrence of 40 cases of poliomyelitis among 6000 inoculated persons during an epidemic in Manitoba in 1953. In 36 cases the disease developed within 7 days of the inoculation. *The Times* (November 16, 1953) in reporting the incident stated that the Manitoba health authorities, while holding that gamma-globulin is useful, concluded that it is not a 'final answer in curbing outbreaks of polio. No one could call this an overstatement.'

'The more favourable results which had been reported in the first of the two trials referred to above were due, it was explained, to the fact that in this trial (1952) the controls were injected with gelatin, while in the second (1953) they were given no injection of any kind. Hammon and his colleagues, who conducted the former, "appreciated the possibility that inoculation of gelatin, like that of many other substances, might provoke paralytic poliomyelitis in certain cases and so give gamma-globulin a false reputation for protective action". (*Lancet*, March 13, 1954, p. 558).'

'It may hardly be credited that, in spite of this scientific proof of the ineffectiveness of gamma-globulin, the President of the National Foundation for Infantile Paralysis, Inc., announced that they were making three million doses of the serum available in 1954 compared with one million in 1953.'

'It is the more extraordinary that in the August 1954 issue of their own bulletin, *Poliomyelitis Current Literature*, (quoted in *Medical Officer*, November 19, 1954, p. 260), they actually published the information that "Dr Graber studied the possible effect of gamma-globulin in a mass inoculation programme in Wisconsin. He comments that there is no evidence that gamma-globulin had any effect in altering the course of the poliomyelitis outbreak or preventing cases of the disease". They also admitted that "following the failure of gamma-globulin in household contacts, this substance is not being provided in Illinois for use in 1954".'

'It was not however on account of its failure as a prophylactic that in 1953 the Glasgow Public Health Department declined the offer of a supply of the serum by the trustees of the United States Roosevelt Memorial

Fund. The reason given was interesting and, according to the *Weekly Scotsman* (January 22, 1953), was that with the comparatively small incidence of poliomyelitis in that city, it would have required the inoculation of 1,250,000 people to prevent an epidemic that might attack, at most, only 250.'

'This alleged prophylatic is one more pitiful example of the unreliability of animal experimentation, for Bodian had found in 1949 that gamma-globulin was highly successful in protecting monkeys against subsequent infection with all three types of virus. (*Proc. Soc. exp. Biol. (N.Y.)*, 1949, 72, 259.'

'As it became more and more clearly realized that animal and human sera were quite ineffective, and that little progress could be expected in this direction, attention was directed towards the production of a vaccine, which might prove successful in preventing the disease.'

'It was in 1949 that a team of Harvard research workers, headed by Enders, reported that they had succeeded in growing polio virus in the kidney tissue of rhesus monkeys. Then Dr Jonas E. Salk, of Pittsburgh, divised a special broth (No. 199) in which to grow the kidney cells.'

'It was already known that there were three main types of virus: (1) Brundhild, (2) Lansing, and (3) Leon, but Dr Salk and his associates isolated and typed 74 strains. By 1952, after he had made experimental vaccines and tested them on monkeys, he was satisfied he had produced one safe enough to be given to human beings.'

'It was on April 12th, 1955, the tenth anniversary of President Franklin Roosevelt's death, that the Foundation of Infantile Paralysis told the world, using every possible means of publicity, that the vaccine devised by Dr Jonas E. Salk was "safe, potent, and efficient".'

'At a meeting of 500 doctors and scientists at Ann Arbor, Michigan, Dr Salk and Dr Francis made such sweeping claims for the vaccine that nearly every American newspaper declared that Dr Salk had abolished poliomyelitis.'

'Only thirteen days after the vaccine has been acclaimed by the whole of the American press and radio, as one of the greatest medical discoveries of the century, and two after the English Minister of Health has announced he would go right ahead with the manufacture of the vaccine, came the first news of disaster. Children inoculated with one brand of vaccine had developed poliomyelitis. In the following days more and more cases were reported, some of them after innoculation with other brands of the vaccine. Then came another, and wholly unlooked-for complication. The Denver Medical Officer, Dr Florio announced the development of what he called "satellite" polio, that is, cases of the disease in the parents or other close contacts of children, who had been inoculated and, after a few days' illness in hospital, had returned home; they communicated the disease to others, although not suffering from it themselves.'

'On June 23rd, 1955 the American Public Health Service announced that there had been 168 confirmed cases of poliomyelitis among the vaccinated, with six deaths, and 149 cases among the contacts of children given the Salk vaccine, with six deaths.'

'But with regard to the "satellite" cases the situation is far worse. According to Dr Florio, children when inoculated with a faulty vaccine may become carriers of the virus. He estimated (*Daily Express*, May 16, 1955) that all of the 1,500 vaccinated Denver children had become carriers. "We have created a group of carriers", he said, "and then there will be another group and so the cycle will go on. It is very distressing". Some of the contacts acquired the disease in its deadliest form.'

'The interval between inoculation and the first sign of paralysis ranged from 5 to 20 days, and in a large proportion of cases it started in the limb in which the injection had been given. Another feature of the tragedy was that numbers developing polio were far greater than would have been expected had no inoculations been carried out. In fact in the state of Idaho, according to a statement by Dr Carl Eklund, one of the Government's chief virus authorities, polio struck only vaccinated children, in areas where there had been no cases since the preceeding autumn; in 9 out of 10 cases the paralysis occurred in the arms in which the vaccine had been injected. (*News Chronicle*, May 6, 1955).'

'An article in *Time* (May 30, 1955) commented: "In retrospect, a good deal of the blame for the vaccine fiasco also went to the National Foundation, which, with years of publicity, had built up the danger of polio out of all proportion to its actual incidence, and had rushed into vaccinations this year with patently insufficient preparation".'

'Few people probably, will recollect that twenty years

ago (1935) Dr J. P. Leake, then Medical Director of the United States Public Health Service, reported a series of 12 cases of poliomyelitis in children who had been inoculated with a chemically treated anti-poliomyelitis vaccine. The onset of the disease occurred 6-14 days after the first or second injection. Five died and three were left with severe paralysis. Dr Leake, who was writing in the *Journal of the American Medical Association* (1935, 105, 2.152) added the comment: "Many physicians will feel that these cases make undesirable the further use of poliomyelitis virus for human vaccination at present".'

'Even the *British Medical Journal* (April 4, 1936) declared, in a leading article, that "it seems probable that these disasters will defer any further attempts of this kind for a considerable time. That such attempts should have been made at all is only to be explained by the enthusiasm of the transatlantic public for methods of specific immunisation". The editor concluded: "He will be a bold man, therefore who proposes to renew the attack on this problem in the clinical field". He underestimated the short memory of the public, its suggestibility by well-planned press publicity, and the pertinacity of the research workers' one track mind.'

'The reader will have noted that in many reports on the Salk vaccine the word "potency" is frequently used and reference made to the stimulation of antibodies in the blood of the vaccinated child. The fallacy of the assumption that antibody formation is a measure of immunity was fully demonstrated in a report issued by the Medical Research Council in May 1950, entitled 'A Study of Diphtheria in Two Areas of Great Britain". In this report by nine doctors (Percival Hartley, W. J. Tulloch, M. Anderson, W. A. Davidson, J. Grant, W. M. Jamieson, C. Kenbarrer, R. Morton, and G. H. Robertson) it was stated that the occurrence of diphtheria in the inoculated "led to the investigation into the immunity state, and the behaviour of the immunity mechanism".'

'In view of the extreme importance of this question, and because so many tests with various vaccines are likely to be made, both in this country and in others, in which it is taken for granted that the antibody formation can be correlated with immunity, it seems desirable to give a brief resumé of the Medical Research Council's findings.'

'It appears that in the course of the study conducted by these nine doctors, inquiry was made into "clinical diphtheria in 95 fully inoculated persons at Newcastle and Gateshead, with special reference to the antitoxin concentration of the serum of these persons, and of hospital nurses, familial contacts, and carriers".'

'There had already, it is stated, been an investigation in 1939 and in 1940-42, of "The antitoxin concentration of the serum of 62 inoculated persons who contracted diphtheria in different areas in England and Wales", but in the first period of the investigation:'

'Some of the results obtained were so unusual and unexpected, so contradictory, and indeed paradoxical, that the inquiry as originally envisaged and put into effect, had to be brought to a close".'

' "The paradox", they said, "was this: on repeated occasions it was found that a sample of serum, taken from a patient with a clear history of inoculation who had yielded diphtheria bacilli from nose or throat swabs, and who according to the clinical history exhibited some or other of the classical symptoms of true diphtheria, was found to contain quite large quantities of diphtheria antitoxin. Now according to Schick, persons whose serum contains not less than one-thirtieth of a unit of antitoxin per ml. or, according to workers in this and other countries, not less than one-hundredth of a unit of antitoxin per ml., should not contract diphtheria. Yet of 62 of the patients investigated prior to April 1942, no less than 25 (40 per cent) were found to contain one-tenth of a unit, or more, of diphtheria antitoxin per ml. of serum, and of these, 5 contained 10 units or more, 7 contained 1-4 units and 13 contained 0.1-0.8 units per ml. of serum . . .".'

'In explanation of this was was suggested that a mistake had been made somewhere but —'

'critical examination of the procedures used for the determination of the antitoxin content of samples of blood and serum failed to reveal sources of error which could account for the high titres".'

'They therefore decided to renew the investigation of Tyneside and to take the greatest possible care in the selection of patients and collection of pathological material and in its examination. But still they found as many as 30 persons with clinical diphtheria, in whom the antitoxin content of the serum was one-twentieth of a unit, or more per ml.'

'They encountered another paradox, "namely, the occurrence of several instances of non-inoculated persons,

having no circulating antitoxin, harbouring virulent organisms, and yet remaining perfectly well, of nurses with little
or no circulating antitoxin, regularly employed in diphtheria wards and remaining free from diphtheria; of
persons previously inoculated or not, with little or no
circulating antitoxin, living in intimate contact with diphtheria in their homes, and yet remaining perfectly well. It
was confidently expected that cases of diphtheria would
arise, either among the nurses, or among the real relations
of patients, and thus provide the material for this part of
the inquiry, but this expectation did not materialise".'

'Part III of the Report deals with the diphtheria outbreak
in Dundee, 1941-2, and here there is also a reference to
the occurrence of diphtheria in persons whose serum
contained an appreciable amount of antitoxin. The facts
disclosed in this Report proved the fallacy of the theory
that the presence of antibodies in the blood shows
protection against a particular disease; but in all the reports
recently published, regarding the testing of immunity
against poliomyelitis infection, they appear to have been
conveniently ignored, and the assumption made that the
theory is firmly established.'

'There has been a long controversy over the question of
whether a virus killed by formalin and given intramuscularly, or a modified (attenuated) live virus given by
mouth, is likely to be the most effective vaccine. According
to the *Lancet* (May 15, 1955, p. 1018) "Dr Jonas Salk and
Dr Albert Sabin have long held opposing views about
vaccination against poliomyelitis . . . but this year it looks
as though Sabin may be right. He favours the use of
attenuated-virus vaccine given by the natural route of
infection (by mouth)".'

' "Sabin has contended that intramuscular injections of
killed vaccine will not confer life-long immunity, and that it
would be impracticable to re-vaccinate each time the short-
lived artificial immunity runs out. If children received such
a short-term vaccine, he argues, there would soon be a
population of young adults with no protection against
poliomyelitis; and as the disease is more severe in adults
than in children, a vaccine which confers only a short
immunity might eventually result in many severe illnesses
when the children grow up".'

'On the other hand, the whole of Dr Sabin's claims as to
the effectiveness of his vaccine are based upon estimates of
the antibodies present (as the result of vaccinations) in the

blood-serum of the chimpanzees and human "volunteers" taking part in the experiment.'

'The fallacy underlying this method of assessing the degree of immunity induced by vaccination has already been fully described, so that it may justly be argued that the efficiency of the attenuated live vaccine is so far entirely problematical.'

'The main argument, against the use of an attenuated, or modified, vaccine of any sort is that put forward by the late Professor McIntosh, who was Professor of Pathology at London University. He stated before the Royal Society of Medicine on October 19, 1926:'

' "Scientifically it cannot be disputed that from every point of view the injection of a virus capable of multiplying in the body of the individual is bad. When multiplication of the virus occurs, then there is no possibility of estimating the dose to which the patient has been subjected. Thus the effect cannot be controlled, and in susceptible individuals may lead to unforeseen results." Commenting upon this address, the editor of the *Lancet* (May 24, 1930, p. 1138) wrote: "The reintroduction of the use of an attenuated virus in tuberculosis was described by Professor McIntosh as a retrograde step. Who knows, he said, for how long an attenuated bacillus can lie dormant and then assume its former virulence".'

'These scientific criticisms apply equally to the inoculation or ingestion of any living virus, and are as valid to-day as when they were made.'

'In spite of repeated assertions that it was quite impossible for the attenuated form of the polio virus to return to its original toxicity, Dr Sabin himself found that when 26 volunteers, between the ages of 21 and 30, were given a minute droplet of a single strain of polio virus it changed in the subjects' bodies to a somewhat virulent form. (*Time*, May 23, 1955).'

After looking closely at the situation obtaining to the incidence of polio in various countries Dr Bayly turned his attention to the situation in the UK where the relative risk of polio was said to be very small indeed and the disease itself, as described by medical experts, not usually of any great importance.

'The actual figures given by the Registrar General show that during the years 1943-53 the average annual number of cases of poliomyelitis notified in England and Wales was 3,328, giving a monthly average of only 227 in a population of 42,290,000 or 6 per million.'

'According to Dr Dennis H. Geffern, OBE, MD, DPH, of every 100 people who become infected with the virus, 90% remain symptomless; 9% show some slight sign of the disease, such as sore throat or stiffness of the neck, whilst only 1% develop definite paralysis. He is reported in *Public Health* (March 1955), to have told the Metropolitan Branch, Society of Medical Officers of Health, that "we are apt to forget that poliomyelitis is the least serious of all infectious diseases with the exception of that one complication, or extension of the disease, which destroys motor cells in the brain and spinal cord and causes paralysis. Apart from this it appears to be a mild infection lasting a few days, the symptoms of which are probably less serious than a cold in the head, and from which recovery is complete and immunity lasting. If we could be sure that an individual contracting poliomyelitis would not become paralysed then there might be much to be said for spreading the disease in order that a community might develop natural immunity".'

Predisposing Host-factors

'Dr Geffern is Medical Officer of Health for St Pancras, and in his address from which the foregoing has been quoted he had some very interesting things to say about the importance of predisposing factors in the host as compared with that of the infecting virus. He gave a list of four main host factors which predispose a person to developing the disease:

1. Operations for the removal of tonsils and adenoids.
2. The condition of pregnancy.
3. Undue exertion, fatigue and chill.
4. Small injuries such as the inoculation of vaccines, injection of drugs like penicillin. In these cases paralysis is usually observed in the limb which has received the trauma.'

'A large amount of enquiry, he said, had convinced Gaylord Anderson, Professor of Public Health in Minnesota, U.S.A., of the following facts:'

'a) Persons with bulbar type of polio give a history of removal of tonsils and adenoids more frequently than do persons with other forms of poliomyelitis.'

'b) If a person who has had tonsillectomy develops poliomyelitis, the likelihood of bulbar involvement is 4 times as great as in one where the tonsils are in situ.'

'c) The proportion of bulbar cases in tonsillectomized persons occurs at all ages and regardless of the time that has elapsed since operation. (Dr R. V. Southcott (*Med. Journ. Aust* 1953, ii, 281) believes that a child whose tonsils were removed at the usual age of 5-7 years suffers trauma to the nerves of the pharynx which increases susceptibility to bulbar poliomyelitis for at least ten years. In an outbreak in South Australia in 1947-48 he found that in 35 out of 39 cases of bulbar poliomyelitis the patient had been tonsillectomised).'

d) The higher proportion of bulbar cases in older persons is due primarily to absence of tonsils rather than to age per se.'

'The theory is that any injury to the body causes changes in the nerve-cells supplying the part so that they are rendered less able to resist infection with the virus. Dr Geffen has himself observed that persons contracting polio after appendicectomy develop paralysis of the abdominal muscles or even of the muscles of the intestine. He is convinced that the injection of diphtheria-pertussis vaccine not only localizes the paralysis of persons infected with virus, but also increases the attack-rate. There can be little doubt, therefore, that even the vaccination of children against poliomyelitis itself may provide the very conditions which favour an attack, and so increase the incidence of the disease. And this risk is by no means confined to the first injection. As a correspondent in the *Lancet* (March 6, 1954, p. 516) pointed out: "A child who is injected three times is at risk three times; there is replication of exposure . . . ." '

'He also referred to experiments which showed that castration in monkeys included a greater susceptibility to the intra-nasal inoculation of the virus. It also appears to be a matter of clinical observation that human beings suffering from a deficiency of Vitamin B6 have a lowering resistance to infection. A considerable number of monkeys were subjected by Bodian (Bodian D. 1948, *Amer. Jour.*

Hygiene, 48, 87-93), to an investigation in which they were deprived of this vitamin (pyridoxin) and then exposed to infection. The results seemed to confirm clinical experience.'

'It was after the publication both of the Francis report on the value of the vaccine, and of the tragic events which had followed the launching of the vaccine on the public in America, that one of the greatest authorities on the subject in this country, W. Ritchie Russell, CBE, MD, FRCP of the Department of Neurology, Radcliffe Infirmary, Oxford, wrote in a letter to the *Lancet* (May 21, 1955, p. 1071): "It may also be pointed out that however dead the virus may be, the giving of any kind of inoculation is likely to precipitate paralytic poliomyelitis in a relatively small number of children who perhaps are already harbouring the virus. One is led to believe that these dangers are less than the benefits of protection, but when the protection is by no means 100% the merits of the method and its statistics become debatable".'

'Dr Ritchie Russell favours the use of a live virus, for, he says: "It is certainly more effective than the Salk method, and may even involve less risk, for should an oral vaccine lead unexpectedly to a febrile illness, there are still many changes that no paralytic disease will develop . . . When, however, poliomyelitis is precipitated by an inoculation the natural defences of the nervous system seem to be ineffective, and nearly all illnesses develop into a paralytic form of the disease, affecting especially the limb used for the injection".'

'Dr Bayly concludes his notes on this subject with a plea against the continued exploitation of animals in this area of science, which he describes in heart rending detail. He asks for the use of human tissue cultures, if research is to be done, and there is now abundant evidence that this could be done, thus relieving the suffering of the millions of laboratory animals, used annually for experimental work and the production of vaccines etc. The commercial element in the vaccination story is also discussed. This involves the astronomical profits enjoyed by the manufacturers of the various sera and vaccines, as well as the commercial aspect of the export of huge numbers of monkeys from India (in the case of polio vaccine). The current situation, in which the debate between those who favour Salk vaccine over Sabin, and vice-versa, continues unabated despite a thirty year proving period since the disastrous launch of Salk vaccine. This is evidence, as Dr Mendelsohn maintains, that they are both probably correct in their assertions as to the other's ineffectiveness and potential danger. This should provide a salutory example of vaccine mania at its worst. Doctors are of course aware of inherent dangers in vaccination and contraindications are recognized in some cases. Specific contraindications to the use of various vaccines are given to doctors and include the following advice:

In the case of live vaccine, these should not be given:

1. If there is any evidence of acute infection or temperature.
2. In the case of pregnancy (unless risks of not using vaccine outweigh risks of giving it).
3. When the immune system is malfunctioning.
4. If there is malignant disease, and if hormonal treatment such as cortisone is being employed. In the case of measles vaccine this should not be given if the child, or its brothers or sisters, or parents, have a history of convulsions, any sensitivity to eggs, or if TB is active. Polio vaccine should be avoided if there is diarrhoea or vomiting, allergy to penicillin, or other drugs such as neomycin. BCG vaccine should be avoided if there is any sign of local sepsis on or in the body. Rubella vaccine should be avoided by children allergic to such drugs as neomycin, or by women who might become pregnant within 12 weeks of the vaccination. Whooping cough vaccine should be avoided if there is a history of fits or convulsions, or irritation or damage to the brain. If parents, or other children in the family, have a history of fits or if the child has a history of neurological diseases or developmental delay, which could relate to neurological defects, then vaccination against whooping cough is thought to be unwise. Diphtheria toxoid should not be given to anyone over ten years of age without prior tests. Tetanus toxoid should not be given unless the patient has had a booster dose within the last 12 months, and

influenza vaccine should not be used on children younger than 9, or to those allergic to eggs.

Specific reactions and dangers to vaccines are officially said to be as follows (*General Practitioner*, April 19, 1985) Polio: although rare there is a danger of vaccine related paralysis in contacts, and so parents should be vaccinated at the same time as children if previously unvaccinated. (Note: there is evidence that many paralytic polio cases result from vaccination itself or from contact with the person immunized). Measles vaccination: A measles-like syndrome may result about a week after vaccination, with rarely, convulsions and brain damage. Risk is estimated to be 87,000 to 1 of serious complications (Note: In life there is seldom an 'all or none' situation. If severe reactions and results occur at that range of probability, then all ranges of reaction occur between that level, and none at all. Thus many mild and more serious complications must also result. However because the individual is in a growing and developing stage, such events are not always associated with the vaccination, even by observant parents. As will be seen, serious long-term potentials exist for chronic disease as a result of measles vaccination. See Chapter 6.)

Cholera vaccination is of interest since this has gradually fallen out of favour in the UK. The requirement to have an International Certificate was abolished in 1973, because of the limited value of the vaccine in controlling the spread of the disease. (Note: If medical authorities say that a vaccine is of limited value it really must be useless, based on observation of their continued devotion to vaccines which are of dubious value.) According to Dr Leonard Roodyn (writing in *The General Practitioner*, May 10, 1985), on the subject of the vaccinations for travellers, 'Protection from this vaccine (cholera) is probably no greater than 50%, and the immunity lasts for only six months'. He notes that individuals such as airline personnel, who have had the vaccination frequently, sometimes develop quite severe reactions.

What claims are currently made for some of the other vaccinations commonly required for tourists and travellers? Recalling Bernard Shaw's comments (see page 5) these are to be seen as less than permanent definitions of efficacy. Typhoid: Having been vaccinated twice with a month gap, there is said to be a three year protection. Cholera: A single dose is said to protect the 50% in whom it is effective, for six months. Polio: Three doses, each separated by one month, are said to provide a 5 to 10 year immunity. Tetanus: A basic course of three injections, with six weeks between the 1st and 2nd, and six months between the 2nd and 3rd, gives immunity for 5-10 years, it is claimed. Hepatitis A and B, varies with the pattern of injection, and the strength of the dose, and gives protection for a limited time. Yellow fever is said to be effective for 10 years. Many of these claims are disputed however. The material from which vaccines are made are often quite nauseating to contemplate. For example: diphtheria toxin and antitoxin is derived from putrifying horse blood; pertussis vaccine from mucus taken from throats of infected children; typhoid vaccine is derived from decomposed fecal material, taken from typhoid victims. Salk polio serum was taken from the infected monkeys kidneys. The discredited vaccine, used ineffectively against swine flu, which had such dreadful effects on the recipients, was derived from infected rotten eggs. These are the materials and the methods used to provoke a response in the complex defence mechanism of the body. There are frequent untoward reactions, some of tragic dimensions. The effectiveness is in dispute, and the history of the methods is, to say the least, supportive of this doubt. The methods of vaccination should be compared with the process of naturally acquired immunity.

In discussing natural immunity the authors of the booklet *The Dangers of Immunization* published by the Humanitarian Society of Pennsylvania, make the point that there is evidence that in normal life, the number of infectious episodes which occur and of which we are aware, are outnumbered approximately one hundred to one, by subclinical infections. These minor, unapparent, infections, have the effect of maintaining the immune function in a prepared state. (The evidence for this is derived from research described in Maxcy-Rosenaw: *Preventive Medicine and Public Health*, 10th edition. Published by Appelton-Century-Crofts, 1973.) Thus it is assumed that minute repetitive infections occur as infectious material escapes the attentions of the first line of defence, such as the tonsils, the lymph nodes and the intestinal immune functions. These stimulate the production of a response by the immune system, which does not reach sufficient intensity to make us aware of the battle. This is direct contrast to the large scale insult which vaccination produces, and which challenges, the system on a massive scale, depleting its reserves (for no system or organ has unlimited reserves of materials or functional ability). It should also be remembered that the body can cope with toxic and infectious materials adequately in one form, but less so in another. Many bacterial infections which occur naturally have their onset in the bowel, and yet the vaccination procedure usually introduces the invader via the blood stream. This can be compared to the difference between the ingestion of snake venom, which would have hardly any effect, and the introduction of this into the blood stream, which would have a highly toxic result. We also should be aware that the infant immune system is not fully developed, and it slowly evolves to its full potential via exposure to myriad micro-organisms in a natural environment. To assault the immune system before it has had time to develop and mature naturally would seem to be courting disaster. The resources and materials of this immature defence capability are unable to adequately deal with the large-scale introduction of toxic materials, and the response weakens its long term efficiency. This could be a major factor in the observed increase in immune-deficient children, with their myriad allergic complaints and behavioural disorders.

Before we turn our attention to the immediate reactions and dangers of immunization, the area in which dramatic illhealth can overtake the recipients, and in which death is also possible, especially in infants, we will examine claims and counterclaims as to the efficacy of these methods. The evidence in this area is damning.

Leaving aside the ineffectiveness of the procedures, and the long-term devastation which can occur, (see Chapter 5) the heartbreaking results of some forms of vaccination should have resulted in the discrediting of these methods long ago.

The reader is asked to bear in mine the information relating to the ineffectivenss of vaccination which was presented in this chapter, relating especially to BCG (TB) vaccines, polio vaccination, and the notes on diphtheria, which Bayly included in his description of the polio vaccine fiasco, as we examine the facts as to the 'success' of other forms of immunization.

CHAPTER 4

Claims and Counterclaims of Immunization's Success

Leaving aside all other considerations for the moment, it is important that a close look be taken at the claims for the success over the past century or so, attributed to vaccination and immunization methods. One of the great triumphs of medical science is said to involve the eradication of smallpox. The fact that it was in decline before mass vaccination was instituted is conveniently forgotten, as are the many cases of fully immunized individuals contracting the disease (see below). Dr Glen Dettman states (*Health Consciousness*, October 1986) 'It is pathetic and ludicrous to say we vanquished smallpox with vaccines, when only 10 per cent of the population were ever vaccinated.' If the tens of thousands of lives that have been saved, ostensibly by these methods, are genuinely the result of vaccination and immunization, then the evidence of short- and long-term damage, which is suggested, requires that we weigh carefully the pros and cons of the case. If however the protection, ascribed to these methods, is indeed largely apparent, and has little basis in reality, then the case against immunization becomes far more clearly defined.

Bernard Dixon in his book *Beyond the Magic Bullet* states,

'Immunisation against diphtheria, introduced on a large scale around 1940, appears to have had a dramatic effect on the incidence of the disease. The number of cases in Britain fell by between fifty and sixty thousand each year, until 1955, since when there have been only sporadic outbreaks. However if we take a longer time scale, over the past century, and alter the criteria, we see a different picture. Diphtheria deaths in children went down continuously from 1300 per year in 1860, to under 300 per year in 1940, with a particularly large drop around 1900, the year when antitoxin was first used. Yet the steepest decline was between 1865 and 1875 — before the diphtheria bacillus had even been isolated'.

Many authorities have pointed out this self same anomaly, that diphtheria and the common infectious childhood diseases, such as measles, scarlet fever, and whooping cough have, in the same time scale, shown a steady and seemingly inevitable decline in incidence and severity, which has been little affected by the introduction of either immunization or antibiotics. This is not to say that either antibiotics or immunization are ineffective, but rather that, in the true perspective of the natural history of the diseases mentioned, they have played but a small part.

The virulence of a number of the micro-organisms which take part in these infections has changed. There was a time when scarlet fever was of such serious import that isolation hospitals housed those affected. It is known that the evolution of the micro-organisms to a milder form has resulted in the condition now being of minor importance only. The death rate in the late 19th century, from this disease, was in the region of 1500 per year, per million of the population (in the UK) and is now under 0.5 per million of the population. This was achieved without any immunization, and the decline has been steady and dramatic for most of this century, long before antibiotics were introduced. The causes of the decline of scarlet fever can be seen to be a combination of greater ability of the host to combat it, due to improved general health (better nutrition, reduction of unhygienic slum living, etc.) as well as on an evolutionary change in the nature of the causal micro-organism, one of the streptococcus family. Had a vaccine been developed, no doubt it would have reaped the credit for this dramatic change, and for the many lives thus saved. As it is no single factor can attract this credit, but it can be said with absolute certitude that it was not due to vaccination. In fact some might seriously say that the decline of the disease was due to non-vaccination.

Bernard Dixon makes the point that for early man the smaller, wide spaced families, in a sparser total population, together with better nutrition, meant that infection was of little importance in his overall condition. This remains true for wild animals today. In crowded unsanitary conditions, with poor nutrition, the opposite obtains, and this was the reason for the massive incidence of infectious diseases in urban man in the past. It is pointed out by Professor T. Mckeown that, 'The modern improvement in health was initiated and carried quite a long way, with little contribution from science and technology, except for epidemiological investigations of environmental conditions in the 18th and early 19th centuries'. With the increase in food production, the introduction of hygienic measures and clean water, as well as control of the size of families, there was a dramatic change in the pattern of disease of an infectious nature, and therefore a decline in both incidence and death, which had little to do with immunization methods and practices.

Typhoid is often introduced into discussions as one of the great successes of immunization. A close look at this claim reveals the opposite. The bacilli used in the combined TAB vaccine are three in type. These are typhoid itself (which comprises bacilli cultured from faeces from an infected individual) which is combined with bacilli from paratyphoid A and B cases, to make up a dose containing in excess of five hundred million bacilli. Typhoid immunization was widely used in the First World War, and claims for its success are first noted at this time. During the earlier Boer War, the British troops suffered some sixty thousand cases, of whom over 8000 died. It has often been stated that typhoid vaccine was not used at this time, but the facts are that the vaccine developed by Sir Almroth Wright was used, and over 400,000 doses were dispatched to South Africa, and a high proportion of the troops were inoculated. Among the evidence against its effectiveness was the statement from a Dr J. Washbourne, who was present with the troops at the time. He said: 'Mild, severe and fatal cases (of typhoid) can occur among the inoculated and the uninoculated, and as far as one can judge, with the same frequency'. The compulsory use of typhoid vaccination of soldiers was withdrawn in 1902, after this debacle, and reintroduced in 1914 on a voluntary basis. During the trench warfare the majority of the troops were indeed vaccinated, and it is noted with triumph, by the proponents of the method, that there were only a little over 20,000 cases, and 1200 deaths, from typhoid in the Great War. This, in proportion to the number of men involved in the Boer War, represents a vast improvement, but the real reason for the decline in incidence and deaths is given by Sir Malcolm Morris, in his Chadwick Lecture in 1921, when he stated: 'In the main the armies on the Western front, in the late war, were preserved from the ravages of dysentery, diarrhoea, typhoid and cholera by good sanitation'. This provision of a wholesome environment was far more important than the vaccine which had failed in 1900, and which would have done so again had not hygiene preserved the troops. The evidence for this statement is based on the fact that where sanitation broke down, as it did in Gallipoli and Mesopotamia, the vaccine was ineffective, and completely failed to protect the troops from crippling outbreaks of intestinal disease and typhoid.

An interesting fact emerges from these outbreaks, which casts doubt on many of the figures relating to the purported 'successes' of vaccination methods. When faced with a case of a disease from which the individual has been given 'protection' by immunization of one sort or another, the doctor faces a dilemma, and will often, with no ulterior motive, diagnose something else rather than the disease. This has occurred in many situations, most recently in the USA when children protected against polio by the current methods of immunization, and yet displaying all the symptoms of acute poliomyelitis, are seen. Doctors have found a number of convenient ways of describing this in other terms. In the case of typhoid we have a remarkable confession made by medical men at the time. Drs Martin and Upjohn stated that 'having 325 typhoid cases to classify in 1917, we regarded those who had been inoculated with suspicion, and managed to cast out 300 of them, leaving only 25 as admitted typhoid cases'. Other army doctors, like Lt-Col. Donegan, CB, have confessed that they were told by their superiors to classify inoculated typhoid cases as something else, and that they did so. This makes a nonsense of those medical statistics trotted out in support of vaccination, under such circumstances. The incidence of typhoid during World War II was low. The efficiency of the provision of clean water and sanitation had been perfected, and this was the major reason for this low incidence. There were odd outbreaks however, and one of these is illustrative. The *Lancet*, 18 September 1945, reported that an outbreak had occurred in the army of liberation, and that 80 personnel had been affected, of whom over half required hospitalization, with two deaths. Of these personnel *ALL* had been vaccinated against typhoid on at least three annual occasions, and the majority had had four or five inoculations.

The evidence would seen to point to typhoid vaccine being singularly ineffective, and this is supported by the numerous demonstrations that have been made in which huge oral doses of the organisms have failed to produce disease. This was done in 1916 in Toronto when a Dr Fraser, and a group of his collaborators, showed their disdain for the micro-organisms, by swallowing millions of typhoid bacilli without harm.

The solution to typhoid is in public and personal hygiene. The *British Medical Journal* of 22 July 1933, stated 'It may be pointed out that in the UK reduction of typhoid began before the carrier, or even the bacillus typhosis, was recognized, and that it was due to the improvements in sanitation carried out by the local government board'. We will look at the untoward effects of this particular vaccination in a later chapter, but for the moment will pass on to another 'success' story in the vaccination saga.

Diphtheria vaccination has been shown not only to be ineffective (see previous chapter) but to carry serious risks. Diphtheria declined in the UK during the war. This was credited by the medical fraternity to immunization. However some doctors were opposed to this view. Indeed, before the war, a group of over 50 doctors in Guernsey signed a petition against compulsory diphtheria immunization, on that island, pointing out that the disease had virtually disappeared in Sweden without any immunization being employed. The results of immunization in various European countries seem to indicate a reverse of the desired result. In Germany, where immunization was compulsory, there was a vast increase in the incidence during the chaos and dislocation in 1945. The number of cases increased from 40,000 to over a quarter of a million, despite the comprehensive immunization programme. In Paris, in 1944, the increase in incidence of diphtheria was 30%, despite compulsory vaccination. In Hungary where compulsory immunization had been the rule since 1938, there was a rise of 35% in incidence over a two year period. In neutral Switzerland, the canton of Geneva had a trebling of cases between 1941 and 1943, despite compulsory vaccination since 1933.

The situation in Germany at the outbreak of the war is contrasted with that of Norway, where there was no vaccination, and where only fifty cases were noted at the same time as Germany was experiencing 150,000 cases.

Publications by the World Health Organization show that diphtheria is steadily declining in most European countries, including those in which there has been no immunization. The decline began long before vaccination was developed. There is certainly no guarantee that vaccination will protect a child against the disease, in fact over 30,000 cases of diphtheria have been recorded in the United Kingdom in fully immunized children.

We will be discussing the side effects of immunization later but it is worth recording that cases have occurred of a form of disease which is indistinguishable from poliomyelitis, as a direct result of diphtheria vaccination (see 'Provocation Disease' page 94). Medical propaganda will have us believe that only unvaccinated children contract the disease, but the phenomenon of 'rediagnosis' occurs here as well. This is when, having arrived at a diagnosis of diphtheria (for example), and then subsequently learning that the child had been immunized, the doctor feels obliged to alter the name of the disease. It has been noted that such alteration of original diagnosis has reached 60% of cases at times. This has never been denied by the authorities, despite its repetition by those opposed to vaccination.

George Bernard Shaw, writing in *The Nation*, 10 Feb. 1923, explains how statistics were often used to confuse the issue as to the effectiveness of such procedures as vaccination,

'In ordinary hospitals some of the Pasteurian inoculations produced a glaring statistical contraction. According to medical statistics they wipe out all the diseases to which they were applied, irresistibly and triumphantly. According to the returns of the Registrar General they either produced no effect or made matters worse. When this was pointed out, the Pasteurians were rash enough to retort that whereas the Registrar General's returns gave only simple mortality, the real test was the *case* mortality. Thus, if in a community of a hundred souls a single case catches diphtheria and dies, the case mortality is 100%, and this leads to the introduction of the inoculation, with the result that the whole population is afflicted with diphtheria and eighty of them die, the reduction in the case mortality from 100 to 80% must be taken to indicate an enormous advance in hygiene produced by the inoculation'.

It can be seen that a combination of the practice of cases being diagnosed to fit into the fact, as seen by the doctor, that despite all the signs and symptoms, the patient cannot be suffering from a particular disease, because he has been 'protected' from it by these methods; together with the use of statistics in such a way as to indicate that success has been achieved, when it has not, makes difficult the task of convincing the uninitiated as to the validity of the assertion that immunization, of some types, actually made things worse. Shaw's exaggerated example of what is a very real phenomenon, highlights what he himself called the 'fallacies and illusions' of statistics. Thus we have a disease which, like typhoid, has decreased, with or without vaccination, and for which there is evidence of greater incidence when vaccination was compulsory. It is also shown that rediagnosis makes a mockery of official figures, which are purported to indicate that only the unvaccinated contract the disease. This coupled with the suggested side-effects, of which more later, makes the case against the mass application of this form of immunization fairly comprehensive.

One of the major triumphs of medical science is claimed to be smallpox eradication. The question remains strong as to whether the decline in the condition's prevalence is related to immunization, and whether there are not other factors involved, as in the examples discussed above.

Smallpox had declined dramatically in the United Kingdom by the end of World War II. The extent of this was such that more children were dying of vaccination, than from the disease. A report dated February 12, 1964, from the Registrar General, indicated that in the 25 years ended December 1962, nearly two thirds of the children born in England and Wales remained unvaccinated against smallpox. In this period four children under the age of five died of smallpox, whilst out of the group of one third of vaccinated children, no less than 86 died from vaccination reactions (children under the age of five) and many more were seriously injured by it. At face value this would seem bad enough a comparison, and yet it hides a monstrous truth. In the figures provided by the Government of the day, it was stated that no children under five years of age had, in the year of 1962 itself, died from vaccine effects. And yet there are a number of recorded cases taken from the Chief Medical Officer's report, which shows this to be a misrepresentation. This report explains the nature of the particular complication of vaccination as follows:

'Vaccinia gangrenosa. This condition, also known as chronic progressive vaccinia, is one in which a primary vaccination lesion fails to heal, becomes necrotic and therefore increases in size. Similar lesions appear on the body from which vaccinia virus can be recovered. After weeks or months death frequently occurs.'

. . .The medical officer's report goes on,

'A fatal case occurred in a boy vaccinated at the age of 4 months; his disease followed the described pattern and he died three months later. At no time was vaccinial antibody demonstrated in his blood, and he revealed an abnormally low gamma globulin level'. Other cases are described and the report then continues to look at the condition known as post-vaccinal encephalomyelitis. It states 'In all there were sixty reported cases (in 1962) of post vaccinal encephalomyelitis, of which five ended fatally. The first death occurred in a male child aged 8 months. This child became ill ten days after vaccination with projectile vomiting and obvious general malaise. The next day on admission to hospital there was obvious bronchitis, but no other abnormal signs. A day later he had a right sided convulsion and developed torsion movements. There were subsequent convulsions and he died early the next morning'.

Case after case is described and yet none of these appeared in the report of the Registrar General for that year. This indicates again the folly of relying too heavily on official figures, when attempting to 'prove' the case for or against anything. However, what is clear is that in the post-war years, until the merciful end of the procedure, vaccination against smallpox killed more children than died of the actual disease which, if Shaw's personal experience is anything to go by, was no less accessible as a result of the procedure than if no vaccination had taken place at all.

It would be as well to have the evidence, at this stage, of a Professor of Preventive and Social Medicine at the University of Otago, Dr C. W. Dixon, who was himself a strong believer in vaccination procedures, and who wrote as follows in 1964.

'If vaccination was, or could be made, an entirely innocuous procedure, the routine vaccination of infants and school children, a quite practicable proposition, although not affording much protection from spread, would have advantages. Although an individual could still die or have a severe attack of smallpox, the population as a whole would have lower mortality, and severity figures.' 'It is a fact', he continues, 'of which we are pretty sure, that risk, even after close contact, of contracting smallpox, in those who have had a successful primary vaccination, or a successful vesicular revaccination, within three years of either event, is exceedingly low, but as the time interval increases we are less able to predict what would happen'.

He discusses the belief of doctors who, having themselves been successfully vaccinated and revaccinated, are convinced that they are permanently immune.

'I have no such illusions', states the professor, 'I have just been revaccinated for about the fiftieth time, and have a good accelerated vesicular reaction response, which has left a small scar'.

The main point of Dixon's assertion was that mass vaccination was the cause of widespread illness; that it accomplished little in containing outbreaks; and that large scale infant vaccination resulted in a combined death rate from vaccination effects and smallpox, far greater than could be expected if vaccination were abolished.

Thankfully smallpox vaccination is now out of use, as the disease is said to have been abolished from the earth. Effective drug therapy is also now available for its containment, and so the arguments surrounding the employment of vaccination in relation to smallpox, are academic only. However we can learn much from its history regarding muddled thinking, and the juggling of statistics to support a particular viewpoint. Early medical researchers, such as Pasteur, Koch and Ehrlich, cast the mould which has largely determined the manner in which modern medicine has chosen to view the natural history of infectious disease. The concentration and emphasis has been on the role of the infecting agent, and not on the host. The fact is that at the time of the identification, by Koch, of the organism which was involved in tuberculosis, most city dwellers in Europe carried in their bodies this dangerous bacillus. It was only when, through nutritional depletion, fatigue and unhygienic conditions, the body became susceptible, that it was able to proliferate and to begin to produce disease. In modern times it can be shown that in the bowel, or salivary excretions, of most people there exists a variety of highly pathogenic micro-organisms. There is no disease however, until other events take place which give rise to suitable conditions in which the organism can expand its activities unchecked. Then disease is manifest. AIDS is said to have infected some ten times more people in America and Europe than are ever going to display its dreaded symptoms. It requires alterations to take place in the checks and controls which the healthy body exerts, before the disease itself will be evident.

It is not the same thing to say that a bacterium causes a particular disease, and to say that it takes part in it, and indeed that it cannot occur without that particular bacteria. There is no cholera without the particular cholera bacillus, but there are many individuals with that organism present in their body, who do not have the disease, and who are unlikely to develop it. Many factors need to coincide before infection takes place, and these are not greatly influenced by immunization against the particular bacterium. Attention to physical and mental hygiene, overcrowding and nutrition (to include clean potable water), are the primary factors which will raise the defence capabilities of the body, and which will allow it to successfully combat infection if it does take place. Immunization can be seen to deal with a peripheral aspect of the problem, and the evidence of infectious disease declining over the best part of the last century, can be seen to have little if anything to do with such procedures. It is the alterations in public health and nutrition which have been the major influence, and which requires emphasis. It is for these reasons that brave workers such as Pettenkoffer, and the Russian Metchnikoff were able to consume vast amounts of pathogenic micro-organisms, with no ill-effects. It is for this reason, combined with the evidence of the unacceptable side-effects involved, that parents should pause before unconditional surrender to pressures to have immunization performed. We will be looking at some individual immunization procedures and the reported side-effects of these, later in the book. At this stage it is apt that we should consider the purported benefits of some of these, and compare these claims with evidence which shows a very different story.

Pertussis (whooping cough) immunization is controversial, as the side effects have received a great deal of publicity. The counter claim is that the effectiveness and protection offered by the procedure far outweigh the possible ill effects. A glance at the graph showing annual deaths, per million children, from this disease over the period from 1900 to the mid-nineteen seventies, shows that from a high point of just under 900 deaths per million children (under age 15) in 1905, the decline has been consistent and dramatic. There had been a lowering of mortality levels of approximately 80% by the time immunization was introduced on a mass scale, in the mid-nineteen fifties. The decline has continued, albeit at a slower rate, ever since. No credit can be given to vaccination for the major part of the decline, since it was not in use. The degree of efficacy of pertussis immunization is disputed by many authorities, for immunized and non-immunized children show an equivalent incidence of the disease in many outbreaks. The disease shows itself to have mild symptoms in most basically healthy children, and is amenable to conservative therapy. A recent report in the medical journal, the *Lancet* (5 October, 1985, p. 776) states that a group of children infected with whooping cough (and confirmed by identification of micro-organisms from nasal swabs) most were immunized. Most of the cases were mild whether immunized or not and few were admitted to hospital, says the report. This is not a serious disease in well nourished children, of good basic health, and the risk factor attached to the method (see Chapter 5) makes its continued use a dubious benefit. The facts relating to the decline in whooping cough incidence is paralleled by all other acute infections, supposedly protected by immunization. The decline is also noted in diseases such as scarlet fever for which there has been no immunization. Professor Gordon Stewart of Glasgow University, is head of a department of community medicine. He has studied whooping cough vaccination extensively. The following are his views as to its efficacy (we will be looking at his evidence as to the dangers of this vaccine in Chapter 5).

> 'The contrary view, with which I am identified, is that vaccination has been at best only partially effective in controlling whooping cough, and has never been proved to be adequate in protecting infants below one year of age who are, in the United Kingdom at least, the only group of children whose health is seriously menaced by whooping cough.'
>
> 'As I view the problem, the marginal advantages of the vaccine in children over one year of age have to be offset against adverse effects of the vaccine itself, which are very common indeed and may be followed occasionally by irreversible brain damage, paralysis and mental deficiency. Because of this danger, or for fear of it, many parents and doctors are reluctant to vaccinate their children.'
>
> 'In assessing the rise or fall of any infectious disease, it is essential firstly to look critically not only at its prevalence now, but also at what has been happening in the past.'

'When this is done, it becomes clear that most of the major infectious diseases, especially those of childhood, have decreased in prevalence and mortality in all developed countries more or less continuously for fifty years, or more.'

'There was a time when whooping cough, in common with scarlet fever, diphtheria and measles, caused many deaths or gave rise to complications followed by ill health for years, sometimes permanently. These days passed, in Britain at least, 30 or more years ago. Deaths from any of these diseases are now very infrequent indeed. Health damaging complications are also rare, most attacks being brief though still distressing at the time, especially the misery of measles and the paroxysms of whooping cough. But the essential fact is that the decline in prevalence and severity of these major infections, and several others, occurred before there was any national vaccination programme.'

'It is self-evident that factors other than vaccination play a large part in the decrease in prevalence and severity of infectious diseases.'

'So the questions began to be asked as to what extent, if at all, vaccination contributes to control, as compared with other factors, and to what extent its benefits — if any — are neutralized by dangerous or potentially dangerous side-effects.'

Professor Stewart states that in 1974/5, and 1978/9, outbreaks in the UK, and in the 1974 outbreaks in USA and Canada, the proportion of children developing whooping cough who had been fully vaccinated was between 30 and 50 per cent.

Professor Stewart does believe in immunization, but not against whooping cough in its present form. A more recent statement in the *British Medical Journal* of July 1983 explains this view. Restating his position on whooping cough vaccination, Dr Gordon Stewart, writing in a letter to the editor of the BMJ, makes some pertinent points. 'Pertussis vaccine has a consistent record in the published work and in unpublished reports since 1933, of neurotoxic and other sequelae, unmatched by other vaccines, long before there was any adverse publicity about it in the media' he said.

'Clinical reports from various sources show that in the outbreaks of whooping cough in the '70s and in 1982, many babies with severe infections were admitted to hospital, confirming the fact, also apparent in the American survey, that current vaccination programmes do not necessarily protect infants'.

It is pointed out that the risk of encephalopathy with permanent brain damage after a child actually contracts whooping cough (1:38,000) is within the range (between 1:25,000 and 1:110,000) after vaccination against diphtheria, pertussis and tetanus. It is also shown that the risk of death after whooping cough (1:13,000) is not too different from the risk of death from pertussis vaccine (1:100,000).

Finally, Dr Stewart states,

> 'There is good reason in the data to believe that if deprivation and overcrowding can be abated, the incidence and severity of the disease will diminish, but until then a vaccine is needed. The data shows that the present vaccine does not control the outbreaks. I believe that it is insufficiently effective, and too risky, to be in mass vaccination programmes'.

Dr Julian Kenyon discusses this subject in a letter to the editor of the *Journal of Alternative Medicine* (August 1984).

> 'A recent report by Professor Gordon Stewart, of Glasgow University, concludes that the risks of vaccination to first born babies, in the average household, are as great as those of catching whooping cough itself. The Department of Health has been embarrassed by these findings and has so far sat on the report for eight months. No doubt we will soon be subjected to yet another "vindication" of vaccination policy, notwithstanding that it increasingly appears to fly in the face of the facts.'
>
> 'When the last whooping cough vaccination debate reached its height the issue acquired features of a political campaign, culminating in entrenched statements from the Minister of Health, to the effect that whooping cough vaccination is good for you, so we all must have it or else.'
>
> 'It's curious that this issue should be judged in such a way. Even Prince Charles and Princess Diana succumbed to the official line and Prince William was duly vaccinated in the conventional way, accompanied by lavish media coverage,

all enthusiastically touting the official line. We might have thought that he might have followed his family's interest in homoeopathy, but perhaps he was frightened by the Department of Health's storm troopers.'

'The risks of vaccination vary from minor reactions at the time of vaccination to gross brain damage and even death. Many homoeopaths would claim that long-lasting side effects of different sorts are common following vaccination and that they go unrecognized and therefore unrecorded. My own experience confirms this.'

'The risks from whooping cough similarly are rarely fatal, but can produce severe long-term effects with resulting lung-damage. If I had to choose between brain damage or lung damage, I would plump for the latter, and be thankful "only" to have to cope with daily postural drainage and occasionally coughing up a little blood, and perhaps a little breathlessness on effort.'

'After all, removing the affected lobe of the lung often helps in the worst cases, but what can you do for brain damage?'

'Naturally, both sides worry that if vaccination was dropped then many more children would catch the disease during the next epidemic, which is due in about two years time. Is there any alternative? The homoeopaths say that there is.'

This is an area we will discuss in the chapter on Alternatives to Vaccination (page 127).

In the case of poliomyelitis the graph showing mortality from this disease, for the period six years before introduction of vaccination (in England and Wales) until six years after, indicates that there was a decline prior to the introduction of vaccination of 82% (from a high of 755 deaths in 1950, to 137 in 1956). There was a further drop of 67% in the subsequent six years (to a low point of 45 deaths in 1962). This decline has continued. Again the question requires asking as to whether immunization had anything to do with the progression of the declining incidence of this disease. This form of immunization has the advantage of being administered orally, rather than by injection, and in this respect at least is more desirable. There is some evidence that, as with most forms of illness, there are varying degrees of virulence, and that most cases are almost asymptomatic, involving transient diarrhoea and not much else. The paralytic symptoms have been associated by some workers with infection subsequent to tonsillectomy, and to prior vaccination against diphtheria. This is discussed further in Chapter 3. Once again it can be seen that the factors which decide the severity of infection lie with the host and not with the micro-organism.

Similar comments can be made regarding diphtheria, measles etc., and the crux of the argument remains that there is little evidence to support the claims for efficacy of immunization on a mass scale, as a major element in reducing the incidence of the diseases in question. In the case of diphtheria, for example, the incidence is now very low in industralized countries, and yet immunization is continued, despite evidence aplenty that its benefits are limited, if they exist at all. In an outbreak in Chicago in 1969 the city board reported that 4 of the 16 cases had been fully immunized, and 5 others had had at least one vaccination. In another outbreak it was stated that of three people dying from diphtheria, one had been fully immunized, and of the 23 carriers identified, 14 had been immunized. The long-term side effects of vaccination remain to be discussed, but the evidence as to efficacy of vaccination against this disease, even without those dangers, remains singularly unconvincing. According to figures produced by the British Union for the Abolition of Vivisection, over 30,000 cases of diphtheria, in fully immunized children, have been recorded in the UK in recent years.

Whether we are considering whooping cough or diphtheria, smallpox or polio, we come to the same point of incredulity in the purported efficacy of the method, even before we get to the question of what additional harm is accruing to the body subjected to this unphysiological assault. The evidence relating to typhoid, which was mentioned earlier, especially in the well documented war-time periods, is overwhelmingly supportive of the argument that reduction in incidence related not to immunization, but to hygiene and clean water supplies. During the second world war the incidence of typhoid was low. Sanitation was a major factor, indeed it was a court martial offence to use water, other than that supplied by army mobile water tankers, in the British Liberation Army.

The first measles vaccine was licenced in the USA in 1963. As we will see in later chapters one of the dangers of the vaccine has been shown to parallel the alleged major danger of the disease itself, in being the cause of encephalitis in a great many cases. In terms of its protective efficacy it also leaves much to be desired. Dr Robert Mendelson states the case as follows: 'I would consider the risks associated with measles vaccination unacceptable, even if there was convincing evidence that the vaccine works. There is not. While there has been a decline in the incidence of the disease, it began long before the vaccine was introduced. In 1958 there were about 800,000 cases of measles in the USA, but by 1962 the year before a vaccine appeared the number of cases had been dropped by 300,000. During the next four years, while children were being vaccinated with an ineffective and now abandoned "killed virus" (see pages 92/3) the number of cases dropped another 300,000'. The death rate from measles had declined equally dramatically, independently of vaccination. In 1900 there were 13.3 measles deaths per 100,000 population. By 1955, before the first measles vaccination, the death rate had declined by 97.7%, to only 0.03 deaths per 100,000 of the population. Mendelsohn continues,

'Those numbers are dramatic evidence that measles was disappearing before the vaccine was introduced. In 1978 a survey of 30 states showed that more than half of the children who contracted measles had been adequately vaccinated.'

A study which appeared in the *Journal of Paediatrics*, in 1972 (vol. 91 no 2, pp. 317-330) studied the epidemiological and seralogical factors associated with urban measles outbreaks, and contained the following information:

'A measles epidemic, during which 130 children were hospitalized and six died, occurred in St Louis City and County, during 1970 and 1971-74. 430 cases occurred, during a forty week period. In one school, out of 90 children known to have been vaccinated, 19 developed measles, a failure rate of 20%. Clinical data sheets were returned from another 125 children in another school. Thirty five of these (28%) had been vaccinated.'

The authors then advised a revaccination programme for the purpose of vaccinating the failure cases. 'However', they say, 'it is admitted that even this might be useless, as one vaccine failure may have repeated failures'.

During the winter of 1967-8 an epidemic of measles occurred in Chicago. As reported in the *American Journal of Epidemiology* (vol. 91 no 3, pp. 286-293) 'Two characteristics warrant particular attention: 1. The high per cent of cases among vaccinated pre-school children, and 2. The failure of the intensive school immunization program to terminate the measles epidemic. 72% of the case were in children under five years. The immunization programe in Chicago has apparently had no effect on the course of the epidemic.' As we will see in later chapter, measles vaccination, as used at this time, produced a condition known as 'atypical' measles, and is also thought to be involved in a wide range of long-term problems. The failure of the method is sufficiently documented to be beyond reasonable doubt. And yet the procedure continues to be used.

These more recent events are but echoes of the tragedy which befell the British nation in the smallpox outbreak of 1870-1872. A considerable proportion of the population had been vaccinated, at least once, and yet an epidemic which killed 44,000 people took place, and as we have heard from Bernard Shaw this was no respecter of the vaccinated. It was this and other failure, and the many cases of unacceptable side-effects which caused public opinion to force a change in the law away from compulsion in vaccination. This may all be taken as of but historical interest, and yet in late 1961 there was a smallpox outbreak in the UK in which, of the 59 cases, 34 were vaccinated and 25 unvaccinated. The Chief Medical Officer of the Ministry of Health, in 1962, reported on this, and found some comfort in the fact that of the unvaccinated fully 16 patients died, whereas of the vaccinated only 5 died. (These figures do not include the individuals from abroad who imported the disease, and of whom two also died.) Thus chastened by events the pro-vaccination spokesmen retreated from the position in which vaccination was claimed to give full immunity, and stated 'there is still a highly significant difference in favour of vaccination exerting an ameliorating effect on the disease'. The advantage thus gained may well have been at considerable risk of chronic ill-health, as we shall see. It is a far cry however from the heady claims of immunity for life, which first heralded this procedure.

Indeed by the 1960s it was not the individual who was expected to benefit from smallpox vaccination (thankfully no longer with us). This statement is made in *The Medical Officer* Jan 10 1964. 'Much confusion of thought arises from not appreciating the fundamental difference between the value of partial immunity to the individual, and to the community. Although an individual, who has been vaccinated some years before, may well die from smallpox, a group of people who have ever been vaccinated will suffer a lower mortality from smallpox than a similarly exposed group of unvaccinated people'. Even this is questionable, for in the 1962 outbreak there were no secondary cases in some areas which had very low levels of smallpox vaccination, e.g. West Bromwich, where only 7% of infants had been immunized.

We will now turn away from smallpox, to a different hazard which is of equal interest, in terms of the failure of immunization. The disease commonly called german measles (rubella) is not serious to children. It does however pose threats to the unborn child, should a woman become infected during the early stages of pregnancy, where the sequals could involve birth defects. The vaccination, as far as it involves boys, is given in the hope that this will prevent their contracting it naturally, at an inopportune time, when they might thereby infect such a pregnant woman. The idea insofar as girls are concerned is that this will get the disease out of the way before maturity. This denial of natural immunity, which the disease itself offers, is thought by many to actually increase the threat of the woman contracting the disease during child-bearing years. Many studies have shown that there is often a lack of evidence as to the antibody presence in women immunized in childhood. This is confirmed by the fact that many people do in fact contract the disease, who have received vaccination earlier. As Dr Mendlesohn puts it, 'A large proportion of children show no evidence of immunity in blood tests given only four or five years after rubella vaccination. Today, because of immunization the vast majority of women never acquire natural immunity. If their vaccine-induced immunity wears off, they may contract rubella while they are pregnant, with resulting damage to their unborn children'. Mendlesohn points out that since the greatest threat of rubella is to the unborn child, were immunization the answer, one would anticipate that obstetricians would be sure to have had immunization. In this way they could not themselves infect their female patients. In a California survey, reported on in the American Medical Association Journal, more than 90% of the obstetricians and gynaecologists interviewed had refused this vaccination. This condemns the procedure forcibly, yet begs the question as to why the vaccine, with known serious side effects (see Chapter 5) should be foisted on children when many doctors themselves refuse to have it.

An article appeared in *The Australian Nurses Journal* in May of 1978 which made it clear that there was overwhelming evidence against the effectiveness of the vaccine. Dr Beverley Allan, of the University Department, Austin Hospital, Melbourne, Australia, was apparently so stunned by these revelations, after her detailed investigation, that it led her to query the whole question of mass vaccination desirability. She had conducted trials on army recruits, whose immunity to german measles was low, as proved by blood tests.

They were immunized with an attenuated virus, and then sent on to training camp, where in the past regular epidemics of rubella had occurred. Four months after immunization an outbreak occurred which affected 80% of the men who had been 'protected'. A further trial undertaken by Dr Allan, at a mental institution, gave the same results, immunization being unable to prevent the disease. All this of course is done in the name of preventing birth defects, and it could be argued that this factor is the only thing that matters, and that perhaps, in some way, the vaccine allowed this to take place, even if the disease was still in evidence. A statement to the press, by Sir Henry Yellowlees, then Chief Medical Officer of Health (February 26, 1976) makes it clear that this protection is not forthcoming, even to the unborn. The statement said that, in spite of high levels of vaccination there had been no detectable reduction in the number of babies born with birth defects. The evidence is strong that confused and confusing statements have promoted the cause of vaccination. Due regard to the facts show that protection is limited; statistics have of times been manipulated, and that there is strong pressure on doctors to rediagnose, when they realize that immunization against a disease had failed. Despite this there is a suggestion in the *Lancet* (Oct. 12, 1985, p. 828) that this form of immunization (rubella) be introduced in the UK as a legal requirement for a child's entry to school.

The presence of a bacterium does not signal disease. The state of health of the host, the body of the individual, is the deciding factor as to whether or not this will take place. Introduction of toxic material does provoke a response on the part of the body, which may have limited benefits in relation to protection from particular micro-organisms. This is not necessarily a desirable situation, and in the long run has only a marginal effect on the health of most individuals. The risks which we will deal with at length in subsequent chapters, far outweigh such dubious benefits. The propaganda in favour of immunization has won the minds of the masses and has influenced medical thinking, and government and international measures, relating to disease control. This has been at the expense of methods which might have raised the real level of well-being of the people at risk. This begins to impinge upon the realms of politics and economics, for the gains are great in this area, and the truth is not always palatable. The removal of the idea of protection, via immunization, and the implementation of expensive measures to improve nutrition in countries which can hardly make ends meet, would not be welcome themes for politicians, even if they could be made to listen to the facts. In the end it is the education of the people themselves, and the enlightenment of, and via, the media, which may get the message across. The first clear message is that immunization offers only limited protection. We will see at what cost, for our next consideration will be of some of the many ways in which the health of people and of nations has been impaired, and put at risk, by the use of these methods.

CHAPTER 5

Immediate Ill Effects of
Immunization Procedures

In Chapter 3 we looked at some of the evidence relating to the dubious effectiveness of tuberculosis (BCG), diphtheria and polio immunization, in order to illustrate the notes on the manner in which immunization is thought to work. Discussion of those particular forms of immunization are also illustrative of the subject matter of Chapter 4 which deals with evidence relating to the lack of efficacy of such methods, and to this chapter which covers immediate adverse effects. The division of negative findings, relating to immunization, into sections, such as efficacy, immediate ill-effects, and long term hazards, is arbitrary, since they to some extent overlap. In considering any of these areas the reader is asked to also examine the associated chapters so that the evidence and views contained in them are not overlooked.

As we examine the evidence relating to the effects of immunization procedures on the body, we will discover that these can be divided into two broad categories. Some of the effects take place dramatically quickly and can be recognized as directly linked to the vaccination procedure. Other changes take many months or years to manifest, and are more difficult to link with the immunization, until connection is established by means of research, and the observation of trends in known vaccinated people. For example, if a particular condition, such as multiple sclerosis, is being considered, it may be that in tracking back for possible common factors amongst patients, it would be noted that among the elements which these individuals have in common is a particular infection or immunization procedure. In this way the conditions or procedures associated with it would come under suspicion. Some workers, as we
* will see, have indeed come to a tentative conclusion relating

measles virus to MS. There are also changes which may take place as a result of immunization, which are not as clear cut as are immediate reactions, or even involvement in chronic disease years later, but which relate to subtle general changes in particular functions and systems. These too require detective work in order to establish the connection between themselves and immunization methods. These changes are the forerunners of much chronic ill health, and they may include general depletion of immune function, as well as lowered vitality and energy. A major possible change leading directly from the introduction into the body of foreign substances, in vaccines, is that a degree of alteration may occur in the genetic material which governs the replication of cells in the body. This may well be the most serious of all long-term effects of immunization, since it has implications which could link immunization with cellular changes leading to cancer, and to alterations which could make the body recognize such affected cells as being 'foreign', and therefore calling forth an immune response to them. In this way we may come to an understanding of the ways in which auto-immune reactions take place. These are the conditions in which a part of the body appears to be allergic to itself, with consequent inflammatory reactions, such as occur in rheumatoid arthritis (an auto-immune disease). In our considerations of all these areas of reaction and change, we must bear in mind that the scale of human involvement in this mass experiment in protective measures is vast. We are thinking in terms of billions of people, over a time scale of a hundred years or so, with the main thrust of the effort taking place in the last half-century. If we objectively assess the dramatic increases noted, world-wide, in chronic disease, even in young children; the increase in birth defects in industrialized countries, and the massive increase in mental disease, we can begin to appreciate that if there is a provable, or even a tentative, link between these factors and immunization, then we are considering one of the gravest disasters in mankind's history, and one which has been self-inflicted.

Sudden Infant Death Syndrome

Our first consideration will be to the possible link between vaccination and that most tragic of events, Sudden Infant

Death Syndrome (SIDS). Many workers have noted that the sudden, inexplicable, death of an apparently healthy baby often takes place within hours or days of vaccination of one kind or another (but with some cases showing more of a link than others). Time and again this has called forth warnings and protests without any real impact on the consciousness of the medical fraternity, or the public at large. This is despite a well documented project in Australia (which we will describe in detail later) in which the incidence of child death following vaccination, which was reaching horrifying proportions, was brought under control by means of a simple nutritional change, the introduction of vitamin C supplementation.

Dr Robert Mendelsohn has stated categorically:
'My suspicion, which is shared by others in my profession, is that the nearly 10,000 SIDS deaths that occur in the United States each year are related to one or more of the vaccines that are routinely given to children. The pertussis (whooping cough) vaccine is the most likely villain, but it could also be one of the others'. It was noted by Dr William Torch, of the University of Nevada School of Medicine, that the DPT (diphtheria, pertussis, tetanus vaccine) may be responsible for SIDS deaths. He noted in one survey that two thirds of 103 children, who died of SIDS, had been immunized with DPT vaccine within three weeks of each death. Many died within one day of the procedure. He states that this was not a coincidence, but that there is, at least in some of the cases, a causal relationship. In 1979, during a vaccination campaign in Tennessee there were eight cases of SIDS, immediately following routine DPT vaccination, which occurrence was followed by intervention of the US Surgeon General, stopping use of the particular vaccine. Of this group, five children died within one day of vaccination. Despite this very strong link an official finding was that there was no relationship between the procedure and the deaths. This sort of bureaucratic pronouncement is not uncommon in medical matters, and requires a little consideration of its own. In this particular instance the official denial of a link between vaccination and the Tennessee deaths, was stated to be because a further analysis, of other cases, led them to a belief that pertussis vaccination could not cause SIDS.

There is no way in which strong evidence of a connection in one case can be denied by findings in another survey. And yet this is what happened. In an address to the Society of Homoeopaths in 1985, Harris Coulter PhD (co-author with Barbara Loe Fisher, of *DPT: A Shot in the Dark*, Harcourt-Brace-Jovanovich) stated the following in relation to this very situation. 'The method used was "retrospective case control": 400 cases of SIDS were collected, and for each of these dead babies two living "controls" were selected, matched by birth date, birth weight and race. When the vaccination histories of the two groups were compared, it was found that in the SIDS group only 38% had been vaccinated, while of the control group 56% had been vaccinated. The CDC director stated to a congressional committee in July 1983, that this strongly supported the view that DPT immunization is not a factor in the etiology of SIDS'.

What Dr Coulter and Mrs Fisher point out so forcibly is that this proves nothing of the kind. The two groups were not matched adequately. Such factors as genetic, nutritional, physiological and other variables make one infant more susceptible than another, and these have nothing to do with date of birth or race. Even such factors as whether or not a child is breast fed is of major importance in subsequent vulnerability to immunological insults. The example above shows what Coulter describes as 'our medical establishment's pursuit of scientific truth, taking on Alice in Wonderland characteristics'.

A study undertaken in 1979, at the University of California, Los Angeles (UCLA), under the sponsorship of the Food and Drug Administration, and which has been confirmed by other studies, indicates that in the USA approximately 1000 infants die annually as a direct result of DPT vaccination, and these are classified as SIDS deaths. These represent about 10 to 15% of the total number of SIDS deaths occurring annually in the USA (between 8000 and 10,000 depending on which statistics are used).

Far and away the most important practical work in this area has been done by Dr Archie Kalokerinos and Glen Dettman, PhD, in their work with aboriginal children in Australia. This is described in Dr Kalokerinos' book, *Every*

Second Child (Thomas Nelson, Australia, 1974). Aboriginal infant death rates had shown a dramatic increase in the early 1970s, having doubled in 1970 and gone even higher in 1971, and there was a situation where, in some areas of the Northern Territory, the infant death rate was reaching 500 out of every 1000 babies. This was a quite unacceptable level, and yet there seemed no answer to the problem. Dr Kalokerinos was asked by the area's Minister of the Interior, to advise. He describes how the answer came to him, 'Suddenly it clicked. "We have stepped up immunization campaigns", Ralph the Minister had said. My God! I had known for years that they could be dangerous, but had I underestimated this? Of course I had. There was no need to go to Alice Springs. I knew. A health team would sweep into an area, line up the aboriginal babies and infants and immunize them. There would be no examination, no taking of case history, no checking on dietary deficiencies. Most infants would have colds. No wonder they died. Some would die within hours from acute vitamin C deficiency, precipitated by the immunization. Others would die later from "pneumonia", "gastro-enteritis", or "malnutrition". If some babies and infants survived, they would be lined up again in a month, for another immunization. If some managed to survive even this, they would be lined up again. Then there would be booster shots, shots for measles, polio and even TB. Little wonder they died. The wonder is that any survived'.

This is to be sure an unusual population, and the problems they face are not common to other groups. Their level of nutritional deficiency is spectacular. They do however point us towards a clearer understanding of the nature of SIDS, or cot deaths, or whatever this obscene insult to modern standards of compassion and care is to be called. The thoughts of Kalokerinos might be dismissed as mere speculation were it not for the fact that he and Dettman were able to almost completely eliminate the infant death problem, by the simple expedient of nutritional supplementation with vitamin C. In relating the experience of aboriginal children, who were dying of what is called immunological shock, or paralysis resulting from nutritional-immunological interactions, to the widespread phenomenon in developed countries, of SIDS, Dr Kalerinos says, 'I have no doubt that some so-called "cot deaths" are in fact acute vitamin C deficiencies, and that these occur even if the diet is adequate . . . and their response to vaccines against infections is not always good. First, there is an increased utilization of vitamin C, and this, particularly when associated with dietary deficiency or failure of intestinal absorption, may precipitate deficiency. This deficiency lowers immunity, and the immunizing agent adds to this temporary lowering. An infection such as pneumonia or gastroenteritis is likely . . . thus an infant may die a few days after being immunized.'

Whatever the mechanisms involved it is at least now proved that many infants who are nutritionally compromised do die after immunization. Dr Kalokerinos mentions that there might be a deficiency even on a good diet. How could this be? One explanation is that there is now a well-established awareness of what is termed 'biochemical individuality'. This knowledge stems largely from the work of Dr Roger Williams, of Texas University, which is described fully in his book *Biochemical Individuality* (Texas University Press). In his research Williams showed that, for genetic reasons, as well as acquired reasons, we all have particular idiosyncratic requirements for certain nutrients, which may make our needs many times greater than someone else of comparable age, sex and circumstances. In just this way babies may have requirements for particular nutrients which are not being adequately supplied by what appears to be a balanced diet. This might place such a child in a situation where a challenge, such as that posed by immunization, could not be adequately coped with, and there could result immunological shock, disturbance of the central nervous sytem with consequent effects on the involuntary act of breathing, leading to the tragedy of SIDS or cot-death. The best answer to this appears to be that breast feeding should be undertaken whenever possible, for as long as possible, and that nutrition should be seen to be of the best (for mother and child) with no nutrient deficient refined foods involved. It is an irony that in the affluent West and North of the world, malnutrition of overconsumption should be manifest, whilst in the underdeveloped world the malnutrition of underconsumption is seen. In both worlds the infant is at risk from immunization, as evidenced by SIDS incidence in the USA and Europe, and the sort of incidents described by Dr Kalokerinos. As we will see in our examination of the evidence of neurological reactions to immunization, nutritional imbalance is a factor underlying this phenomenon. This is infinitely more widespread than SIDS, which may in fact represent the extreme neurological reaction, resulting in collapse and death.

In 1985 a pair of baby twin boys died in Scotland within 24 hours of receiving triple vaccination. Post mortem suggested SIDS and the vaccine was removed from use for examination of the batch involved. The results indicate the narrow vision of the investigators. The vaccines were tested for impurities, or other factors which might have affected quality. In the words of the Institute for Biological Standards 'The retesting of these vaccines has been completed and no abnormal results were found'. They were therefore restored to availability and use in Scotland. The company which manufactured the vaccine, Wellcome Foundation, said that 'As 2.5 per 1000 live born infants die of SIDS, and two thirds of the infant population receive three doses of DPT vaccine, it would be expected that five to ten children a year will die, by chance, within 24 hours of receiving vaccine. Twins are particularly at risk.' Now anyone with but a glimmering of intelligence should be able to see that if SIDS is often the result of vaccination, then of course there will be a co-incidence between vaccination and infant death. If there is an assumption that the two factors (death of infants and vaccination) are unrelated, then the double talk emanating from the company could be seen to make a degree of sense. The evidence is however that there is often a link, and that the vulnerable child will succumb to a severe immunological shock, directly related to the vaccination procedure. This is the evidence which was so clearly spelled out in Australia. Twins would have almost identical nutritional deficits. Twins in Scotland are likely to be more deficient than in most parts of the UK (apart from Northern Ireland) since the diet is shown to be very poor in fresh vegetables and fruits, and high in refined foods. The maternal health levels would be transmitted to the children, in terms of deficiencies (especially of vitamin C). This is not known to be the case in the twins mentioned above, but it a general observation relating to Scotland, and to twins. The chances are that like the aboriginal children described by Kalokerinos, these children had little chance of surviving the assault by the pathogenic vaccine. That the vaccines were found to be 'normal', and therefore 'safe', is even more horrifying therefore than had they been found to be imperfect in some way. The tragedies go on.

Neurological and Brain Damage as a Consequence of Immunization

In their major research work, dealing with the effects of DPT vaccination, Dr Harris Coulter, PhD, and Barbara Loe Fisher have painstakingly catalogued the typical acute reaction, although they state that there was an astonishing variety of reactions noted. The most typical mild reactions include the following: rash, swelling at the site of injection, mild fever, unconsolable crying and ear-ache. These are usually self-limiting conditions, and are accepted as 'normal' by the physicians administering the immunization. When reactions are more acute, and more severe, they often involve high fever (104-105 degrees), as well as collapse, convulsions, and often a peculiar type of crying which is described as encephalitic crying, or high pitched screaming. Death may also occur in such cases. If a child who has a severe reaction survives he/she may develop serious chronic problems. The least worrisome of these are likely to be chronic ear problems, allergies (multiple), asthmas and sleep disturbances. The more serious long-term effects are likely to include mental retardation, infantile spasms (possibly petit mal or grand mal), hemiplegia or paraplegia (partial paralysis), damage to the organs of sense (hearing, speech and visual disturbances, to include the possibility of deafness or blindness). These sensory disturbances may result in a condition known as 'infantile autism', in which the child appears to be unable to communicate, and to withdraw into a private world. In less severe situations the impairment of sensory perception results in learning disabilities, including dyslexia and hyperactivity. The UCLA/FDA study (mentioned in the section on SIDS) suggested that some eleven to twelve thousand cases of permanent neurological damage take place annually, as a result of DPT vaccination. This is a gross under-estimation of the scale of the disaster, according to Coulter and Fisher. They point out that some 15 to 20% of American school children are officially classified as suffering from learning disability. Some three million children in the state school system in the USA are enrolled annually in special teaching programmes. Many of these children, it is asserted, as the result of pertussis vaccination damage, and so the level must be greatly higher than the estimation of the survey quoted. It is noted that when children are diagnosed as congenitally mentally retarded, or as suffering from congenital seizures (fits), this usually takes place after some months, when normal developmental standards are seen to be absent, or slow in achievement. This, Dr Coulter and Mrs Fisher observe is usually after the baby has had a number of vaccinations, which are given at 2, 4 and 6 months of age. Is it fair to simply describe a survey, by a major educational establishment, as being inaccurate because its findings do not fit with estimations made elsewhere? Not if this is done in a purely off-hand manner, without examination of the methods involved. These methods can however be shown to be questionable in certain instances, and to confirm Coulter and Fisher's assertion that they gravely under-estimated the degree of damage and death accruing from pertussis vaccination. For example, the survey asked Los Angeles MDs to report all reactions taking place within 48 hours of the vaccination (over a two year period). The question is asked as to why a 48 hour limit, since no studies have been undertaken to show that vaccine reactions do not occur outside of this time scale. It is noted that as a result of this cut-off period, 2 children who died shortly after vaccination were not included in the statistics. One of these became ill within four hours of vaccination, and died four days later. This was outside the 48 hour limit. The other became ill three days after vaccination and died the next day. This child also was excluded from the survey. Apart from death, there were many other reactions which might have been included in the statistics of the survey but which were not. These include 9 infants whose reaction was of convulsions and collapse, but these were excluded because they were 'not severe enough'. A further 17 cases are recorded in which high-pitched screaming was manifested (this is thought to relate to cerebral irritation). These too were excluded from the survey, and there was no effort made to follow up, to see whether there were long-term deficits in these children. In this way Dr Coulter and Mrs Fisher, and others, are critical of the results announced, although these do still indicate a large degree of harmful reaction to the vaccine.

Coulter and Fisher observe that with the exception of the State of Maryland, there are no laws that require doctors to keep records as to the manufacturer's name, or the lot or batch number, of the vaccines they use. This makes attempts to trace batches which produce severe reactions difficult and at times impossible. They maintain that the FDA and manufacturers have known for decades that the only tests used to screen the pertussis vaccine for safety in the USA, the so-called mouse toxicity test, is meaningless, because it does not correlate with the vaccine's ability to causes death and brain damage in children. Safer tests have been developed as to toxicity, notably in Japan, but the one used in the USA may leave one vial of vaccine as much as 400% more potent, and therefore potentially more toxic, than another, and still remain legally usable. The only FDA attempt to evaluate the more than 40 years of reported adverse reaction to pertussis vaccine, was the UCLA-FDA study, and although the finding published in 1981 in the *Journal of Paediatrics*, showed adverse reactions ranging from rashes to ear infections, to high fever, severe convulsions, brain damage and death, this report was never made available to the general public!

Mumps vaccine, says Dr Mendelsohn (*The People's Doctor*, Newsletter) is of extremely questionable value, for although it may decrease the incidence of the disease, in the children to whom it is given, it does so at the risk of exposing them to its dangers later on, as the protective effects are less than likely to last a lifetime. The dangers of mumps are exaggerated, and the chances of male sterility almost nil, since the possibility of the rare accompanying symptoms of orchitis (inflamed testes) almost always involves only one testis and, as Dr Mendelsohn points out, 'A man can populate the world with the remaining one'.

Dr Robert Mendelsohn points out that a number of vaccines other than pertussis can produce neurological reactions. These include measles and mumps vaccination which, he says, may also expose children to central nervous system involvement, including febrile seizures (fits relating to high temperature), unilateral deafness, and encephalitis. Although such risks are small, they are infinitely less acceptable than the minimal dangers of the condition which they are supposed to be protecting against. The major reason for the use of measles vaccination is the prevention of the side-effects of the disease (which are incidentally very very rare in well nourished children) such as encephalitis. The official estimation is that children who contract measles suffer encephalitis about once in 1000 cases. This is disputed however by such workers as Dr Mendelsohn, who claims that this may be true in children living in poverty and malnutrition, but does not relate to well nourished children in hygienic situations, where the level of this complication is likely to be no more than one in 100,000. The truth, as asserted by Drs Kalokerinos and Mendelsohn, is that the vaccine itself carries a high risk of producing encephalitis, as well as other serious conditions such as subacute sclerosing panencephalitis, which is almost always fatal, involving as it does a hardening of the brain substance. It is also suggested that measles vaccine may produce such severe reactions as ataxia (lack of co-ordination of movement), mental retardation, meningitis, convulsions and one-sided paralysis. These are just the short term possibilities for, as we will see later, the chance of long term neurological degeneration, such as occurs in multiple sclerosis, has been linked to measles vaccines. These allegations occur in the face of mounting evidence that the vaccine is not even effective in protecting against measles, and that the decline in incidence of the disease has little relation to the vaccine's use. (USA figures show 800,000 cases in 1958, which declined to 500,000 cases in 1962, which was the year prior to the introduction of the vaccine. The decline in incidence has continued since its introduction.) We have already examined briefly the controversy over polio vaccination, and whether live or killed vaccine is more desirable (see Chapter 3). As we have seen they both carry risks. Perhaps the view of the developer of the killed vaccine, Dr Jonas Salk, would be of interest, insofar as it concerns the rival vaccine developed by Dr Sabin. Salk stated, in *Science*, April 4, 1977,

> 'The live polio virus vaccine has been the predominant cause of domestically arising cases of paralytic poliomyelitis in the United States since 1972. To avoid the occurrence of such cases, it would be necessary to discontinue the routine use of live polio vaccine.'

Unfortunately we do not have to hand Dr Sabin's view on Salk's vaccines, which together with the above might lead us to the conclusion that neither should be used.

In the UK a major voice against the use of pertussis vaccine has been that of Professor Gordon Stewart who, as Professor of Public Health at the University of Glasgow, stood out against his colleagues and challenged the use of this method, due to its unacceptable risks. He stressed not only the dangers inherent in the vaccine, but also its inadequacy in offering protection. He stated, in 1980 (*Here's Health*·March 1980, pp. 87-90).

> 'Pertussis vaccine was given along with diphtheria and tetanus toxoids as a "triple vaccine". Introduced in 1957. This vaccine had been administered to 70% of infants by 1960 and over 70% of all children by 1969.'
>
> 'The vaccination programme was monitored from 1957-1968 by the Public Health Laboratory Service. In 1969 they reported that the vaccines were "not very effective", in that they had failed to control outbreaks, or to protect fully-vaccinated children from infection. During this time, the proportion of children vaccinated rose to 80% or more, and it is a matter of record that whooping cough continued to decline in prevalence and severity. But, equally, it is firmly on record not only that whooping cough occurred in fully-vaccinated children, but also that severe adverse reactions to the vaccine were causing problems and concern.
>
> 'If reference be made to events at the time of the earlier trials of pertussis vaccine when given alone (i.e. not as part

of triple vaccine) in the USA and UK, it becomes clear that the inclusion of pertussis vaccine makes triple vaccine much more likely to be followed by adverse reactions involving the heart and nervous system. Such reactions include shock, collapse, convulsions and screaming fits, all of which had been recorded in some of the children who received pertussis vaccine alone in the earlier trials.'

'More light was thrown on this problem when Professor W. Ehrengut in Hamburg, and Dr John Wilson and colleagues, at the Hospital for Sick Children, Great Ormond Street, London, reported independently that signs of severe brain damage began to appear in some children soon after adverse reactions to triple vaccine. At about the same time, a number of reports appeared in the press from different parts of the UK about children who were previously well, but had become mentally retarded or paralysed soon after receiving triple vaccine. The Government, on the advice of its advisory committees, responded to these reports by re-affirming the efficacy and safety of pertussis vaccine, and by insisting that this component be retained in triple vaccine. They insisted also that a high level of vaccination among children of all ages must be maintained if epidemics were to be averted.'

'At that time, in 1974, vaccination levels generally were about 80%, seldom below 70%, and often above 90%. The last outbreak of whooping cough had been in 1970-71 and, as epidemics are currently liable to occur every three or four years, another epidemic was expected and did in fact occur in 1974-75. This provided an opportunity for reviewing the efficacy of pertussis vaccine. It soon became apparent that protection was again incomplete, and at best temporary, in that in all reports published at that time, a considerable proportion (30-50%) of cases, occurred in fully vaccinated children.'

Professor Stewart continues by explaining that reports of brain damage in children, immunized in this way, were continuing to cause anxiety in the early 1970s. Compensation for vaccine damaged children was introduced in 1978. During the 1970s the pertussis complement of the triple vaccine was often not used, and only tetanus and diphtheria were being given, instead, as a double vaccine. In anticipation of the expected epidemic many doctors were urging a return to pertussis vaccination. When a major outbreak did occur in 1977-1978, and into 1979, this danger was confirmed, and yet it was noted that despite an increase in the numbers contracting whooping cough, the mortality rate was the lowest ever. A very high proportion of those infected had been immunized. The same pattern was taking place abroad. In Canada and USA pertussis vaccine was widely in use, with claims that the disease was disappearing. However large outbreaks occurred in 1974, in which between 30 and 50% of those infected were found to have been fully immunized. In West Germany, as a result of anxiety regarding toxicity and adverse reactions, some areas abandoned using the vaccine. This happened in Hamburg, for example, where no difference was noted in incidence or mortality after stopping the vaccine. A similar pattern emerged in Italy and Egypt, where the disease continued to decline without extensive vaccination.

Professor Stewart concludes his survey of this progression by stating that, having had his four children vaccinated in the normal way, between 1951 and 1956, he would not dream of doing so now, after his experience and research. His statement in this regard is clear and unequivocal:

> 'There is no doubt in my mind that in the UK alone some hundreds, if not thousands, of well infants have suffered irreparable brain damage needlessly, and that their lives and those of their parents have been wrecked in consequence.'

Could anything be more poignant and heartbreaking than to see the life of a dearly loved child smashed as a result of a procedure which is being performed to protect him? What anguish and misery this has caused.

Neurological damage is almost worse than death. The living death of a child, reduced to a vegetable-like existence, is beyond the comprehension of those who have not experienced it.

The degree of the side effects of pertussis vaccination was discussed by Dr Vincent Fulginiti, chairman of the American Academy of Paediatrics, Committee on Infectious Diseases, in a 1976 paper *Controversies in Current Immunization Practices*. Among his comments were:

'Attempts have been made periodically to record all complications in a given group of patients (receiving pertussis immunization) in a systematic fashion. The results are as divergent as those recorded for efficacy (see Chapter 4). Strom in Sweden detailed 36 instances of significant neurological disease, post-pertussis vaccine, among 215,000 recipients, an incidence of approximately 1 in 6000. Immediately his analysis was challenged as a reworking of his data suggested an incidence of 1 in 5000. In other countries the estimates varied from none, to 1 in 100,000. Amazingly in the US we do not know the incidence, despite the recommendation that every child receive the vaccine.'

Dr Fulginiti reports that taking account of all adverse reactions, to include both trivial and severe, 'The total number of all reactions in one Medical Research Council study was 70%'. The doctor explains why there is sometimes doubt as to the link between subsequent serious illness and the vaccine:

'A confusing factor is the time relationship between vaccine administration and adverse event. How long an interval is possible in a vaccine induced central nervous system infection, or other untoward event? Strom recorded data in some patients who first fell ill with neurological problems one week after receipt of vaccine. Is that disease relatable to vaccine? Most experts accept an interval of 24 hours between vaccine and onset of encephalopathy; a few suggest 2-3 days as an acceptable delay in onset. But there is no good proof for any interval. In fact, the very nature of post-pertussis encephalopathy is not clear, even in infants who have died. In patients who survive such an episode there are no certain diagnostic tests which link pertussis vaccine and observed neurological disease. It is little wonder that confusion exists as to the incidence of this complication'.

It is also little wonder that parents, whose children have been permanently brain damaged, or who have died within a few days of receiving such immunization feel that there is a link. For when doctors differ it is the patients and the public who suffer. It is also little wonder that the public has been voting against the use of this form of immunization in particular, by refusing to expose their children to it.

Pertussis vaccination stands condemned by these disasters, and it should be stopped forthwith for it is now routinely administered. The evidence against other vaccines may not be so clear-cut, insofar as neurological damage is concerned, although the lack of clear evidence does not stop them from being suspect. As we will see in the later examination of long-term damage (i.e. damage which does not begin to show itself until long after vaccination) there is evidence against others. If we take together the evidence of Professor Stewart, Drs Mendelsohn, Kalokerinos and Coulter, we have at the very least cause for anxiety, and a case to be answered. This is too late for the brain damaged children who have been sacrificed on the altar of immunization. No matter how positive the motives, this has been a chapter of incompetence and criminal insensitivity, in the face of adequate evidence as to the damage being done. It must not happen again.

We will next examine some of the evidence relating to other reactions to immunization, which although less dramatic than those involving brain damage and death, can often severely damage the affected child. Among these are the cases of impaired immune function, arthritis and pseudoarthritis which follow some forms of immunization.

Impaired Immune Function and Tetanus Vaccine

One of the keys to the health of the immune system is the ratio between the T-helper and the T-suppressor cells, in the lymphocytes of the body. The helper T-lymphocyte aids the B-lymphocyte in its formation of antigens, and also assists in the function of the destruction of viruses or tumour cells by the T-lymphocytes.

Suppressor T-lymphocytes modify and regulate the degree of the response to any antivirus or antitumour activity. Between them they harmonize immune function. Approximately 60 per cent of the T-cells are helpers and between 20 and 30% are suppressor cells. This ratio is very important, and if there is a change in it, it can be seen to indicate a severely compromised immune system.

The ratio between helper and suppressor cells, is one of the key methods of assessing early signs of AIDS (Acquired Immune Deficiency Syndrome). The *New England Journal of Medicine*, January 19, 1984 carried a report that there had been a study on 11 healthy individuals, to determine the effects of routine tetanus booster vaccinations, on the ratio between helper and suppressor T-lymphocyte cells. The method used to determine this was the sophisticated one of indirect immunofluorescence study, before and after vaccination. The results showed that the ratio had dropped markedly in four out of the eleven (healthy) subjects, with the lowest levels being seen between 3 and 11 days after immunization, after which there was a return to normal of the ratios. Even though the effects are temporary, this shows a severe compromising of the immune function. What effects similar to this may occur in infants remains for further research, but it is impossible to avoid the conclusion that the repeated vaccinations, of one type or another, to which infants are subjected, especially in the first year of life, must involve some degree of alteration between levels of helper and suppressor cells. This could be a factor in the increase in allergic responses in young children (of which more later in this chapter).

Such reactions remain unmonitored by the medical fraternity, and should be seen by parents as one more reason for considering carefully just what they are doing in complying with the advice to immunize their children.

Arthritis and Rubella Vaccine

Rubella is not a serious disease, and yet the side effects of the vaccination which (inefficiently it seems) is designed to protect children from it, are sometimes very serious indeed. These include arthritis, arthralgia (painful joints) and the painful condition of polyneuritis, in which there is a burning, tingling numbness in many nerves. These symptoms are usually of limited duration, but may last for several months, and may not start until a few months after vaccination. How widespread is the phenomenon? There is no telling, but one piece of strong evidence comes from America, as reported in the journal *Science* (March 26, 1977). 'The HEW reported in 1970 that as much as 26% of children receiving rubella vaccination, in national testing programs, developed arthralgia or arthritis. Many had to seek medical attention and some were hospitalized to test for rheumatic fever and rheumatoid arthritis. In New Jersey this same testing program showed that 17% of all children vaccinated developed arthralgia and arthritis'. The report in this prestigious journal continues by pointing out that during the previous year there had been, in the entire USA, 87 cases of congenital birth defects, resulting from rubella infection in the expectant mother, but that the figures quoted above indicated that in the state of New Jersey alone 340,000 children were placed at risk of serious ill-health by virtue of the protective measure against the disease which had resulted in but 12 cases of birth defect in that state in the previous year. This seems an unacceptable price to pay, even if it could be shown to be a valid protective measure which all the evidence denies. Reports in other countries show that the rubella virus is associated with arthritic development. For example, Glen Dettman, PhD, is quoted in the book *Dangers of Immunization* (Humanitarian Society, Quakerstown, Pennsylvania, 1983) as describing a figure of 30% of adults in Canada, given rubella vaccine, suffering from arthritic attacks within 4 weeks. Some of these were crippling in intensity. Dr Dettman states that live rubella viruses have been found in one third of children and adults suffering from rheumatoid arthritis.

The *New England Journal of Medicine* (vol. 313 no 18, of October 31, 1985, p. 1117) carried a research report entitled 'Persistant rubella virus infection associated with chronic arthritis in children'. This confirms that 'infection *or immunization* with rubella virus has been recognized as producing an acute synovitis, which although normally self-limited has been reported to recur in certain persons for months or years after the acute stage'. It is reported that it is often possible to isolate the virus from affected joints in children, vaccinated against rubella, many months after the vaccination. This report tells of the isolation of viruses from the peripheral blood of women with prolonged arthritis, which followed vaccination.

The viruses in their blood were found up to eight years after the vaccination procedure, *although there had been a normal immune response*. This, it is suggested, could account for the chronic joint problems of many people. In children it was found that fully 35% of those suffering from chronic joint disease were carrying rubella virus particles in their lymph cells. Rheumatoid arthritis in juveniles is a particularly horrible disease, destroying young joints permanently, and this association with vaccination must make for a good deal of disquiet on the part of both parents and doctors. The women mentioned in the report had been immunized in order to prevent their having the disease, and thus placing possible offspring at risk of deformity. The hazard to the mother, in these cases, can be seen to make this a decision of some importance. The types of disease noted by this research as being associated with the presence of rubella virus included juvenile rheumatoid arthritis, spondyloarthritis and polyarticular rheumatoid arthritis. The viruses were not found in normal individuals, or in people with joints problems of a mechanical nature (strains, injuries, etc.) or with other connective tissue diseases. Most of those involved in the assessment had been vaccinated in the past. The fact that not all individuals, with these diseases, were able to display virus particles in the tissues examined, is not thought to rule out their presence elsewhere in the body. It is pointed out that other inaccessible sites may be the main reservoir for these viruses since, in rabbits, rubella virus particles were found to be concentrated in hyalin cartilage tissues, which are not easily amenable to assessment by investigators in human subjects, as surgery would be required to reach them. The evidence seems overwhelmingly to support the role of immunization in the production of some destructive joint diseases, in children and adults.

Nobel Prize winner Dr John Enders, writing in the *New England Journal of Medicine* states that the vaccination of young girls makes the chances of their contracting rubella when they grow up greater, not less, since vaccination only confers partial protection, unlike the naturally acquired disease which gives full protection from reinfection.

In some cases it had been shown that immunization against a particular disease calls forth a situation in which the same disease is seen to occur later, but in a modified form. Measles is such an example. The following sequence of events is described in *The Journal of the American Medical Association* (vol. 1244, no 8, pp. 804-6, 1980). A killed measles virus vaccine was used in America for protection against this disease between 1963 and 1968. Some 750,000 children received this vaccination. A vast number of these children are now subject, as young adults, to what is called 'atypical measles'. This is a very severe form of the disease in which it appears that, because of the vaccination, there is a heightened susceptibility to measles viruses, resulting from damage to the immune response. Incidence of 'atypical measles' have been noted up to 16 years after the vaccination procedure. It seems that some 50% of the children vaccinated in this way (when under twelve months of age) suffered damage to their immune systems causing permanent alteration to their ability to respond to this particular virus. Whether this also applies to the ability to respond normally to other micro-organisms is not known, but according to research on animals such a possibility is strong. Atypical measles often results in encephalitis, the possibility of which the vaccination was supposed to nullify. The following statement was made by Dr Marshall Horowitz, a virologist at the Albert Einstein College of Medicine, 'There is no way to predict when this will stop. I will not predict that it will get milder as we get farther away from the initial vaccination. There have probably been hundreds (or thousands) of unreported cases of atypical measles, and it is confusing to the doctors who often diagnose it as Rocky Mountain Spotted Fever'. If it is confusing to the doctors let it be clear that it is also confusing to the public.

Unlike measles the chance of contracting diphtheria in a modern industrialised society is slim. Should such a disease be contracted there are available antibiotics which are effective against it. As we have seen (Chapters 3 and 4) the effectiveness of immunization against diphtheria is extremely doubtful, and yet tens of millions of vaccinations are undertaken annually against this disease. A large number of 'immunized' individuals develop the disease, whenever a rare outbreak occurs, and the dangers inherent in all vaccinations would make it seem that this is an indefensible situation. The dogma of modern medicine however requires that such procedures are continued. Smallpox vaccination continued for many years after the disease itself had disappeared, producing the anachronistic obscenity of no less than 115 children, under the age of five, dying from smallpox vaccination over a 28 year period up to 1961, during which not a single child born in England or Wales died of the disease (reply of Minister of Health in Parliament, Oct. 24, 1963). The same situation can now be seen to obtain as far as polio vaccination is concerned, with the majority of cases reported in the USA being the direct result of vaccination.

Provocation Disease

It seems that many years must pass before the machinery can be slowed down and a procedure which is causing more harm than good stopped. This is the case with diphtheria vaccination. Statistical evidence is overwhelming as to the continuation of the previous decline in the incidence of diphtheria, which began long before immunization was started. One of the oddest side-effects of immunization procedures, such as diphtheria, is that they may provoke the incidence of other forms of infection, such as poliomyelitis. In his book *The Hazards of Immunization* Sir Graham Wilson, in 1967 discussed what is called 'provocation disease'. This takes place when there is already present in the body of the individual being vaccinated, a latent, or incubating, infection, which might either be about to become manifest, or with which the defence mechanisms of the body would deal adequately without patent infection being displayed. Should a vaccination against, say diphtheria, be received at such a time the incubation period of the other disease (say polio) is shortened, or a latent infection which might not have ever been seen as an active disease, is activated, and the symptoms of infection by this micro-organism may become evident in an acute form. The two diseases in which this form of provocation has been most noted are typhoid fever and poliomyelitis. According to Sir Graham Wilson, other diseases may also, in this way, be activated by vaccination. He says, 'Evidence exists to show that it may be operative in other diseases, such as tuberculosis, and rickettsial infections'. Many cases have been reported of poliomyelitis becoming evident immediately after vaccination against diphtheria or pertussis. Paralysis which results from such infections is often noted in the limb which was used for the inoculation. Should there be a latent virus present, in a suitable susceptible individual, (say someone with nutrient deficits or generally lowered vitality and well-being) then a variety of possible changes could occur.

An article in the *New England Journal of Medicine* (vol. 283, no 22, p. 1209, 1970) discussed meningoencephalitis (inflammation of the brain) following vaccination against influenza. This it is thought results from invasion of the nervous system by a virus, and it is considered that this might be a dormant virus which was harboured by the nervous system, and which was activated by the vaccine. Provocation of latent viruses is seen to be a potentially dangerous eventuality of all and every vaccination procedure.

Wilson suggests the following mechanism for the occurrence of provocation disease: 'The mode of action of the injected vaccine is open to doubt. The most probable explanation is that it acts like a fixation abscess, and allows viruses circulating in the bloodstream to settle down at the site of the injection and thence to proceed, via the nerve fibres, to the spinal cord. The greater the irritation effect of the vaccine, the more likely this is to happen'.

We have therefore the irony of protection against one disease stimulating the action of other virus particles, which may be resident in the child's body, with horrible consequences. There is no way of knowing when such latent or incubating situations may be operating, and therefore no way of knowing when a vaccination may produce this sort of provocation.

Apart from Wilson's theory as to how this might take place, there is also the possibility that due to the large compliment of the immune systems defending agents (T- and B-lymphocytes) which the procedure of vaccination monopolizes, this may well leave the system unable adequately to continue to deal with the micro-organisms with which it was already engaged, prior to the vaccination. The lymphocytes may become inert, and thus unable to react efficiently against other toxins or infective agents. It can be seen that if a child has been subjected to a number of repetitive vaccinations and boosters, there could be a reduction in the total reserve of immunologically active cells.] An ironical weakening of defences could be seen to have taken place as a result of an effort to increase defences. This would be compounded by the common nutritional deficits seen in so many children, who eat little fresh fruit and vegetables, and whose major source of nutritional intake is refined carbohydrate of one sort or another.

Flu Vaccination Reactions

The changes are that few people, unless affected by it through personal experience, have heard of Guillain-Bàrre syndrome. This is a self-limiting devastating disease which affects the nervous system, via inflammation of nerves. The infection may be due to a wide array of micro-organisms, and may occur in either sex at any age. It usually follows respiratory infection, developing rapidly. Paralysis may affect all four limbs and is usually symmetrical in distribution. Artificial ventilation is often required. In a period of mass vaccination against an influenza epidemic (swine-flu) in the USA in 1976, there was noted a massive increase in the incidence of Guillain-Bàrre syndrome. Authorities have tended to make dismissive comments regarding this fact, despite the national outcry which followed the scandal. (Documented in *Journal of Neuroimmunology*, by C. Poser and P. Behan, 1982.) The enormous claims for compensation, which resulted from this tragedy, slowed down the process of mass immunization against influenza, and greatly increased public awareness of the dangers inherent in flu vaccination. The following thoughts from the medical journal *Annals of Internal Medicine* (vol. 97, no 1, p. 149) in 1982, indicate the manner in which this vaccine disaster has directed some medical thinking. 'Is it possible that an antigen in the swine-influenza vaccine evokes, in some patients, an immune response to myelin basic proteins — those that surround the peripheral nerves in patients who develop Guillain-Bàrre syndrome, and those around the central nerves, in patients who develop a similar disorder to multiple sclerosis?' This possibility, and others which we will touch on later, seem to show that some of the diseases for which, as yet, there are no known causes (or cures) may have origins in the insult to the immune system which vaccination induces.

Several years after the first disaster with swine flu vaccine, efforts were made to start a second programme. Fortunately Congress refused to sanction this. Financial considerations were involved for the Government had underwritten the indemnity of the manufacturers and were paying out some four hundred million dollars in compensation at the time.

Just why the American nation was first stampeded into mass immunization against influenza is illustrative of the way in which passions and fears may be mobilized to this end. In February 1976 there was a not uncommon outbreak of influenza, in a military camp in New Jersey. A young serviceman, reportedly exhausted after participation in strenuous exercise, died of pneumonia. Some 500 people, out of 12,000 persons at the camp, contracted what was labelled 'swine-flu'. (The infecting organism was named swine flu virus A/NJ/76.) It was noted that a few others at the camp were also infected by another flu virus, which was then infecting many people in the USA (AV/Victoria). It was claimed that the major outbreak in the New Jersey incident was the result of a virus very similar to that which had been responsible for the great flu pandemic of 1918-19, which had killed millions of people. This similarity, and the death of the servicemen, aroused the fear of a return of this epidemic. This resulted in President Ford announcing that the Federal Government would appropriate some 135 million dollars, in order to support the development of a vaccine, so that the entire population of the United States could be vaccinated against influenza. There were a great number of mild reactions, and some acute reactions, early on in the vaccination campaign. This caused a refusal by insurance companies to provide cover for the manufacturers of the vaccines, who then appealed to the government to provide this, which request was granted. This led to widespread speculation as to the safety of the whole programme. Concurrently questions began to be asked as to just how likely a pandemic was. Influenza has shown very little variation over half a century, and the high mortality of the 1918-19 epidemic was seen to have perhaps been the result of other factors than only the virulence of the virus itself. These factors may have had more to do with malnutrition and stress after the First World War, than the virus. A reappraisal, as well as the incidence of severe reactions involving Guillain-Bàrre syndrome, brought the vaccination programme to a halt. It can be seen that the manufacturer's fear of law suits for compensation, by victims of the vaccine, was the major reason for the ending of the campaign. Tests subsequently showed that the New Jersey outbreak was less virulent than the common influenza-A virus, and that there was in fact little danger of an epidemic. The death of the young serviceman was seen to have been more the result of his exhausted state, than of the virus itself. The fiasco was allowed to pass into history, hopefully to be forgotten, apart from by those those lives had been wrecked by the experience.

The body's immune function is not concerned with infection alone, but is also in the front line of surveillance against malignancy. Should there be an impairment of immune capacity, this would be weakened, with a greater chance of cancer developing. As we will see this may be one of the major dangers resulting from immunization, of all sorts. Vaccination procedures stand accused of being responsible for alterations to the genetic material body cells, as well as being a factor in the reduction of overall immune efficiency. This combination of results from mass immunization, makes the procedures prime a suspect of being behind the rising tide of malignant diseases in children. The dangers of alterations taking place in body cells, in a way which makes them appear 'foreign' to the immune system, has been mentioned as a possible cause of auto-immune disease, such as rheumatoid arthritis. A further change which is noted, in such conditions, is what is called immune-deficiency. This might for example, involve the thymus gland, which is responsible for the production of hormonal secretions which are vital for the production in lymphocytes of specialized alterations in their ability to defend the body. Without thymosin, from the thymus, the T-cells do not become the highly specialized fighters which we depend upon. There is no way of knowing at this stage what long-term effects are produced in such functions, by artificial stimulus of the immune capacity via vaccinations. It is strongly suggested by many researchers that a combination of events may occur, in some people, which leads not only to the immune function being aimed against the cells of its own body, in an auto-immune response, but also that the T-lymphocyte function might be deficient at the same time. Both of these changes may be a result of immunization procedures. The increase in childhood cancers is one major area in which immunization may be a major factor. Other alterations in immune function bring forth the auto-immune disease. Less speculative are the noted increases in the incidence of allergies in general, which have been seen to rise to vast proportions in the industrialized world. Such changes are not likely to have but one cause, and are probably multi-causal in origin. Many allergists speculate as to the link between the vast array of allergic symptoms, seen in children today and the use of toxic foreign proteins in vaccination procedures. There is evidence that this is indeed so. For example, in adults receiving flu immunization, there have been observations of a worsening of allergic symptoms. This was noted, in one survey, to occur in six out of seven people immunized (report by Dr Robert Gouch of Baylor University, Houston, Texas, to US Public Health Committee in 1982). A variety of other symptoms were also seen to be worse after immunization, including aggravation of high blood pressure, diabetes, gout and Parkinson's disease. The allergic factor though seemed to receive the greatest exacerbation.

Allergy represents a response on the part of the body which is excessive and undesirable. Since the main mediator of allergic reactions involved the immune system it is not unreasonable to hypothesize that there is a link between the way it functions and the things that are done to it. One of the major aspects of life which it is currently called on to cope with is the introduction of foreign toxic substances, in the form of vaccines, from a very early age.

We have seen in this chapter some of the possible consequences, in terms of death and disease which have been shown to result from one or another of these substances being used. Allergy is increasing, and this is evidenced by such surveys as that described in the *British Medical Journal* (September 17, 1983, pages 775-6). This showed that of some 12,500 children born in a single week in 1970, fully twelve per cent were reported as having atopic eczema by the time they were 5 years old. This was more than twice the proportion reported in a similar study 12 years previously. This is factual and demonstrable. Allergy is increasing. There are of course factors which may be involved other than vaccination (diet, pollution, drugs and antibiotics in particular, and the decline in breast feeding). However, immunization is a strong contender for the key cause of this change in health in the population at large.

Dr Robert Mendelsohn asks the following rhetorical question, 'An auto-immune disease can be explained simply as one in which the body's defence mechanism cannot distinguish between foreign invaders and ordinary body tissues, with the consequence that the body begins to destroy itself. Have we traded mumps and measles for cancer and leukemia?' In order to come to some sort of understanding as to how such a terrible eventuality might have taken place, we must look at the evidence which shows just what changes could occur in the cells of the living body as a result of immunization, which could lead to this.

CHAPTER 6

The Long-Term Dangers of Immunization: Leukemia, Cancer, Multiple Sclerosis etc?

For many years naturopathic and far seeing medical thinkers have been warning of the dangers inherent in immunization. One of the repetitive warnings was that in some way the introduction of alien micro-organisms directly into the bloodstream was likely to create long-term hazards, with cancer and degenerative disease frequently mentioned as possibilities. It was however not until recent times that indications began to emerge, from research efforts, which support these thoughts. In 1961-2 the report of the Medical Research Council (UK) included an article entitled 'Cell transformation by a tumour virus'. This included the following:

> 'The most important is SV40 virus or vacuolating agent. This virus occurs naturally in monkeys, and it causes sarcomatous tumours experimentally in hamsters. Its particular importance lies in the fact that monkey kidney cells are used extensively for the production of virus vaccines such as poliomyelitis vaccines'.

The report continues by stressing the importance of making certain that only monkey tissues, completely free of this undesirable virus, are used. Whilst stating that it is unlikely that the virus would cause tumours in many people, it does say: 'There have been recent reports that it causes a change in behaviour of human cells grown in tissue culture'. There is no indication of the precautions taken to prevent the presence of this virus particle in cells used for the manufacture of polio vaccine, or when they were instituted. It is worth reflecting that the origins of the development of AIDS, is said to be from viruses occurring endemically in Green monkeys from central Africa. No connection is suggested between AIDS and poliomyelitis vaccination, but that both polio vaccine, and the virus which has started this epidemic in compromised bodies, should derive from monkeys could give us cause to think about the dangers inherent in transmitting noxious material of this sort into the systems of our children. The long term effects are unknown, the short term dangers are known however, and are sufficient to call into doubt the practice.

In 1971 there appeared reports of a major development in our understanding of the processes of alteration of the genetic material in cells, via contact with bacteria (*World Medicine*, September 22, 1971, pp. 69-72). The article described how Japanese bacteriologists discovered that bacteria of one species could transfer their own resistance to specific antibodies to bacteria of a different species. Further research at the Department of Plant Physiology, at Geneva University, has proved that the genetic transfer of information is not confined to bacteria, but occurs also between bacteria and higher plants, and animals. This process involves the 'shedding' of DNA material (the genetic material, deoxyribonucleic acid, which instructs each and every cell in the body as to its structure and role) which may be taken up by other cells in the organism. Turning from plants to animals the researchers extracted frog tissues and immersed this in bacterial suspensions. They found that ribonucleic acid and deoxyribonucleic acid (RNA and DNA) the genetic material of cells from the bacteria, became 'hybridized' with genetic material from the frog tissues. The results were explained in this way,

'Since we know that no bacteria got into the frog auricles, we can only conclude that the bacterial DNA must have been exuded from the bacteria and absorbed by the animal cells. This transfer phenomenon, or "transcession", as it has been called, is very probably a general one, otherwise the synthesis of bacterial RNA would hardly have been successfully achieved with animal tissues at the first attempt'.

A question was posed in this article which is of interest:

'What connection does trancession from bacteria to our own cells have with disease? Could the heart damage that can follow after rheumatic fever and similar bacterial infections be the result of the body's immunological system reacting to its own cells producing an alien RNA?'

Research has continued along these lines, and it is confirmed that there does occur a spontaneous release of DNA by human blood lymphocytes, in laboratory conditions. This process takes place, and has been consistently demonstrated, between a variety of different cells and species. DNA transfer occurs between bacteria and animals and man and also between the cells of higher organisms (*International Review of Cytology*, vol. 51, 1977, Academic Press). The possibility that all this activity might have implications relating to the development of cancer is obvious. It has been postulated that DNA material may occur in a free form, circulating in the blood stream or lymph, and that there might be a take-up of this genetic material, by cells, with implications relating to tumour development.

In 1975 the Nobel prize was awarded to David Baltimore and Howard Temin for their work in showing that cancer-causing viruses used, as part of the process involved in this causation, a substance called reverse transcriptase (an enzyme). This was used to enable the virus to attach itself to the DNA of cells which they infect. Thus incorporated into the genetic material of the cell of an animal, cancer development may begin. The understanding of how virus particles can actually become integrated parts of invaded cells explains what was previously a mystery. This process has now been shown to also take place without cancer developing. This phenomenon also takes place without the use of reverse transcriptase, and the cells thus formed (cell DNA and virus RNA) is known as a 'provirus'. It is thought that this capacity to link with invaded cells is inherent in the virus RNA of influenza, mumps, measles and polio viruses. Dr Robert Simpson of Rutgers University, New Jersey, has shown in tests, under laboratory conditions, that proviruses, derived from measles virus for example, can exist in invaded cells without any sign of alteration in that cells function or structure. The question is raised by Simpson and others as to whether the introduction of viruses of influenza, mumps, polio etc. to the body, in vaccination programmes, may not be 'seeding' humans with virus RNA. This would allow the development of proviruses which could lie dormant in cells throughout the body. The activation of these, at a later stage, might it is thought, be responsible for such diseases as multiple sclerosis, Parkinson's disease, cancer and others. This is a form of natural (and in the case of vaccination unnatural) genetic engineering. Leaving out the dangers of contamination by viruses of a type such as those in monkey kidneys, it appears that, by means of vaccination into the blood stream, of a variety of virus and bacterial materials, mankind has indeed managed to engage in a massive experiment in genetic engineering. The repercussions of this will be felt for generations as the latent provirus cells, and other cells whose DNA has been altered, began to produce the inevitable consequences of their presence.

What are the diseases which might be seen to result from such a scenario? Dr Mendelsohn maintains that long-term effects related to measles vaccine, for example, include multiple sclerosis, juvenile onset diabetes and Reye's syndrome. (This is a serious complication occurring in childhood, of infections such as influenza. It has been noted recently that the administration of aspirin to young children during the development of influenza, increases the risk of Reye's syndrome. Thus aspirins, in the USA, now carry a warning on the package as to this danger.) This complication i.e. Reye's syndrome, consists of acute encephalopathy accompanied by fatty degeneration of organs such as the liver, kidneys and sometimes the heart and pancreas. It typically occurs in children under the age of 16, recovering from influenza or varicella. The cause is unknown, except as mentioned it occurs more frequently when aspirin has been used. Fatalities are common with this complication. Dr Robert Mendelsohn states,

'Reports linking immunization to Reye's Syndrome continue to appear. In an epidemic of this, affecting 22 children in Montreal, five had received vaccines (measles, rubella, DPT and Sabin polio vaccines) within three weeks prior to their hospitalization with Reye's syndrome'.

'While the Center for Disease Control has been quick to suggest a relationship between Reye's syndrome and certain flu outbreaks, they have not, to my knowledge, given equal time to consideration of an association between the disease and the flu vaccine itself'. (*San Francisco Chronicle*, May 22, 1978).

We have previously examined some of the pioneering work of Drs Dettman and Kalokerinos (see Chapter 5) in relation to the prevention of SIDS (cot death) in aboriginals receiving immunization. This area of work led them to examine further the whole subject of immunization and its results. In the Australian *Nurses Journal*, December 1977, Dettman wrote about the research involved, and of the SIDS results, in which they virtually stopped the incidence by use of vitamin C supplementation, (see *Medical Journal of Australia*, April 7, 1973). The suspicions which their research aroused led them to the following thoughts,

'It is now seriously suggested that the slow virus may be the cause of a number of degenerative diseases including rheumatoid arthritis, leukemia, diabetes and multiple sclerosis. It is further possible that some of the attenuated strains of vaccines that we advocate may be implicated with these diseases.'

Of polio immunization, Dr Fred Klenner (of North Carolina) has stated,

'many here voice a silent view that Salk and Sabin vaccines, being made of monkeys kidney tissue, have been directly responsible for the major increase of leukemia in this country'.

This suspicion, as to the long term effects of virus particles in the blood stream, or latent in cells elsewhere in the body, is echoed by other researchers. A major article appeared in the *British Medical Journal* (Apr. 11, 1967, pp. 210-213) entitled 'Multiple Sclerosis and Vaccination'. This comment sums up the theme:

'German authors have described the apparent provocation of multiple sclerosis by vaccinations against smallpox, typhoid, tetanus, polio and tuberculosis, and after injections of anti-diphtheria serum. Zintchenko (1965) reported 12 patients in whom multiple sclerosis first became evident after a course of anti-rabies vaccinations'.

Dr Klenner, writing in the *Cancer Control Journal*, vol. 2 no 3, 1974, states,

'Many theories have been advanced relating to the causative agent in multiple sclerosis, the virus theory taking precedent over all others. What virus? Kempe from the University of Colorado School of Medicine, as reported in *Medical World News*, believes that it is the vaccinia virus. We have patients under treatment for MS who have never received this vaccination. Dr Alter, reporting in *Medical Tribune*, suggested the "sleeping" virus syndrome. Most of the theory rests with the circumstantial evidence that filterable, transmissible agents, having slow virus properties, are present in other diseases. We propose that multiple sclerosis is caused by the Coxsackie virus. One of our patients was diagnosed as having poliomyelitis, having experienced total paralysis, but made a complete recovery. Six years age he was definitely diagnosed as having MS. Another patient under our care was diagnosed as having poliomyelitis when she was 19 years old. At age 28 she was diagnosed as having MS. The neurologist who made the original diagnosis of MS, believes that what she has now was her real pathology at age 19. Both diseases can cause paralysis, but only Coxsackie virus allows recovery without residual evidence'.

It seems a number of viruses are capable of involvement in MS. The Coxsackie virus is one of a large group, or genera, of viruses, which includes the polio virus (of which there are three different types). Coxsackie viruses are divided into two groups, comprising about 30 different types of virus particles. They are involved in a wide variety of diseases ranging from common colds to pneumonia, meningitis and paralytic poliomyelitis. They are often present in subclinical infections, are distributed worldwide, and are present in most people. It is the presence in the blood of the more virulent types which may lead to severe illness. According to Dr H. Weaver (as reported in *Medical News*, May 22, 1967)

'circulating antibodies are responsible for some destruction of the myelin sheath in MS. Moreover cell culture tests reveal that an unidentified blood protein destroys the myelin, but when the protein factor is removed, the myelin is rapidly repaired. MS patients have probably had prior infection such as measles and mumps. A delayed auto-immune reaction in the central nervous system could be involved'.

Thus we can see that a number of researchers are pointing to a latent virus in the body, which when activated, causes damage to the myelin sheath around nerve structures, leading to the dysfunction and paralysis of multiple sclerosis. It is interesting to note another aspect of the weakening of the immune defence capability which increases the risks of MS in later life. This is the removal of the tonsils. According to Dr David Poskanzer of Harvard Medical School's Department of Preventive Medicine and Neurology, the risk of developing MS is nearly double if the tonsils are absent. (The findings of research into this were published in *The Lancet*, December 18, 1965).

Dr Poskanzer suggested that a virus may be active in the body of an individual in childhood, and that this might relate to the situation which called for removal of the tonsils. These structure are filters which defend the body against bacterial and viral infection, and their absence increases the opportunities for such micro-organisms to penetrate into the deeper recesses of the digestive tract. This is one of the reasons for the current opinion in medicine which maintains that tonsils should almost never be removed. Is there any real evidence for the supposition that viruses remain dormant for many years and become reactivated later?

An article in *The Lancet* of Saturday 5, January 1985, based on research in Denmark, helps us to understand more of this phenomenon. Its title is 'Measles Virus Infection Without Rash in Childhood is Related to Disease in Adult Life'. What the researchers found was that when they investigated the histories of people who claimed not to have had measles when they were children, a number were found to have present in their blood antibody evidence of such an infection. Some of these had after exposure to infection, been injected in childhood with immune serum globulin. This may have suppressed the infection which was at that time developing in their body. A high proportion of such individuals were found in adult life to have developed immuno-reactive diseases such as sebacious skin disease, tumours and degenerative disease of bone and cartilage. These included cervical cancer, skin cancers and cases of multiple sclerosis. It seems that the fact that the normal progression of measles having been stopped by injection of serum globulin, forestalled the natural destruction of the viruses, which process it is now known takes place in the spots by which the disease is characterized. The significance of the measles rash (and of other rashes associated with childhood infectious diseases) becomes clear as we study the report. It states,

> 'It is assumed that the rash is caused by a cell-mediated immune reaction, which damages cells infected with measles virus. If this association is correct, absence of a rash may imply that intracellular virus escapes neutralization during the acute infection, and this, in turn, might give rise to developmental disease subsequently'.

Put simply this means that, as part of the process of neutralizing the invading virus, the body literally 'burns' up the cells which contain these. This incineration takes place at the site of the spots or rash, which measles are known for. If this is stopped in some way (as by inoculation with serum globulin) then the rash is prevented and the virus survives and lives on in the body, only to cause havoc later. A number of individuals who reported that they had not had measles as children, yet who showed antibody evidence of previous virus activity, were able to confirm that they had indeed received immune serum globulin after being exposed to measles. Among the diseases they displayed in adult life, in consequence, were lupus erythematosus, Scheuremann's disease and chondromalacia which are all chronic degenerative diseases. The authors of this research article are firmly in favour of vaccination, but issue cautionary warnings that there needs to be reconsideration of two particular aspects of routine measures. These are that if their hypothesis, as described above, is correct (and they require more research before being certain) then the routine giving of immune serum globulin to children, who have been exposed to measles might need to be stopped, since this could well prevent incubating measles from being expressed, with all the consequences, as described, being risked. The second comment made by the researchers is, 'Measles vaccine contains live virus, but *should* be safe when given after the disappearance of maternal antibodies'. This means that the evidence suggests that immunization which takes place when there are antibodies present may include a long term suppressive effect, and measles virus may remain in the body to do its damage later. We now know that there is no assurance that a vaccinated individual will not contract measles, as we have seen from the evidence of numerous authorities. Once vaccinated there will be antibodies in the blood. Subsequent infection may therefore not be expressed in a typical measles rash, and this is quite likely to lead to the sequence of events as described above. This research confirms the worst fears of those who have speculated on the possibility of viruses remaining dormant for many years after immunization. It also shows the folly of suppressing a seal-healing mechanism, such as is displayed by the healthy body in response to infection. A healthy child will suffer no ill-effects from infection by measles virus. A child whose immune function has been modified and impaired by immunization methods, will be unable to adequately deal with such a virus, and may later suffer chronic degenerative disease, of one sort or another. This is no longer mere speculation but is, of course, not proved beyond all doubt. However, there is sufficient evidence to allow for the calling of a halt to the direction in which immunization is taking the human race, and to ask for emphasis to be restored to that aspect of the defence mechanism which has been neglected, the nutritional effort which can boost defences without harmful potentials. As this survey of suppressed measles rash indicated, the aspect of immunization damage, which was discussed earlier, in which auto-immune reactions might take place, is apparent in some of the conditions exhibited by the patients. Such conditions as lupus erythematosus are included in this category. A combination of changes and potential dangers would seem to follow from immunization, in which alterations in cells leads to the immune system being directed against the tissues of its own body. As well as this damage and changes taking place in genetic material, leading to possible malignant changes, aggravated by a less than adequate immune function. To this we have to add the chance of viruses remaining in the body for many years until such time as circumstances are suitable for their becoming active, in various tissues and systems of the body, with a wide range of destructive possibilities.

Could cancer result from any of the changes discussed above? In 1964 it was shown (*Journal American Medical Association*, Nov. 23, 1964, pp. 721-6) that a tumour producing virus, called the polyoma virus, could result in malignant changes in hamster cells, by virtue of the persistent effects of DNA material which had been transferred from the virus to the hamster cells.

We have seen earlier that the possibility exists for transfer of genetic material from viruses in the body, to the cells of the body, thus altering their code and their future pattern of reproduction. If malignant changes are part of that new genetic code, then that is what will be produced as the cell reproduces. A further hazard should also be noted. Common non-tumour inducing viruses, such as polio virus, Coxsackie B4, and others, have been shown to increase the degree of carcinogenicity of materials, when supplied in combination with them to experimental animals. Thus, carcinogens (cancer causing substances) which in themselves are too weak to cause harm, are noted to be made much more potent when combined with these common viruses (*Science*, December 15, 1961). This makes the presence in the body of the virus particles from vaccines highly undesirable, even if they have been inactivated. Remember that the polio virus is given live, if weakened. Smallpox virus was another shown to be a cocarcinogen in this report.

We have seen many aspects of the possible danger of introducing protein particles, of virus or bacterial origin into the human system in the form of vaccines. Let us briefly return to the work of Antoine Béchamp and see whether his ideas can shed further light on this scenario. A study of this has been made by Australian physicians and their work will be quoted from below.

Béchamp's Hypothesis: Modern Supporting Evidence

The following is an extract from an article by Ian Dettman, Dr Glen Dettman and Dr Archie Kalokerinos which appeared in the *Journal of the International Association for Preventive Medicine* (Vol. 4, 1 July 1977) entitled 'Mycrozymas, Micro-organisms and the Cause of Disease'.

'Is there any modern day biochemical and microbiological evidence to support Béchamp's concepts? Béchamp's mycrozymas may be equated with DNA (deoxyribose nucleic acid) or its breakdown components which constitutes much of the chromosomes that determine the nature of cell differentiation. In common with bacteria and viruses our genes determine our protein structures and the genes of bacteria-viruses and human cells have a lot in common. For example the DNA triplet, UUU(Uradine-uradine-uradine) coded for phenylalanine (an amino acid), and the triplet CCC(Cytidine-cytidine-cytidine) codes for proline (another amino acid) whether the trinucleotide is in human, guinea pig, or bacterial or viral cells. Therefore it is biochemically sensible to maintain that the genetic structure of such widely diverse cells as human and bacteria have similar origin. That is, the DNA is composed of nucleotides, which in turn consist of a phosphate ester of deoxyribose and a nitrogenous base.

It is not necessary to have a complete DNA molecule consisting of thousands of nucleotides to make a functional protein molecule. For example a single tripled polyuridine could code for a polypeptide of phenylalinine. Furthermore most enzymes and hormones have active sites which may be as few as a half a dozen amino acids which could be coded for a maximum of a half a dozen DNA triplets. Chemically such oligopeptides can be produced in the test tube, not requiring complex cellular RNA molecules, polyribosomes or endoplasmic reticulum. It is not impossible

111

that given the right nutrient and energetic environment that a polynucleotide of a few amino acids could occur using a DNA oligonucleotide as a code for the amino acid sequencing. Very little modification of the DNA oligonucleotide is required for it to become an RNA oligonucleotide which could serve as a messenger RNA substitute for oligopeptide formation.

Béchamp's mycrozymas may be as small as oligonucleotides or, in order to most easily conceptualize the maintenance of inherited characteristics of an organism, he may have been referring to polynucleotides consisting of several gene pairs, or he may have meant the whole chromosomes. It is easier in modern biochemistry reasoning to believe that Béchamp meant whole chromosomes when describing the mycrozymas, but as already suggested it is not biochemically impossible that he was referring to poly- or oligonucleotides. Most cells contain packets of degradative enzymes such as proteases, glycosidases or nuclases; therefore, the potential exists for internal polymerization of the DNA macromolecule. It is of some interest that in the interphase nucleus the chromosomes appear to disperse into diffusely staining chromatin granules. The state of aggregation of the DNA in the resting nucleus of higher organisms is not well understood.

Does Current Literature Support Béchamp's Thesis?

'Are there any examples in the current orthodox literature to directly support Béchamp's concept of internal genesis of viruses and bacteria in particular their evolution from the DNA of the cell?

Firstly and possibly one of the most convincing arguments is the well researched and documented latent viruses. The DNA of the latent virus is incorporated into the chromosome of human cells. Here it may sit for some considerable time before microenvironmental changes which may be nutrient, hormonal or emotionally based, can cause the viral DNA to spring into life and take over the host cell's DNA, directing it to produce DNA and viral protein. This is the method of action in the many adeno viruses which may cause a variety of upper respiratory infections and is also probably the way in which herpes outbreaks occur. At a slightly different state of microbial evolution there are a good many examples of pathogenic organisms existing as spores in the tissues, including *Clostridum welchii*, a not uncommon "cause" of food poisoning, which can be commensal of the large intestine. There is also *Clostridum tetani*, supposedly the cause of tetanus. Other "pathogenic" organisms *commonly present in the body without causing disease states* include; *Neisseria gonorrhhoea*; *Corynebacterium diphtheriae*; *Treponema palladum*; *Mycobacterium tuberculosis*; yeast (*Candida albicans*); *Vibrio cholera*; *Salmonella*; pertussis; coagulase positive; staphylococci; beta haemolitic streptococci; various pox viruses; flu viruses; herpes; poliomyelitis; hepatitis; measles, roto virus.

Clearly there must be other factors than just the microorganism or its devolutionary states such as spores, or latent DNA, which cause the state of disease in a susceptible person.'

Whether such bacteria/viruses find their way into the body (via infection or immunization procedures) and then become latent, or whether they are formed from basic genetic material, it seems obvious that vaccination/immunization has little prospect of controlling ultimate chronic disease processes which may result. It is the status of the host which is critical in this regard.

The virus report in *Time* magazine (November 3, 1986) makes it clear that the whole area of latent virus activity is a mystery to modern science. They state,

'In so called latent infections the viral genes lie low, becoming active only intermittently, but throughout a lifetime. Occasionally, *for reasons which are poorly understood but that usually involve stress, fatigue, sexual activity, and even sunburn*, the immune system can no longer keep the hibernating viruses in check; they awaken, reproduce and head for the skin' (the behaviour of herpes viruses was being considered). As Bernard Roizman, a herpes researcher of the University of Chicago states, 'as long as they remain latent in the ganglia (where they hide), it remains shielded, and no permanent cure for herpes exists and none is in sight'.

Whilst modern science finds latent virus behaviour a mystery, Béchamp's work explains it.

These are the long-term potentials of immunization of all sorts and the fact that some of these dangers remain to be fully proved does not make the case for rethinking immunization procedures less urgent. The direction in which immunologists are moving is so worrying as to make the urgency of a thorough investigation into all these possibilities very great indeed.

As infectious diseases become less of a health problem, for a variety of reasons touched on in earlier chapters, so do the thoughts of immunologists turn to new pastures. There is now serious consideration of introducing vaccination against dental caries. The bacterial nature of the production of plaque on teeth, a major factor in dental and gum disease, makes this target a suitable one for their methods, they maintain. The fact that nutritional care and dental hygiene are a more natural manner of preserving teeth seems unimportant, and a campaign in this direction can be expected.

Another area, far more difficult to imagine, in which immunology is directing its efforts, is almost upon us. This is the area of slimming. Recent research experiments in Scotland have shown that a single vaccination can reduce fat deposits in experimental animals by 50%. How is this done? Fat storage cells were removed from rats and injected into sheep. The sheep reacted by producing antibodies against these foreign cells. The antibodies, removed from the sheep, were then injected into rats, which stimulated their immune systems to attack and destroy their own fat storage cells. This research was carried out at the Hannah Dairy Research Institute, Ayr, Scotland. According to the researchers the original research was designed to look at the role of body fat in pregnancy, but has led on to the idea that these methods can be used to produce leaner meat. The main obstacle to the use of this method in humans is said to be the severe adverse reactions which could occur. This is to be overcome, the researchers think, by using a technique called monoclonal antibody production. This is done by making an antibody-producing cell immortal, by fusing it with a cancer cell. This allows an endless reproduction of the material produced in this cell. This would then be injected into humans to allow their immune system to attack their fat storage cells, leading it is anticipated to a slim, fat-free future. So far the techniques of genetic engineering which will produce this marvel have succeeded only in cells from mice and other small mammals. Man's cells are proving harder to master, but given time doubtless the task will yield the substance which will end obesity. What else it will do to the body's economy and metabolism does not bear thinking about. These are some of the directions in which immunology is hoping to take mankind. Whether mankind wants to take that route remains to be seen.

Our aim should be to enhance natural immunity, and to bring an end to the methods which have been shown to be largely ineffective, dangerous in the short- and long-term, and which have sown seeds of ill-health for generations to come. We will consider methods which might be used in the reproduction of higher levels of immunity and better health, in the next chapter. Before doing so I would like to quote from the words of Henry Lindlahr MD, who wrote in 1924 in his book *Natural Therapeutics* (vol. I Philosophy),

'At present the trend of allopathic medicine is undoubtedly towards serum, antitoxin and vaccine treatment. Practically all medical research tends that way. Every now and then the medical journals and the daily papers announce new serums and antitoxins which are claimed to cure or create immunity to certain diseases. Suppose the research and practice of medicine continues along these lines, and are generally accepted; or as the medical associations would have it, are forced upon the public by law. What would be the result? Before a child reached the age of adolescence it would have had injected into its blood the vaccines, serums and antitoxins of smallpox, hydrophobia, tetanus, cerebrospinal meningitis, typhoid fever, diphtheria, pneumonia, scarlet fever, etc. If allopathy were to have its way the blood of the adult would be a mixture of dozens of filthy bacterial extracts, disease taints and destructive drug poisons. The tonsils and adenoids, the appendix and probably a few other parts of the human anatomy would be extirpated in early youth, under compulsion of the health departments. Which is more rational and sensible. The endeavour to produce immunity to disease by making the human body a swill pot for the collection of all sorts of disease taints and poisonous antiseptics and germicides, or to create natural immunity by building up the blood on a normal basis, purifying the body of morbid matter and poisons, correcting mechanical lesions and cultivating the right mental attitude? Which one of these is more likely to be disease building – which more health building?'

The answer to this question, which although couched in language and images which confirm the author as living in another period of time, should identify the reader's attitude to health and healing. For those who would follow the path suggested by Lindlahr, the chapters 8 and 9 will attempt to give guidance.

CHAPTER 7

AIDS: Could Immunisation Have Started It?

A major change has occurred in the number of type of infectious diseases over the past few decades, especially regarding sexually transmitted diseases and some respected scientists have concluded that factors relating to immunisation procedures have probably been involved in the evolution of new viral agents. Some even hypothesise that AIDS might be the result of one such mutant strain.

Dr. R. de Long, of the Department of Biology, Del Mar College, Corpus Christie, Texas, explained how this might have occurred (A possible cause of AIDS and other new diseases. Medical Hypothesis 13:395-397 1984) when he stated that AIDS and other new diseases might be caused by,

'The probability of genetic recombination between live vaccine viruses and between live vaccine viruses and other viruses'.

He continued,

'Since 1961 we have been immunizing the human population with attenuated (live) viral vaccines en masse. Such unparalleled use of live viral vaccines may be the reason for the appearance of new diseases.'

Michael Culbert D.Sc, in his monograph AIDS: Terror, Truth, Triumph (Bradford Foundation 1988) expanded on this possibility of an AIDS/Vaccination connection when on page 87 he commented:

'As if echoing his (de Long's) thoughts a 1985 report in the Nutrition Health Review, New York, reported that "ironically a rather interesting coincidental relationship exists between the rapid outbreak of AIDS and another program of the past decade. In 1978 a group of physicians tested a vaccine for the Hepatitis-B virus in Greenwich Village, New York, on a group of homosexual volunteers. The most perplexing result of this study was the death of two subjects who had taken the serum, not of hepatitis, but from an 'unidentified virus'. Could this have been the beginning of AIDS?" '

Or could simple, accidental, contamination of human vaccine have resulted in genetically altered viral particles which tiggered AIDS?

Dr Eva Sneed (Immunization Related Syndrome (Monograph Metro Medical Publications, San Antonio, Texas 1987) points out that at the time of the identification of HIV (the purported viral cause of AIDS) it was said to be very similar to SV40 (Simian virus number 40) which was commonly found in African Green monkeys (and others).

She also reminds us of the little known fact that large batches of polio vaccine used in the late 1950s and early 1960s, which had been cultivated on monkey kidney tissue, were contaminated with SV40, and that this is well documented in medical publications over the past 20 years.

The contamination of hundreds of thousands of Europeans and Americans by SV40 was confirmed in parliament in answers (mostly evasive) by various health ministers in response to questions posed by Peter Rost MP (questions were published in the Journal of Alternative and Complementary Medicine in their issues of March, October and November 1988 and in June and July 1989 having been compiled for the Mr. Rost and the Journal by the author in cooperation with Simon Martin, with whom he co-authored *World Without Aids* [Thorsons 1988]).

On July 25 1988 the first question was asked:

'Whether polio vaccine used in the UK in the late 1950s or early 1960s was contaminated with SV40 and what effects this known enhancer of genetic change in other microorganisms is considered to have had in its recipients?'

The Minister answered:

'I am advised that some of the polio vaccine used in the UK at that time contained SV40. However I am also advised that there is no evidence of adverse effects on recipients. In particular two large studies in the USA have shown no evidence of adverse effects on people who were given polio vaccine containing SV40 in the late 1950s and early 1960s'.

(Please take note of this answer for it is misleading as further questions and comments make clear.)

In April 1989 the following follow-up questions were asked:

'Since the two large studies conducted in the US mentioned in his answer of July 25, on the contamination of polio vaccine by SV40, both refer to carcinogenicity and not to AIDS, and since one of them (Fraumeni et al *An evaluation of the carcinogenicity of SV40 in man*, Journal of American Medical Association vol. 185 no. 9 pp. 85–90) also states: *"since the latent period may be longer than the four years of observation studies here, it will be important to keep cohorts in question under continued observation"* and therefore that *"it would be premature to conclude from this study that SV40 is innocuous to man"*, will the Secretary of State for Health now state whether there has been any continued observation in the UK on those babies, and others, contaminated with SV40 in the late 1950s and what proportion of these people now have AIDS, and to ask if no observation has been carried out, why not?'

The Minister answered:

'1a AIDS had not been identified in the human population at the time the studies referred to were undertaken. The studies were directed to look for evidence of carcinogenicity in the population exposed to SV40.
1b There has been no separate continued observation of those people in the UK who might have received vaccine contaminated with SV40. We have relied on the results of the studies in the USA'.

Simon Martin and I (still acting on behalf of the Journal of Alternative and Complementary Medicine) pressed on by asking yet another supplementary question, through the good offices of Peter Rost MP.

On June 7 1989 the following question was asked:

'As there has been no continued observation of SV40 babies, despite this being the recommendation of the US studies referred to by the minister, is there any way of now assessing what proportion of such people have AIDS/ARC or other immune system related diseases?'

The Minister answered:

'Since the population who received poliomyelitis vaccine containing SV40 is not identified, there is no way of assessing what proportion of people have AIDS/ARC or other immune related diseases.'

We commented (JACM July 1989 page 36):

The Minister has just shot himself in the foot. If people contaminated with SV40 cannot be identified, then the minister lied when in reply to one of our previous questions he told the house that there was no evidence that the department's mass inoculation of people with a vaccine containing a tumour-causing monkey virus had caused any health problems.

Why have no efforts been made to trace the effects of SV40 in the people injected with it? If the minister cannot find out who received contaminated vaccine how can he possibly state that there have been no ill-effects?

It is clear that the British government's health department complacently and deviously continues to assert *no danger* when in fact they should have stated *no data*.

In fact they could undertake research of the blood of people with AIDS/ARC for evidence of SV40 contamination (looking for what is called the SV40 genome) as this would at worst clear up the unsavoury suspicion of a cover-up which the answers to these questions indicate, and at best point to SV40s involvement in the evolution of this disease.

Why do we feel so strongly that SV40 could have been involved?:

In 1960 the World Health Organisation stated in a bulletin that there could be unexpected and undesirable viruses encountered in vaccines and the next year live virus vaccination of polio was commenced.

In December 1963 there appeared reports in Science Digest describing a 'near disaster' relating to the polio vaccination programme, involving simian viruses, Arthur Snider the writer stated,

> 'It is now almost certain that a recently discovered virus, unwittingly put into hundreds of thousands, if not millions, of doses of early Salk vaccine will not cause cancer in human beings. But for a while the evidence pointed the other way.'

With hindsight we may say, perhaps not cancer, but AIDS.

In 1964 a Hungarian report spoke of this virus being excreted by people who had received the Salk live vaccine (Horvath B Fornosi F Acta Microbiologica Scientera Hungary Vol. 11:2171–5 1964–5). It described its findings thus,

> 'SV40 virus has been recovered from 10 out of 35, nine to twelve month old babies primovaccinated orally with type 1 attenuated poliovirus vaccine contaminated with SV40 virus'.

In 1964 a report appeared in the Russian journal Voprosi Virusologyi (vol.9 pp. 1–5) which states,

> '374 samples of human sera were examined . . . in the test with SV40 using the plaque method. Antibody to SV40 has been found in 50% of persons given a three dose course of Salk vaccination.'

It continues by reporting on the possible dangers of malignancy development (later discounted) due to this viral contamination.

Dr. Snead points out that in 1977 the Atlantic Monthly discussed the contamination of millions of Americans with SV40, offering this as 'food for thought'. It is perhaps coincidental that the first AIDS case was reported in 1977.

SV40 is particularly interesting as it is commonly used by scientists to induce genetic changes in other viruses with which it is brought into contact.

Did genetically altered viral material, part of the cocktail of such material swilling around inside all those subjected to mass vaccination over the past quarter century or more, interact with SV40 to produce HIV? Dr. Snead thinks so.

She summarises her hypothesis and research findings, saying:

> 'SV40 may predispose towards secondary viral infection by destroying the immune system at the outset. SV40 hybridizes with other viruses, especially Epstein-Barr, infectious mononucleosis etc. SV40 causes severe immunosuppression. Since SV40 was present and passed undetected in the early specimens of Salk and Sabin vaccine, viruses other than SV40 could have done the same. No studies exist. If SV40 contamination of some batches of immunizations are the cause of the development of AIDS and other diseases, whether by itself or by activating or being activated by other substances, it would be found to cause each and all symptoms associated with these diseases.'

Does it?

SV40 is immunosuppressive. In animals it causes large numbers of develop sarcomas.

SV40 decreases protein production in animals infected with it, leading to muscle wasting. These are symptoms of AIDS.

Viruses are more or less comprised of genetic material and not much else and have a greater or lesser degree of ability to genetically link with the genetic material in the cells they infect, as well as with other virus particles.

SV40 has this ability in an enhanced form.

As mentioned on page 101 in 1961/2 a report appeared by the Medical Research Council (UK) entitled, 'Cell transformation by a tumour virus'. This discussed the importance to human health of ensuring that only monkey tissues which were completely free of a particularly undesirable virus, which had strong abilites to alter the genetic structure of any cells it infected, should be used in polio vaccines.

The virus they referred to was of course SV40. They stated,

> 'SV40 occurs naturally in monkeys and causes sarcomatous tumours experimentally in hamsters. Its particular importance lies in the fact that monkey kidney cells are used extensively for the production of virus vaccines such as poliomyelitis vaccines'.

As we now know SV40 contaminated vaccines were used in millions of individuals and this microorganism which is known to be capable of genetically altering other virus particles (especially let it be noted with Epstein-Barr and Cytomegaloviruses) and cellular genetic material. This virus entered the bodies of a generation now in young and middle adult life.

People born and immunised in the 1950s and early 1960s, who were thus contaminated, are the major group of people with AIDS.

Dr. Snead asks why no major effort has been made to search for evidence of SV40 in AIDS patients although its ability to 'hide' is well known. As she puts it,

> 'Lack of detection (of SV40) has no meaning since it may disappear and not reappear until triggered or promoted by another virus or chemical. This phenomenon by which cell cultures in which SV40 was studied may exhibit continued production of abnormal cells even in the absence of the virus and/or antibody, is clearly stressed by Harvey N. Shein and John F. Enders from the department of Bacteriology and immunology of Harvard Medical School, as communicated in the Proceedings of the National Academy of Sciences of the USA Vol 48 July 1962. They state on page 1170, "There is more reason to believe that SV40 induces an

123

inheritable cellular metamorphosis. This concept is supported by data indicating that both viral multiplication and cell transformation are associated with changes in the nucleus. Fluorescent antibody studies indicate the virus is present only in the nucleus" '.

It should be realised that this examination of Dr. Snead's hypothesis relating to this particular episode (SV40 and polio vaccine) represents but one possible link between AIDS and immunisation.

Dr. Harold Buttram suggests other links (Vaccinations and Immune Malfunction. Textbook of Natural Medicine [editors Joseph Pizzorno and Michael Murray] John Bastyr Publications Seattle 1986) He says,

'There are grounds for believing that Western vaccines introduced since World War II into native African populations may have catalized the change of the AIDS virus from latent to active state.'

Buttram links the infection factor and AIDS with immunisation as follows.

'It is known that HIV preferentially infects the helper T-lymphocyte subpopulation (T4-cells) taking up long term residence in these cells. It does not multiply however until some other infection activates the T-4 cells to fight this. Thus as long as the infected person (infected with HIV) has no other infections or other demands on the immune system the AIDS virus remains dormant. Once the T-4 cell is activated and the virus begins multiplying the cell soon dies and releases many new AIDS viruses that then invade other T4 cells.'

Eventually a 'last-straw' infection results with the full manifestation of AIDS.

This concept explains the vulnerability of all groups most at risk who have either recurrent infection (gay men and IV drug users) or weakened immune systems or both, due to a variety of other reasons (leukemia patients receiving blood transfusions; infants with undeveloped immune function and Haitians usually living in abject poverty, resulting in both malnutrition, poor hygiene and recurrent infections).

It also has implications for the population at large of course. The American scientist who discovered HIV, Dr. Robert Gallo, says that vaccines may 'trick the immune system into manufacturing antibodies and can be a risk for people infected with HIV'. (Report in The Washington Post, February 2 1986 in an article entitled AIDS: A monster that can sleep for years [B. Rensberger].) In this he is comparing the activation of a dormant HIV by naturally occurring infection with the artificial infection by immunisation methods.

Yet another Vaccination/AIDS connection has been proposed, as reported in The Times (London May 11 1987) in which its science editor Pearce Wright stated,

> 'The AIDS epidemic may have been triggered by the mass vaccination campaign which eradicated smallpox. The W.H.O. which masterminded the 13 year campaign is studying new scientific evidence suggesting that immunization with the smallpox vaccine *vaccinia awakened the unsuspected dormant human immuno defence virus infection (HIV).'*
>
> *'Some experts fear that in obliterating one disease*, another disease was transformed from a minor endemic illness of the Third World into the current pandemic.'
>
> 'An adviser to the WHO who disclosed the problem told *The Times* "I thought it was just a coincidence until we studied the latest findings about the reactions which can be caused by *vaccinia*. Now I believe the smallpox vaccine theory is the explanation to the explosion of AIDS." '

AIDS may or may not be the result, in total or partially, of vaccination/immunisation procedures, past and present. However the horrific scenario painted by Dr. Snead, based on completely verifiable data from numerous medical authorities, as well as some of the other theories touched on in this chapter, should at the very least alert us to the risks we are taking when mixtures of killed or partially deactivated viral and bacterial particles are pumped into delicate, undeveloped, immune systems. The long term effects of the transmission of such noxious materials are unknown (although the short term dangers are clear) and should at the very least call into doubt this whole practice, for the consequences could make AIDS look mild in comparison, as new and more monstrous viral mutants evolve.

CHAPTER 8

Enhancing Immune Function and Alternatives to Immunization

(Homoeopathy, Botanic Medicine, Osteopathy, Acupuncture, Nutritional Methods etc.

The general findings which this book has attempted to lay before the readers are that immunization procedures are:

1. Largely ineffective and not the major reason for the decline of the incidence of the diseases for which they are given.
2. The cause of a great many side-effects which can range from trivial to fatal.
3. The cause of long-term changes in the immune system, and in cellular and genetic structure, with unimaginable repercussions, in terms of future health.
4. A major factor in people surrendering responsibility for their health status to the medical profession, with consequent avoidance of health promoting measures, such as sound nutrition, adequate exercise, etc.

The general findings are supported by a wide range of specific and circumstantial evidence, hopefully of sufficient weight to produce an altered attitude, if they are found acceptable and accurate.

We have looked at the evidence which shows that there are repetitive failures of various immunization procedures to offer true immunity from the diseases they are aimed at. We have seen that other factors notably hygiene, clean water and better living conditions etc. have been the major reason for the reduction in incidence of these diseases in Western society. We have looked at some of the many examples of the known and suggested side-effects of vaccination etc., in both immediate effects and long-term degenerative trends.

The hazards are seen to range from the threat of brain damage and death, to cancer, and other diseases of a severe and destructive nature. We have also seen how the juggernaut of immunization rolls on, despite failure and disaster; lurching from fiasco to dissension within the medical fraternity, and yet managing to continue to appear as the saviour of mankind, and to have dreams of immunizing us against everything from toothache to obesity. It is time to cry stop. It is time for those who oppose these methods and practices to demand a review of the sort of examples of muddled thinking and unscientific double-talk which have characterized many aspects of immunology over the past half-century. It is time to have objective answers to the very real questions as to the long-term implications of immunization procedures. It may well be that there are benefits to be derived, and some degree of protection to be gained, from these methods, but the cost may be too high in terms of risks, for many people. It is not for others to decide whether these hazards are to be faced by your children or mine, unless they acknowledge the dangers and accept the responsibilities. This would include stating that we are henceforth deprived of our rights as caring and thinking parents, to make decisions in this regard. The removal of such rights from parents would, I believe, be found to be unconstitutional in the USA, and to fail to stand the test of objective justice in the courts of any democratic society. There should be no compulsion or pressure on parents to have their children immunized. There should be free and open availability of information, as to the real hazards and risks, and a great deal of research into the genetic and cellular changes, and the effects on the immune system as a whole, long-term, of these methods.

It is also time to spend research money on alternative methods of raising the health of individuals to a point where they can cope with infection, should it arise, and where they have a greater chance of not becoming ill at all, in consequence of their improved health status. A concerted effort is called for in health education and publicity, by all means possible, as to the methods by means of which real immunity, via good health, may be obtained. This would be a dramatic change of course for medical and government agencies. This is the logical future. Preventive medicine, in terms of its involvement with immunization, can be seen to be one of the major causes of ill-health in the world today. This may appear to be harsh judgement. I believe the evidence presented thus far substantiates this judgement. At the very least it should be sufficient to cause some rethinking, and redirection of effort. In terms of alternatives to the current methods there are two main lines of thought. The first concerns the use of homoeopathic and other non-drug methods, by which immune function may be enhanced specifically or generally. The second involves nutritional methods.

Homoeopathic Enhancement, of Immune Function

There are varying views as the role of homoeopathic methods in achieving enhanced immune function, expressed as an ability to withstand infection or deal adequately with infection should it occur. In brief these two major differences may be described as representing firstly, a view which says that homoeopathic strengths of suitable materials may be used to enhance the defence capability of the body against specific infection, leading to a greater degree of resistance. There is a variation of this in which orthodox immunization methods are used, in some sort of association with homoeopathic medicines. The second major direction which homoeopathic thinking takes would be to avoid the use of the two options mentioned above and to concentrate homoeopathic attention to the enhancement of overall health, via treatment of constitutional (i.e. inborn) weakness. In order to understand these two quite different viewpoints, and some of the methods involved, a brief explanation as to what constitutes homoeopathic treatment is necessary.

Homoeopathy uses medicines which have been prepared from a variety of materials and which have been success-ively diluted to form a final dilution, which may represent anything from one part in ten (lx) of the original substance to the hundredth dilution (lc) or even to the thousandth (1M). After a degree of dilution in this way (performed in a manner in which the material is either shaken or succussed) there is possibly no demonstrable molecule of the original material present. The potency of the medicine is said to increase with its progressive dilution. The latent energy of the substance is claimed to be released via this method of dilution, so that the effect on the body is related more to its energy pattern than to its physical characteristics.

The principle of vaccination has a surface resemblance to that of homoeopathy, in that a small amount of a substance is being used in order to provoke a response by the body which is thought desirable. The difference is that the vaccination model calls for a very real presence of toxic, material or micro-organisms, whereas homoeopathy uses infinitely smaller quantities. Anyone who wishes to further study the ostensibly strange theories and methods of homoeopathy should consult a suitable book (see book list, page 152).

Homoeopathic thinking ascribes much ill-health to inborn taints and miasms, which have been inherited from previous generations. These set the pattern of health and these are the major constitutional areas which the practitioner attempts to deal with, rather than just the specific symptoms which the patient is displaying. In arriving at a choice of suitable medicines, the homoeopathic practitioner will closely examine and question the patient as to a great many variables in their feelings, likes, dislikes, etc., and also as to what factors aggravate or improve their general well-being, as well as their symptoms. In this way remedies will be found which approximate the picture gained from the patient. The remedy will be based on the principle of 'like cures like', which is illustrated in the following example. Should a patient present with a variety of symptoms and characteristics which closely approximate the symptoms and characteristics which would be anticipated, in a normal individual, were they to consume a dose of a particular substance, then it would be anticipated that a homoeopathic dose of that substance would have a curative effect. The symptoms and characteristics of a vast range of substances have been 'proved' over the past 200 years, by their administration to volunteers, who carefully note the effects. By marrying the overall signs of the patient and his symptoms, to the pictures of the available remedies, the homoeopath arrives at a prescription. It is then a matter of skill and experience to choose an appropriate potency of the medicine. This oversimplified explanation gives an indication as to the methods used in homoeopathy. The one certainty, noted by sceptics, is that with such small doses, homoeopathic medicines will not cause any harm, unlike the drugs used by orthodox practitioners. In dealing with the question of immunization we can do no better in our attempt to gain an understanding of the variations in the methods used, than to look at the views of experts in that field. One is a leading British MD, who is also a practising homoeopathic physician, Dr Andrew Lockie, MB, Ch.B, MRCSGH, MFHom. In an article in the *Journal of Alternative Medicine* (January 1984) he described his personal approach to immunization as follows:

'Immunisation, is one of the few areas of medicine where homoeopathy and orthodoxy come in contact, and where similar forces may be seen to be in operation, albeit on different levels. It has been viewed with suspicion by homoeopaths for years, although some early English homoeopaths appeared to have embraced vaccination against smallpox. (J. Epps, MD, *Homoeopathy and its Principles Explained* (Bloomsbury) 1882). Others, while noting that the process by which noxious agents were attenuated was akin to the Hahnemannian concept of potentisation, dismissed it in practice as uncertain, unseen, unreliable and unmeasurable in its effect on the infinitely complex human Organism. (S. Close, MD, *Lectures in Homoeopathic Philosophy* (Boericke & Tafel) 1924).'

'J. Compton Burnett (*Vaccinosis* (London Homoeo-pathic Publishing Co.) 1984), traced the onset of many chronic complaints to smallpox vaccination and others have reported similar long-term sequelae to other immunizations such as rabies, measles, polio, influenza. TAB and even tetanus (G. Vithoulkas, *The Science of Homoeopathy* (Grove Press) 1980).'

'These effects can often be "antidoted" by giving the corresponding nosode (disease product) such as Variolinum for smallpox, or a remedy which covers the symptom picture, e.g. Thuja, Maladrinum or Silica, in the case of smallpox vaccination.'

'There can be little argument that many of the diseases where prophylactic immunization is employed are potentially lethal. As far as I am aware there has been little research on the role of the other factors e.g. genetic, nutritional, psychological, in the severity of disease caused by these infections. There is however, always a spectrum in the degree of morbidity arising from the same infecting organism.'

'Unfortunately, "herd immunization" is the rule, not protection of individuals, and the concept of chronic sequelae, as opposed to acute reactions, is hardly ever mooted. There are signs of change, however; in Germany for example, they immunize against whooping cough only those felt to be at risk.'

'The options facing the homoeopathic physician seem to be as follows:

1. Use orthodox procedures only.
2. Use orthodox procedures, but immediately antidote with a non-specific remedy, e.g. Thuja, to prevent long-term complications.
3. Use orthodox procedures, but antidote using specific remedies which are known to act as epidemic remedies.
4. Use homoeopathic nosodes instead of orthodox vaccines.
5. Use constitutional treatment to maximise the total health of the individual, so that they will cope with any infection.
6. Use the epidemic remedy to protect contacts of an infected individual.

Antidotes do not appear to greatly affect the acute reaction to orthodox vaccines.

In practice I employ all the above measures, bar No. 1.'

'*Diphtheria, Tetanus, Polio*
Orthodox immunizations plus
Merc. cyan. 30.
Hypericum 30. 1 dose.
Gelsemium 30, immediately.'

'*Whooping Cough*
Pertussin 30 (homoeopathic nosode) 1 dose 12 hourly, for three doses, then one dose every three weeks from autumn

to spring. If there is an epidemic dose more frequently, especially if incubating the disease.'

'*Measles, Mumps*
Morbillinum, Parotidinum. As above for Pertussin, or treat constitutionally.'

'*Rubella*
Orthodox immunization plus Pulsatilla 30, one dose immediately.

B.C.G.
Orthodox BCG plus constitutional remedy or Silica 30 to antidote.

Colds and Flu
Homoeopathic nosode prepared from current and old Influvac plus nosodes of Staphylocci etc. plus Bacullinum 30. Give as for Pertussin.'

'*Travel Immunization*
Some orthodox immunizations are inefficient, e.g. cholera and paratyphoid, while others are efficient, e.g. typhoid. I give the useful ones and antidote them with the appropriate epidemic remedy, e.g. Baptisia for typhoid.'

'The use of homoeopathy in conjunction with, or as an alternative to, orthodox immunization is a very changeable area, and the above is my personal view at this time. Little attempt to clarify the issues has been made. Certainly the remedies are easy to give, especially with children. They are cheap and non-toxic. They do, however, have to be repeated more frequently and are not proven in the orthodox sense of the word. Indeed there has only been one trial of homoeopathic immunization published, so far as I am aware. In it homoeopathic cold and flu tablets were shown to reduce the number of days lost from ill-health in a factory. With children, full discussion with the parents of all the factors involved is essential, and may modify the above.'

Dr Lockie subsequently wrote about the work of one of the world's leading homoeopathic practitioners, the Greek physician, George Vithoulkas, whose views regarding immunization would seem to centre on the use of constitutional treatment (as in point 5, in Lockie's article). He described Vithoulkas's views as follows (*Journal of Alternative Medicine*, January 1985).

'He passionately believes that all immunizations are capable, in susceptible people, of so distorting the Vital Force that it is weakened, in some cases beyond repair.'

'It has been described by one of his colleagues as being likened to committing a defending army to battling with a very minor trouble-spot, while a huge army is massing for attack in another area. Like many homoeopaths, he believes that the diseases against which children are immunized will only occur in children who are susceptible to them, and will only become dangerous in those children who are already weakened by constitutional factors or previous allopathic treatment.'

'He believes it unnecessary to immunize children who have been treated constitutionally with homoeopathic remedies, because their defence mechanisms will be capable of dealing with the infection, and they can also be treated by homoeopathy.'

'From his own experience, he gives examples of illness such as rheumatoid arthritis and multiple sclerosis, which he believes have resulted from immunizations. He also points to the increase of AIDS (Acquired Immune Deficiency Syndrome) and the rise in frequency of auto-immune diseases, as being possible sequelae to immunization.'

'Although he has not actually done the research, he believes that if one were to study the incidence of multiple sclerosis in Israel, where immunization is wide-spread, and compare it with the incidence of MS in their Middle East neighbours, where it is not, one would find a wide difference in incidence.'

'He describes how immunizations in children may lead to a weakening of the immune system, which makes them more prone to upper respiratory tract infections, recurrent otitis media, and bronchitis, etc. When the onset of these illnesses can be traced back to immunization and the appropriate nosode is exhibited, it is common to find that the child is no longer susceptible to these illnesses.'

'Vithoulkas argues that, by antidoting the immunization and producing a change in the immune system, it follows necessarily that they are no longer immune to the disease against which they have been previously protected by the immunization. This would be easily proven by measuring antibody titres before and after exhibition of the nosode.'

'He is very contemptuous of the practice of giving orthodox immunization, followed by a homoeopathic anti-dote, and equally contemptuous of the practice of attempting to immunize, using only homoeopathic potencies of nosodes. The reason he gives for this is that he believes that in order to produce a protective influence by giving the remedy, one would have to make the patient sick'.

It can be seen from these views that homoeopathic treatment directs its efforts more to the patient as a whole, than to the specific disease process, and this would be more in line with the approach which is advocated by those to whom preventive medicine means building up the patient's immune system, without the dangers inherent in many current medical methods. Dr Julian Kenyon, MD, MB, OB, in the *Journal of Alternative Medicine* (August 1984) discussed the homoeopathic approach to whooping cough vaccination as follows:

'They (Homoeopaths) claim that giving homoeopathic whooping cough (Pertussinum) at six months, one year, two years and at five, is a safe method of vaccination free from side-effects. No continued side-effects of any sort have been reported following homoeopathic vaccination.'

'The problem remains that this method is unproven, as nobody has done any trial, worthy of the name, using Pertussinum. Yet I remain confident that it works, having given it to all of my own children, and to many patients.'

'On numerous occasions the patient develops short-lived symptoms, typical of mild whooping cough. My youngest child gave two or three highly characteristic whoops the day after taking Pertussinum.'

'These observations are impressive. They counter the cynics who claim that the remedies are too dilute (the ones I have used are so dilute that there is no possibility of any of the original molecules of pertussis remaining) to produce any effect. Surely the stage is set for a large, well designed placebo controlled double-blind trial, to objectively assess homoeopathic vaccination.'

There have been a number of trials which seem to indicate that the homoeopathic approach has a part to play in enhancing immune function. In the 1970s a systematic trial was carried out in which alternative child patients, attending a group of doctors for routine smallpox vaccination, prior to commencing schooling, were given homoeopathic substance Variolum, orally or intramuscularly. Four to six weeks later each child was given the normal smallpox vaccination. Those children who had previously received the homoeopathic medication all had a typical response, which indicated what the doctors involved called an 'accelerated' response, indicating immunity. There were no outward reactions. One of the doctors involved, Dr Henry Williams MD, of Lancaster, Pennsylvania, stated that all the doctors involved achieved the same results. This same group of doctors subsequently produced, in co-operation with a major London homoeopathic pharmacy Nelsons, a homoeopathic substance comprising the 30C dilution of all the influenza strains known. This was administered, on a monthly basis, during autumn and winter, with only mild reactions reported. The results indicated that this was a reasonably effective method of immunizing against influenza, without dangers. These trials were reported on in *Alternatives to Vaccination: Vaccination and Immune Malfunction*, by Harold Buttram MD and John Hoffman (Humanitarian Publishing Co., 1983).

A critical review of homoeopathic research was published in the July 1984 issue of the *British Homoeopathic Journal,* by A. M. Scofield MSc, PhD, in which a wide range of trials and experiments, on humans, animals and plants, were described. Of particular interest are those relating to infection in animals. These include the following:

'*Infections*
Jeanes et al. (1972) reported that FSH 9c* (follicle-stimulating hormone) was effective, in treating the crisis induced in guinea pigs and rabbits infected with coli bacillus. There was no statistical analysis in this or in the work of Baranger and Filer (1971) who claimed success with potentized Geraniol in the treatment of chicks infected with a virus.'

'Nasi et al. (1982) studied the effect of homoeopathic remedies on the parasitaemia and life span of mice, infected with the protozoan blood parasite *Trypanosoma cruzi*. They

* Note: This is the 900th dilution of the substance.

claim that a nosode prepared from the blood of infected mice and given for ten days before infection reduced parasitaemia and protected the mice from the lethal effects of the infection. All control mice died. A variety of treatment regimes was tried, but the nosode given at other times was not effective. A nosode prepared from *T. cruzi* itself was also effective in reducing parasitaemia and prolonging the life of mice, but only when given before or at the same time as infection. Unfortunately no statistical analysis of the data was made. In view of the fact that one treated group had no parasites in the blood and no deaths, whilst at the same time controls had a heavy parasitaemia and ultimately died, the work should be repeated.'

The effects of homoeopathic medication on cells and bacteria are also of interest and including the following:

'Moss et al. (1982) tested the effect of five homoeopathic remedies, normally used in treating mild bacterial infections, in the range 2×10^{-7} to 10^{-13} g. 1^{-1} on the movement of guinea pig macrophages or human leukocytes in vitro. In four series of experiments, 47/533 tests showed a statistically significant modification of cell movement. With human leukocytes, 5/50 tests from four subjects were significant. In some experiments movement was facilitated, whilst in others it was inhibited. The largest effects were obtained with a few sensitive guinea pigs and one human. The magnitude and direction of the effect appeared to depend on the batch of animals being tested, rather than the set of remedies used. These results suggest, like those of Poitevin et al. (1983), that the effectiveness of homoeopathic remedies may well be influenced by the sensitivity of the individual. The incidence of significant results in these experiments was low, but Moss et al (1982) point out that homoeopathic remedies would normally be used to treat ill subjects, who would be expected to have a higher sensitivity to the remedy than healthy subjects, such as were used in the experiments.'

'Cells other than blood cells have been used in culture as test systems for homoeopathic remedies. Boiron et al. (1981) cultured epithelial cells and fibroblasts in vitro in the presence of concentrations of $HgCl_2$ which depressed the mitotic index. Protection against the depressing effect of the chemical was found for $HgCl_2$ 5c* but not for 15c. The experiment was statistically analysed.

At the very least these experiments indicate that some

---

* Note: This is the 500th dilution of the substance.

homoeopathic methods have a positive effect, despite the dilution of the substance employed. Further research could well make this a valuable alternative for those who see the need for some form of outside aid, to those most in need of protection, because of circumstances, poverty, reduced health status, malnutrition etc, or in the event of epidemics.

Andrew Lange ND has written ('*Homoeopathy*'. *Textbook of Natural Medicine*. Pizzorno and Murray, 1985, John Bastyr College of Naturopathic Medicine) succinctly defining it thus: 'Homoeopathy is a method of specific induction of non-specific resistance, which stimulates the body's inherent defence and self-regulatory mechanisms, rather than, by taking over a function of the body (and thus) initiating dependency on the medicine itself.'

Botanical Medicine

In terms of enhancement of immune function there are other methods available which are safe and well tested. Among these is the use of medicinal plants such as *Echinacea angustifolia*. There are others, and a detailed study of books on botanical medicine (herbal medicine) would yield much information on this subject to the interested reader (see book list). *Echinacea* is described as follows (*Textbook of Natural Medicine,* as above).

'*Echinacea angustifolia:* Purple coneflower contains inulin, betaine, echinacein, echinacoside (a caffeic acid glycoside) and fatty acids, and affects many parameters of non-specific immunity. Its major component, inulin, is an activator of the alternate complement pathway and thus promotes: chemotaxis of neutrophils, monocytes and eosinophils; solubilization of immune complexes, neutralization of viruses; and bacteriolysis. Complement plays a crucial role in non-specific resistance to infection. Other inulin containing plants include *Arctium lappa* and *Innula helenium*. Echinacea enhances phagocytosis, activates natural killer cells, and increases properidin levels'

This indicates something of the research activity that has been undertaken in botanical medicine, and which is available as an alternative to those who would use largely non-toxic methods of prevention and therapy.

A combination of botanical and homoeopathic medicine can be seen to offer methods, via which enhancement of immune functions might be achieved. These methods however cannot replace the fundamental underlying requirement for sound immune function, which is adequate nutrition. This will be considered briefly below since it is not the role of this book to instruct in these methods, but simply to offer possible alternatives for consideration. There are other methods whereby immune function may be stimulated, either in a nonspecific manner or, in the case of existing infection, to assist in the defence of the body.

Osteopathic Enhancement of Immune Function

The lymphatic system is a vital route of communication and drainage in the body, with a special role in case of infection. When infection takes place bacteria are taken, via the lymphatic system, to the lymph nodes. Within the lymph nodes are areas called sinuses, which are lined with macrophages which can engulf and destroy bacteria and other toxic materials. It is in the lymphoid tissue of these lymph nodes, as well as in the spleen and bone marrow, that the T- and B-lymphocytes are produced. It is the T-lymphocytes which are the highly specialized sensitizing agents invading micro-organisms. The B-lymphocytes aid in the production of antibodies against these invaders. The free flow of lymph is critical to the defence efficiency of the body. Anyone who has had a sore throat will be familiar with the hard, indurated and sensitive nature of the 'glands' in the neck. These are lymphoid structures, which are dealing with the infection and the by-products of the process, and are at that time congested, and as a result the movement of lymph is sluggish. In a wider picture, similar processes are going on wherever the body is fighting infection, and dealing with consequent toxic debris. Anything which can increase the movement of lymph through the nodes will enhance the defence capability. As antigens pass through these structures the production of antibodies increases by between 4 and 7 times. There are a variety of methods which osteopathic practitioners use in order to aid the movement of lymph. These include techniques which, together, can be called 'lymphatic pump techniques'. These may involve techniques which address the fascial or connective tissues, which surround the lymphatic vessels, as well as mechanical pumping techniques which exaggerate the respiratory function, and use this as a motive force for actively moving the lymph. These methods are extremely efficient, and are used extensively in cases of infection, especially in children. They are described by osteopathic practitioner Simon Fielding MRO, in the *Journal of Alternative Medicine,* December 1983 (pp. 10-11). Modifications of these methods may be taught to parents of children and employed regularly during infectious episodes. Research has shown that pumping techniques used in the spleen region, will increase the number of leucocytes in the blood by an average of 2200 cells per cubic millimetre. This will have a dramatic effect on the ability of the body to cope with active infective processes of all types. According to Fielding,

'The efficiency of the lymphatic pump techniques has been demonstrated clinically, innumerable times, and recent research studies support clinical experience. John Measel PhD, has shown experimentally, in human studies, that the lymphatic pump does have an advantageous effect on the body's immune system'. *(J. of American Osteopathic Association,* Sept. 1982 Vol. 82 (No 1) pp. 28-31).

In this research report Dr Measel explained the methods and objectives as follows:

'The purpose of this study was to reinvestigate the lymphatic pump technique, with the use of pneumococcal polysaccharide as an antigen, in normal medical students, with subsequent investigation of the immune response to the antigen'.

The result showed that the lymphatic pump technique did indeed have an effect on the immune system, specifically on the B-lymphocyte component, of the immune response.

The researchers believe that the increased antibody levels that arose because of the method, would increase phagocytosis and this aspect of the effect was the next area which they were going to investigate. The effect was significantly different in individuals receiving the lymphatic pump techniques, as compared with controls in the trial. The technique involved applied pressure to the anterior chest wall, with the patient lying face upwards. This procedure was applied fifty times per minute, with a quick release, for five minutes, twice daily, for one week. This is a simple measure, which any parent can learn to apply to their child in a matter of minutes.

As mentioned previously similar techniques, over the spleen area, have been shown to have marked effects on the levels of white blood cells. This, and other more gentle, but equally effective techniques, more suitable to babies, may be used, in any childhood (or adult) infectious condition. They have been shown to reduce the time scale of the infection, as well as the severity of the symptoms. Combined with homoeopathic and botanical medicine, as well as additional non-suppressive measures, the handling of infectious diseases becomes much less stressful for parents. This is not to say that standard antibiotics are not also of value in such situations. Antibiotics however have no effect on viral infections, and have been shown to have become less effective in many bacterial infections in recent years, as the micro-organisms have become conditioned to their use, and have genetically altered themselves into more resistant strains. Antibiotics should be reserved for situations in which they are strongly indicated, rather than being used as a matter of course. In viral infections their use, as a means of forestalling secondary bacterial infection, may be found to be unnecessary if the methods advocated above are employed, together with the use of intravenous vitamin C as mentioned in Chapter 3 (page 24).

Acupuncture Methods in Enhancing Immune Function

A number of research trials have shown that acupuncture methods have a very marked effect on immune response and function. A report in the *American Journal of Acupuncture* (no 21, pp. 67-70, 1973) described a trial in which phagocytic and fibrinolytic activities in human subjects were measured before and after acupuncture. It was found that phagocytic activity increased by 56% as a result of the procedure. The scientists undertaking the trial reasoned that the results were caused by stimulation of the hypothalamic diencephalic centres in the brain, which regulate phagocytic activities. A variety of the biochemical effects of acupuncture are reported, by Louise Wensel MD, in her book *Acupuncture in Medical Practice* (Reston Publishing Co., 1980). These include a number of trials in which leucocytosis was enhanced by acupuncture, and hormonal and immunological functions were beneficially affected. Acupuncture may be seen to offer some positive assistance in the enhancement of immune function, notably at the time of infection. It is worth noting that in dealing with children there is no need to use needles to achieve the effects described, for pressure techniques, and stimulation of specific areas by hand, can achieve the same ends. The use of acupuncture, and osteopathic methods, can be seen to have more relevance to situations in which infection is already active, whereas homoeopathic methods offer the potential to deal both with preventive measures, as well as being applicable to current problems of infection. The other major area in which both preventive and therapeutic advantages may be obtained, is that of clinical nutrition.

Nutrition and the Immune System

A study by the World Health Organization maintains, 'The best vaccine against common infectious diseases is an adequate diet' Poor nourishment is regarded universally as the single most common cause of immune system deficiency. This is commonly thought to relate more to the undernourished populations of the third world. However research attention is beginning to focus on the subclinical deficiencies of the populations of the industrialized nations of the world, who suffer frequently from the undernutrition of overconsumption. One of the great British physicians of this century, Sir Robert McCarrison, wrote the following in 1936,

'Obsessed with the invisible microbe, virus, protozoa, as all important excitants of disease, subservient to laboratory methods of diagnosis, hidebound by our system of nomenclature, we often forget the most fundamental of all rules for the physician, that the right kind of food is the most important single factor in the promotion of health, and the wrong kind of food the most important single factor in promotion of disease'.

It is known that there exists, in all people, a degree of biochemical individuality, which makes standard dietary advice likely to leave one aspect, or another, in less than optimal supply. The scientist who researched and published the findings, showing the biochemical individuality was universal in man, plants and animals, was Professor Roger Williams. His two major books *Biochemical Individuality* (Texas University Press) and *Nutrition Against Disease* (Bantam Books) are required reading for anyone who wishes to gain a real understanding of this most vital of subjects. In relation to infectious disease Williams used tuberculosis as an example, and says,

'We know a good deal about this disease. Considerable and valuable efforts have been made in isolating the guilty bacillus, studying its habits, and trying to find chemicals that will kill or disarm it, without at the same time injuring the person it has infected. Yet for all that, our knowledge of tuberculosis is curiously lopsided. We do not know why some people seem far more resistant to tubercular infection than others, and we certainly do not know how this resistance works. We are aware that people with inadequate diets are statistically more vulnerable to the infection than others, and we know that adequate diet is an essential part of the treatment for tuberculosis. Regarding the scientific interpretation of all this we remain ignorant, for medical research has never seriously bothered to explore the matter'.

Williams proposes the following model of how his theories, as to the nutritional origin of much disease, may be applied to the question of TB. He says,

'One might put the hypothesis like this. Those individuals who are susceptible to the disease have, because of their biochemical individuality, distinctive patterns of nutritional needs that are not adequately met when they eat in their accustomed manner. Such deficiencies make these individuals easy prey for the tubercle bacillus. They furnish a peculiar environment to which these organisms can readily adapt, and the individual's own tissues lack the wherewithal to combat the specific enemy attack'.

An example of a situation in which nutritional deficit may result in common infection is given by Dr Carl Pfeiffer in his book *Zinc and Other Micronutrients* (Pivot, 1978). He says,

'Patients who are zinc deficient have body swellings, which even extend to the face, to involve the hollow sinuses and tubes. As a result the patients have a constant nasal twang, which goes away when zinc and vitamin B6 are given'.

He continues,

'Children with recurrent medical ear infections do not have these infections when they get adequate vitamin B6 and zinc. In this instance the control of the infection is partly mechanical, because of the relief of the swollen tissues, but zinc has other actions which enhance immunity and may be directly bacteriocidal.'

He quotes extensively from his, and other research workers' findings, to support this. He mentions the work of Dr Robert Pecarek, of Trace Metal Laboratories, who showed that lymphocytes from the thymus gland are impaired when zinc is deficient. Animals with this deficiency show increased susceptibility to infection, especially of viral origin. This is corrected by supplying zinc in adequate amounts. Research in Texas has shown that the immune reaction of the body depends on adequate zinc presence.

It should be noted that this is but one example of many nutrients which are involved in a variety of ways, in immune function. The interaction of zinc and vitamin B6 is but one example of the chain of interacting dependency which nutrients have with each other. Should this be weak at any point, through deficiency, then the overall function is diminished. The hard fact is that among many people in our society there exists a demonstrable deficiency of certain vital nutrients, and zinc is one of the commonest. The research work of scientists, such as Dr Jeffrey Bland of the Linus Pauling Institute of Science and Medicine, is so overwhelming in this regard, that there can be no argument once the evidence is examined. A random survey, conducted in the USA, using the very conservative levels of the recommended daily allowance (RDA) of nutrients, as a yardstick of adequacy, found that 88% of those interviewed (healthy population group) showed at least one deficiency, and 59% had two or more deficiencies *(American Journal of Clinical Nutrition* vol. 17, pp. 259-71). Many other surveys of this kind, in Europe and all developed countries, show a similar pattern, and the trend is for this to get worse, not better, as time goes by. The findings overall, as to the areas in which nutrition is linked to immune function, may be summed up thus:

Protein. Protein is seen to be fundamental to adequate immune function. This area is less likely to produce problems in industrialized societies, where overall protein consumption is excessive, rather than deficient.

Sugar. Sugar consumption can be shown to speedily reduce the efficiency of the neutrophils in their phagocytic function. This is not noted when other carbohydrate is consumed. Research shows that these effects of sugar consumption start within half an hour, and last for over five hours. At the peak there is a loss of phagocytic activity of 50%. This is about two hours after the consumption of approximately 100 grams of sugar, whether it be glucose, fructose, sucrose (including common sugar, honey, or fruit juices such as orange juice). Phagocytosis represents the part of the defence process in which foreign invading micro-organisms are ingested by the defending neurophils (polymorphonuclear leucocytes). These comprise nearly three quarters of the total white blood cell population, and their reduction in efficiency can be seen to seriously compromise that function. Other aspects of immune function are also affected. This reported effect of sugar *(American Journal of*

Clinical Nutrition, vol. 26, pp. 1180-4, 1973) is particularly relevant in the USA and Western Europe, where intake of sucrose alone is in the region of a 100 to 150 grams daily, with a variety of other sugars also being consumed. This is vitally important in the early stages of infection, as it can make the difference between contracting a serious infection, and avoiding it. This is evidenced by a well documented event, which occurred in the USA in 1949. This is described graphically in a book called *Diet Prevents Polio* (Lee Foundation for Nutritional Research, Milwaukee, 1951) by Dr Benjamin Sandler. During a polio epidemic in North Carolina, in 1949, Dr Sandler was able to promote the view that sugar was a major contributory factor in the contracting of this disease. With the aid of local radio and newspaper publicity he urged parents to stop the intake, by their children, of ice cream, sweets, soft drinks and sugar as such, especially during hot weather. Fortunately the fear of the epidemic caused the heeding of the warning, and polio incidence in North Carolina dropped by 90% in 1949, as compared with surrounding areas, and previous outbreaks. Animal trials were conducted by Dr Sandler, which showed that animals which were normally resistant to polio became infected easily, when made hypoglycaemic by the use of insulin. Low blood sugar is a normal consequence of the ingestion of large amounts of sugar, since this brings about a response by the body of extra production of insulin, in order to reduce blood sugar levels. It is in the hypoglycaemic state (which starts soon after ingestion, but reaches its peak about two hours later) that infection is most likely, as a result of reduced efficiency of the phagocytic neutrophils. It should also be noted that insulin and vitamin C seem to have exactly opposite effects in this regard. Thus if a deficiency of vitamin C were to coexist with a high sugar intake (not unusual in sweet eating, soft-drink consuming, and non-fruit and vegetable eating, youngsters) then the chances of infection would be greatly enhanced. (Note: Caffein containing foods (chocolate, cola drinks, coffee, etc.) encourage hypoglycaemia, because they stimulate the release of sugar into the blood stream). A change of dietary habit, with supplementation of vitamin C at times of epidemic (ideally not only then), can be seen to be a prudent measure.

Fats. There is a general depression of immune function in response to increased levels of fats in the blood. These can, to a large degree be offset by a diet which contains ample quantities of fibres. This would include unrefined carbohydrates such as 'brown' rice, whole grain products, as well as vegetables of all sorts, pulses (lentils, beans, etc.) and fruit (to include the skin, if not contaminated by toxic sprays and preservatives). Excess fats, especially of animal sources (milk, cheese, meat) can be shown to be undesirable, unless kept to moderate levels.

A number of nutrients have a special relevance to immune function, and these include:

Vitamin A. This enhances a number of immune functions, including phagocytosis, thymus gland function, antibody response, etc. This is also true of the vitamin A precursor, beta carotene.

Vitamin C. This is vital in immune function, and has antiviral and antibacterial effects. Generally it improves the body resistance level. It should always be taken together with bioflavenoids, which occur with it in nature (if it is taken as a supplement). The ideal dosage of vitamin C, when used orally for therapeutic effects, can be ascertained by slowly increasing the daily dosage. Starting with a gram a day, this can be stepped up by a further gram each day, until diarrhoea is noted. This is the level at which intolerance begins. One gram less than this is the ideal daily dose for the time being. As infection or stress reduces, so will the need for higher levels of intake, and the dose may be lowered accordingly so as to always remain within the limits of bowel tolerance.

Vitamin B (Thiamin). Deficiency lessens the spleen's ability to respond adequately as part of immune functions.

Vitamin B2 (Riboflavin). When deficient results in a smaller thymus gland, and few antibodies.

Vitamin B12. Reduces the blood's antibacterial activity, when deficient.

Biotin (a B vitamin). Is necessary for T-cell function.

Folic acid (a B vitamin) is essential for white cell function.

Pantothenic acid (vitamin B5). Helps in the production of antibodies.

Vitamin E. This is noted for its enhancement of cell mediated immunity. In excessive amounts it depresses

A, C B, B2, B12, Biotin, folic   147
acid & Vitamin E - deficiency can
can cause attack on immune function.

immune function, therefore doses of no more than 250 iu daily, should be taken supplementally, in period of exposure to infection.

Pyridoxine (B6). Vitamin B6 deficiency has been shown to greatly reduce immune function. It is known to be low if a diet contains high levels of protein or alcohol. This and the other B vitamins are essential to immune adequacy. William Philpott MD, discusses the nutritional methods which he employs in the treatment of a wide variety of conditions in which the immune function is weak. His methods include what he terms 'supernutrition'. He combines this with avoidance with those foods, chemicals and inhalents, which aggravate the symptoms of the individual, as well as by using autogenous vaccines. These are derived from micro-organisms which are found on or in, the patient, and which are then cultured and used in intramuscular injections to stimulate immune function. This is only done when the patient is also receiving the additional support of nutritional methods, such as those outlined below. Dr Philpott describes this briefly thus *(A Physician's Handbook of Orthomolecular Medicine,* Keats, 1979), 'Pyridoxine and Pantothenic Acid (Vitamin B6 and B5) are necessary for immunological defence, since antibodies cannot be formed when these are deficient. These central vitamins of course require adequate support from other nutrients, especially riboflavin, zinc, magnesium, and manganese. Vitamin C in adequate supply is known to suppress infectious invasion.'

Minerals. A number of these are critical to immune function. Minerals which enhance the immune system:

Calcium (and calmodulin, a calcium activator) is essential for the destruction of foreign substances once they are engulfed by white blood cells.

A decreased number of antibody producing cells is observed in mice with severe as well as a marginal *copper* deficiency.

Cobalt helps white blood cells ingest and destroy toxins.

Iron deficiency, or excess, increases the susceptibility to infection, particularly the ability to kill bacteria.

Manganese helps white blood cells ingest and destroy toxins.

Selenium in modest excess stimulates antibody production. The Memorial Sloan-Kettering Cancer Center, reported that zinc is an essential element for maintenance of normal T-lymphocytes and other immune function. Selenium is also shown to have specific effects in the defence against tumour development.

A number of other nutrients, such as the amino acids *leucine, histidine, arginine,* etc., have been shown to have immune function involvement, and to be capable of enhancing phagocytosis and antiviral activity. The tripeptide *glutathione peroxidase,* is known to be important in this regard, as well as being a detoxifying agent.

Fasting. Fasting as a therapeutic measure is much neglected. It is now known that this traditional naturopathic measure is a most important aid to immune function, if not prolonged. During the first 36 to 60 hours of an infection there should be fasting on water only. This brings about an increase of up to 50% in phagocytic activity. This is one of the most important first-aid measures which can be introduced by parents (reported on in *American Journal of Clinical Nutrition,* vol. 26, 1973).

In understanding that a sound nutritional pattern reduces the risk of infection we have the key to avoidance of much of this problem. It is also seen to be a major factor in the efficient handling of infection, should it arise, and this too is important knowledge, if we are to adequately protect the well-being of ourselves and our children. It is suggested that the books recommended at the end of this work be studied for further information in this regard. No specific advice is given as to nutritional intake, since this is not the role of this book. It is hoped that the general survey given above will create the desire for further investigation of what is a very large and important subject. There are other areas of importance in consideration of immune function, and these include the overall stress levels of the individual, and the question of adequate exercise, fresh air, sunlight and basic hygiene. These are mentioned but not discussed in detail, which does not mean they are not thought to be vital. They are areas which the individuals should investigate for themselves, for there is ample literature on these topics.

As well as considering the areas discussed above it is of importance that we are aware of those factors in our lives and environments which mitigate against a sound immune system, and which therefore contribute singly, or in combination, to the likelihood of infection. These include the following:

Use of drugs and stimulants, such as alcohol and nicotine. Even 'second hand' smoke is found to have this effect. Children of individuals who smoke are far more likely to develop respiratory infections than children in smoke-free homes, for example. *Use of the 'pill'.* This lowers immune function as does the use of hormone containing drugs.

Exposure to air or water pollution by heavy metals (lead, etc.). Anyone living in an industrial area, or a large city, where atmospheric lead from petrol is likely to be excessive, should increase their intake of nutrients which help to counteract this (e.g. Vitamin C, selenium, calcium). Similarly city water should be avoided and spring (bottled) water consumed, as high levels of contaminating metals have been noted in tap water in most cities in industrialized areas.

Excessive sunbathing has a marked lowering effect on immune function, making infection risks much higher. This can be seen by anyone with herpes simplex virus infections (cold sores, etc.) which will be more in evidence after sunbathing.

Stress in all its forms is lowering for the immune function, and a method of stress reduction (see book list) is suggested. This might include relaxation and/or meditation techniques, applied regularly. Also such methods as yoga and Tai chi chuan have a relaxing and beneficial effect.

Inadequate sleep is a further factor of which we should be aware. A sound nutritional pattern plus adequate exercise helps to promote this.

Exposure to electromagnetic radiation, in more than moderate amounts, has been shown to have a lowering effect on immune efficiency. Thus extra precautions are required (nutritionally and in other ways touched on above) for anyone working in front of a video display screen, or exposed to microwaves, X-rays, telephones, radar, television, computers, and all low frequency electronics. A major controversial area, which is now known to have the potential for markedly lowering the efficiency of the immune systems functions, is *the danger of mercury being absorbed* into the body via the silver amalgam fillings used in dentistry. This subject is receiving great attention, and can be studied by all those whose fillings are potential health hazards, by reading up on the subject (see book list). These and other factors should be born in mind when considering the overall implications of the need for enhanced immune function. This calls for both positive action and the avoidance of negative factors, as outlined.

The message that this survey is hopefully carrying is that the direction in which medicine has taken us, with the best of intentions, is not one which ultimately will be seen to have benefited mankind. Rather it will be seen that it has lowered the overall health level of the population thus involved and has mitigated against the self-involvement in health matters, which is vital if we are to live our lives in harmony with our requirements. To some extent we must return to a point where we accept responsibility for our health, leaving medicine to operate in the areas in which it is best suited, which is crisis care and management, and first aid. The area of preventive medicine belongs in the hands of the people involved, you and me. With the knowledge now available we can begin to work towards better health levels, and ultimately aim for optimum health. In this scheme of things immunization will become largely unnecessary. Those who wish to indulge in immunization will do so, but those who do not will be left free from pressure or compulsion.

CHAPTER 9

Conclusions and Questions

Immunization as a procedure has some positive virtues. It does offer a degree of protection against the incidence of the disease for which it is designed, to a greater or lesser degree. This protection is bought at the cost of endangering the recipient, both in terms of immediate effects and, more profoundly, in terms of long-term dangers. The magnitude of this is only slowly beginning to be appreciated. The cost is too high in the main. There are alternatives, albeit not fully proven, to the actual procedure of immunization, using homoeopathic medications. These appear to be effective, if for a short time only, and certainly appear to have no inbuilt hazards, unlike modern vaccines. Overall a strategy of health promotion would seem to be the most effective method of immunization, and some of the aspects of this have been discussed. There remain a number of areas which have been briefly touched on, but not examined which deserve attention. One of these is the question of the commercial implications of vaccination programmes. There are vested interests, to whom the making of money is the prime motivating force. It is not suggested that such enterprises (known as 'ethical' drug houses) would deliberately endanger lives, or that they would knowingly damage children by virtue of falsifying the research and development work which they undertake. However human nature is what it is, and there are many ways of rationalizing and evading the seeing of the truth, especially if vast amounts of money (and careers) depend upon not seeing or acknowledging what is in fact the truth.

How can this be, if we are dealing with trained scientists? The truth is that aspects of 'science', as we know it, are open to various interpretations. In a book in praise of immunization, published in 1964, Dr John Rowan Wilson (*Margin of*

Safety) it is stated: 'To the chemist, or the physician, the standards on which the research biologist has to rely are so imprecise as to be almost laughable. But science is to a large extent measurement, and if there are no precise methods which can be used one has to do the best one can, with what is available'. Dr Wilson was speaking of the difficulties facing Dr Jonas Salk, in his assessments of the efficacy of his 'killed' virus vaccine against polio. Commenting on Dr Wilson's statement, as the 'laughable' imprecision of measuring what cannot easily be measured, K. F. Williamson, Editor of the *Vaccination Enquirer* (Autumn 1964), makes the following points:

> 'Now these "imprecise" measurements, to which Dr Wilson has referred, unfortunately are the very essence of the whole subject, and their import must be faced, must be evaluated, must not be ignored and must not be swept aside on a wave of fanaticism. For it is perfectly true that Salk's measurements of immunity are laughable, but to solemnly average a column of strongly variant values, and to treat the resulting figure of 60% immunity as a firm and significant one, is not laughable, it is a tearful tragedy – and from the scientific point of view the very height of experimental dishonesty'.

Williamson continues by discussing the very heart of the problem, of a scientist who is faced with facts which are unpalatable to his beliefs.

> 'The immunologist is not knowingly being dishonest (speaking of Salk), for he really believes his estimate of immunity does exist, when in truth it is all illusion. The failure to realize and face this fact, forces him into the unenviable position to self-deception; leading to the enforced creating of shockingly, fantastic excuses, and reliance on magical thinking to comfort the soul, when mortality curves go up and then down – a position no scientist would tolerate'.

Not all scientists and pioneers of immunology have been distorters of the truth in true ignorance of that fact. The instigator of smallpox vaccination methods, Jenner, was described by Professor Greenwood, in *The Lancet* (February 2, 1923, pp. 233) as 'guilty of roguery'. This is described by Williamson thus.

'He (Jenner) tried to bluff the Royal Society, and having failed, decided to pull the medical leg. This he did so successfully that the vaccination question is still alive after 170 years of transparent fraud'.

Fraud? Distortion of the truth? Is it possible for scientists to act in such a manner? The answer is that they are human and fallible, and anyone finding themselves backed into a position where their basic belief system is questioned, is likely to either deceive themselves or others, innocently or deliberately.

Leaving aside the question of blatant fraud, there is the question as to why scientists and doctors continue to support methods and systems, long after they are seen by outsiders to be based on false premises. One factor is what is called 'concensus medicine'. Dr Carl Simonton is a physician who was practising orthodox methods of radiology, when he found that there were alternative methods which could assist his cancer patients. He developed and pioneered methods of visualization, via which patients were able, to an extent, to help themselves. He describes the difficulties faced by a doctor, when faced with the pressure of his fellow doctors to conform with current practices, and not to deviate (*Dimensions of Healing Symposium,* U.C.L.A., 1972).

'As I went further into medicine, I discovered that it was very difficult to help people in the way that I would like to be able to help them. On every hand I was being shown that it was impossible, or at least nearly impossible, to make any major breakthroughs in the field of cancer research therapy. I am sure most physicians go through some degree of this when they find out that the good that they are able to do, is much less than they had hoped it would be. While the physician is under all the pressures of current concepts and limitation, both from the system itself and the people who teach him, at the same time he feels a tremendous responsibility to make right decisions. He must always be right, for fear that in being wrong he may endanger someone's health or life. This fear causes him to accept the medical teachings that are given to him. He hesitates to think much on his own, for fear his wrong thinking may cause further ill-health or ultimately death, on the part of his patient. This feeling is largely generalized in our thinking, and during these focal years we have a tendency to be very close minded because of this tremendous overwhelming fear'.

me as a student

The doctor is human as is the scientist. The simple fear of stepping out of line; the fear of rejection by one's colleagues and peers, and of being labelled as a heretic, are powerful reasons for conforming, and not rocking the boat. Thus most do stay in line, and in the main the people who distort results, or alter a diagnosis to fit the 'accepted' facts of how things ought to be, are not dishonest. They honestly believe in the system they are protecting, and can rationalize their actions by means of semantics and professional double talk and double think. Thus, faced with a patient who has all the signs and symptoms of a particular disease, from which they have been 'protected' by immunization, it is obviously difficult to make the diagnosis they would have made if faced by such a case in an unvaccinated person. By calling the disease something else they are protecting their belief system, and the integrity of the theories around which they have built their actions, such as vaccination. The patient patently cannot therefore have this or that disease, and there are such a plethora of alternative names, that finding one which is accurate, but safe, is no problem. All this is done to protect a system, and to help to save the public from having doubt as to the efficacy of methods. Re-diagnosis is a real phenomenon, and happens all the time. In the case of diphtheria this was rampant, and it is interesting to note that it was only the vaccinated cases of diphtheria which were diagnosed as something else. In some epidemics the figure of re-diagnosis reached 60% of cases. It is hard to see what sense can be made of statistics when they are based on inaccuracies of this sort. The reluctance to make a diagnosis, or to state anything, which would reflect badly on the profession is a characteristic which goes back a long way in medicine. In 1874 Dr Henry

May, a proponent of vaccination states (*Birmingham Medical Review,* January 1874) that, 'It is scarcely to be expected that a medical man will give opinions which may tell against, or reflect upon him, in any way'.

Barbara Loe Fischer, co-author of *DPT 'A Shot in the Dark',* writes of the way the medical mind has to cope with the unacceptable. 'Wolfgang Ehrengut, a West German MD and immunologist, has pointed out that the prevailing mentality among physicians, when it comes to pertussis vaccine, is that 'what must not be, cannot be'. In other words,

> 'it *must* not be true that this vaccine, that is supposed to save lives, has been killing and brain injuring children in unacceptable numbers for forty years, because whatever will we do if it is true? How will physicians who have been routinely administering a neuro-toxic vaccine to millions of babies ever live with that knowledge?'

Thus self-denial of obvious truth becomes a built-in defence mechanism, for the trained scientific mind. No ulterior motive. No devious plan to harm and not tell. Just a plain inability to see the facts and to accept them. A very human fault, but not one which parents of brain damaged children are about to easily forgive.

This characteristic is of course not universal. Dr Charles Creighton, in evidence to the Royal Commission on Vaccination stated,

> 'Until I began to look into the subject for the purpose of the article which I wrote in *Encyclopaedia Britannica,* I held the ordinary belief which I had been taught as a student, without any question, and it took me a long time to change it. What made me suspicious at the outset was the nature of cowpox. When I began to ask myself, what is cowpox? I was very much astonished at the nature of the case, and it appeared to me that such a disease as cowpox, on the evidence of those who described it in Jenner's time, and who have described it subsequently, had no relation to smallpox at all. This was the suspicion from which I started, and from that suspicion I went on in the downward path of scepticism, until I landed in total disbelief'.

The commercial pressures which are built into the need to continue the pattern of vaccination promotion are too complex to discuss in detail. The area of commercial interest, monopoly and the vast industry surrounding the research, development and marketing of vaccines, and its interlocking facets with government and educational establishments, is part of the content of a remarkable special report by the Gannet News Service (PO Box 7858, Washington DC 20044). This was reprinted under the title *The Vaccine Machine,* and consists of a number of well-researched reports. It appeared in many newspapers across the USA in the week commencing December 16, 1984, and is available from the agency. It is worthy of perusal for its insights into the uniquely American aspects of the vaccination saga. It is well known that within the interlocking relationship which exists between government agencies, educational and research establishments, and the vast funds available to the latter from commercial interests, there is a code of conduct which is not to be broken. This calls for funds to be made available for research into the promotion of methods which maintain the status quo. No meaningful research is really possible without funds of this sort, and no funds are forthcoming unless the protocols on the research project is to the liking of the providers of the funds. Staffing of the various research, educational and (in the USA) government agencies, such as the FDA (Food and Drug Administration) is also a circuit. Thus the interchangeable personnel in these establishments and organizations are part of the same team, in a sense. The chances of a maverick emerging, and rocking the boat is minimal, as is the chance of their having ready access to the media which supports the dominant, currently held views, of the establishment.

The Gannet News Agency report *The Vaccine Machine* carries a story which illustrates this phenomenon. Dr J. Anthony Morris was a respected research virologist working for the Food and Drug Administration, Division of Biologic Standards. He protested at the idea of the introduction of the swine-flu vaccine in 1976, because he felt it to be ineffective. He was over-ruled. After the fiasco in which 500 or so individuals were left afflicted with Guillain-Bàrre paralysis, he was removed from his positioin, despite his having warned against it. Having established a private non-profit scientific research establishment, he stated that getting fired was a relief. 'I felt I was free for the first time'. He believed that his dismissal was economically motivated as 'the influenza vaccines were the biggest sellers at that time'. After subsequent publicity regarding pertussis vaccine damage, he was asked to appear on the nationally networked Phil Donaghue show. He was at this time doing consulting work for the University of Maryland, and a credit to this effect appeared on the programme, during the show. He was chastized for this by the authorities at the University who stated that it would jeopardize grants to the University from the Federal Government, and that those already granted might be withdrawn. There is freedom of speech, but if toes are stepped on the reaction can be very heavy handed indeed. The Media pushes the popular orthodox line, and this supports the views which are being taught to the next generation of scientists and doctors, who after investing years of their lives to become a part of the established order, are unlikely for many reasons, to be heretics. The system is self-perpetuating, and it is only an informed public which can begin to alter this. Motives are those of ordinary people therefore all the best and worst of humanity is bound up in what is done. Selfishness and deceit are manifested, as is high-minded selflessness. The nature of things though is that change is slow, and that the established order will hang on to its beliefs and methods doggedly. This is the case today.

What is the parent to do? In the USA Barbara Loe Fisher has a part of the answer:

'Today parents in 22 states can exercise a "philosophical objection" to vaccination. That freedom should be protected in those states, and extended to every state. The right not to use a product is the ultimate form of quality control in a free enterprise system, and it is particularly critical at a time when we are seeing research and development of many new vaccines from herpes to AIDS to cancer, many of which will be recommended for mandatory use by children and adults. Will these new vaccines be subject to the same lax research, manufacturing, testing and surveillance standards that apply to the pertussis vaccine? Beyond that question, perhaps we must also begin to ask whether or not the deliberate injection of so many foreign viral and bacterial antigens into children will negatively impact on the genetic structure and immune systems of whole generations of Americans, in ways we may be unable to predict or control.'

A recent report (September 21, 1984, *G.P., Focus on Medicine*) describes another new vaccine – this one will be a contraceptive vaccine.

'The first contraceptive vaccine to be tested on women will probably contain diphtheria toxoid. The other component will be a string of 37 amino acids from one of the beta chain of human chorionic gonadotrophin (HCG). And the chances are that it will work.'

'There are four main targets for a contraceptive vaccine. First, you can try to knock out one or other of the reproductive hormones. This tends to have rather dramatic effects on menstruation and, in the case of gonadotrophins, sexual behaviour.'

'Alternatively, you can go for the unfertilized egg; the fetus itself; or, given that a male Pill remains beset with toxicity problems you can try the next best thing and knock out the sperm when they get to the vagina.

'The HCG vaccine, while acting against one of the reproductive hormones, has the fertilized embryo as its main target since lack of HCG stops the embryo from implanting. Strictly speaking, it is thus a very early abortifacient rather than a contraceptive vaccine.'

'Until recent HCG's structural similarity to luteinizing hormone (LH) ruled it out because of the menstrual irregularities which would result. Monoclonal antibody technology has changed all that. Subtle differences in structure between LH and HCG specific antigens have been identified. Some researchers are continuing to look at LH vaccines in spite of worries about altering pituitary activity.'

'The main alternative to an antihormone vaccine is currently a vaccine against sperm. Again, monoclonal antibodies have pushed this research forward so that 20 antigens have already been identified from the head to the tail of the sperm. Some of these are known to play a role in male and female infertility. The next stage is to work out the immune mechanisms involved and, not least, to determine whether the antigens which have been found really do come from normal sperm, and are not just proteins released by dead sperm.'

'Researchers are optimistic that immunocontraception is a viable proposition but there are many difficulties to be overcome. Not least, is the body's own natural protective mechanisms for eggs and sperms which actually suppress any over-zealous immune reactions against these agents of reproduction. After all, it is only a very few individuals who have a natural immunity to eggs or sperm cells, the rest won't take kindly to interference.'

What sort of impact all this could have on normal function and health is certainly open to question. Individuals need to demand freedom of choice. An informed debate between the various viewpoints in the field of immunization must include the public, since it is they whose children are being asked in the main, to be offered up to the system. The situation in the USA where attendance at public school is forbidden, in many states, unless immunization is complete, had been challenged as unconstitutional. There are grounds in other states on the base of philosophical belief which can allow parents to escape the enforced immunization of their children. They do risk however the local authorities attempting to make their children wards of the state, on the grounds that the parents are unfit to have custody. This is happening now in the US (*see DPT: A Shot in the Dark*). This sort of pressure is unacceptable when the parents have legitimate grounds for questioning the procedures. In the UK there is freedom of choice, but the pressures on the parents to conform is great, and resistance difficult, unless they are articulate and well-informed. Hopefully this book will help somewhat in that direction. As to the future there is the danger of compulsion being introduced where it is now absent, and of other forms of immunization being developed (dental caries is one possibility in this regard as well as AIDS, if a vaccine is developed). We have seen how mass medication via the introduction of fluoridation of water supplies has been enacted, despite the fact that the vast majority of people consuming such doctored water are incapable of deriving benefit from the purported reduction in dental decay, since this is only achieved in childhood. The potential dangers of this method are another story. The principle of mass medication via the water supplies of the nation is very similar to that of compulsion in immunization.

We have worked our way through the complexities of the immunization procedures and have seen from evidence that there is in many cases serious doubt as to its efficacy. There is evidence that there are both immediate dangers from the procedures, and long-term hazards. Immunity is seen to be less simple than the model offered by Pasteur and his followers. There can be immunity without antibody presence, and there can be lack of immunity even when antibodies are present, since the antibody is specific to one antigen, and variants and 'wild' strains can circumvent this apparent immunity. Real immunity relies on healthy well nourished body systems, which nature designed, and which have been co-existing with bacterial and viral enemies (and friends) for all of history. There are alternatives, and they are infinitely preferable to the dangers with which immunization is accompanied. The genetic and cellular alterations of which such methods have been shown to be capable, and the short-circuiting of natural infections (such as measles) may lead to chronic degenerative disease. These elements are true for all people. There are those who are nutritionally deprived and deficient, and whose immune functions are depleted. It is precisely these people who will have the worst reactions to immunization, as noted in the Australian aboriginal disaster. Natural immunity is derived from healthy, hygienic living. Unnatural immunity is a two-edged sword, and its benefits are largely illusory, whilst its hazards are all too real.

Suggested Reading and Sources of Reference

A Note Regarding Sources and References

The reader will find specific references accompanying a number of the quotations and facts contained in this book. There are also many which do not contain individual references as to origins. These have been derived from one of the following sources, which are commended to the interested reader.

I wish to thank the writers and researchers whose work has helped me to concentrate the evidence as to immunization's shortcomings, in this way. The work of the organizations which have opposed vaccination and vivisection in the United Kingdom, over the past century, deserves recognition. A number of vital facts and statistics have derived from their publications and pamphlet. These are:

The British Union for the Abolition of Vivisection (47 Whitehall, London SW1).

The National Anti-Vaccination League (and its journal *The Vaccination Inquirer*) (26-28 Warwick Way, London SW1).

The National Antivivisection Society, and The Lord Dowding Fund for Humane Research (51 Harley Street, London W1).

Books Relating to Immunization used as Sources of Information

The Hazards of Immunisation. Wilson G. Athlone Press 1976.

Beyond the Magic Bullet. Dixon G. George Allen & Unwin 1978.

Vaccination Condemned. Elben. Better Life Research 1981.

How to Raise a Healthy Child In Spite of Your Doctor. Mendelsohn R. Contemporary Books Inc, 1984.
The Dangers of Immunisation. Humanitarian Society, Quaker Town, Pa. 1983.

A Physician's Handbook of Orthomolecular Medicine. Roger Williams and Dwight Kalita. Keats 1979.

Doctors Delusions, Crude Criminology and Sham Education. George Bernard Shaw. Constable and Co. 1932.

Every Second Child. Kalokerinos A. Thomas Nelson Ltd., Australia 1974.

Medical Nemesis. Illich I. Calder and Boyars, 1975.

Béchamp or Pasteur? E. Douglas Hume, 1963.

Mirage of Health. Dubos R. Allen and Unwin 1959.

DPT: A Shot in the Dark. Harris Coulter PhD and Barbara Loe Fisher. Harcourt-Brace-Journovich 1984.

L'Intoxication Vaccinale. Delarue F. Editions de Seuill, Paris, 1977.

Vaccination the Silent Killer. Ida Honoroff. 2901 Les Flores Blvd, Lynwood CA 90262.

Diet Prevents Polio. Sandler B. Lee Foundation of Nutritional Research, Milwaukee Wis. 1951.

Confession of a Medical Heretic. R. Mendelsohn MD. Contemporary Books 1980.

Journals, Articles and Reports used as information sources

Pamphlets from Organizations listed above, also:

Robert Mendelsohn MD, *The Medical Time Bomb of Immunisation against Disease*. East/West Journal, November 1984.

Health Consciousness (Holistic Magazine) Vol. VI, No. 4, August 1985.

The Vaccine Machine, Gannett News Service Special Report (PO Box 7858, Washington DC 10044), 1984.

Kenyon J. *Whooping Cough: Don't Vaccinate,* J.A.M., Aug. 1984 (letter).

Lockie A. *Miasms and Vaccines.* The Vithoulkas View, J.A.M., Jan. 1985, p. 8.

Lockie A. *Protect with More than Immunisation*. J.A.M., Jan. 1984, p.11.

Stewart G. *Danger*. Here's Health, March 1980. pp. 87-90.

Fulginiti V. *Controversies in Immunisation Practices*. Statement to Senate Subcommittee, June 1982.

Morris J. *Guillain-Bàrre Syndrome*. The Lancet, Sept. 16, 1978, pp. 636.

Morris J. *Multiple Sclerosis and Vaccinations*. Br. Med. J. Apr. 22, 1967, pp. 210-213.

Rønne T. *Measles virus Infection with rash in childhood is related to disease in adult life*. The Lancet, Sat. 5 Jan. 1985, pp. 1-5.

Weisbren B.A. *A Swine-Influenza Vaccine*. Annals of Internal Medicine, July 1982, pp. 149.

Baraff L. et al. *Possible Temporal Association between DPT Vaccination and SIDS*. Paediatric Infectious Disease, 2(1)7, 1983.

Fulginiti V. & Helfer R. *A typical Measles in Adolescent Siblings, 16 years after killed measles virus vaccine*. J. of Am. Med. Assoc., August 22/29, 1980, pp. 804-806.

Rosenberg G.A. *Meningoencephalitis following an Influenza Vaccination*. New England J. of Med. v 283(22), pp. 1209.

Wilkins J. & Wehrle, P. *Additional evidence against measles vaccine administration to infants less than 12 months of age: Altered immune responses following active/passive immunisation*. Journal of Paediatrics, June 1979, pp. 865-9.

Linnemann C. et al. *Measles Immunity after Revaccination*. Paediatrics, March 1982, pp. 332-5.

Brody J. Macallister R. *Depression of Tuberculin Sensitivity following Measles Vaccination*. Am. Review of Respiratory Diseases 90:607-611, 1964.

Halsey N. et al. *Risk Factors in Subacute Sclerosing Panencephalitis*. Am. J. Epidemiology, 1980, vol. 111, pp. 415-24.

Viola M.V. et al. *Persistent Measles virus infection in vitro and in man*. Arthritis/Rheum. 1978, 21:46-451 (supplement).

Rebel A. et al. *Viral antigens in osteoclasts from Paget's disease of bone*. Lancet, 1980, ii, pp. 344-46.

Joseph B. et al. *Replication and Persistence of Measles Virus in defined subpopulations of human leukocytes.* J. Virol. 1975, 16:1638-49.

TV

DPT: Vaccine Roulette, 60-minute documentary, produced by Lea Thompson WRC-TV, Washington DC, April 1982 (Transcript $3).
Donahue Report. December 1982. PO Box 2111, Cincinatti OH. 45201 (Transcript $2.50).

Further Reading Suggestions

The books, pamphlets and journal articles referred to above will give a broader basis for understanding the problems involved in immunization. For a better awareness of alternative methods of health enhancement the following books are recommended. Some are more technical than others, and are marked*.

Nutrition

Biochemical Individuality, Roger Williams. Texas University Press, 1978.
Nutrition against disease, Roger Williams. Bantam Books, 1979.
*Medical Applications of Clinical Nutrition, Ed. J. Bland. Keats, 1983.
Nutrition and Vitamin Therapy, Michael Lesser. Thorsons, 1984.
Your Personal Health Programme, J. Bland. Thorsons, 1984.
The Whole Health Manual, Patrick Holford. Thorsons, 1983.
Diet and Disease, Cheraskin, Ringsdorf and Clark. Keats, 1968.
Candida albicans, Leon Chaitow. Thorsons, 1985.
*The Missing Diagnosis, C. Truss. PO Box 26508, Birmingham, Alabama, 1983.

Diet Crime and Delinquency, Alexander Schauss. Parker House, 1981.

Chemical Victims, Richard Mackarness. Pan Books Ltd., 1980.

Food, Mind and Mood. David Shinkin and Michael Schachter. Bobbs-Merrill Co.

Diet and Nutrition, Rudolph Ballentyne. Himalayan International Press, 1978.

*Clinical Ecology, L. Dickey. Thomas, 1976.

*Amino Acids in Therapy, Leon Chaitow. Thorsons, 1985.

Low Blood Sugar, Martin Budd. Thorsons, 1984.

The Toxic Time Bomb (Mercury fillings), Sam Ziff. Thor-sons, 1985.

Books on Alternative Methods of Healing

Homoeopathy: A practical guide to natural medicine. Phyllis Speight. Granada, 1979.

Homoeopathy: Medicine for the new Man. Goerge Vithoulkas, Thorsons 1985.

Green Pharmacy: A History of Herbal Medicine. Barbara Griggs, Jill Norman and Hobhouse, 1981.

Naturopathic Medicine: Roger Newman Turner, Thorsons, 1984.

*A Text Book of Natural Medicine. Joseph Pizzorno and R. Murray, JBC Publishing, Seattle, 1985.

Your Complete Stress Proofing Programme, Leon Chaitow, Thorsons, 1985.

Osteopathy: A complete health care system, Leon Chaitow, Thorsons, 1984.

*Osteopathic Medicine. Hoag, Cole and Bradford, McGraw-Hill, 1969.

*Acupuncture in Medical Practice, Louise Wensel, Reston Publishing Co. 1980.

Journals:

1. Journal of Alternative Medicine, 30 Station Approach, West Byfleet, Surrey.
2. Here's Health, 30 Station Approach, West Byfleet, Surrey.
3. Health Consciousness, PO Box 550, Oviedo, Florida 32775, USA.

Index

aboriginal children, immunization of 77-8
acupuncture 141-2
adeno virus 112
adverse effects 34
African people, immunization of 124
agglutination 33
AIDS (acquired immunodeficiency syndrome) 22, 23, 62
causes 14, 117-26
early detection 90
immunization-associated 117-26
origin of virus 101-2
see also human immuno defence virus infection (HIV)
Albert Einstein College of Medicine 93
alcohol use 150
Allan, Beverley 72
allergies 48, 99, 99-100
allopathic medicine 115
Alternate Complement Pathway (ACP) 24, 138
alternatives to immunization 127-51
American Academy of Paediatrics 30
Committee on Infectious Disease 87
American Journal of Acupuncture 142
American Journal of Clinical Nutrition 145, 149
American Journal of Epidermiology 70
American Journal of Hygiene 46
American Public Health Service 40
amino acid 111, 159
animals
exploitation 46-7
immunization research use 101, 102, 114

subject to infection 18-19, 55
SV40 effects on 122
see also British Union for the Abolition of Vivisection; National Antivivisection Society
Annals of Internal Medicine 96
anthrax 30
bacillus 18, 19
prevention 18
antibiotics 7, 54, 141
allergy-causing 100
diphtheria treatment use 93
excessive use 24
introduction 6
antibodies 21, 26
immunoglobulin 28
in relation to immunity 41, 43
monoclonal 114-15, 158, 159-60
antidote 132, 134
antigen 21, 26
pneumococcal polysaccharide used as 140
swine-influenza vaccine in 96
antitoxins 32-4, 42, 43
Arctium lappa 138
ARC (AIDS-related complex) 120
arthralgia 90,91
arthritis immunization
immediate ill effects/ dangers 90-4
aspirin, dangers 104
'at risk' 124
Atlantic Monthly 122
atypical measles *see* measles, atypical
Austin Hospital, Melbourne 72
autism, infantile
auto-immune disease 75, 98, 100
auto-immune reaction/response 75, 99

B-lymphocyte 95

function 27-9 *passim*, 89-90, 140
bacilli
  consumed by scientists 17, 55, 63
  anthrax *see under* anthrax
  cholera 17
  tubercle *see* tubercle bacillus
bacterial disease 20
bacterial toxin/antitoxin 20
bacteriolysis 138
Bacullinum 133
Baptisia 133
basophils 27
Bayly, M. Beddow, quoted 37-44, 47
BCG (Bacillus Calmette-Guérin) immunization 21
  tuberculosis (TB) against 30-2
  homoeopathic 133
  side effects 32
  vaccine 48
    testing dangers 31
Béchamp, Antoine 9, 10, 11-12, 18
  hypothesis
    current literature 112-16
    modern supporting evidence 111-12
belief system 155
beta haemolitic streptococci 113
betaine 138
beverages, souring 10
  research 11, 17
biotin (B vitamin) 147
Birmingham Medical Review (Jan 1874) 156
Bismark, Chancellor of Germany 5
Bland, Jeffrey 25, 145
blood pressure, high 99
Bodian, D. 39, 46
Boer War (1899-1902) 55, 56
bone 27
bone marrow 139
botanical medicine 138-9
brain damage 8, 9, 48, 64, 66
  immunization-caused 81-9
breast feeding 77, 79, 100
breast milk, immunoglobulin-containing 28

British Homoeopathic Journal (July 1984) 136
British Liberation Army 68
British Medical Journal 41, 57, 65, 100, 105
British Naturopathic Journal and Osteopathic Review (1964) 32
British Union for the Abolition of Vivisection 68
  see also animals; National Antivivisection Society
Brunhild polio virus 39
bulbar poliomyelitis 46
bursa (B) 27
Buttram, Harold 123

calcium 148, 150
calmodulin 148
Cancer Control Journal (1974) 106
cancer
  immunization-caused 98, 100, 104
    childhood 99
  risk increased by immunization 110
Candida albicans 22-3
carbolic acid 11
carcinogens 110
CCC (Cytidine-cytidine-cytidine) 111
cells, alteration of genetic material within 101-4
cellular metamorphosis 124
Center for Disease Control 105
Chadwick Lecture (1921) 56
Charles, Prince of Wales 66
chemotaxis 138
chicken pox (varicella) 104
Chief Medical Officer, Ministry of Health 60, 70
cholera
  bacillus 17
  decline, Europe 6, 6-7
  immunization 48, 50
  homoeopathic 133
chondromalacia 108
chromatin granules 112
chromosome 110, 112

chronic progressive vaccinia (vaccinia gangrenosa) 60
cilia 23
Circassian woman (isopathic methods) 4
Clostridum tetani 113
Clostridum welchii 113
'clumping' 33
coagulase positive 113
cobalt 148
cocarcinogen 110
colds, homoeopathic immunization 133
coli bacillus 136
Committee on Safety of Medicines 34
compulsory immunization 5-6, 160
  collapse of 6, 7
  soldiers of 55-6, 57
  see also mass immunization; propaganda, immunization
conjunctivitis, phlyctenular 32
consensus medicine 154
consumption 6
contraceptive vaccines 159-60
convulsions 48, 81
Copenhagen Tuberculosis Research Team 31
copper deficiency 148
Corynebacterium diphtheriae 113
'cot deaths' *see* Sudden Infant Death Syndrome
Coulter, Harris 77, 81-3
cowpox 4-5, 156
  vaccination (against smallpox) 4-5
Coxsackie virus 106
  B4 110
Creighton, Charles, quoted 156
crystallography 10
Culbert, Michael, quoted 118
Cytidine-cytidine-cytidine (CCC) 111
Cytomegalovirus 123

Daily Express 40
degenerative disease, immunization-caused 8, 105-16, 161
dental caries, immunization research into 114

deoxyribose, phosphate ester of 111
Department of Health 66
Dettman, Glen, quoted 9-10, 14, 91, 111-12
Dettman, Ian, quoted 111-12
developmental delay 48
diabetes 99
diabetes (juvenile onset), measles immunization-caused 104
Diana, Princess of Wales 66
dilution 129-30
diphtheria 7
  'A Study of Diphtheria in Two Areas of Great Britain' 41
  decline 53-4, 57
  immunization absence due 58
  increase due to immunization 57-8
  treatment with antibiotics 93
diphtheria immunization 34-45, 93-4
  disease provoked by 58, 95
  homoeopathic 132
diphtheria toxin 33
diphtheria toxoid 48, 159
disease
  auto-immune *see* auto-immune disease
  bacterial 20
  degenerative *see* degenerative disease
  eczematous 5
  killer 6-7
  poliomyelitis-appearing 58
  provocation *see* provocation disease
  venereal 20, 113
disease, germ theory of 9
disease, natural history of 54-5, 63
  modern medicine's view 62
disease causation, philosophical concept 1
'disease is born of us and in us' 18
disease patterns, study-evolution 2, 7
Dixon, Bernard, quoted 53-4
Dixon, G. W., quoted 61
DNA (deoxyribonucleic acid) 11, 12, 102-4 *passim*, 111

oligonucleotide 112
triplet 111
virus/bacteria evolution from
112-13
doctors, attitudes towards
immunization 154-6
see also rediagnosis
double helix 11
DPT (diphtheria, pertussis, tetanus;
'triple vaccine') 85
ill effects/dangers 81-3, 85-6
Sudden Infant Death Syndrome-
associated 76-7, 80
draining sinuses 32
drug user, intravenous 124
Druid priests 4
Dubos, Rene 17
Dubos (Professor, Rockefeller
University) 14
dysentery, decline in Europe 6, 7

'eating by a cell' 26
Echinecea angustifolia (purple
coneflower) 138
echinacein 138
echinacoside 138
eczema, atopic 100
eczematous disease 5
eggs, sensitivity to 48
Ehrengut, Wolfgang, quoted 46,
86
Ehrlich, Paul 20-1
encephalitic crying 81
encephalitis 69, 84
encephalomyelitis, post-vaccinal 60
encephalopathy 66, 104
Encyclopaedia Britannica 156
Enders, J. F. 39, 92, 123
endogenous 10
endoplasmic reticulum 111
enzymes 102, 103, 112
eosinophils 27
Epstein-Barr 123
epithelial cell 137
'ethical' drug houses 152
exercise 149, 150
exogenous 10

fasting 149
fats 137

FDA *see* Food and Drug
Administration
fibrinolytic activity 142
fibroblast 137
Fielding, Simon, quoted 140
Fisher, Barbara Loe
quoted 158
research, DPT 77, 81-2
fits 48
Florio, Dr (Denver Medical Officer)
40
flu *see* influenza
folic acid (B vitamin) 147
Food and Drug Administration
(FDA), study 77, 81, 83, 157
Francis report 47
freedom of choice 160
frog tissue use 102
Fulginiti, Vincent, quoted 87-8

Gallo, Robert 125
gamma globulin (IgG) 28, 37-9
passim
ganglia 113
Gannet News Agency Service 157
gastroenteritis 78, 79
gay man 124
Geffen, Dennis H.
predisposing host-factors 45-7
quoted 37
Gelsemium 132
gene 10; *see also* genetic material,
alteration of; genetic engineering
gene, viral 113
General Practitioner, The 49
genetic engineering 104, 115
genetic material, alteration of 101-4
Geneva University, Department of
Plant Physiology 102
Geraniol 136
germ theory of disease 9
german measles *see* rubella
Glasgow Public Health Department
38
Glasgow University, Professor of
Public Health 85
globulin 108, 109
glutathione peroxidase 149
glycosidase 112
gonorrhoea, Neiserria 113

gout 99
granulocytes 27
Great Ormond Street, Hospital for Sick Children 86
Great War *see* World War I
Green monkey, African 101, 118, 123
Guilain-Bàrre syndrome 96, 97, 98, 157

Hahnemannian potentisation concept 131
Haitian 125
Hannah Dairy Research Institute 114
Harvard Medical School 107
Health, Education and Welfare (HEW) (now DHSS) 91
health
  decline 151
  improvement 54
  promotion 152
Health Consciousness (Oct 1986) 14, 53
'health depends on right living' 18
health status 1, 8
  enhancement 15-16
  individual responsibility for 14, 15
  reduced 138
helper cell, T- 89-90
heparin 27
hepatitis 113
hepatitis A immunization 50
hepatitis B immunization 50
  vaccine testing 118
Here's Health (March 1980) 85
herpes 112, 113
HEW (Health, Education and Welfare) (now DHSS) 91
histamin 27
histidine 149
homoeopathy
  definition 138
  immunization by 132-3
  treatment explained 129-30
  used to enhance immune function 129-38
  trials 135-8
hormone(s), reproductive 159

hormone-containing drugs 150
Horowitz, Marshall, quoted 93
horsepox 5
host condition 20
  immune function and 7
    AIDS risk 14
  predisposing factors 47-52, 62-3
human chorionic gonadotrophin (HCG) 159
human immuno defence virus infection (HIV) 118, 125
see also AIDS
Humanitarian Society of Pennsylvania 50
hyalin cartilage tissue 92
Hypericum 132
hypothalamic diencephalic centres 142

IgA 28
IgD 28
IgG *see* gamma globulin
IgM (macroglobulin) 28
ill health, multicausal background 16
Illich, Ivan, quoted 2, 6-7
immune complexes, solubilization of 138
immune-deficiency 98-9
immune function/immune system
  deficiency 18-19
  enhancement 7, 115, 127-51;
    by acupuncture 141-3
    homoeopathy 129-38
    nutrition 142-51
    osteopathy 139-41
  explanation of 22-52, 98
  host condition and *see under* host condition
  impairment 95-6, 98, 127, 134
    tetanus immunization by 89-90
immunity
  active 33
  passive 33-4
immunity, natural 50-1, 72, 116, 161
  denial of 71
  'hit and miss' view 14
  immunization procedures compared 50-1

immunity, unnatural 161
immunization
  AIDS/HIV-associated with
    117-26
  cases for avoiding 48-8
  commercial element 47, 152,
    157
  compulsory *see* compulsory
    immunization
  conclusions 152-61
  degenerative disease-causing
    105-10
  doctors' attitudes towards 154-6
    see also rediagnosis
  explanation of 22-52
  history 4-21
  ill effects/dangers
    immediate 74-100
    long-term 101-16
    official views of 34, 49-50
    range of 8-9
  ineffectiveness of: BCG 30-2;
    cholera 49; diphtheria 34-45;
    polio 34-45; rubella 72-3
    also success, counterclaims
    below
  limited protection-providing 49,
    73
  mass *see* mass immunization
  methods/procedures, criticism
    summary 127
  natural immunity compared 50-1
  neurological/brain damage-
    causing 81-9
  propaganda *see* propaganda,
    immunization
  provocation disease-causing 94-6
  questioned 1-3
  questions raised by 152-61
  research
    animal use *see* animals
    new fields 114-15, 158, 160
  success, claims 53-73
  success, counterclaims (*see also*
    ineffectiveness *above*); 53-73
  'hit and miss' view 15
  natural history of disease
    considered 54-5, 62-3
immunocontraception 159-60
  immunoglobulin (Ig) 28

antibody 28
immunological defence system 24,
  25
Immunological Memory 34, 35
immunological shock 25, 78, 79
immunologists 114, 153
immunosuppressive 122
infant 124
infecting agent, emphasis, over
  host condition 62
infection, natural history of 21
influenza (swine-flu) 30
  epidemic 96, 97
  pandemic (1918-19) 97, 98
  Reye's syndrome risk 104, 105
  vaccine 96, 97, 157
    ill effects/dangers 96-100
    virus 113
influenza-A virus 98
influenza immunization
  by homoeopathy 133
Innula helenium 138
insect bites 25
Institute for Biological Standards 80
insulin 146
International Academy of
  Preventative Medicine 9-10
International Review of Cytology
  (1977) 103
intestinal immunity 35
intestines 23
inulin 138
intravenous drug user 124
isopathic 4

Jenner, Edward (1749-1823) 4, 4-
  5, 153-4
Jesty (farmer) 4, 5
joints, painful 90
Journal of Alternative Medicine 66,
  131, 134, 135
*Journal of Alternative and
  Complementary Medicine* 118
Journal of Biological Studies
  (1984) 36
*Journal of the International
  Association for Preventative
  Medicine* (July 1977) 111
Journal of Neuroimmunology 96
Journal of Paediatrics 69, 83

Journal of American Medical Association 41, 72, 93, 110

Kalokerinos, Archie, quoted 9-10, 14, 77, 78, 78-9
Kenyon, Julian, quoted 66-7, 125
killed vaccine 30, 34, 35, 43, 85
killer cells 138
Klenner, Fred, quoted 105, 106
Koch, Robert 6, 19, 62
  postulate (law) 19-20

Lancet, The 17-18, 31, 35 57, 154
  1954 editions 38, 46
  1955 editions 38, 43, 47
  1985 editions 64, 73, 107
Lange, Andrew 138
Lansing polio virus 39
le Duc (historian) 4
lead pollution 150
Lee Foundation for Nutritional Research 146
Leon polio virus 39
leucine 149
leucocyte (leukocyte) 27
  polymorphonuclear 27
leukemia, immunization-induced 100, 105, 124
leukocyte see leucocyte
Levy, Jay, quoted 14
LH (luteinizing hormone) 159
'like cures like' 120
Lindlahr, Henry 4, 5, 18
  quoted 115-16
Linus Pauling Institute for Science and Medicine 25, 145
Lister, Joseph (1827-1912) 11
live vaccine 30, 34-5
  excepted use 48-9
Lockie, Andrew, quoted 131, 133-5
Loe Fisher, Barbara see Fisher, Barbara Loe
London University, Professor of Pathology 44
Long, R de, quoted 117
lupus erythematosus 108
luteinizing hormone (LH) 159
lymph modes 139

lymphadenitis 32
lymphatic pump techniques 140, 141
lymphocyte (s) 26, 27, 96, 98
  B- see B-lymphocyte
  non-granulated 27
  T- see T-lymphocyte

McCarrison, Robert, quoted 142
McIntosh (Professor) 44
McKeown, T., quoted 55
macroglobulin (IgM) 28
macrophage 26, 139
macrophages, guinea pig 137
Maladrinum 131
malnutrition 78, 79
manganese 148
Manitoba 38
Martin, Simon 118, 120
mass immunization 7, 96, 97;
  see also compulsory
    immunization; propaganda,
    immunization
Measel (Dr. John), quoted 140
measles 7, 8, 30, 113
  'atypical' 70, 93
  decline 69
  epidemics 69-70
  immunization 48, 49, 69, 84
  ill effects/dangers 93, 100, 107-10
  rash, absence of 107-10
Medical Journal of Australia 46, 105
Medical News (May 1967) 107
Medical Officer, The 38, 71
Medical Research Council (MRC)
  reports 41-2, 101, 123
  study 88
Medical Tribune 106
Medical World News 106
medicine
  allopathic 115
  naturopathic see naturopathic medicine
  preventative 151
meditation 150
Memorial Sloan Kettering Cancer Center, The 148

Mendelsohn, Robert, quoted on
    immunization dangers 100,
    104-5
  BCG testing 31
  measles 69, 84
  mumps 84
  poliomyelitis 36
  rubella 71-2
  whooping cough 76
meningitis 106
meningoencephalitis, immunization-
    caused 95
mental deficiency 64
Merc. cyan. 132
mercury 150-1
Metchnikoff, Elie 17, 63
middle ear infection, recurrent 144
minerals 148
Minister of Health 39, 66, 94
Ministry of Health, Chief Medical
    Officer 70
monkey, African Green 101, 118,
    123
monoclonal antibody production
    114-15
monoclonal antibody technology
    159-60
monocyte 27, 28
  chemotaxis of 138
Morbillinum 133
Morris, J. Anthony 157-8
Morris, Malcolm, quoted 56
multicausal background to ill health
    16
multiple sclerosis (MS) 8, 29, 74-5
  immunization-caused 104, 106-
    7, 134
mumps immunization 83-4, 100
  homoeopathy use 123
muscle wasting 122
Mycobacterium tuberculosis 113
mycrozyma 10, 11, 111, 112
myelin sheath, damage 107

Nation, The 56, 58
National Advisory Committee, The
    37
National Antivivisection Society 37
  see also animals; British Union
    for the Abolition of Vivisection

National Foundation for Infantile
    Paralysis 38, 39, 40
natural healing pioneer 18
naturopathic medicine 101, 149
Neisseria gonorrhoea 113
Nelsons 136
neomycin 48
neurological damage,
    immunization-caused 81-9
neurological disease 48
neutrophils 27
  chemotaxis of 138
New England Journal of Medicine
    90, 91, 92, 95
New York 6
News Chronicle (May 1955) 40
nicol prism 12
nicotine 150
Nobel prize winners 12, 92
non-granular lymphocyte 27
Norwegian Medical Society 31
nosodes 24, 25, 134, 137
nosode, homoeopathic, 131, 132,
    135
nuclase 112
nucleotide 111
Nurses Journal, The Australian 72,
    105
nutrition, used to enhance immune
    function 142-51
nutritional imbalance 77-81 passim

oligonucleotide 112
oligopeptide 111, 112
oral vaccine 34, 35
osteopathy, used to enhance
    immune function 139-41

Palmer, Carrol, quoted 31, 32
pandemic
  AIDS 123
  influenza 97
Paracelsus, Theophrastus Bombast
    von Hohenheim (1490c-1541)
    4
paralysis 64
paratyphoid bacilli 55
paratyphoid immunization 30
  homoeopathic 133
Parkinson's disease 99

immunization-caused 104
Parotidinum 133
Pasteur, Louis (1822-95) 7-8, 161
  alleged plagiarism 10
  legacy 9-21
pathogenic, definition 12
pathogenic organisms existing in
    body 113
penicillin, allergy to 48
People's Doctor, The 83
pertussis *see* whooping cough
Pettenkofer, Max von 17, 63
Pfeiffer, Carl, quoted 144
phagocytic activity 142
phagocytosis 26, 153, 156
phenylaladine 111
'philosophical objection' to
    immunization 158
Philpott, W., quoted 25, 148
phylyctenular conjunctivitis 32
phosphate ester of deoxyribose 111
pill, the 150
  'male' 139
plasma 33
pneumococcal polysaccharide 140
pneumonia 25, 78, 79, 106
polarized light 12
polyarticular rheumatoid arthritis 92
polio *see* poliomyelitis
poliomyelitis (acute anterior
    poliomyelitis; 'polio') 30, 113
  decline 67
  immunization 21, 34-45, 48-50
    passim
    deaths caused by 39-40, 41
    ill effects/dangers 36, 105
  immunization-induced 85, 94, 95
  types
    bulbar 46
    paralytic 36, 38, 85, 106
    'satellite' 40
  vaccine 41, 101
    AIDS-associated with 118-23
    passim
  viruses 39
poliomyelitis-appearing disease 58
polymorphonuclear leucocyte 27
polyneuritis 90
polyoma virus 110
polyribosome 111

polyuridine 111
potency 41, 130
pox virus 113
predisposing host-factors 45-52
pregnancy 45, 48, 71
preventative medicine 151
proline 110
properidin 138
propaganda, immunization 1, 15,
    31, 72
  see also compulsory
    immunization; mass
    immunization
protease 112
protein 145
provirus 103-4
provocation disease 58
  immunization-caused 94-6
Public Health (March 1955) 37,
    45
Public Health Laboratory Service
    85
Pulsatilla 133
purple coneflower (*Echinacea
    angustifolia*) 138
pyridoxine (vitamin B6) 25

rabies 30
  treatment 18, 19
Radcliffe Infirmary, Oxford 47
radiation, electromagnetic 150
RDA (recommended daily
    allowance) of nutrients 145
receptor 20-1
rediagnosis (56), 58, 59, 155
  see also doctors
  attitudes towards immunization
Registrar General 59, 60, 61
relaxation 150
remedies 131
reticulo-endothelial system (res) 24
Reye's syndrome
  increased risk 104, 105
  measles immunization-caused
    104
reverse transcriptase (enzyme) 102
rheumatoid arthritis 75, 92
  polyarticular 92
riboflavin *see* vitamin B2
rickettsial infection 95

RNA (ribonucleic acid) 12, 102, 111
  oligonucleotide 112
  virus 103, 104
Rocky Mountain Spotted Fever 93
Roodyn, Leonard, quoted 49
Rost, Peter 118
roto virus 113
Royal Commission on Vaccination 1
Royal Society of Medicine 44
rubella (german measles) 30
  immunization 71-3
  homoeopathic 133
  ill effects/dangers 90-4
  vaccine 48, 90
Russell, Ritchie, quoted 47

Sabin, Albert 43
Sabin vaccine 43-4, 122
St Pancras Hospital 45
Salk, Jonas E. 43, 85, 153
Salk vaccine 39-40, 41, 50, 121
Salmonella 113
San Francisco, UCLA 14
Sandler, Benjamin 146
sanitation 55, 63, 68
sarcoma 122
'satellite' poliomyelitis 40
scarlet fever 54, 76
Scheuremann's disease 108
Schick test 42
Science 91, 110
Science Digest (Dec 1963) 121
Secretary of State for Health (UK) 119
sexually-transmitted disease 117
  see also specific diseases
Shaw, George Bernard, quoted 5-6, 58-9
sheep, immunized 18
Shein, H. N. 123
'side chain theory' 21
SIDS see Sudden Infant Death Syndrome
Simian virus number 40 see SV40
Simon, Harold, quoted 32
Simonton, Carl, quoted 154-5
sinuses 139
sinuses, draining 32

skin test 30, 31
sleep, inadequate 14, 150
slimming, immunization research 114-15
smallpox 4, 5
  decline/eradication 6, 53 59-60
  epidemics 5-6, 70
  vaccination (cowpox by) 4-5, 71
    deaths caused by 60-2, 94
    HIV-associated with 125
    multiple sclerosis caused by 106
snake bites 25
Snead, Eva 118, 122
Snider, Arthur, quoted 121
Society of Homoeopaths 77
Society of Medical Officers of Health 45
spleen 139, 140, 141
spondyloarthritis 92
staphylococci 113
Stewart, Gordon T. 29, 64-6, 85, 89
stimulants, use of 150
streptococci, beta haemolitic 113
stress 149, 150
subacute sclerosing panencephalitis 84
Sudden Infant Death Syndrome (SIDS) 29
  immunization-caused 75-81
  DPT vaccine link 76-7
sugar 145-6
sunbathing, excessive 150
suppressor cell, T- 89-90
SV40 (Simian virus number 40) 101, 118-24 passim
  immunosuppressive characteristics 122
swine-flu see influenza
symbiotic 22
synovitis 91
syphilis 20

T-cells, helper/suppressor 89-90
T-lymphocyte (T-4 cell) 95, 124
  function 27, 89-90
  function maintenance 149
TAB vaccine (cholera/typhoid/ paratyphoid) 30, 55

Tai chi chuan 150
TB *see* tuberculosis
Temin, Howard 103
tetanus
  toxin 33
  toxoid 48
tetanus immunization
  homoeopathy use 132
  immune function impaired by
    89-90
The Vaccine Machine (1984) 132
thiamine *see* vitamin B
Thuja 131, 132
thymosin 99
thymus gland (T) 27, 98-9
Time magazine 12, 14, 40, 113
Times, The (Nov 1953) 38
tonsillectomy 46, 107
  tonsils 23
removal *see* tonsillectomy
toxins 32-4
toxoids 32, 34
  side-effects 34
Trace Metal Laboratories 144
travel immunization 50
  homoeopathic use 133
Treponema palladum 113
trinucleotide 111
'triple vaccine' *see* DPT
Trypanosoma cruzi 136, 137
tubercle bacillus 19, 31; 144
  see also tuberculin
tuberculin 19
  see also tubercle bacillus
tuberculosis (TB) 19, 48, 95
  BCG against 30
  decline, Europe 6
  nutritional origin 143-4
typhoid 55
  bacillus 55, 57
  decline, Europe 6, 7
  immunization 30, 50, 56-7
    compulsory 55-6
    homoeopathic 133
  immunization-induced by 94

UCLA *see* University of California,
  Los Angeles
UCLA-FDA study 77, 81, 83
United States Public Health Service 41

United States Roosevelt Memorial
  Fund 38-9
University of California, Los
  Angeles (UCLA) 77
University of Maryland 158
University of Otago, Professor of
  Preventative and Social
  Medicine 61
Uradine-uradine-uradine (UUU)
  111
urinary tract 23

vaccination *see* immunization
vaccination, small-pox 4-5
Vaccination Enquirer (Aug 1964)
  153
vaccine(s)
  contraceptive 159-69
  killed *see* killed vaccine
  killed/live, risks compared 36
  live *see* live vaccine
  materials for 50
  oral *see* oral vaccine
  side-effects/dangers, official view
    34, 49-50
  specific cases for avoiding 48
  vaccinia 106, 125
  vaccinia gangrenosa (chronic
    progressive vaccinia) 60
vacuolating agent 101
vagina 23
varicella (chicken pox) 104
Varidinum 130, 136
venereal disease 20, 113
Vibrio cholera 113
virus
  adeno 112
  roto 113
  SV40 101
  vaccinia 106
virus, neutralization of 138
visualization 129
Vital Force 134
vitamin
  B5 (pantothenic acid) 147
  B6 (pyridoxine) 25, 146
    deficiency 46, 148
  B12 147
  C 147, 148
    deficiency 78, 79

supplement 76, 78, 105
E 147-8
Vithoulkas, George, quoted 134-5

Wallgren (Professor), quoted 31-2
Washbourne, J., quoted 55
Washington Post, The 125
water, fluoridation of 160-1
Weaver, H., quoted 107
Weekly Scotsman (Jan 1953) 39
Wellcome Foundation 80
Wensel, Louise 142
WHO *see* World Health
  Organization
whooping cough (pertussis) 7, 30,
  113
 decline 63
 immunization 63-7
  brain damage caused by 85-9
  disease-causing 94
  risks 67, 76
 vaccine 8, 9, 48
'wild virus' 36

Williams, Roger, quoted 143-4
Williamson, K. F., quoted 153,
  154
Wilson, Graham, quoted 94-5
Wilson J. R., quoted 152-3
World Health Organization (WHO)
  58, 121, 125
World Medicine (Sept 1971) 102
World War I ('Great War'; 1913-
  18) 55, 56, 98
World War II (1939-45) 6, 57,
  59, 68
Wright, Almroth, vaccine 55
Wright, Pearce 125

yeast (*Candida albicans*) 113
  see also Candida albicans
yellow fever 30
  immunization 50
Yellowlees, Henry 72
yoga 150

zinc/zinc deficiency 144-5, 149